AF378261

The 1921 ANNUAL of ADVERTISING ART

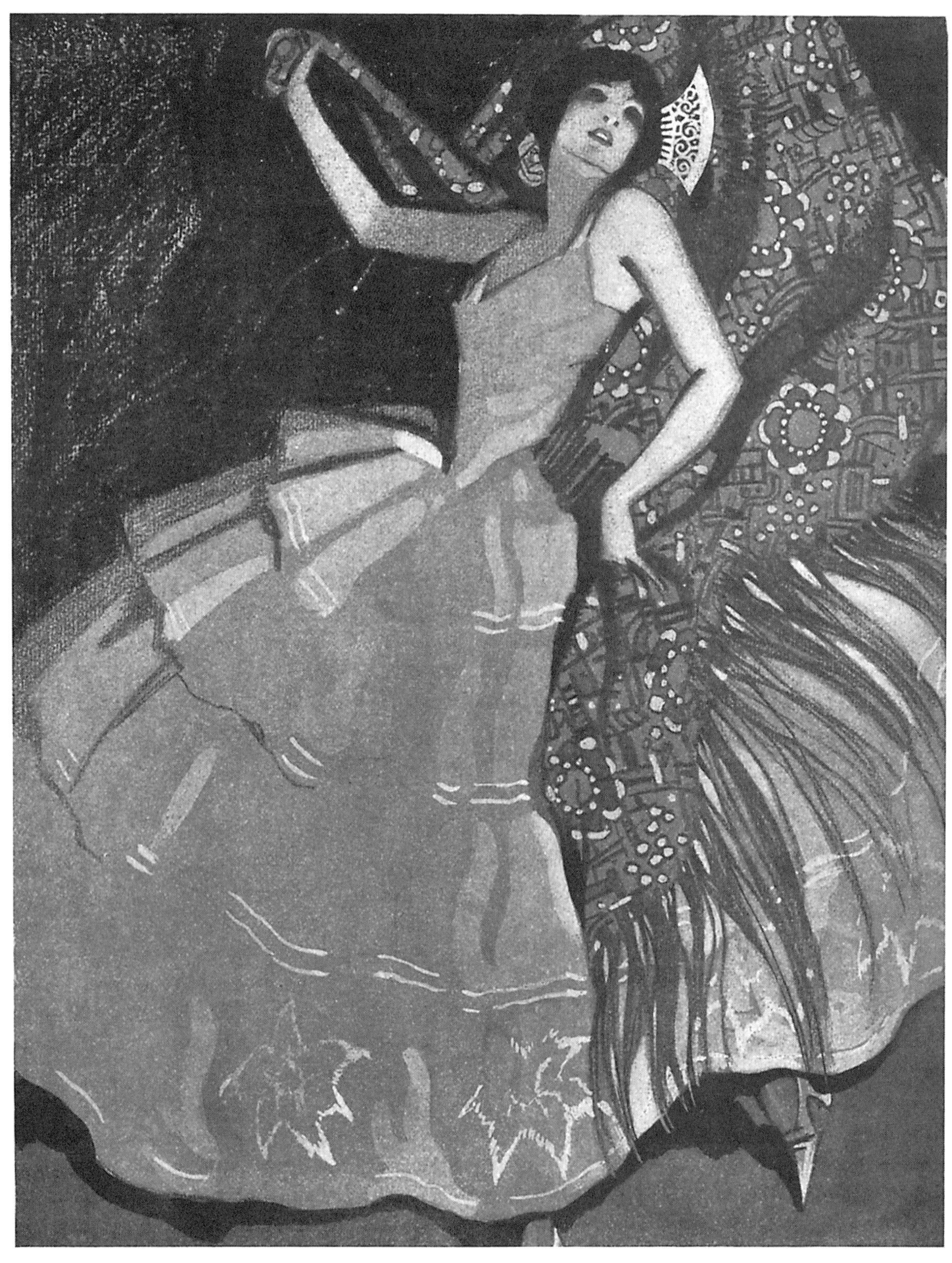

A.   The First Award in Section II for Paintings and Drawings in Color
Carmen—*W. E. Heitland*
Loaned by Columbia Graphophone Company
Exhibited by George Batten Co., Inc.

The 1921 ANNUAL *of* ADVERTISING ART

The Catalog of the First Exhibition

• HELD BY •

THE ART DIRECTORS CLUB

DOVER PUBLICATIONS, INC.
MINEOLA, NEW YORK

Bibliographical Note

This Dover edition, first published in 2018, is an unabridged republication of *Annual of Advertising Art in the United States: 1921,* originally published by Publishers Printing Company, New York, 1921, for The Art Directors Club. For this edition, the front matter has been rearranged, and both a Contents and a sixteen-page color insert have been added.

Library of Congress Cataloging-in-Publication Data

Names: Art Directors Club (New York, N.Y.)
Title: The 1921 annual of advertising art : the catalog of the first exhibition held by the Art Directors Club.
Other titles: Annual of advertising and editorial art, 1921.
Description: Mineola, New York : Dover Publications, 2018. | Includes index. | "This Dover edition, first published in 2018, is an unabridged republication of Annual of Advertising Art in the United States:1921, originally published in 1921 by Publishers Printing Company, New York, for The Art Directors Club."
Identifiers: LCCN 2018025040| ISBN 9780486829197 (paperback) | ISBN 0486829197
Subjects: LCSH: Commercial art—United States—History—20th century—Exhibitions. | BISAC: ART / Annuals. | ART / Collections, Catalogs, Exhibitions / General.
Classification: LCC NC998.5.A1 A692 2018 | DDC 741.6074/7471—dc23
LC record available at https://lccn.loc.gov/2018025040

Manufactured in the United States by LSC Communications
82919701   2018
www.doverpublications.com

CONTENTS

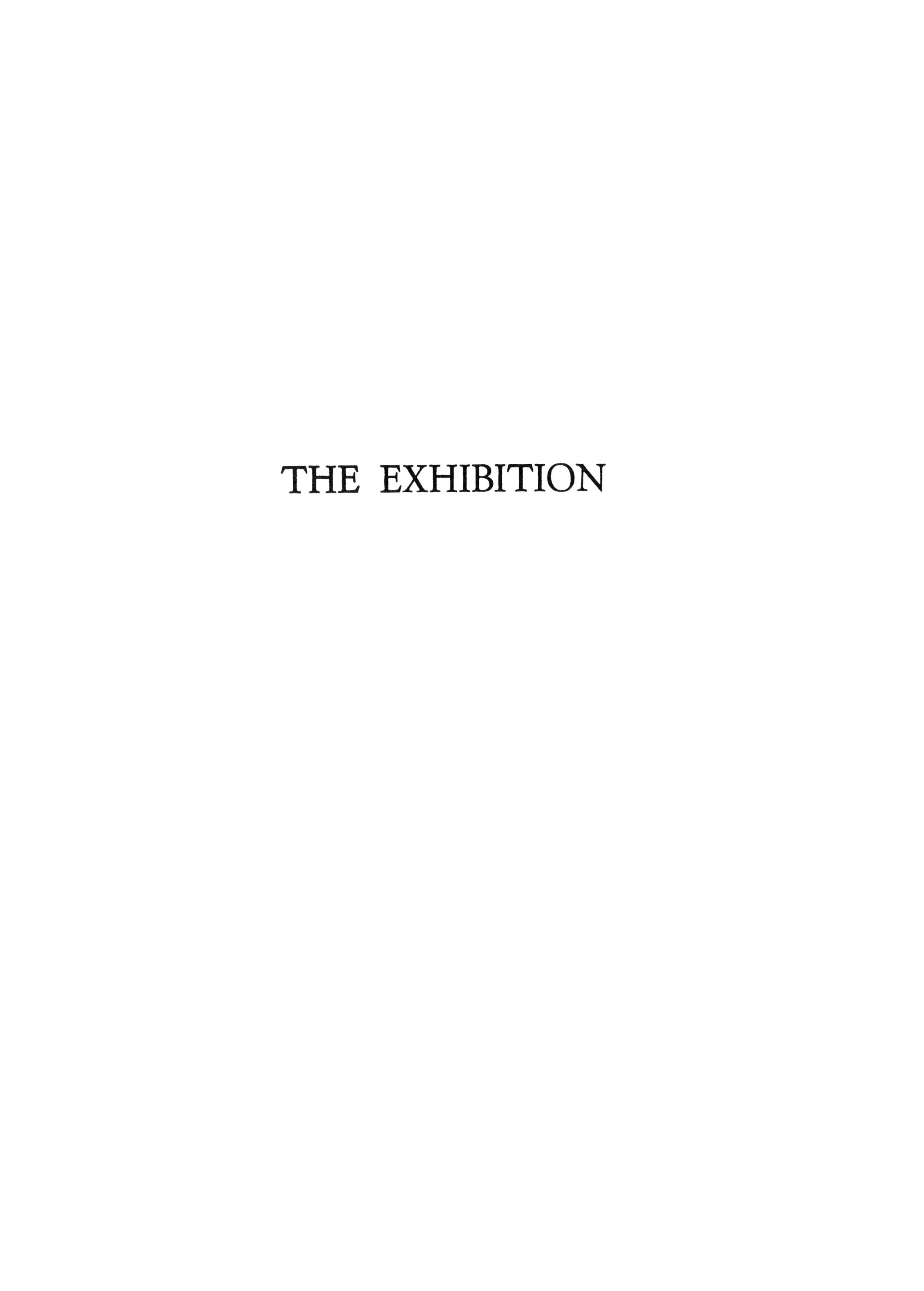

THE EXHIBITION

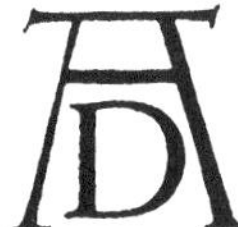

THE ART DIRECTORS CLUB

HEYWORTH CAMPBELL, *President*
J. H. CHAPIN, *Vice-President*
STANFORD BRIGGS, *Second Vice-President*
JAMES ETHRIDGE, *Secretary*
RALPH SHULTZ, *Treasurer*

Executive Committee

FRANKLIN BOOTH   GUY CLARK
THOMAS BOOTH   RAY GREENLEAF

DURING the last fifteen years there has been developed the highly specialized vocation of advising commerce in the use of art and of interpreting to art the requirements of commerce. Advertising agencies and publishers were among the first to encourage this specialization, but today "art directing" is a professional and well-defined work, often entirely independent of any other.

The Art Directors Club was organized early in 1920 by a group of men ambitious for the progress of art in advertising and industry, who believed they could contribute to the best interests of art and advertising by collective participation in art affairs.

The club recognizes as an art director one who counsels in the buying, selling and creation of art work and whose services have been accepted by any reputable organization.

The officers of the club during its first year were: Richard J. Walsh, President, Thomas Booth, Vice-President, Guy Clark, Second Vice-President, Egbert G. Jacobson, Secretary, William Schaefer, Treasurer.

THE EXHIBITION

IN November 1920 the Art Directors Club sent invitations to those who it thought would be interested in submitting proofs, clippings or other reproductions of advertising illustrations worthy of being included in an exhibition of original paintings and drawings used in American advertising.

The first Art Committee of the club, which originated and set in motion plans for the exhibition, consisted of:

RALPH SHULTZ, *Chairman*   J. H. CHAPIN
STANFORD BRIGGS   RAY GREENLEAF
EGBERT G. JACOBSON   OTTO REBELE
EDWARD A. WILSON   WALTER SMITH

The following regulations governed the exhibition:

Each proof, clipping or other reproduction submitted was to show not merely the illustration but the advertisement in which it appeared.

No illustrations or designs were to be exhibited which had not actually appeared in a magazine or newspaper advertisement, or as a poster, or in an advertising booklet or circular, or other medium.

While the committee would try to limit the exhibition to work which had appeared within the past two years, it would accept illustrations of particular merit even though several years old.

THE PURPOSES OF THE EXHIBITION WERE:

To show forcefully that good art and good advertising are consistent and that successful advertisers are using as high a standard of art as that used in illustration or shown in the average exhibition of studio painting.

To encourage the entrance into the field of advertising illustration of painters who still feel that commercial work is unworthy of their interest.

To encourage and educate students and inexperienced artists.

To give advertisers and advertising executives the opportunity of reviewing from year to year the tendencies of advertising illustration, that they may better utilize the work of artists.

To emphasize the importance of illustration and its intelligent handling in advertising.

The exhibits were divided into three sections as follows:

1. Black and white illustration and design—oil, pen and ink, wash, pencil, photographs, etchings, wood-cuts, etc.

2. Paintings and drawings in color.

3. Posters of all sizes, including car cards.

PATRONS OF THE EXHIBITION

The first annual exhibition was made possible through the financial support
of the following, who contributed generously to the fund
for awards and other expenses:

American Lithograph Co.
Barrows & Richardson
Barton, Durstine & Osborn, Inc.
George Batten Co., Inc.
Beck Engraving Co.
Harvey Blodgett Co.
William J. Boardman
Stanford Briggs
Stanford Briggs Co., Inc.
Arthur William Brown
Bush-Krebs Co., Louisville
Calkins & Holden
Charles E. Chambers
J. H. Chapin
Cluett, Peabody & Co.
Crowell Publishing Co.
Curtis Publishing Co.
Albert Frank & Co.
Franklin Printing Co.
Sam Moss
Byron Musser
H. K. McCann Co.
New Columbus Litho. Co.
Newell-Emmett Co.
William Oberhardt
Patterson Andress Co.
L. C. Pedlar, Inc.
Photo Engravers' Board of Trade
John O. Powers Co.
Rebele Studios
David Robinson
F. J. Ross Co.
Paul J. Sachs
Sterling Engraving Co.
Street & Finney
J. Walter Thompson Co.
Walker Engraving Co.
N. C. Wyeth

COMMITTEE ON FIRST ANNUAL EXHIBITION

FREDERIC J. SUHR, *Chairman*
HEYWORTH CAMPBELL, *Secretary*
JOHN DEVRIES, *Treasurer*

ANNOUNCEMENTS
John DeVries, *Chairman*
Everett R. Currier
Ray Greenleaf
Richard J. Walsh

FINANCE
John DeVries, *Chairman*
Stanford Briggs
James Ethridge
Richard J. Walsh

PUBLICITY
Heyworth Campbell, *Chairman*
F. DeSales Casey
Ray Greenleaf
Walter Smith
Richard J. Walsh

HANGING
Byron J. Musser, *Chairman*
M. B. Aleshire
Guy Clark
Peter A. Juley
William Oberhardt

MAILING LISTS
Ralph Shultz, *Chairman*
Heyworth Campbell
Gerald Page-Wood
Walter Whitehead

DINNER
J. H. Chapin, *Chairman*
John Clyde Oswald

AWARDS
J. H. Chapin, *Chairman*
Franklin Booth
Heyworth Campbell
F. DeSales Casey
Ray Greenleaf
August Hutaf

PROOFS
Robert Parkes, *Chairman*
Franklin Booth
Samuel Moss
Ralph Shultz
E. A. Wilson

ORIGINALS
F. DeSales Casey, *Chairman*
Ray Greenleaf
Peter A. Juley
Samuel Moss
William Oberhardt

CATALOGUE
Heyworth Campbell, *Chairman*
M. B. Aleshire
F. DeSales Casey
Fred Farrar
Otto Rebele
Richard J. Walsh

POSTER
August Hutaf, *Chairman*
Otto Rebele
E. A. Wilson

REPORT
OF THE JURY OF AWARDS

IN ANNOUNCING its awards, the jury wishes to make the following observations:

1—A number of paintings and drawings have been hung which were received at the Gallery after the Jury had adjourned and were not, of course, considered.

2—The awards have been made only with regard to the merit of the subjects as paintings or drawings and without attempting to judge their value as advertisements. The fact that they have been used for advertising has necessarily been accepted by the Jury as prima facie evidence of their advertising value.

3—The Jury feels that the exhibits should have been sub-divided into a greater number of sections, particularly in the black and white section, where oil, pen and ink, wash, pencil, photographs, etchings and wood-cuts were all to be considered together. There were so few photographs, etchings and decorative designs that the Jury did not attempt to make any awards in these classes of subjects. It awarded one honorable mention in the wood-cut classification. It recommends that in future exhibitions wood-cuts and etchings be considered separately from drawings and paintings.

4—The Jury decided, with reluctance, that it must make its awards without taking into account the reproductive possibilities of the subject. No complete set of proofs or other reproductions of the exhibits was available. It is recognized that the failure to obtain proper reproduction might be chargeable to the engraver, the printer or to the requirement of haste in handling which unfortunately obtains in most advertising production, to the great detriment of quality. It is equally true, however, that many artists do not have sufficient knowledge of, or give sufficient consideration to, processes of reproduction. We strongly recommend that in future exhibitions of this character provision be made for judgment of the exhibits with regard to their possibilities for successful reproduction.

5—The Jury was authorized to award a medal for the best exhibit in each of three divisions and has done so. It was also given discretionary power to award one or more special medals but sees no occasion for doing so. It has, however, because of the great variety of the exhibits, increased the proposed number of honorable mentions.

RICHARD J. WALSH, *Chairman*
ROBERT HENRI
CHARLES DANA GIBSON
E. H. BLASHFIELD
ARTHUR W. DOW
JOSEPH PENNELL

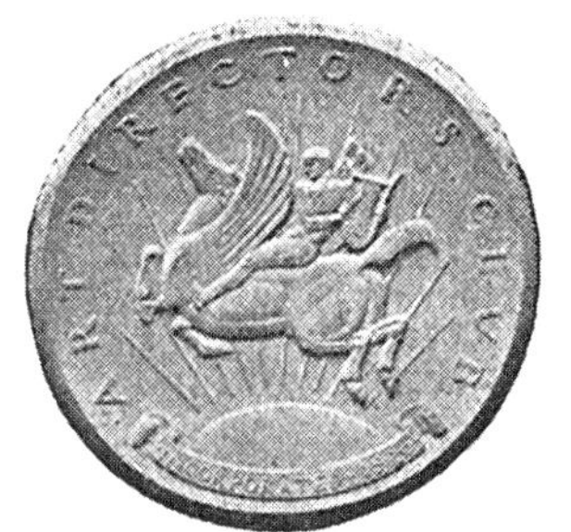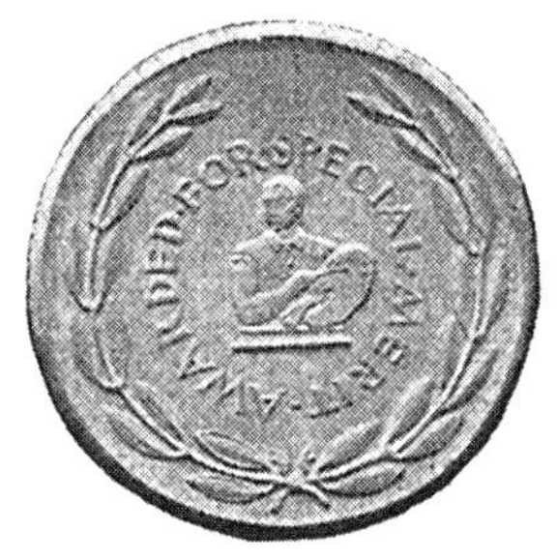

AWARDS

Section I.

Black and White Illustration and Design.

The First Award—Medal—to Frederic R. Gruger for black and white drawing —"Curtain Fire"—used in newspaper advertising by the Curtis Publishing Company. Plate B, page xii.

Honorable Mentions:

Franklin Booth—for a pen drawing made for the Victor Talking Machine Company through the Franklin Printing Company. Plate 253, page 86.

Wallace Morgan—for a drawing made for Ovington through Barton, Durstine & Osborn. Plate 117, page 37.

John J. A. Murphy— for wood-cuts made for the Ritz-Carlton Hotel through the Irving Press. Plates 291-292, page 97.

Henry Raleigh—for a drawing made for Arbuckle Bros. through the J. Walter Thompson Company. Plate 33, page 10.

Section II.

Paintings and Drawings in Color.

The First Award—Medal—to W. E. Heitland for painting made for the Columbia Graphophone Company through the George Batten Company. Frontispiece.

Honorable Mentions:

C. C. Beale—for a drawing, in colors, made for the Chickering Division of the American Piano Company through the Bricka-Ford Company. Plate 178, page 61.

Dean Cornwell—for a painting made for the Andrew Jergens Company through the J. Walter Thompson Company. Plate 61, page 19.

J. C. Leyendecker—for a painting made for Cluett, Peabody & Co. Plate 132, page 44.

Maxfield Parrish—for a painting,"Primitive Man", made for the Edison Lamp Works of the General Electric Company through Barton, Durstine & Osborn. Plate 267, page 91.

Section III.

Posters of All Sizes Including Car Cards.

The First Award—Medal—to René Clarke for poster drawing made for Crane & Company through Calkins & Holden. Plate 114, page 36.

Honorable Mentions:

Elizabeth Shippen Green Elliott—for a poster made for the Fleischmann Company through Donovan & Armstrong. Plate 104, page 32.

Edward Penfield—for a series of four posters made for the Franklin Printing Company. Plate 128, page 42.

Adolph Treidler — for an automobile catalog design made for the Pierce-Arrow Motor Car Company through the Bartlett-Orr Press. Plates 162-3-4, page 55.

FOREWORD

FROM the beginning, usefulness has been the criterion of vitality in art. The exhibits in our museums of fine art today are for the most part exhibits of ancient and medieval applied and industrial art. The ceramics, sculpture, furniture, armour, tapestry, jewelry, painting and stained glass, whose beauty we admire, were primarily developed by a demand for articles of use. The origin of ceramic art is essentially a response to need, yet its highest development, in Chinese porcelain, exhibits the same regard for utility as the clay bowls of primitive man.

The tombs of Egypt are found rich in magnificent sculpture, not because the Egyptians worshiped beauty but because they believed in immortality and required sarcophagi and tombs for their royal families. Beauty at first was a minor consideration; but ever since beauty became an end in itself, even the most exquisite examples of art have been judged by their functional fitness no less than by the design and craftsmanship displayed.

In this country the only art which can claim the distinction of national expression is one of the most highly useful arts in any civilization — architecture. Not country house nor city residence architecture, for both of these are very strongly reminiscent of European models; but commercial architecture, structures such as railway terminals, hotels, and office buildings. Commerce, facing the prohibitive cost of land and the crowding for space in defined areas, realized the economy of the skyscraper, the triple level terminal and the large hotel, and called for a new architecture. The result was a real contribution to art. It is significant that commerce should have been responsible for this important contribution.

Just as in Greece the wealth and power of the state enabled it to patronize art, just as in Italy and France the riches and power of the church enabled it in turn to command the services of art, so today in the United States, where encouragement from government, religion and private wealth is infrequent, the need and wealth of commerce have empowered it to assume the patronage of art.

This book is a catalog of an exhibition of paintings and drawings not only prescribed by commerce but made for the purpose of stimulating commerce. Commerce has seen the value of making known its wares through advertising and has been quick to perceive the usefulness of art in presenting these wares attractively.

Mr. Ernest Elmo Calkins, writing of the exhibition, said in part: "More artistic ability is now available for the advertiser's use than he is using—than he even realizes. Thousands of pictures were submitted for the purposes of this exhibition. Only three hundred were thought good enough from among them. But good as they are, they are not as good as they could be. They are not the best that can be done. What is needed is a better atmosphere—a better attitude toward good work—a better understanding of the selling power that can be put into pictured advertising —a less stiff and condescending state of mind on the part of the world's greatest artists—a less intolerant and narrow-minded attitude on the part of the world's greatest advertisers."

As commerce has engaged the best architects to meet the requirements of utility and by that has evolved a national architecture, it will engage the best artists to produce its advertising pictures, and thus a second great national art expression based on usefulness will be developed.

EGBERT G. JACOBSON

CATALOGUE

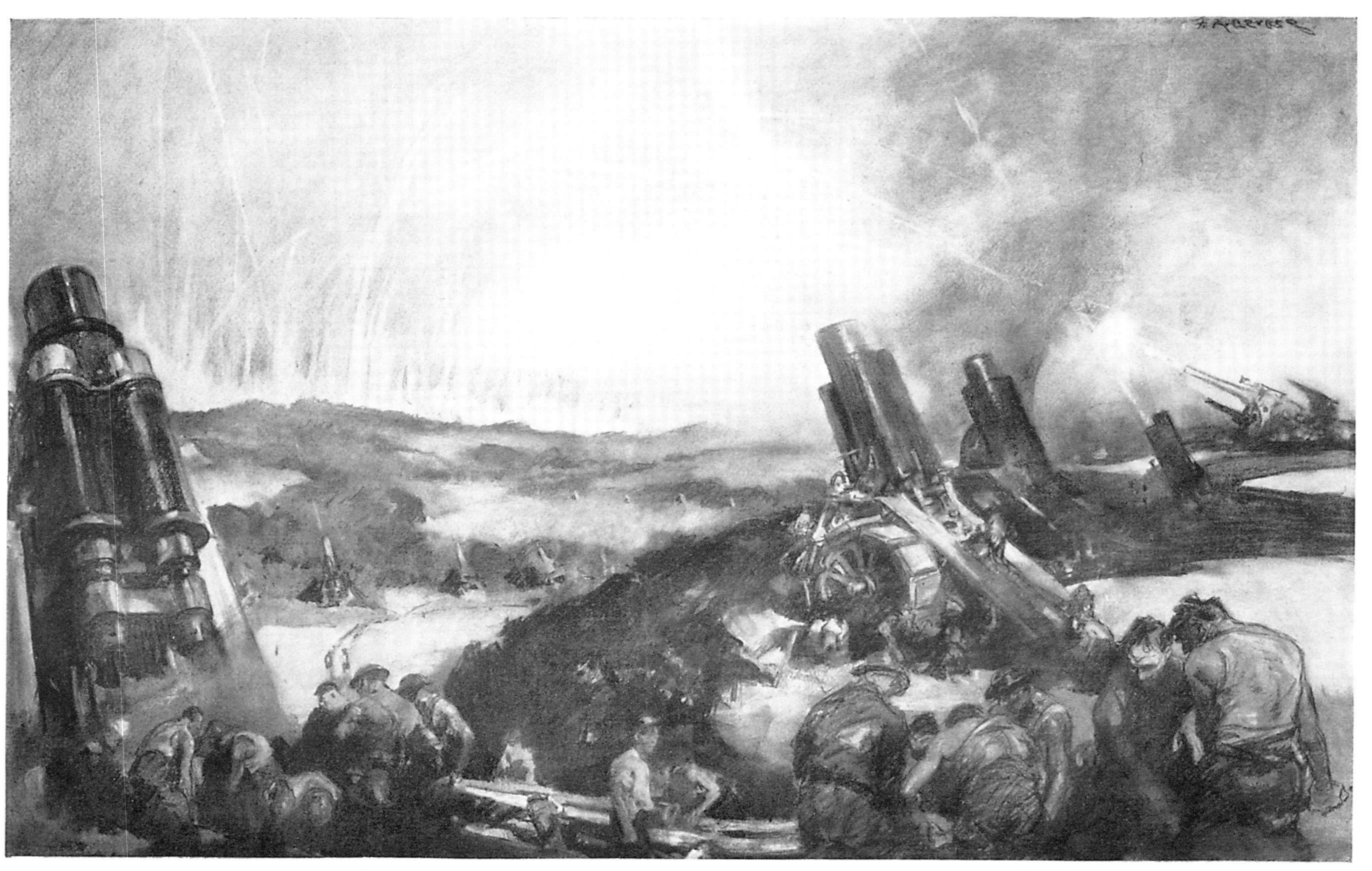

B.   The First Award in Section I for Black and White Illustration and Design
"CURTAIN FIRE"—*Frederic R. Gruger*
Exhibited and loaned by the Curtis Publishing Company

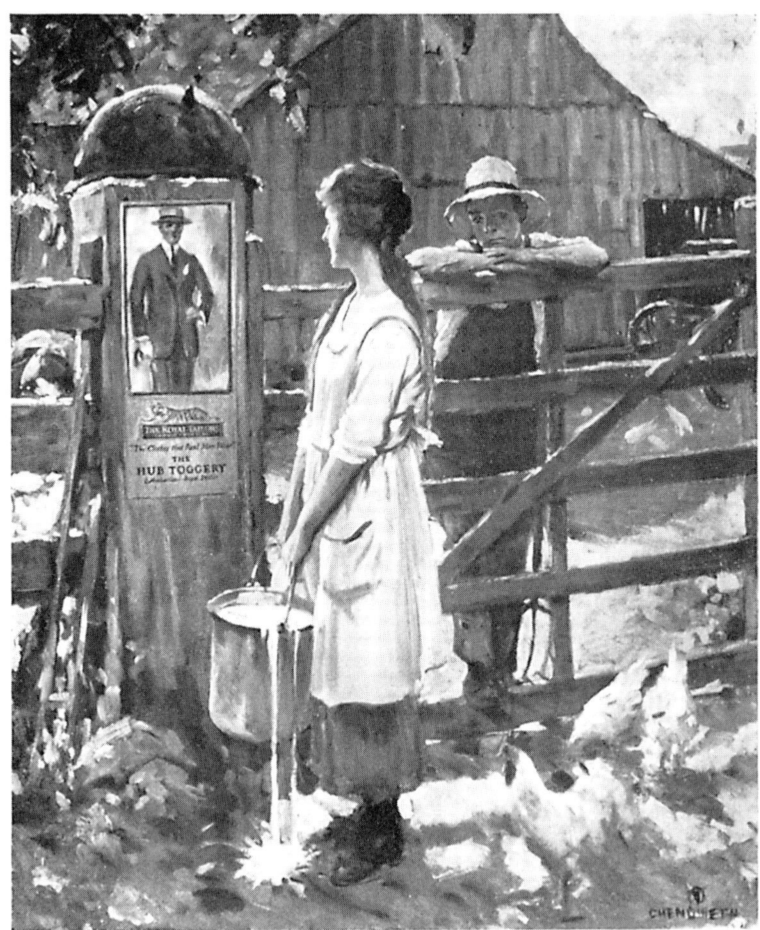

1 "Rivals"—*J. Chenoweth*
Loaned by The Royal Tailors
Exhibited by Bertsch & Cooper

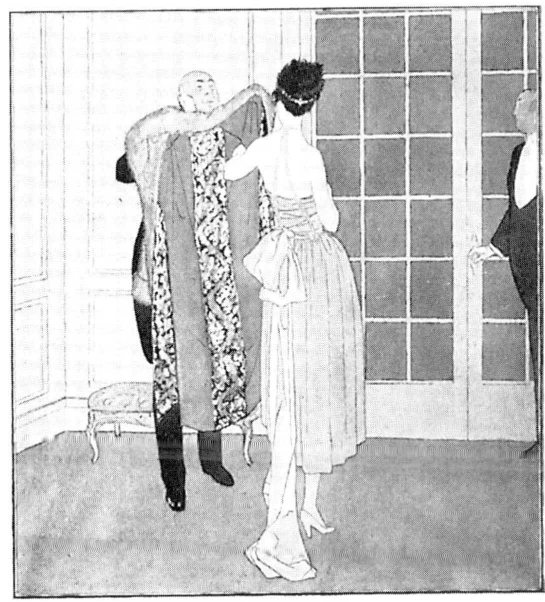

2 French Satin—*Carl Erickson*
Loaned and exhibited by Pelgram & Myer

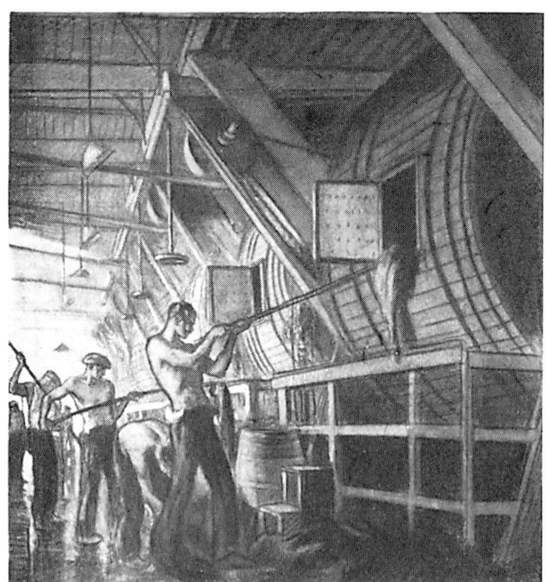

3 McElwain Shoes—*Wallace Morgan*
Loaned by W. H. McElwain Co.
Exhibited by Barton, Durstine & Osborn, Inc.

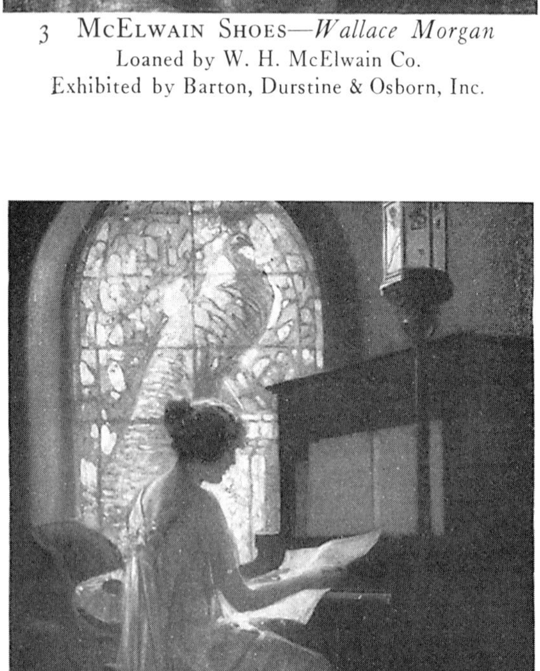

5 Packard Pianos—*Andrew Loomis*
Loaned by The Packard Company
Exhibited by Charles Everett Johnson Co.

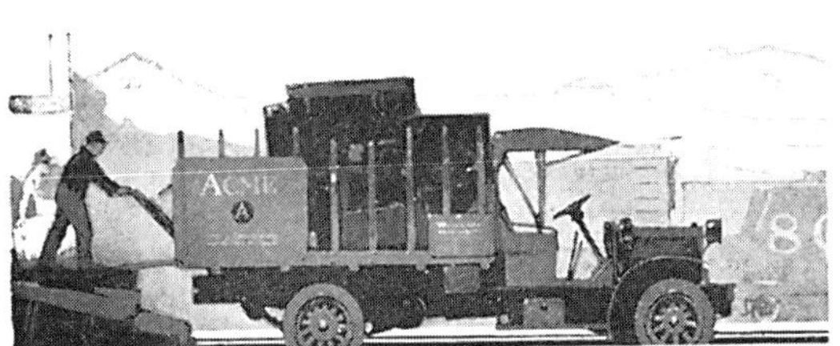

4 White Trucks—*E. G. Teale*
Loaned and exhibited by the Caxton Company

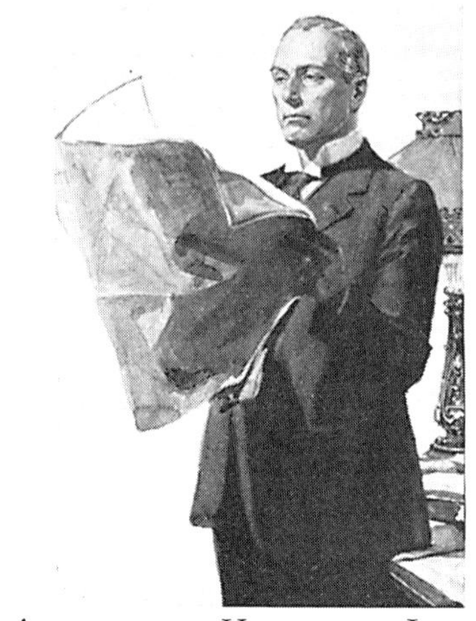

6 Alexander Hamilton Institute
Arthur William Brown
Loaned by the Alexander Hamilton Institute
Exhibited by Barton, Durstine & Osborn, Inc.

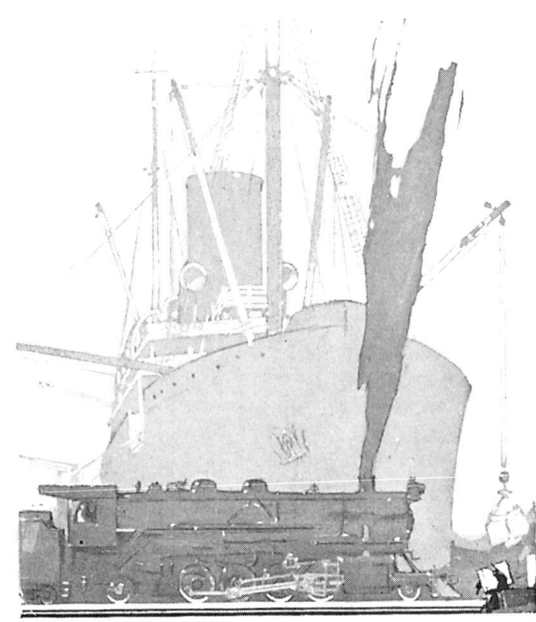

7 Burroughs Adding Machines—*Harry Lees* 8
Loaned and exhibited by the Burroughs Adding Machine Co.

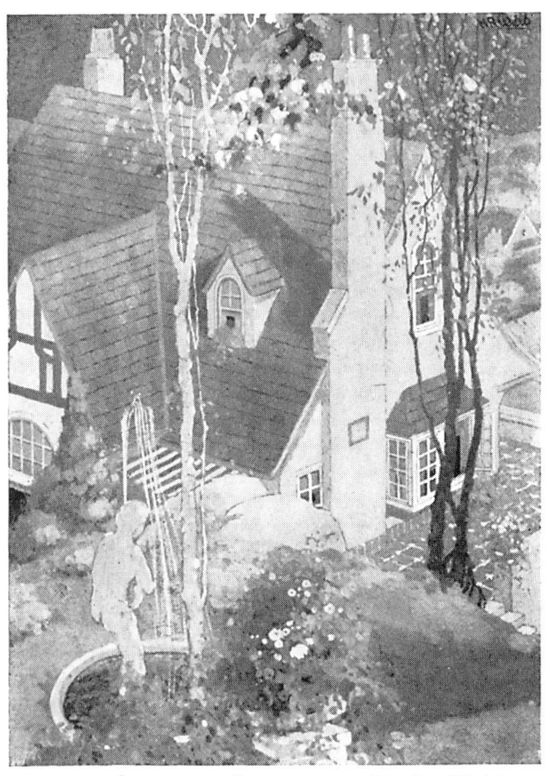

9 Asbestos Shingles—*H. R. Weld*
Loaned by the Johns-Manville Co.
Exhibited by Newell-Emmett Co., Inc.

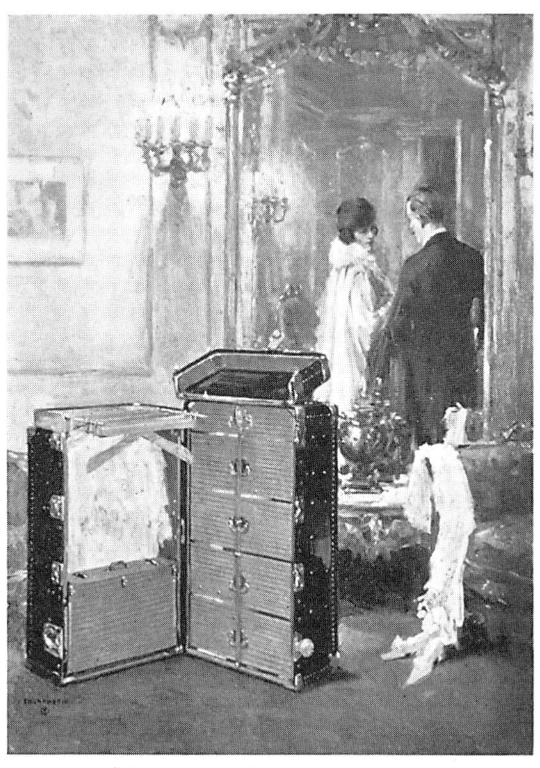

10 Hartmann Trunks—*J. Chenoweth*
Loaned by the Hartmann Trunk Co.
Exhibited by the Wm. H. Rankin Co.

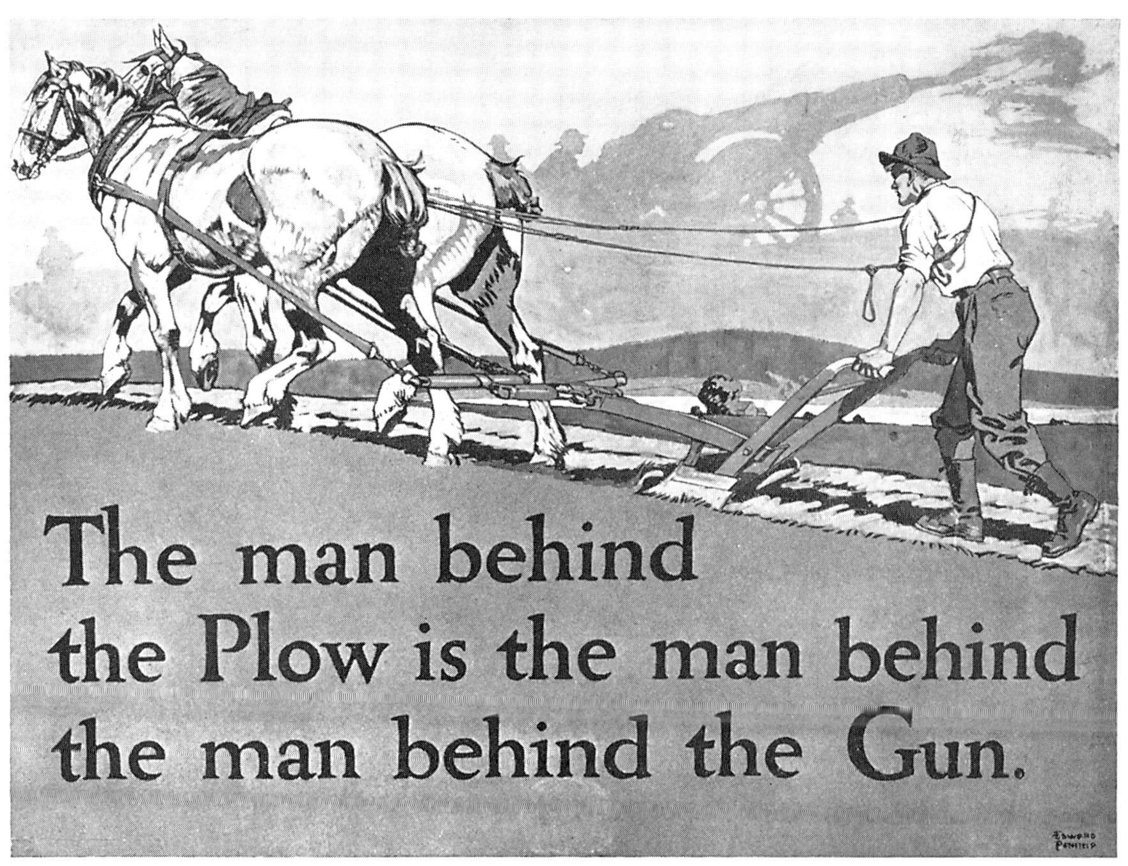

11 Department of Agriculture, U. S. Government—*Edward Penfield*
Loaned and exhibited by Edward Penfield

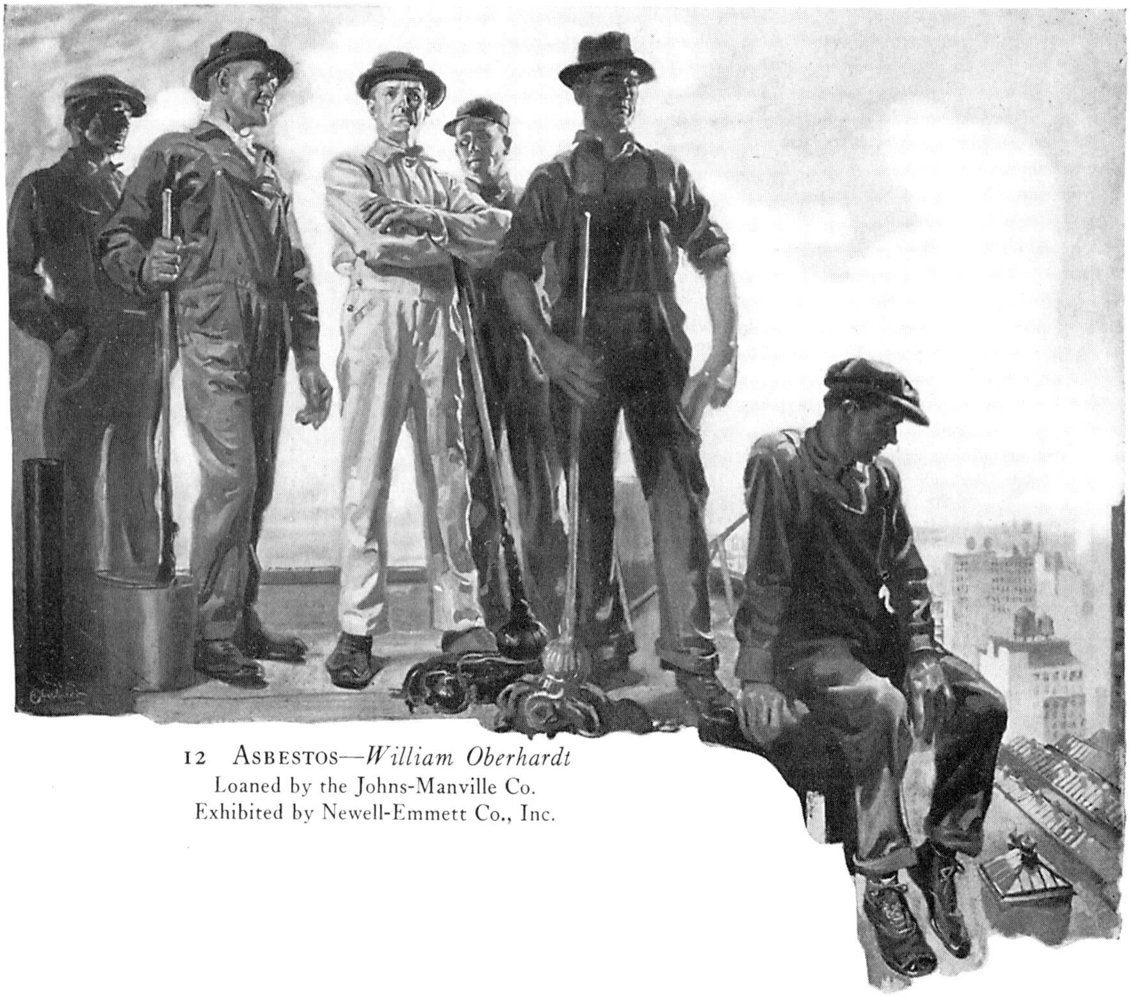

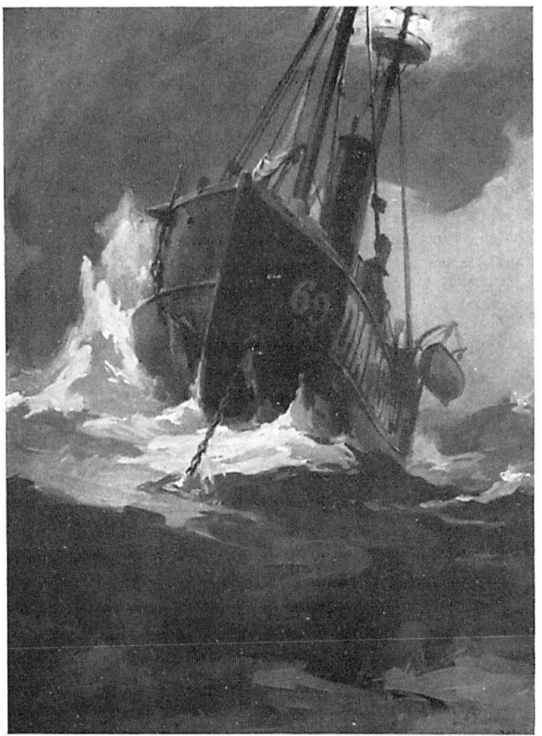

12 ASBESTOS—*William Oberhardt*
Loaned by the Johns-Manville Co.
Exhibited by Newell-Emmett Co., Inc.

13 PAINT AND VARNISH—*L. A. Shafer*
Loaned by the Paint and Varnish Association
Exhibited by the F. J. Ross Co., Inc.

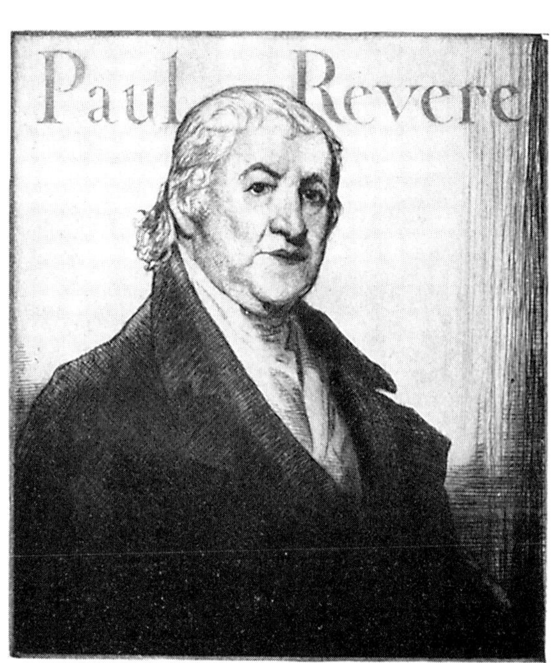

14 ETCHED PORTRAIT—*Percy Grassby*
Loaned and exhibited by the Franklin Printing Co.

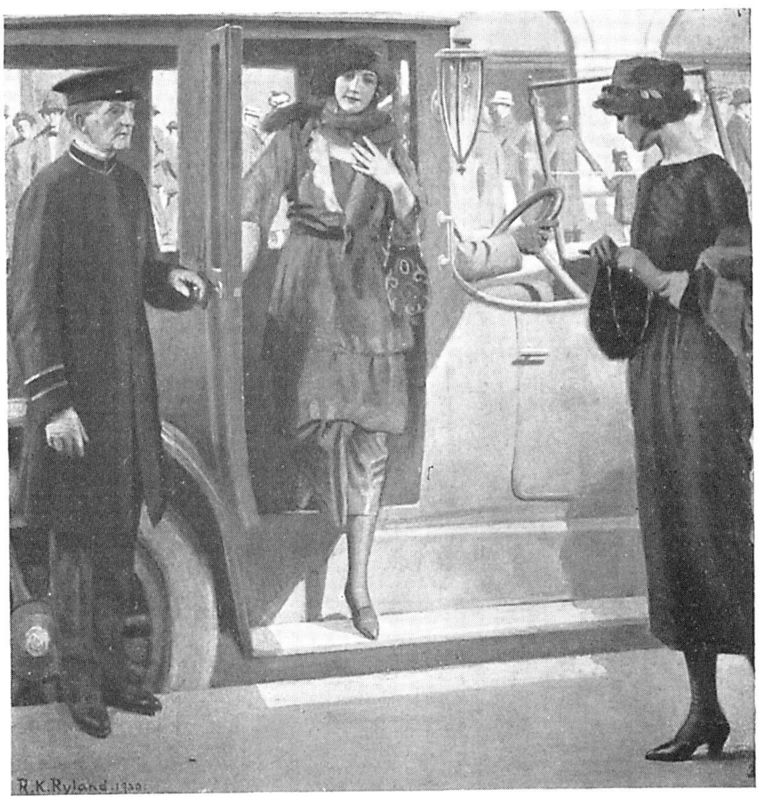

15   VODE KID—*R. K. Ryland*
Loaned by Standard Kid Manufacturing Co.
Exhibited by the George Batten Company

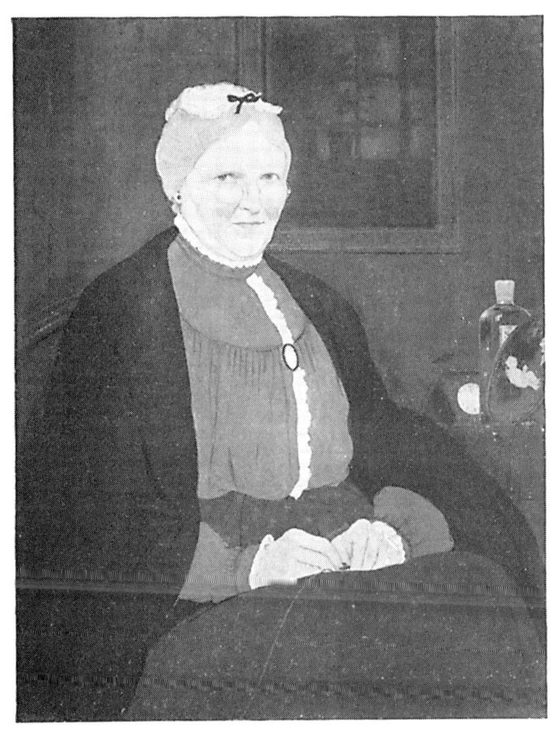

16   NUJOL—*Walter Dean Goldbeck*
Loaned by the Nujol Laboratories
Exhibited by The H. K. McCann Co.

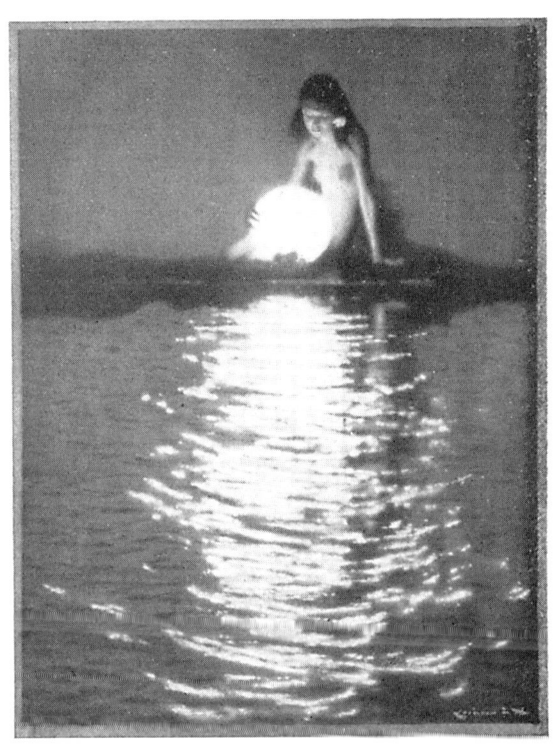

17   "MOON-GLO" SILK—*Lejaren à Hiller*
Loaned by J. A. Migel
Exhibited by Street & Finney

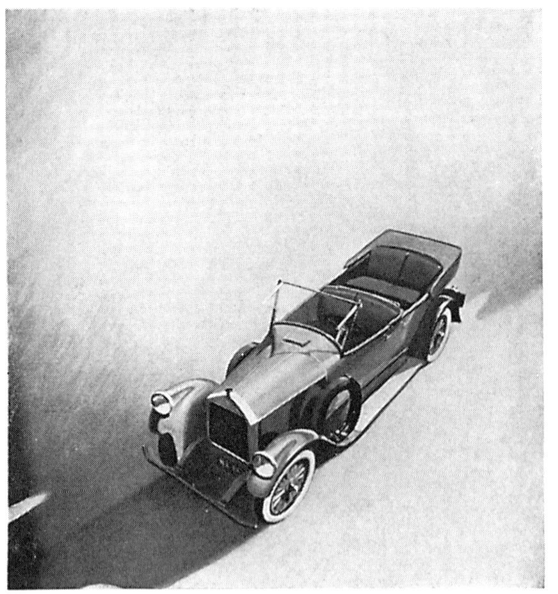

18   PIERCE-ARROW MOTOR CAR
Edward A. Wilson
Loaned by The Pierce-Arrow Motor Car Company
Exhibited by Calkins & Holden, Inc.

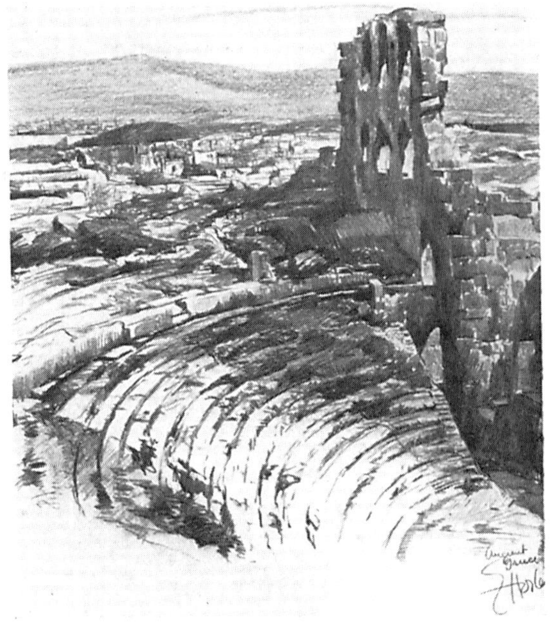

19   ELDORADO PENCILS—*Earl Horter*
Loaned by the Joseph Dixon Crucible Co.
Exhibited by N. W. Ayer & Son

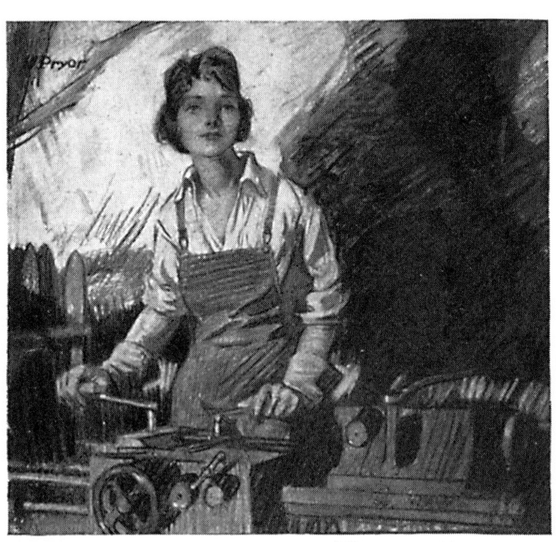

20   —*Warrant Pryor*
Loaned and exhibited by The Amsden Studios Co.

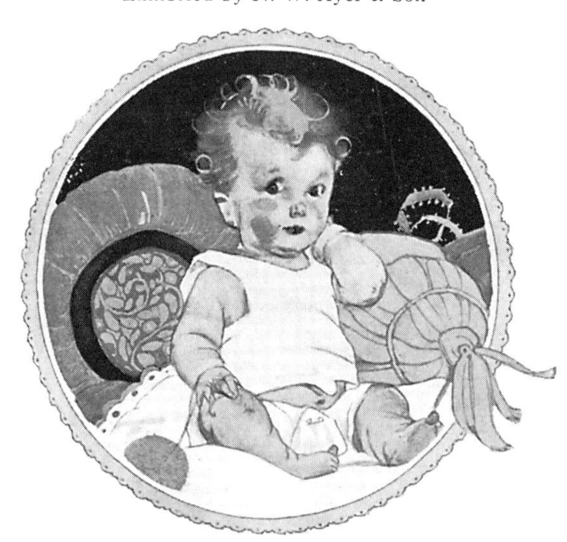

21   LUX—*Lucile Patterson Marsh*
Loaned by the Lever Bros. Co.
Exhibited by J. Walter Thompson Co.

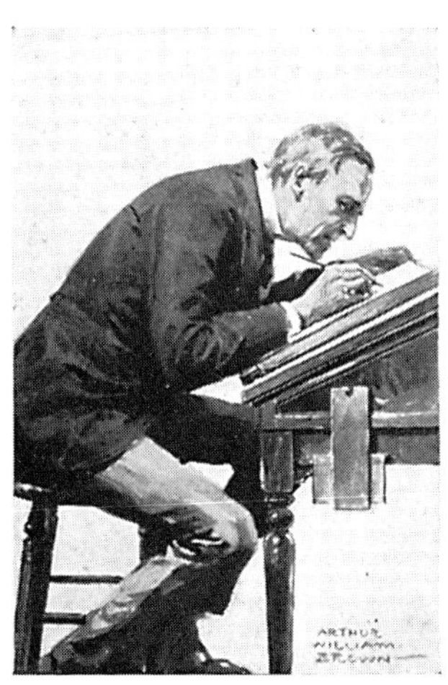

22   ALEXANDER HAMILTON INSTITUTE
Arthur William Brown
Loaned by the Alexander Hamilton Institute
Exhibited by Barton, Durstine & Osborn, Inc.

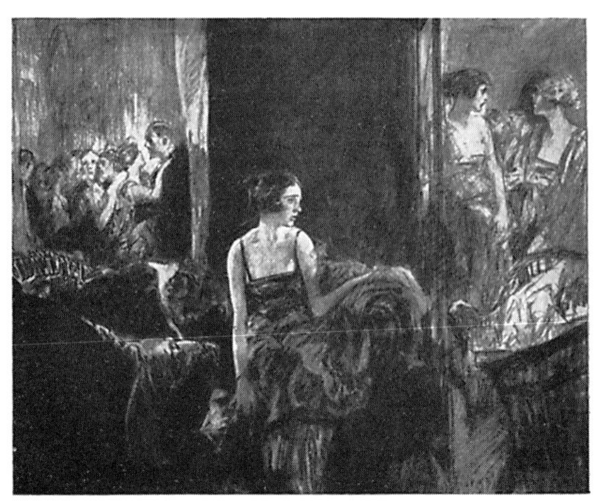

23   ODORONO—*F. R. Gruger*
Loaned by the Odorono Co.
Exhibited by J. Walter Thompson Co.

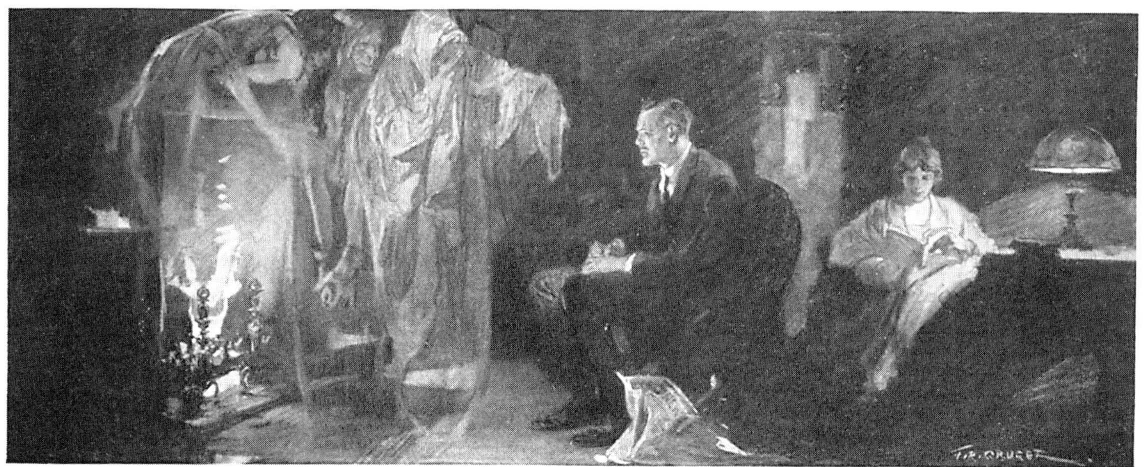

24 ALEXANDER HAMILTON INSTITUTE—*F. R. Gruger*
Loaned by the Alexander Hamilton Institute
Exhibited by Barton, Durstine & Osborn, Inc.

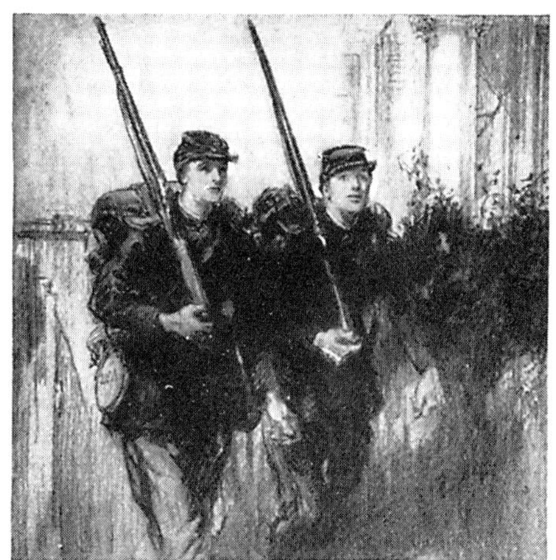

25 ALEXANDER HAMILTON INSTITUTE
Arthur William Brown
Loaned by the Alexander Hamilton Institute
Exhibited by Barton, Durstine & Osborn, Inc.

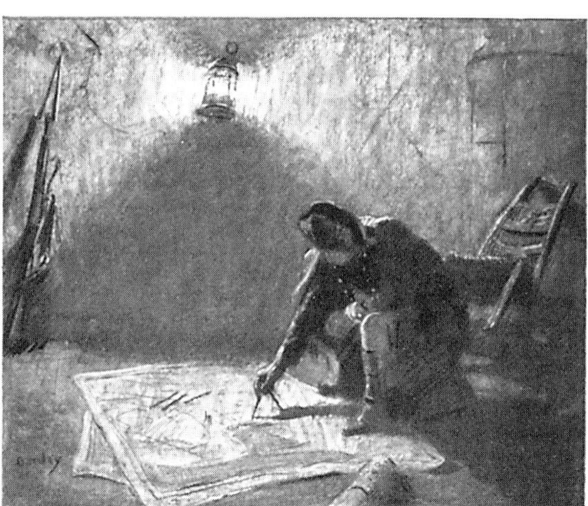

26 NAPOLEON BONAPARTE
MacClelland Barclay
Loaned and exhibited by Charles Everett Johnson Co.

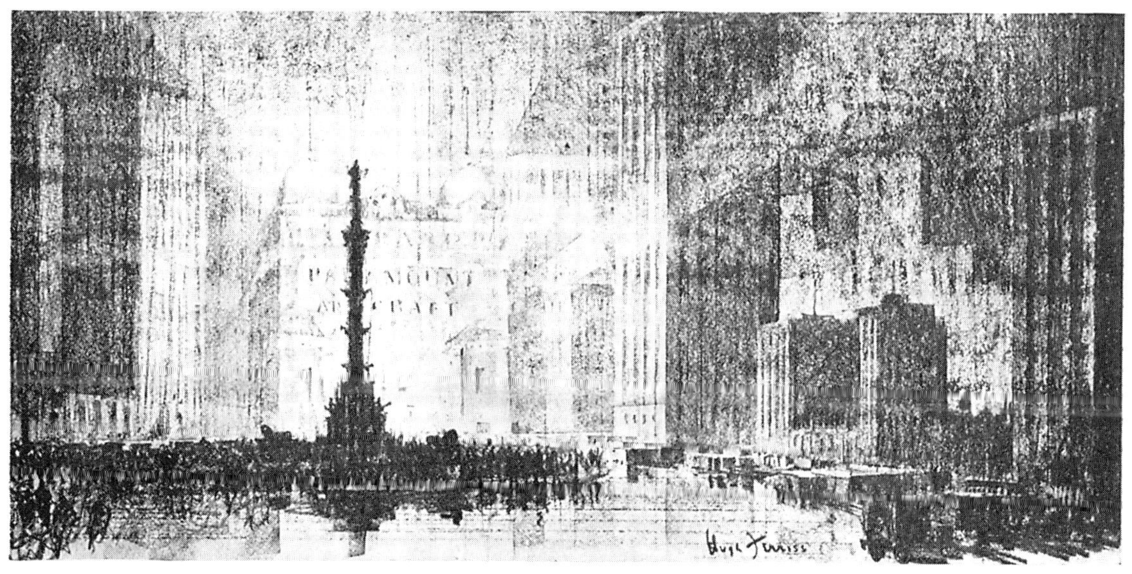

27 PARAMOUNT PICTURES—*Hugh Ferriss*
Loaned by the Famous Players-Lasky Corporation
Exhibited by Hanff-Metzger, Inc.

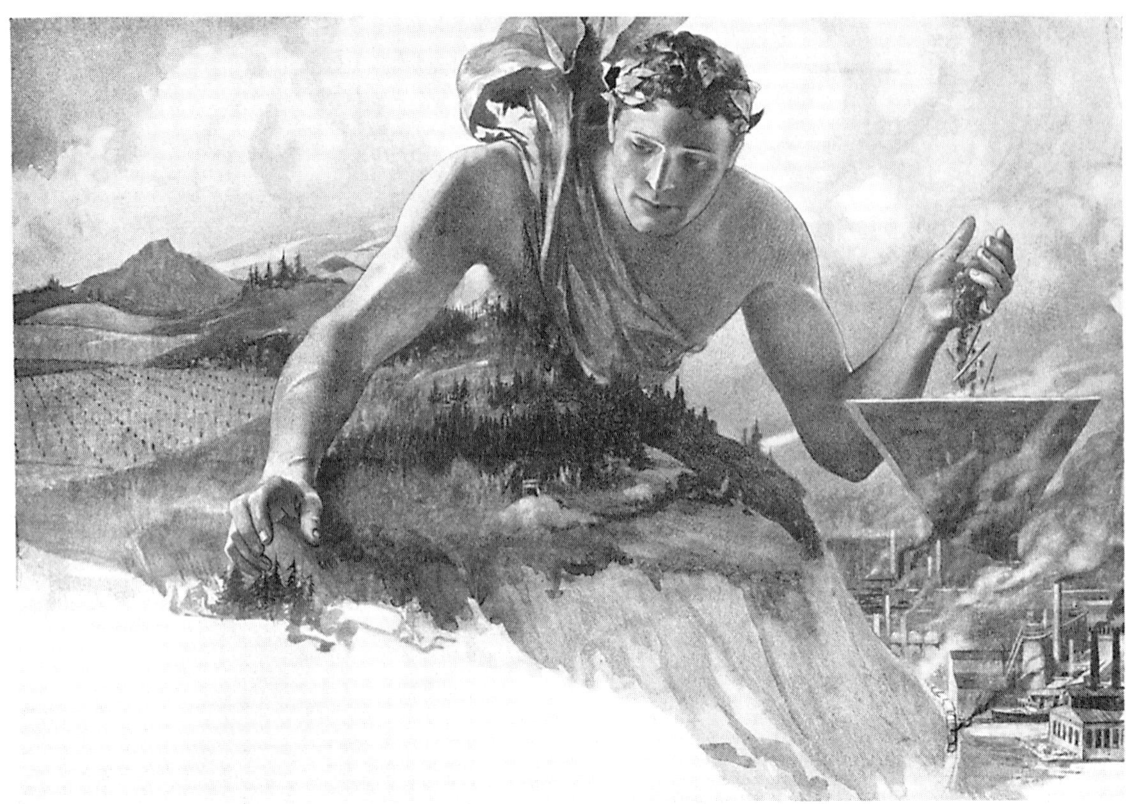

28   SECURITIES—*A. E. Foringer*
Loaned by the National City Co.
Exhibited by The Blackman Co.

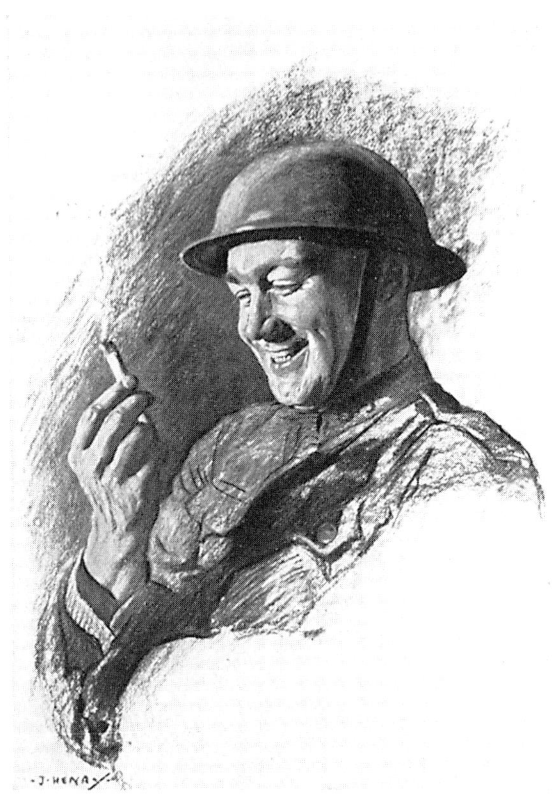

29   EVER-READY SAFETY RAZOR
J. Henry Bracker
Loaned by the American Safety Razor Co.
Exhibited by the Federal Advertising Agency, Inc.

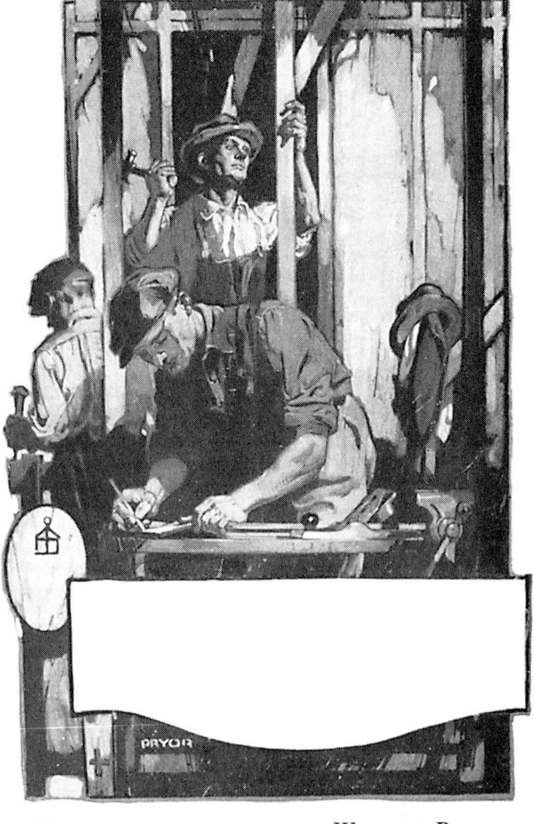

30   —*Warrant Pryor*
Loaned and exhibited by The Amsden Studios Co.

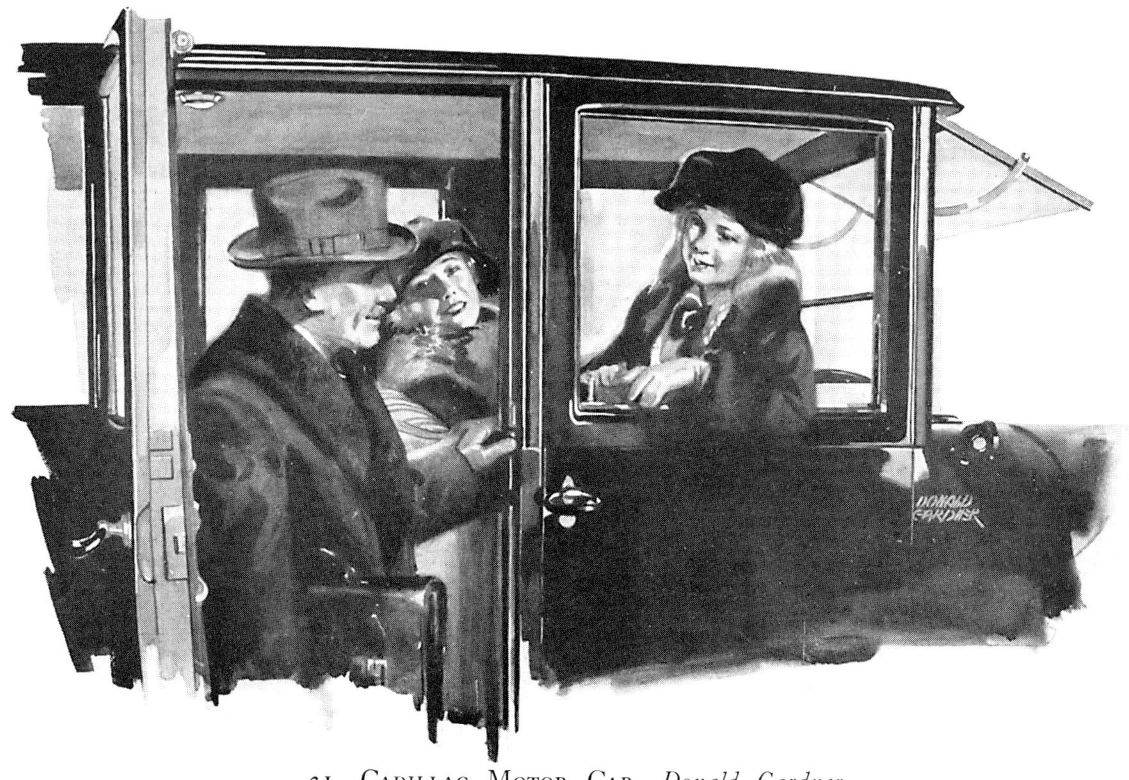

31　Cadillac Motor Car—*Donald Gardner*
Loaned by the Cadillac Motor Car Co.
Exhibited by T. F. MacManus, Inc.

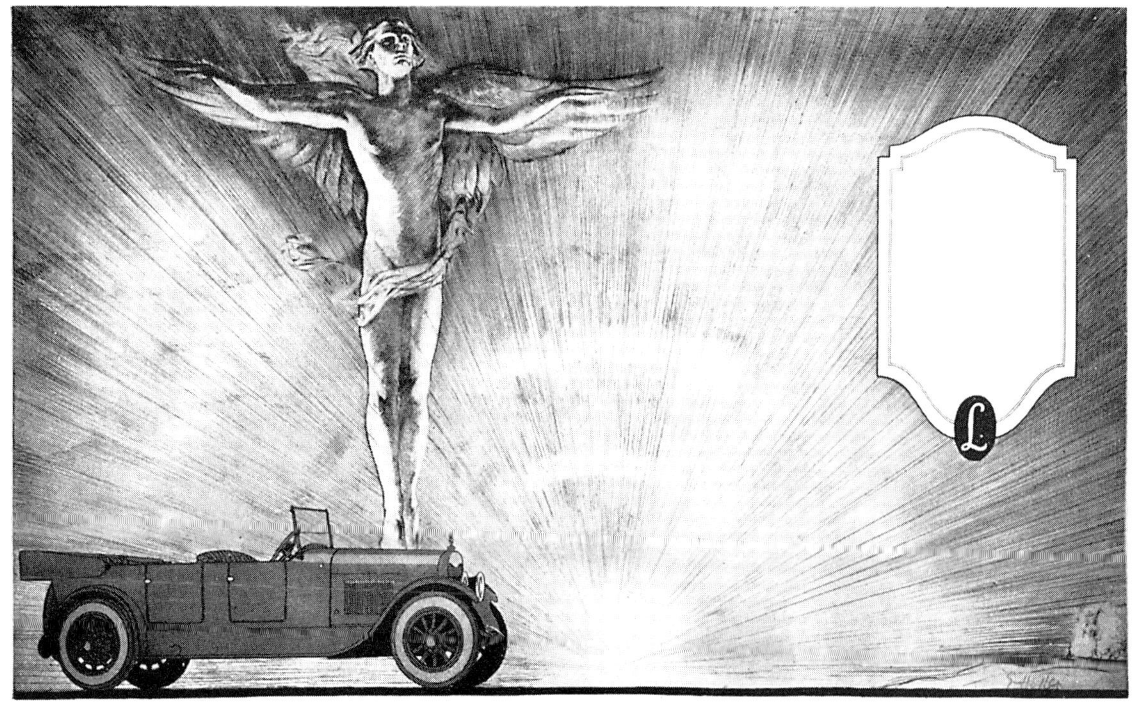

32　Lincoln Motors—*Earl Horter*
Loaned and exhibited by the Lincoln Motor Co.

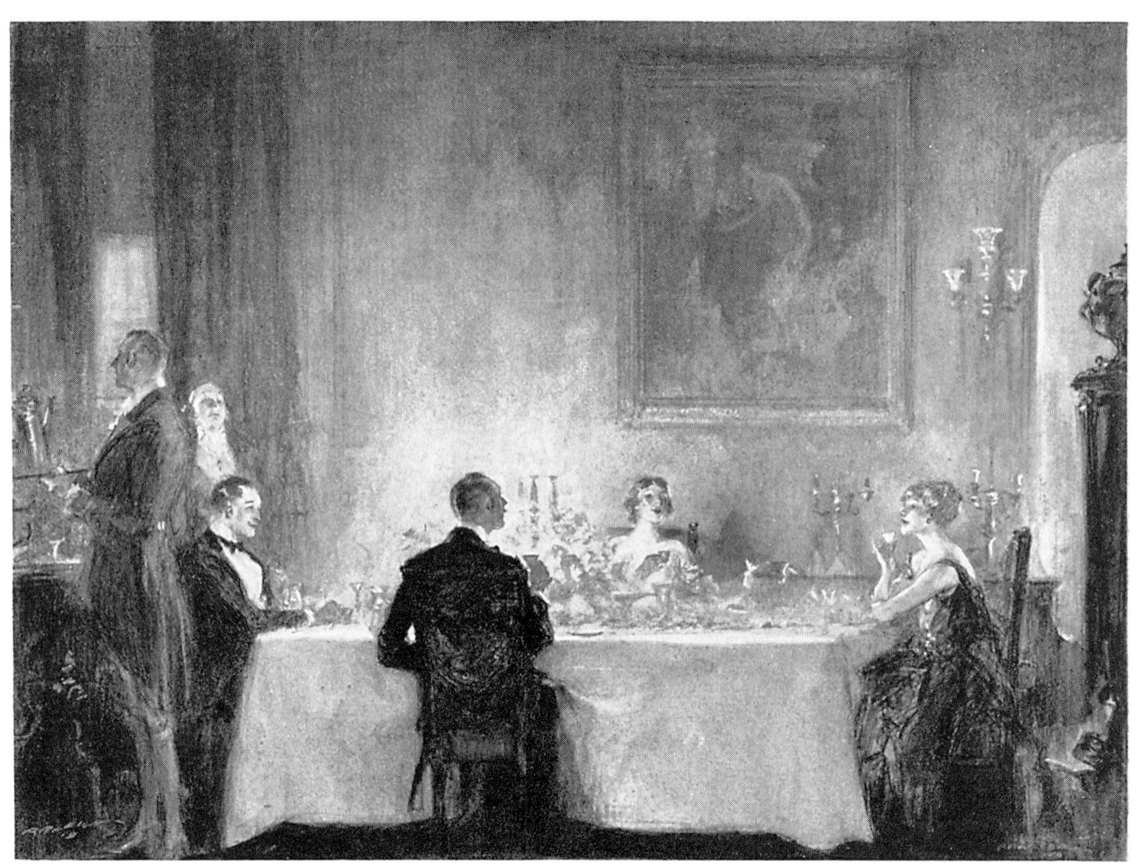

33 YUBAN COFFEE—*Henry Raleigh*
Loaned by Arbuckle Bros.
Exhibited by J. Walter Thompson Co.

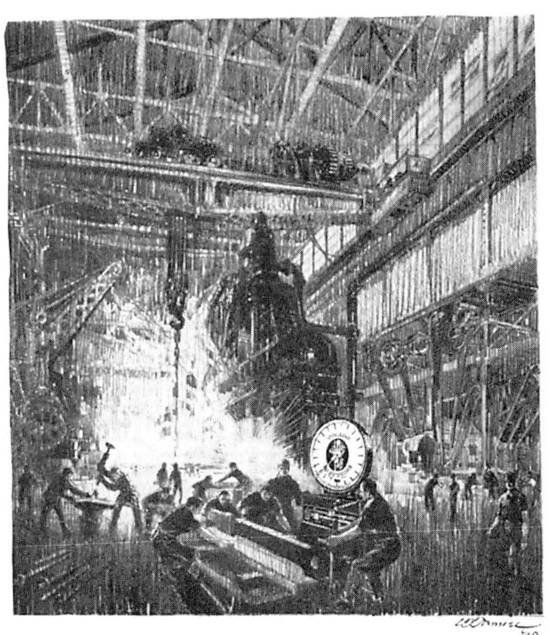

34 AUTOMATIC SCALES—*A. T. Tornrose*
Loaned by the Toledo Scales Co.
Exhibited by The Blackman Co.

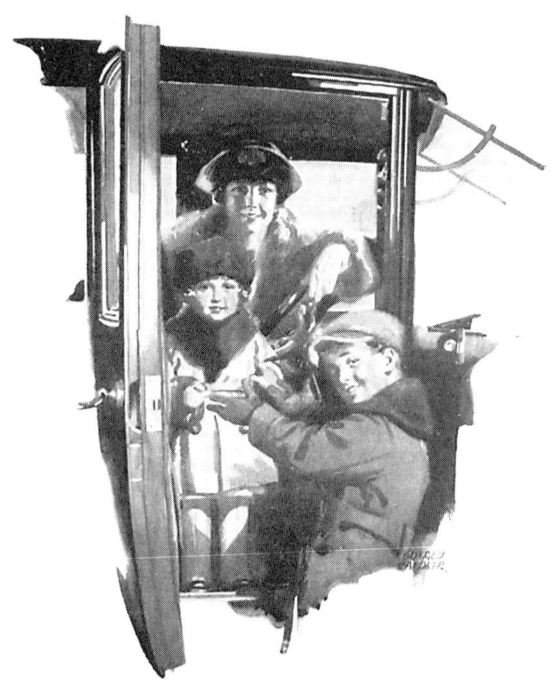

35 CADILLAC MOTOR CARS—*Donald Gardner*
Loaned by the Cadillac Motor Car Co.
Exhibited by T. F. MacManus, Inc.

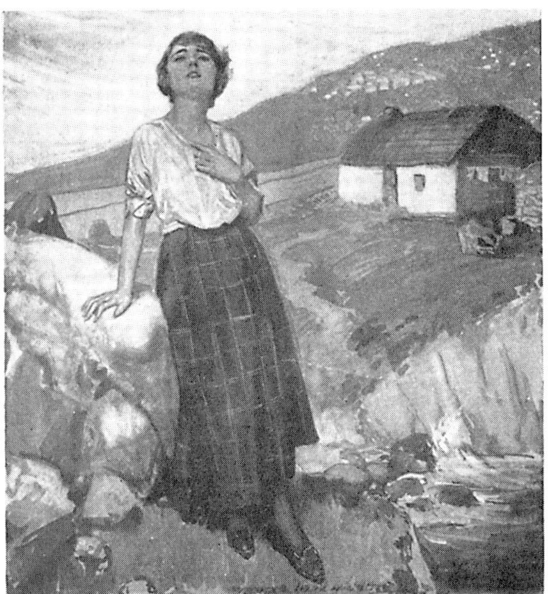

36 VICTOR RECORDS—*Vaux Wilson*
Loaned by the Victor Talking Machine Co.
Exhibited by the Franklin Printing Co.

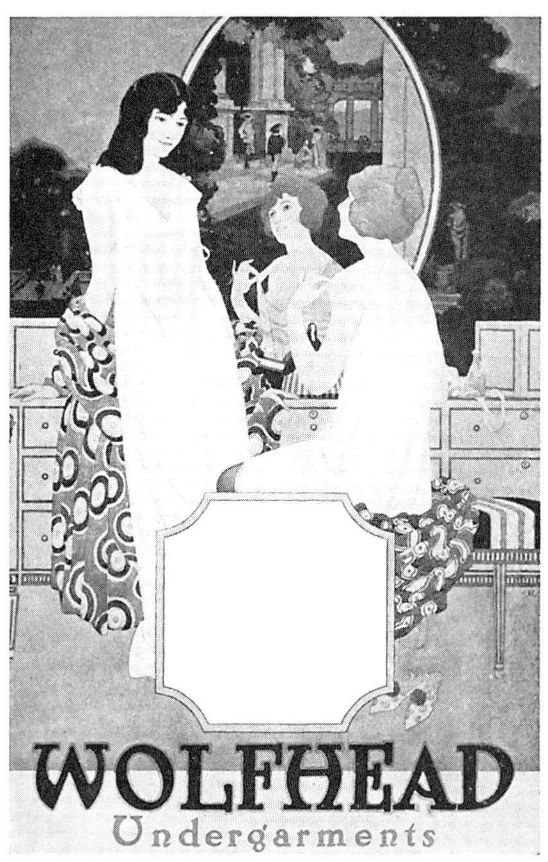

37 WOLFHEAD UNDERGARMENTS—*The Reeses*
Loaned by The Wolf Co.
Exhibited by Barrows & Richardson

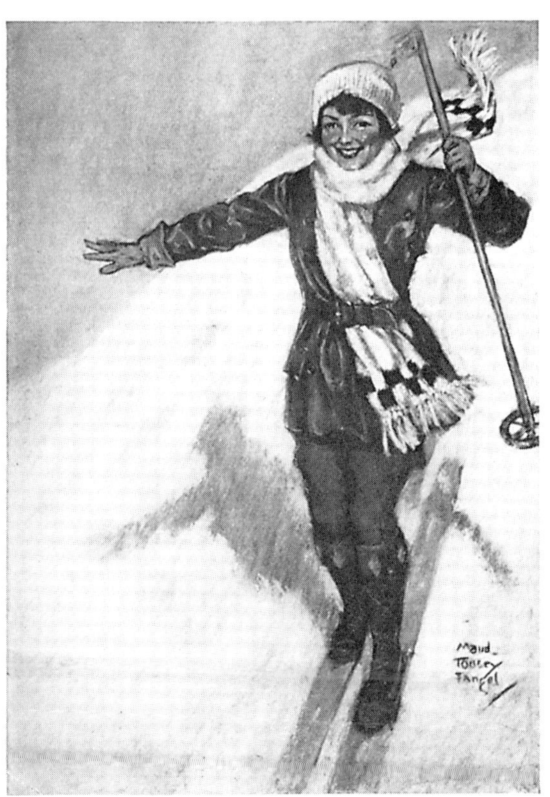

38 FACE CREAM—*Maud Tousey Fangel*
Loaned by Colgate & Co.
Exhibited by Frank Seaman, Inc.

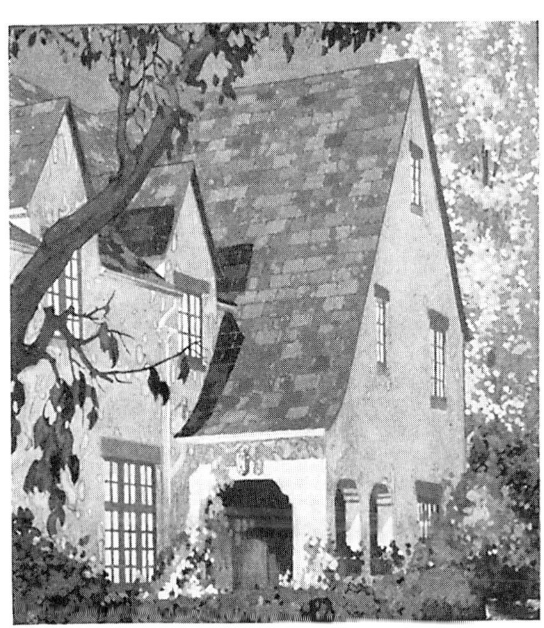

39 ASBESTOS SHINGLES—*Stanley F. McNeill*
Loaned by the Johns-Manville Co.
Exhibited by Newell-Emmett Co., Inc.

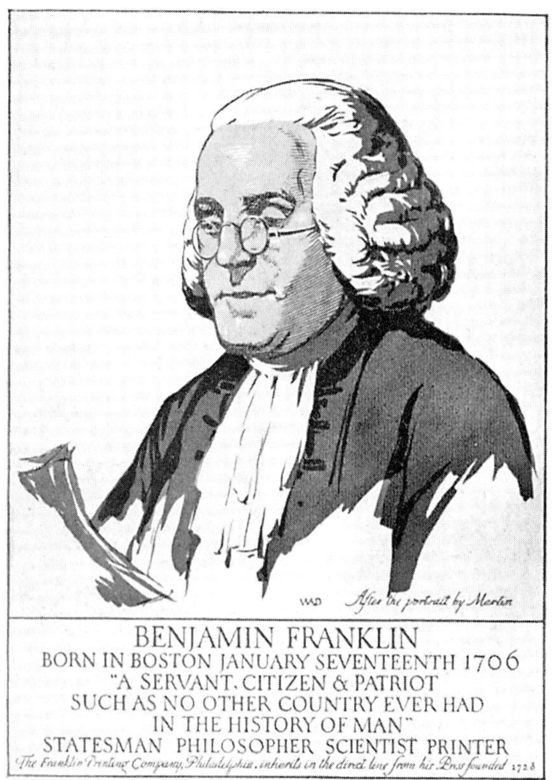

40 PORTRAIT—*W. A. Dwiggins*
Loaned and exhibited by the Franklin Printing Co.

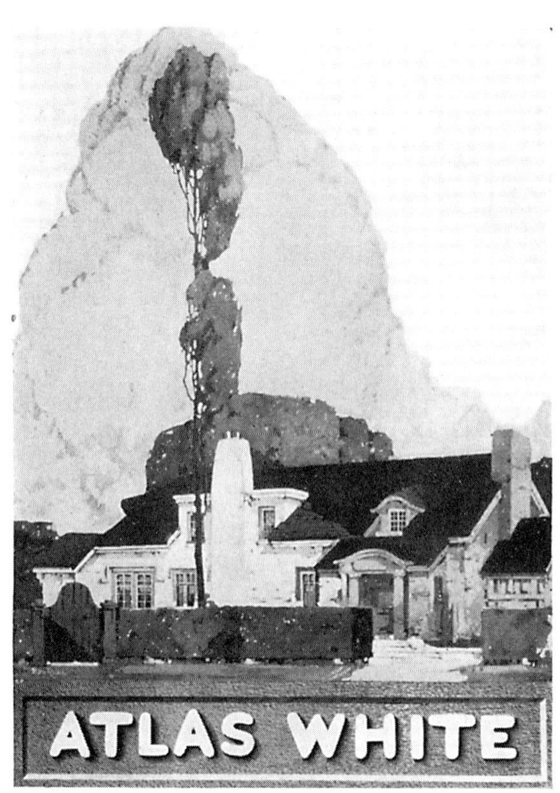

41 ATLAS PORTLAND CEMENT
Thomas D. Ben Rimo
Loaned by the Atlas Portland Cement Co.
Exhibited by Frank Seaman, Inc.

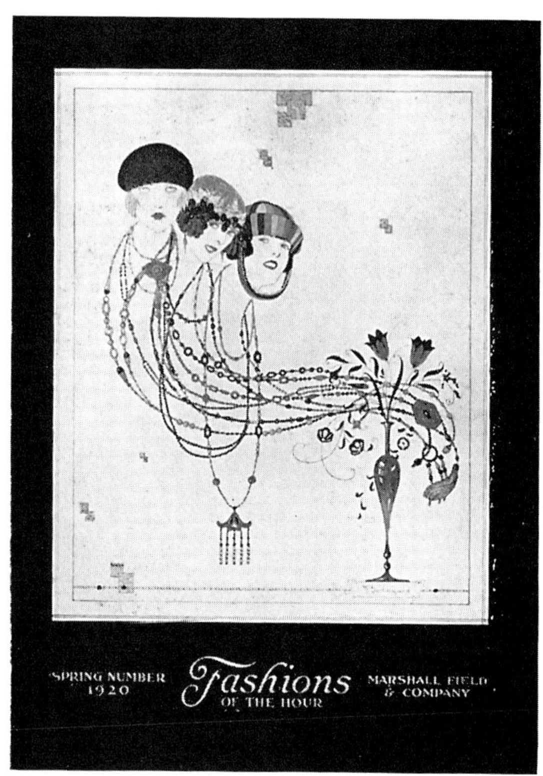

42 COVER DESIGN—*Joseph Bolegard*
Loaned by Marshall Field & Co.
Exhibited by the Wm. H. Rankin Co.

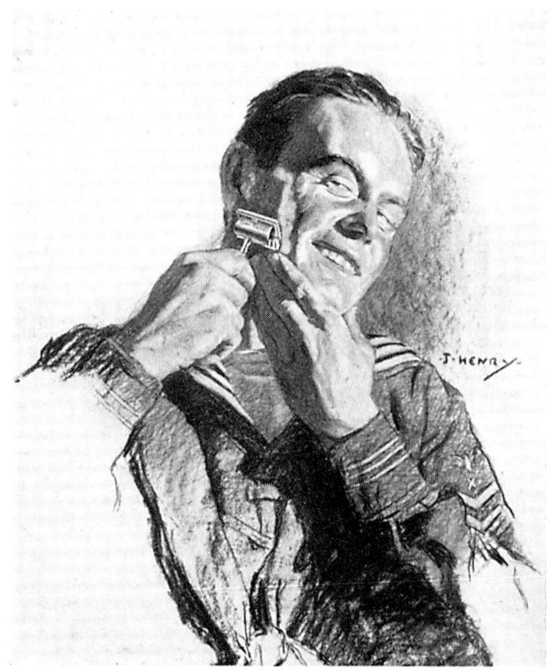

43 EVER-READY SAFETY RAZOR
J. Henry Bracker
Loaned by the American Safety Razor Co.
Exhibited by the Federal Advertising Agency, Inc.

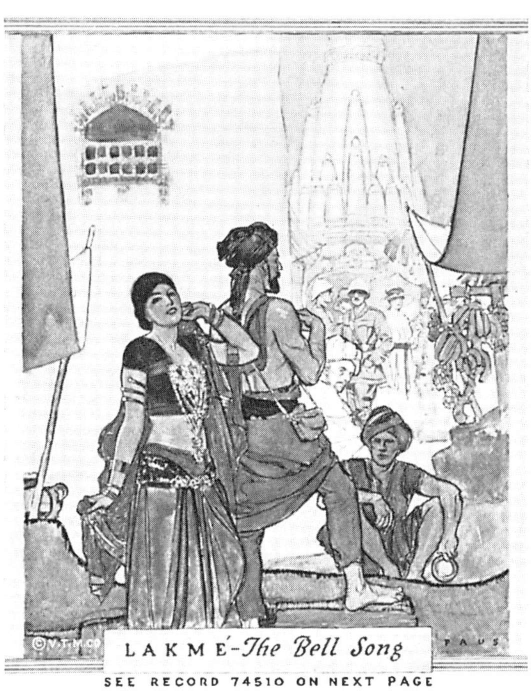

44   VICTOR RECORDS—*Herbert Paus*
Loaned by the Victor Talking Machine Co.
Exhibited by the Franklin Printing Co.

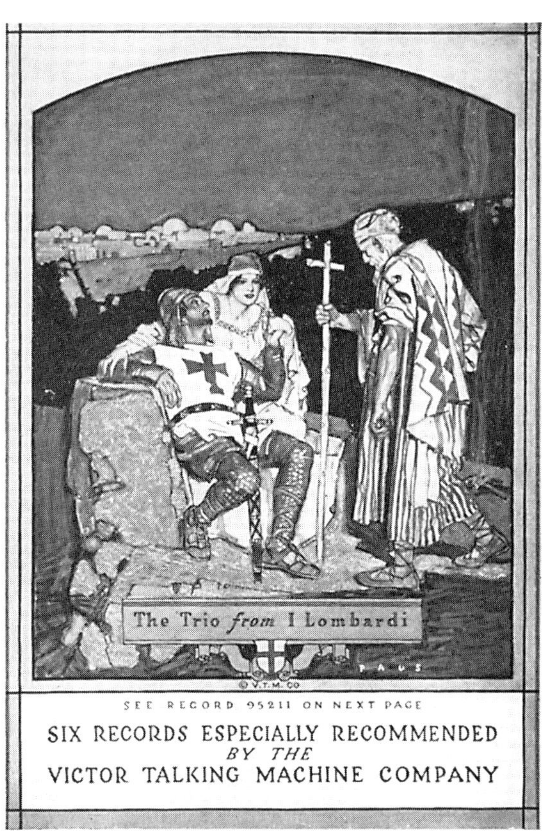

45   VICTOR RECORDS—*Herbert Paus*
Loaned by the Victor Talking Machine Co.
Exhibited by the Franklin Printing Co.

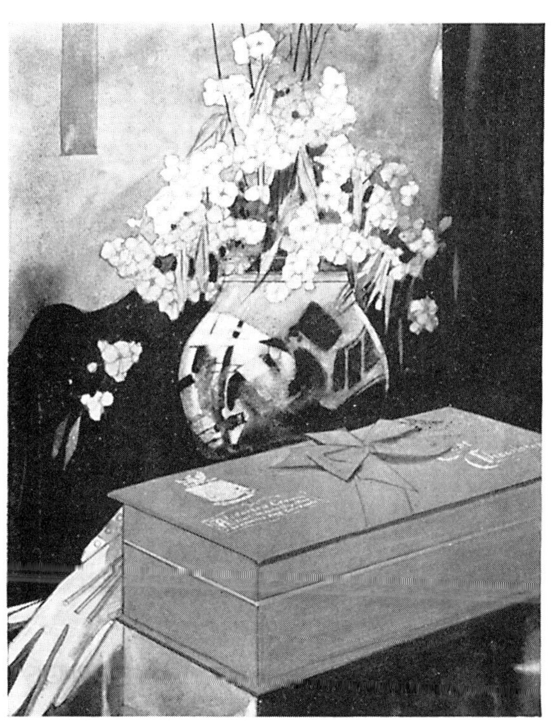

46   LOWNEY'S CHOCOLATES—*Wm. Rienecke*
Loaned by the Walter Lowney Co.
Exhibited by The Blackman Co.

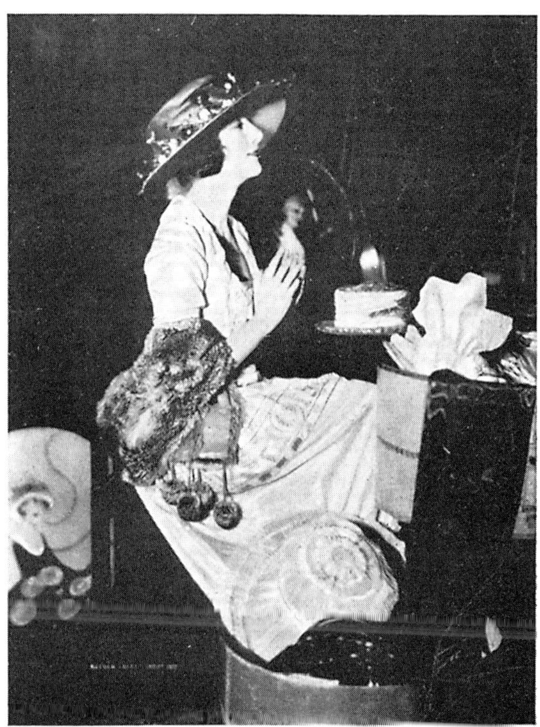

47   WOMEN'S HATS—*Alfred Cheney Johnston*
Loaned and exhibited by Dobbs & Co.

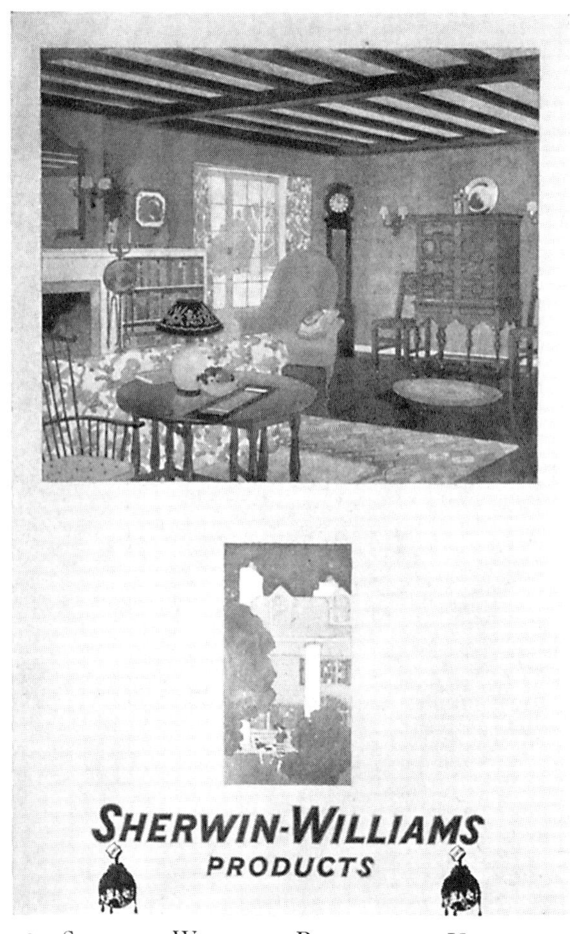

48   SHERWIN-WILLIAMS PAINTS AND VARNISHES
The Reeses
Loaned by The Sherwin-Williams Co.
Exhibited by Calkins & Holden, Inc.

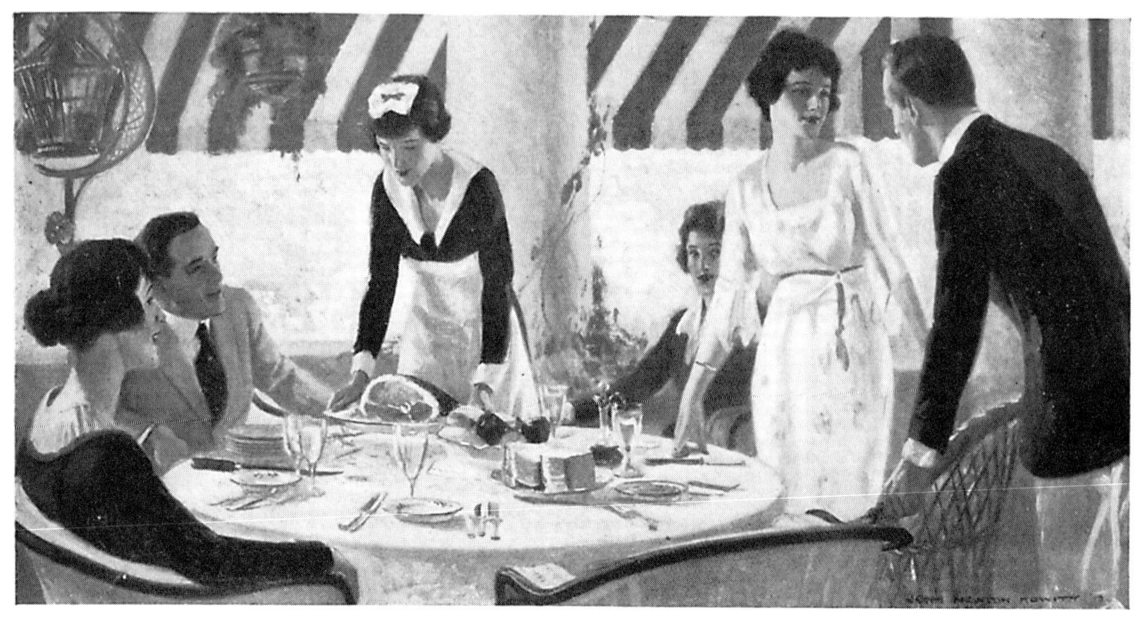

49   SMOKED HAM—*John Newton Howitt*
Loaned by Swift & Co., Inc.
Exhibited by J. Walter Thompson Co.

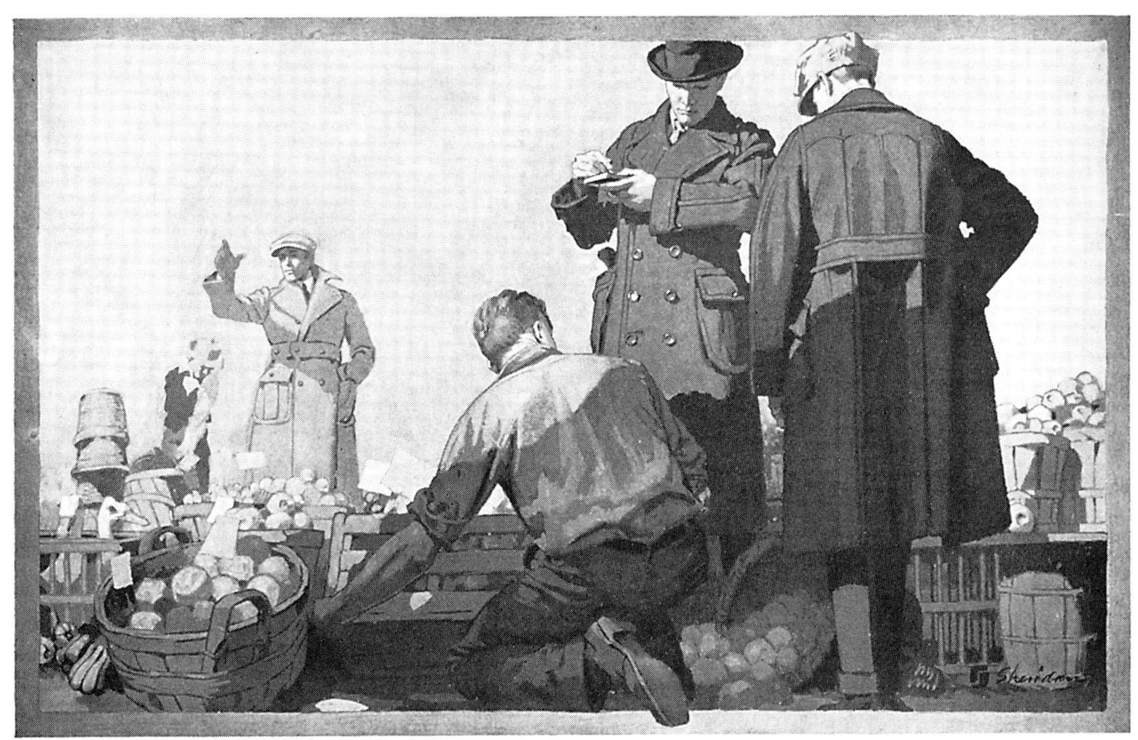

50 Men's Clothing—*John E. Sheridan*
Loaned and exhibited by Hart Schaffner & Marx

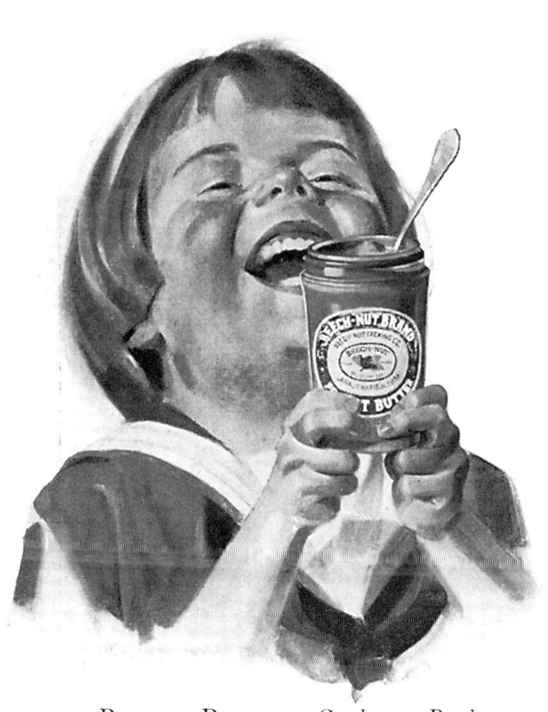

51 Peanut Butter—*Cushman Parker*
Loaned by the Beechnut Packing Company
Exhibited by The H. K. McCann Co.

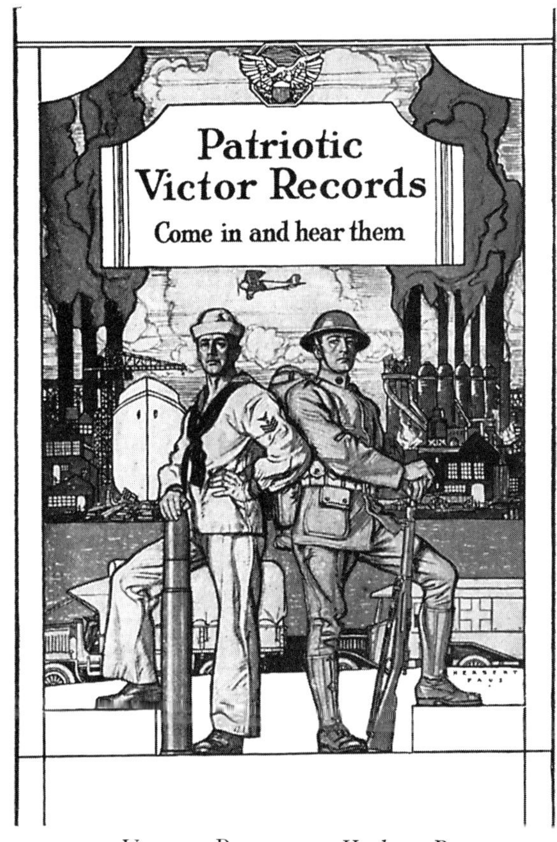

52 Victor Records—*Herbert Paus*
Loaned by the Victor Talking Machine Co.
Exhibited by the Franklin Printing Co.

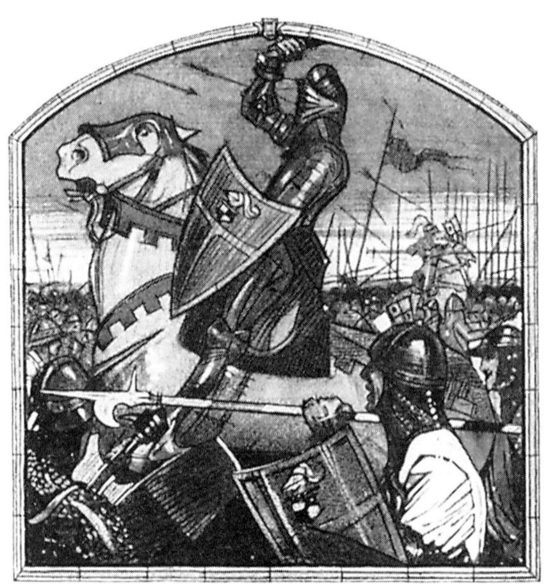

53 LIBERTY TAPE—*Edmund G. Davenport*
Loaned by the Liberty Paper Co.
Exhibited by The H. K. McCann Co.

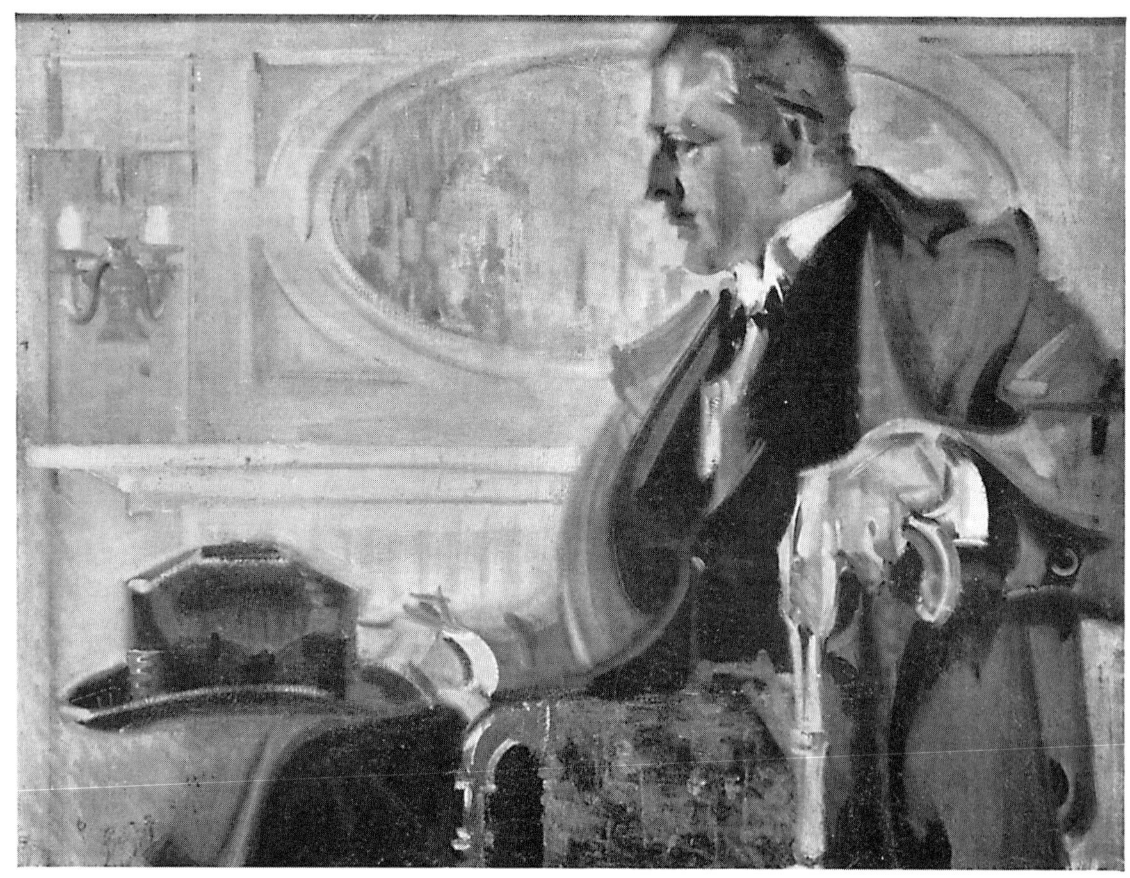

54 MALLORY HATS—*Leon M. Gordon*
Loaned by E. A. Mallory & Sons, Inc.
Exhibited by George Batten Co., Inc.

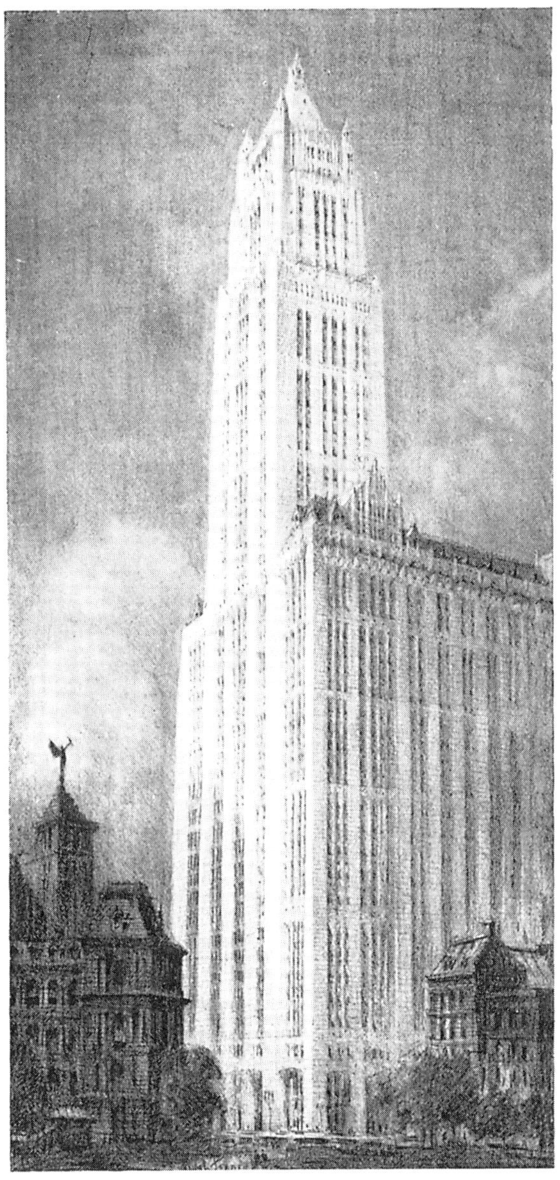

55   TERRA-COTTA—*Hugh Ferriss*
Loaned by the National Terra-Cotta Society
Exhibited by The Erickson Co.

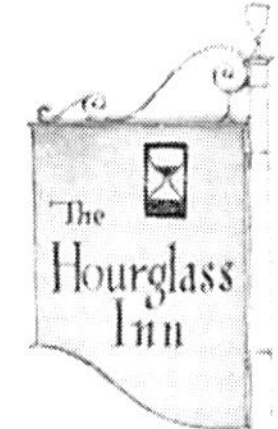

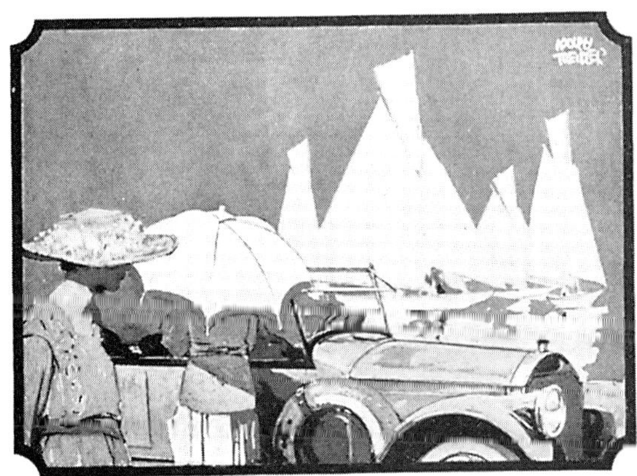

56   PIERCE-ARROW MOTOR CARS—*Adolph Treidler*
Loaned by The Pierce-Arrow Motor Car Company
Exhibited by the Bartlett-Orr Press

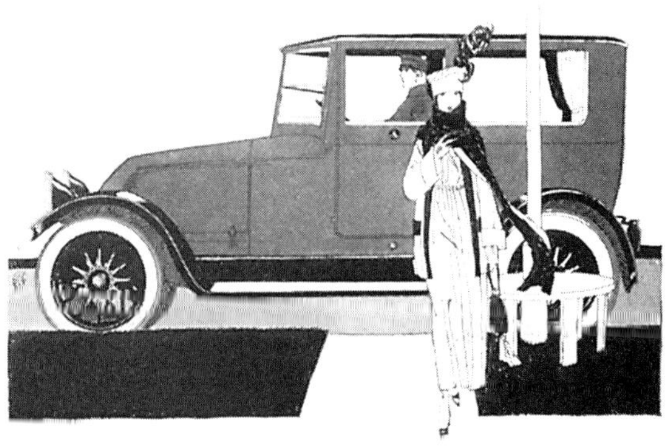

57   FRANKLIN MOTOR CARS—*F. T. Chapman*
Loaned by the Franklin Automobile Company
Exhibited by Patterson-Andress Co., Inc.

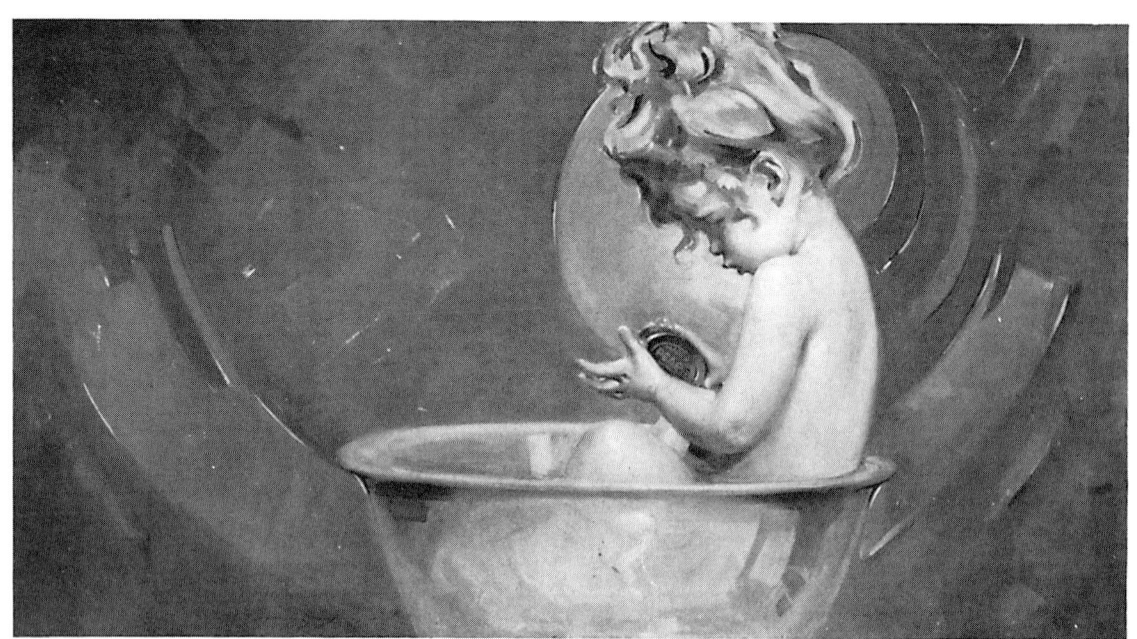

58   PEARS SOAP—*Charles E. Chambers*
Loaned by the Walter Janvier Co.
Exhibited by George Batten Co., Inc.

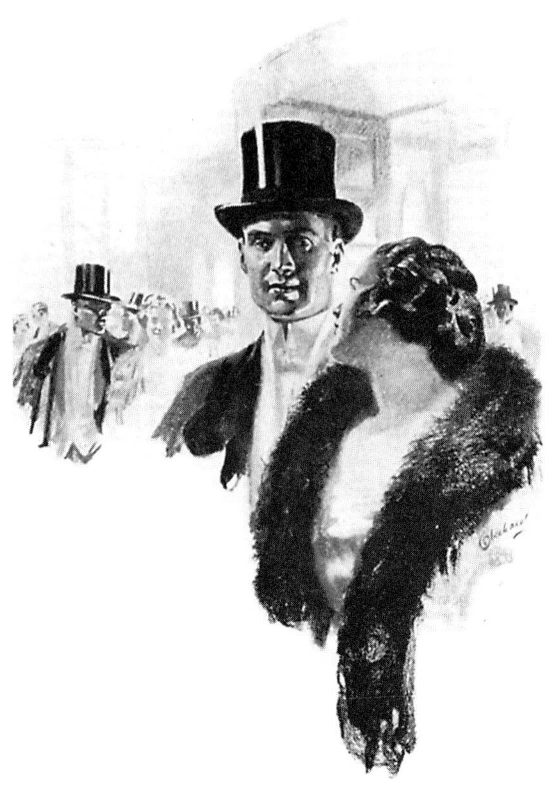

59   FATIMA CIGARETTES—*Wm. Oberhardt*
Loaned by the Liggett & Myers Tobacco Co.
Exhibited by Newell-Emmett Co., Inc.

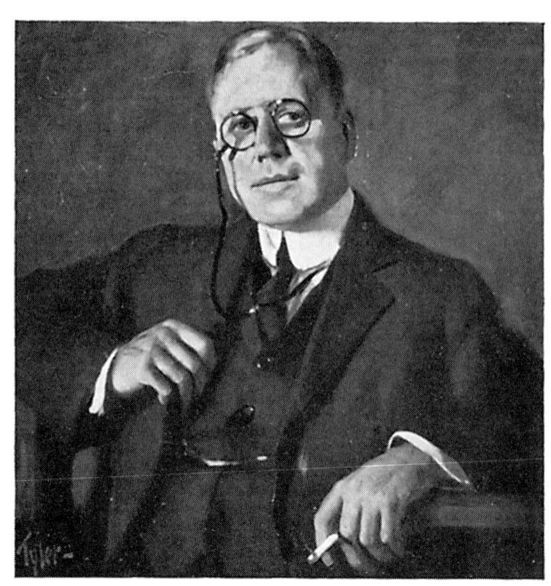

60   FATIMA CIGARETTES—*Audubon Tyler*
Loaned by the Liggett & Myers Tobacco Co.
Exhibited by Newell-Emmett Co., Inc.

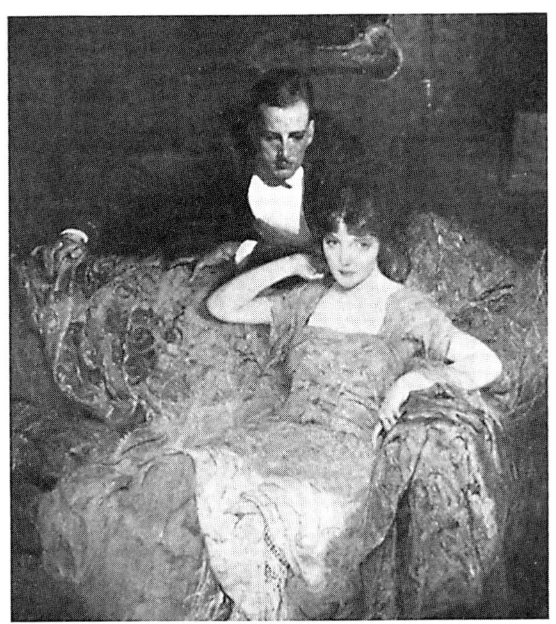

61   WOODBURY'S FACIAL SOAP—*Dean Cornwell*
Loaned by The Andrew Jergens Company
Exhibited by J. Walter Thompson Co.

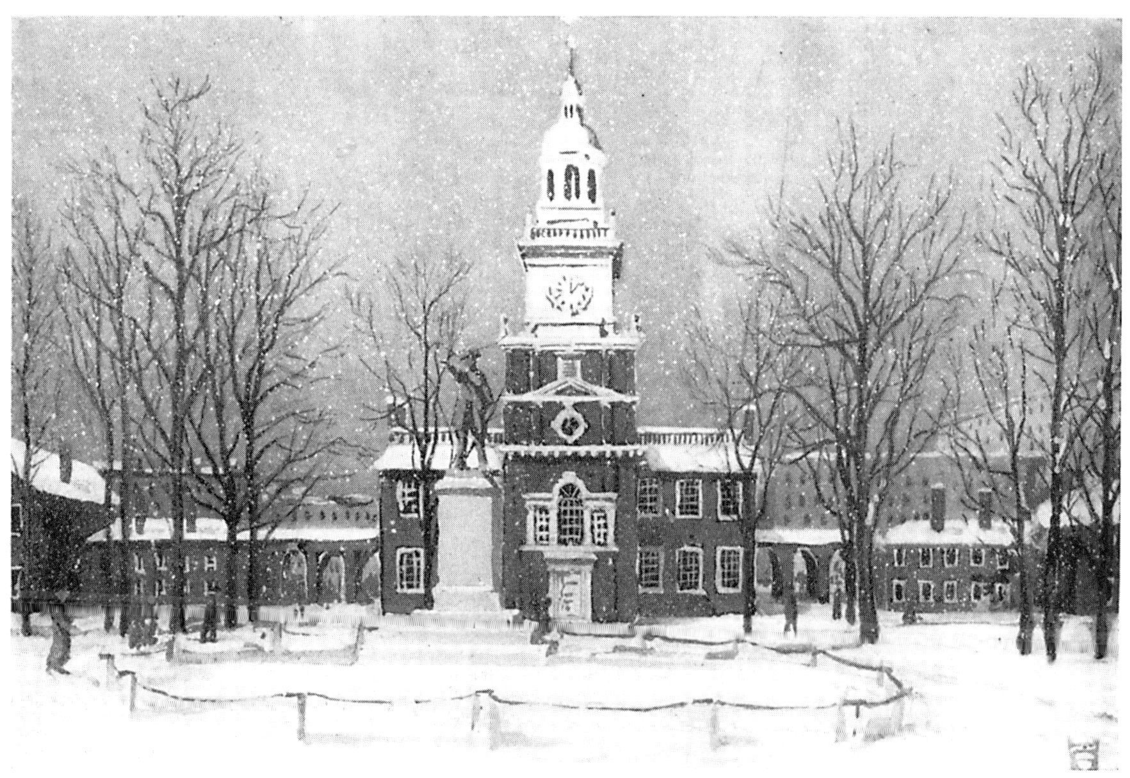

62   INDEPENDENCE HALL—*Charles R. Paul*
Loaned and exhibited by the Franklin Printing Co.

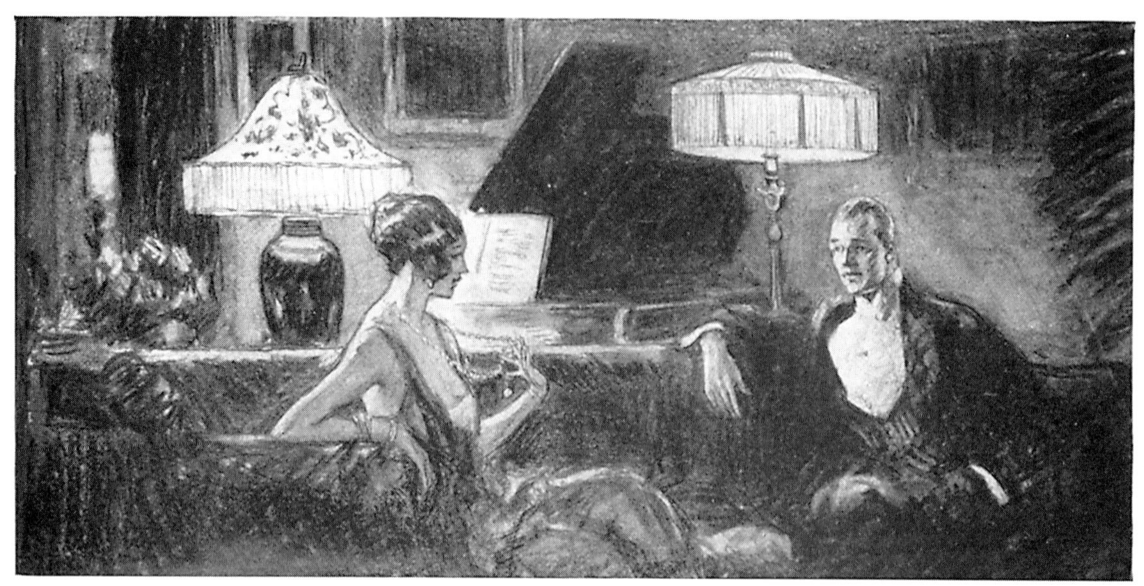

63 OVINGTON'S—*Wallace Morgan*
Loaned by Ovington Bros. Co.
Exhibited by Barton, Durstine & Osborn, Inc.

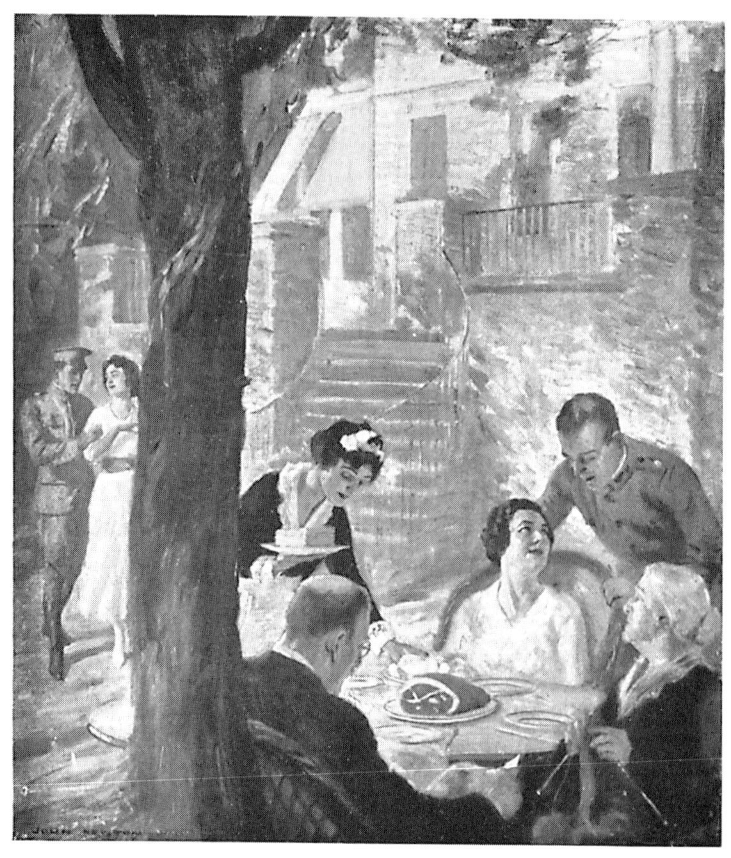

64 SWIFT'S HAM AND BACON
John Newton Howitt
Loaned by Swift & Co., Inc.
Exhibited by J. Walter Thompson Co.

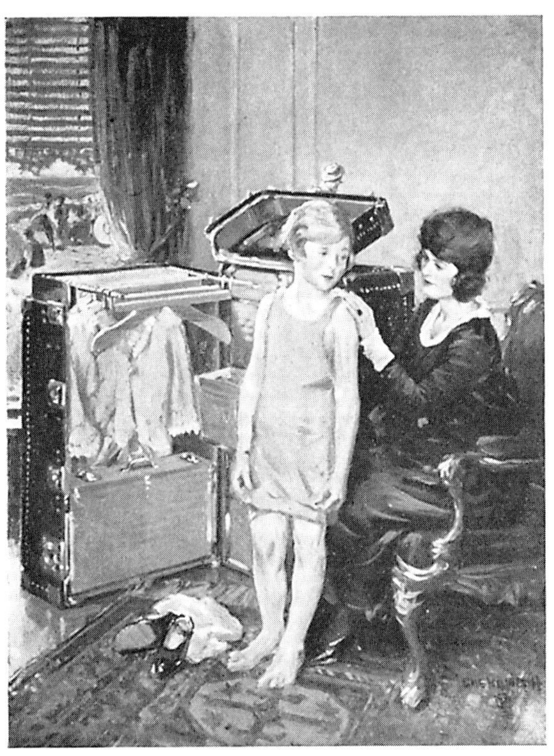

65 HARTMANN TRUNKS—*J. Chenoweth*
Loaned by the Hartmann Trunk Co.
Exhibited by the Wm. H. Rankin Co.

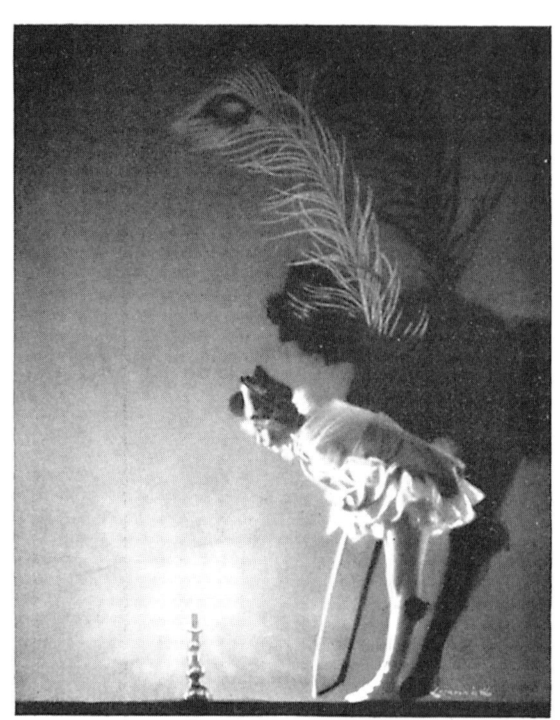

66 PIERRETTE SILK—*Lejaren à Hiller*
Loaned by J. A. Migel
Exhibited by Street & Finney, Inc.

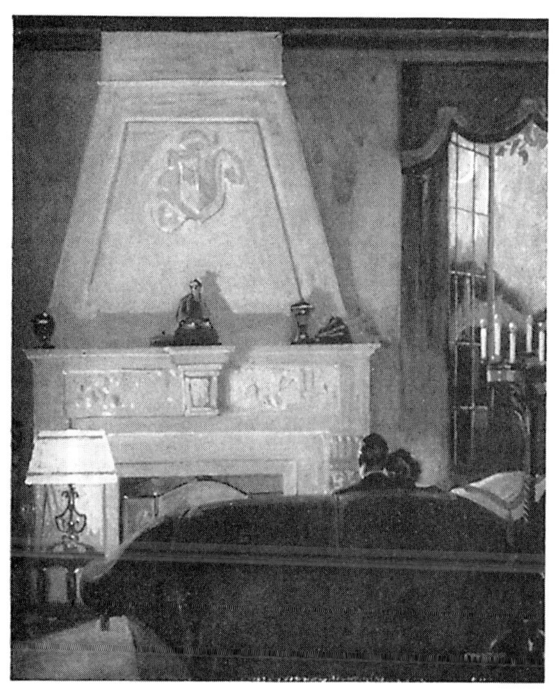

67 JEWELRY—*Roy Spieter*
Loaned by the National Jewelers Board of Trade
Exhibited by the Vanderhoof Advertising Agency

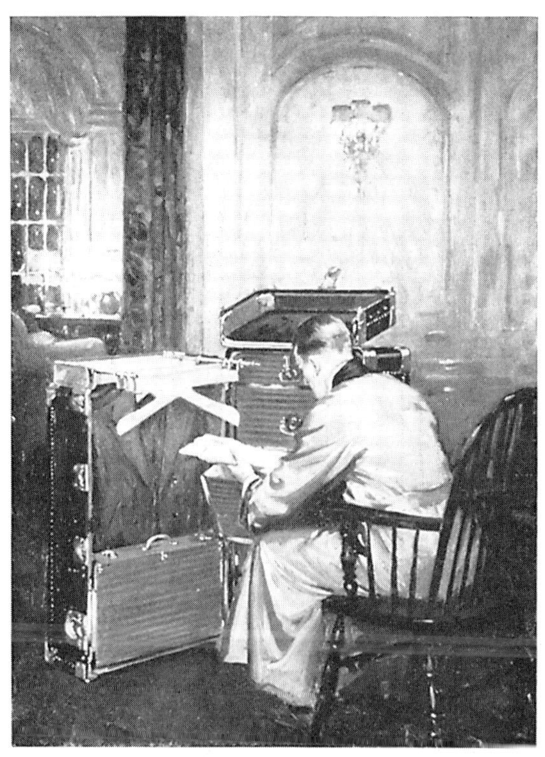

68 HARTMANN TRUNKS—*J. Chenoweth*
Loaned by the Hartmann Trunk Co.
Exhibited by the Wm. H. Rankin Co.

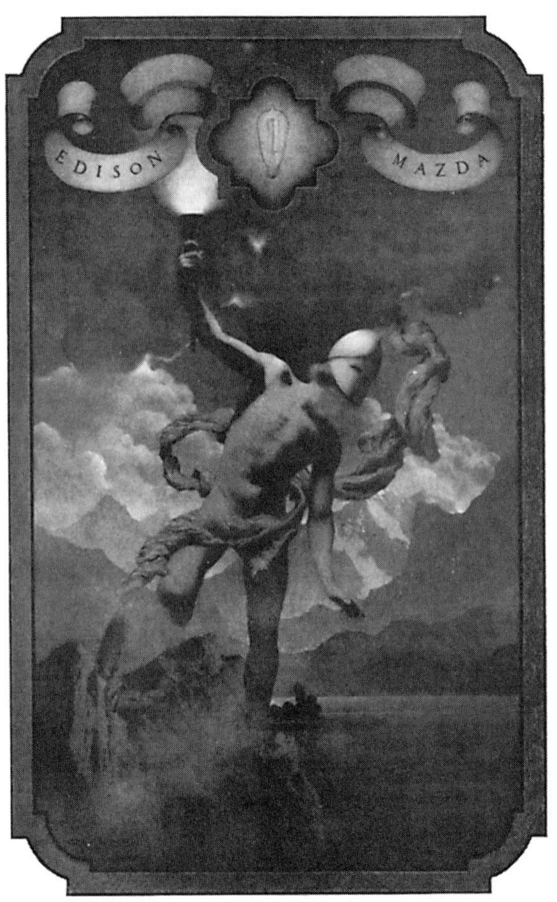

69 EDISON MAZDA LAMPS—*Maxfield Parrish*
Loaned by the Edison Lamp Works of General Electric Co.
Exhibited by Barton, Durstine & Osborn, Inc.

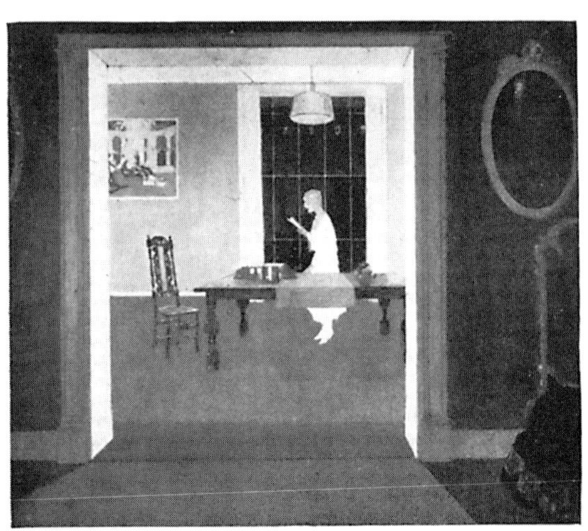

70 DUPLEX LIGHTING FIXTURES
George J. Illian
Loaned by the Duplex Lighting Works of General
Electric Co.
Exhibited by Barrows & Richardson

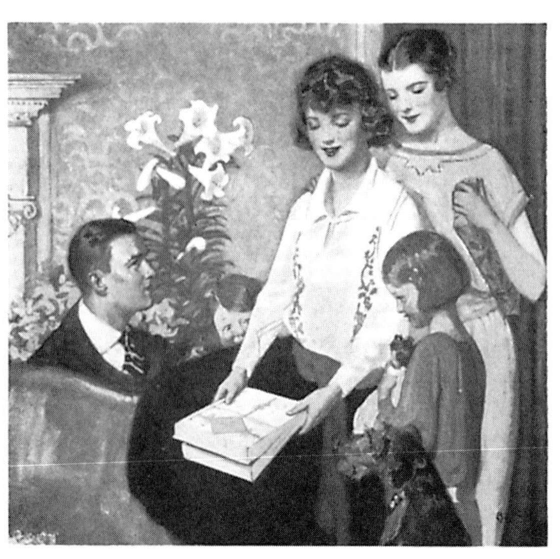

71 CRANE'S LINEN LAWN AND EATON'S HIGH-
LAND LINEN—*MacClelland Barclay*
Loaned by the Eaton, Crane & Pike Company
Exhibited by Calkins & Holden, Inc.

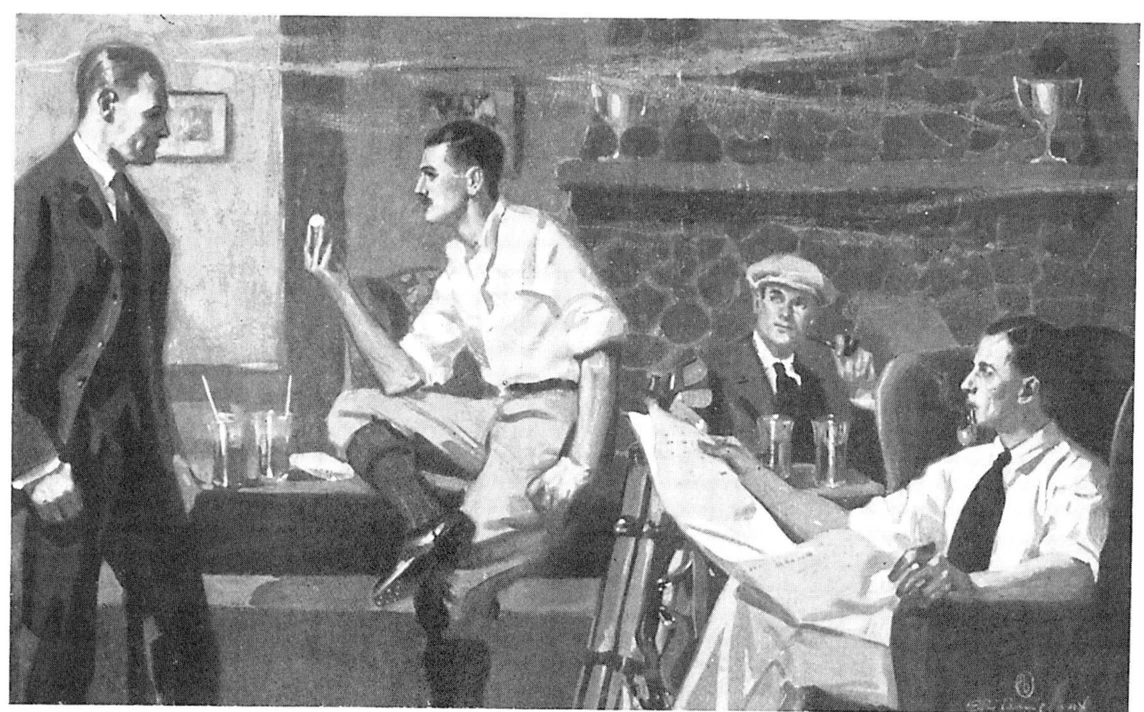

72   U. S. Golf Balls—*E. R. Burgraff*
Loaned by the U. S. Rubber Co.
Exhibited by The H. K. McCann Co.

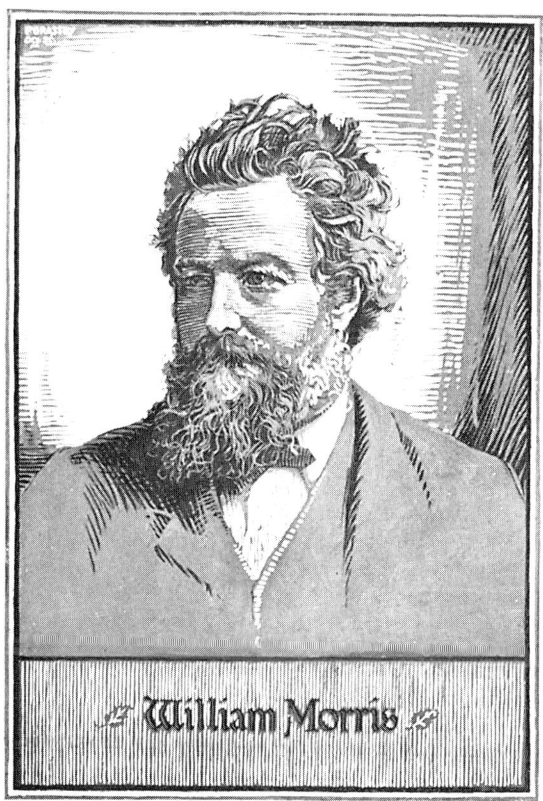

73 Wood Engraved Portrait—*Percy Grassby*
Loaned and exhibited by the Franklin Printing Co.

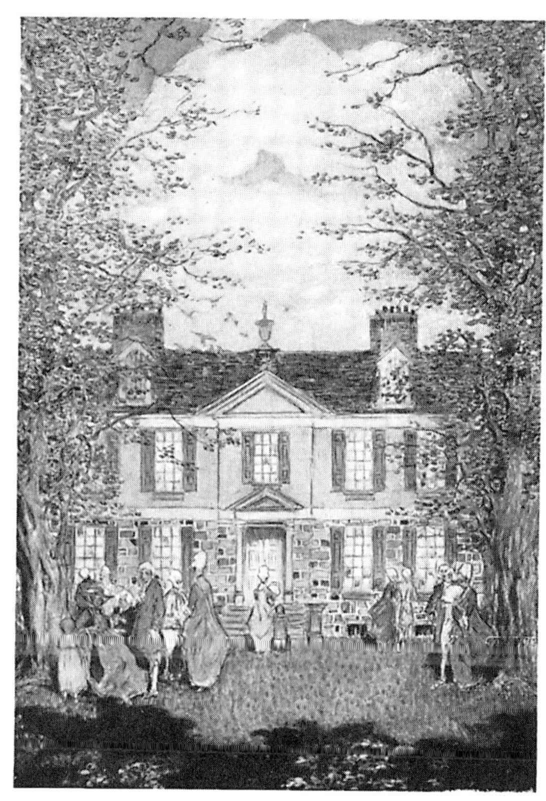

74 Calendar Illustration—*James Preston*
Loaned and exhibited by the Beck Engraving Co.

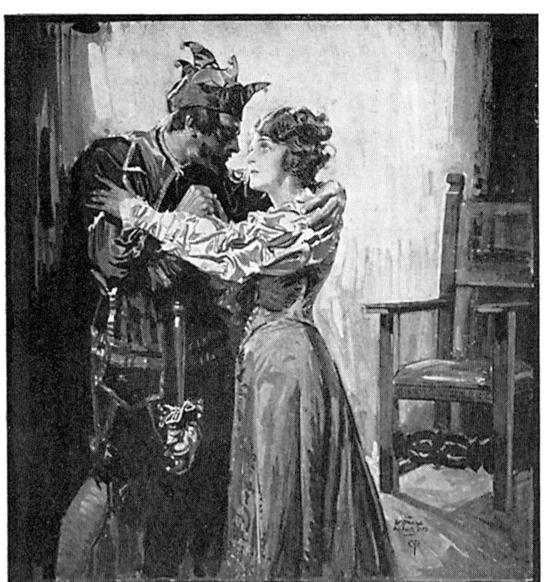

75 VICTOR RECORDS—*Vaux Wilson*
Loaned by the Victor Talking Machine Co.
Exhibited by the Franklin Printing Co.

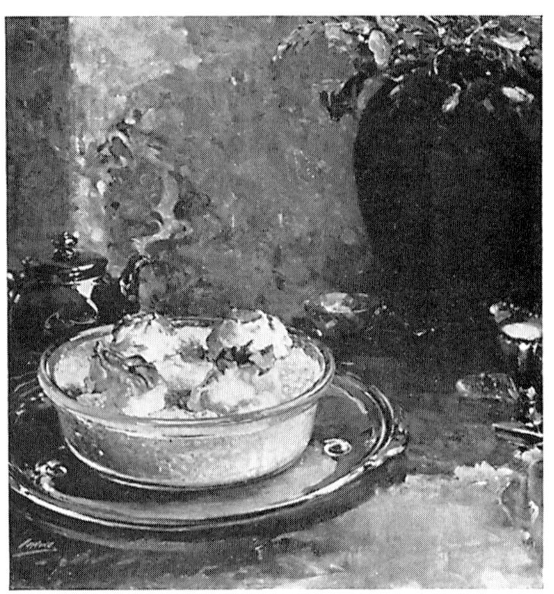

76 MINUTE TAPIOCA—*Charles Irvine*
Loaned by the Minute Tapioca Co.
Exhibited by George Batten Co., Inc.

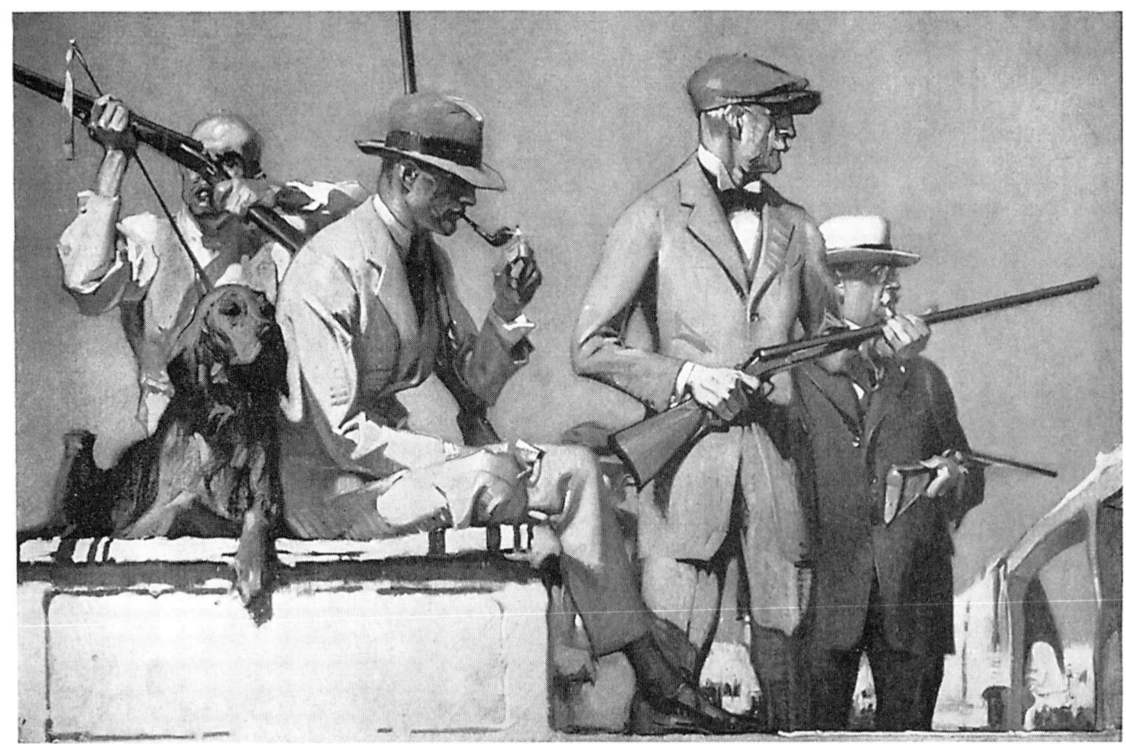

77 MEN'S CLOTHING—*S. N. Abbott*
Loaned and exhibited by Hart Schaffner & Marx

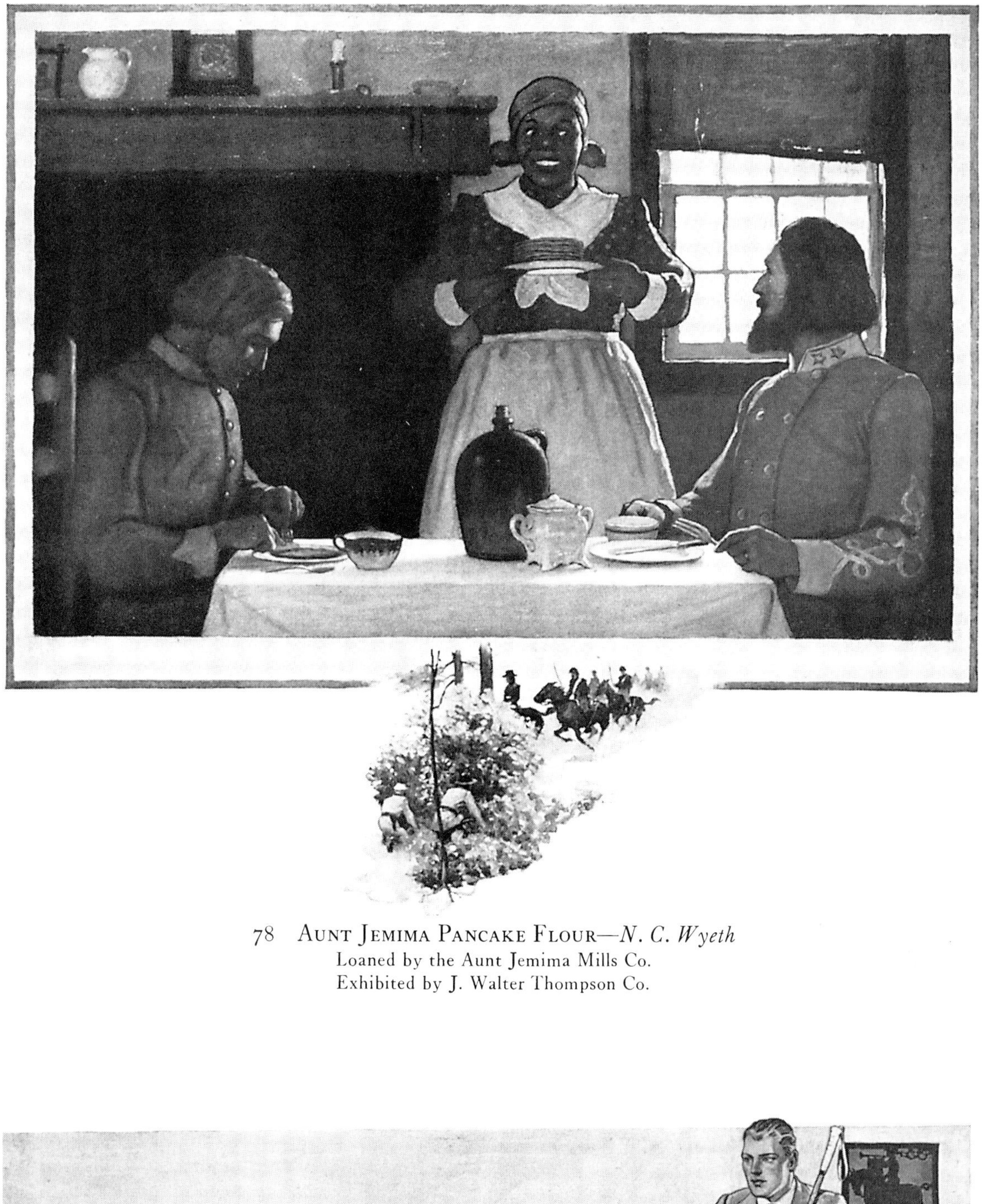

78   Aunt Jemima Pancake Flour—*N. C. Wyeth*
Loaned by the Aunt Jemima Mills Co.
Exhibited by J. Walter Thompson Co.

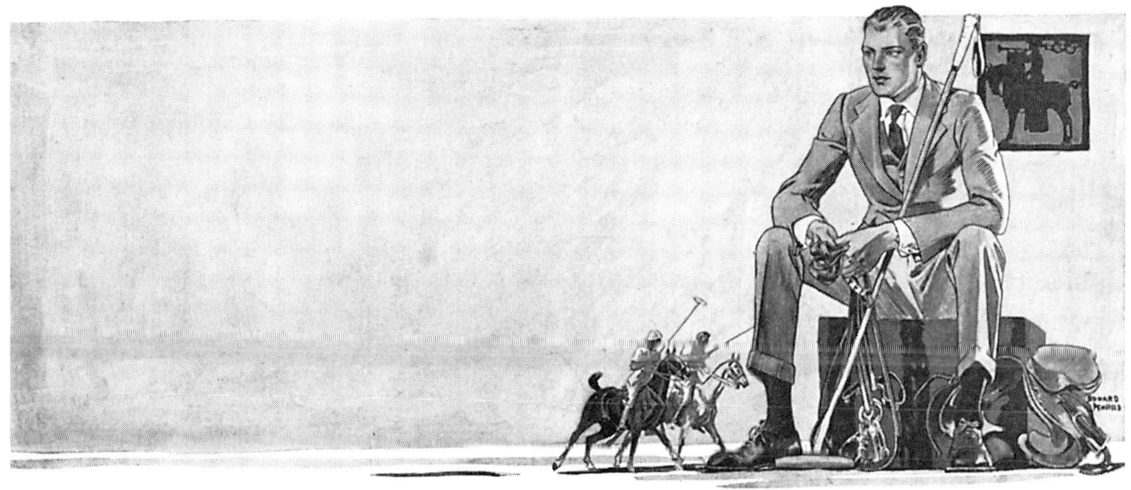

79   Men's Clothing—*Edward Penfield*
Loaned and exhibited by Hart Schaffner & Marx

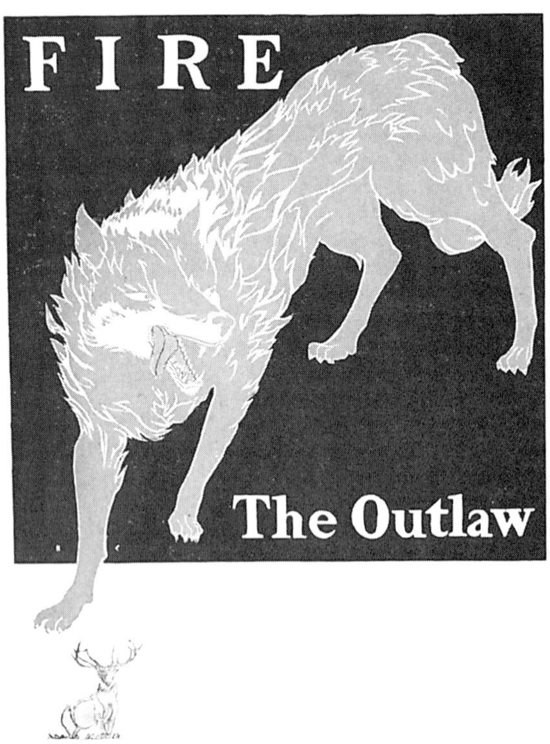

80   HARTFORD FIRE INSURANCE—*René Clarke*
Loaned by The Hartford Fire Insurance Co.
Exhibited by Calkins & Holden, Inc.

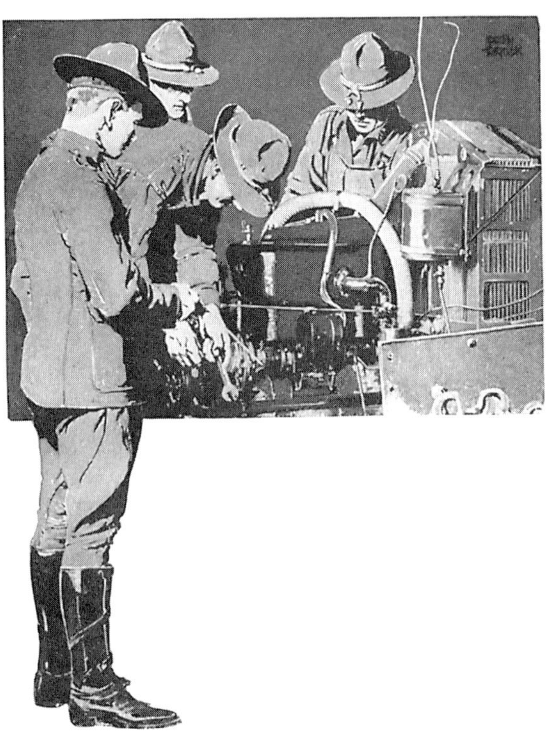

81   U. S. ARMY TEACHES TRADES—*Adolph Treidler*
Loaned by the U. S. Army
Exhibited by Calkins & Holden, Inc.

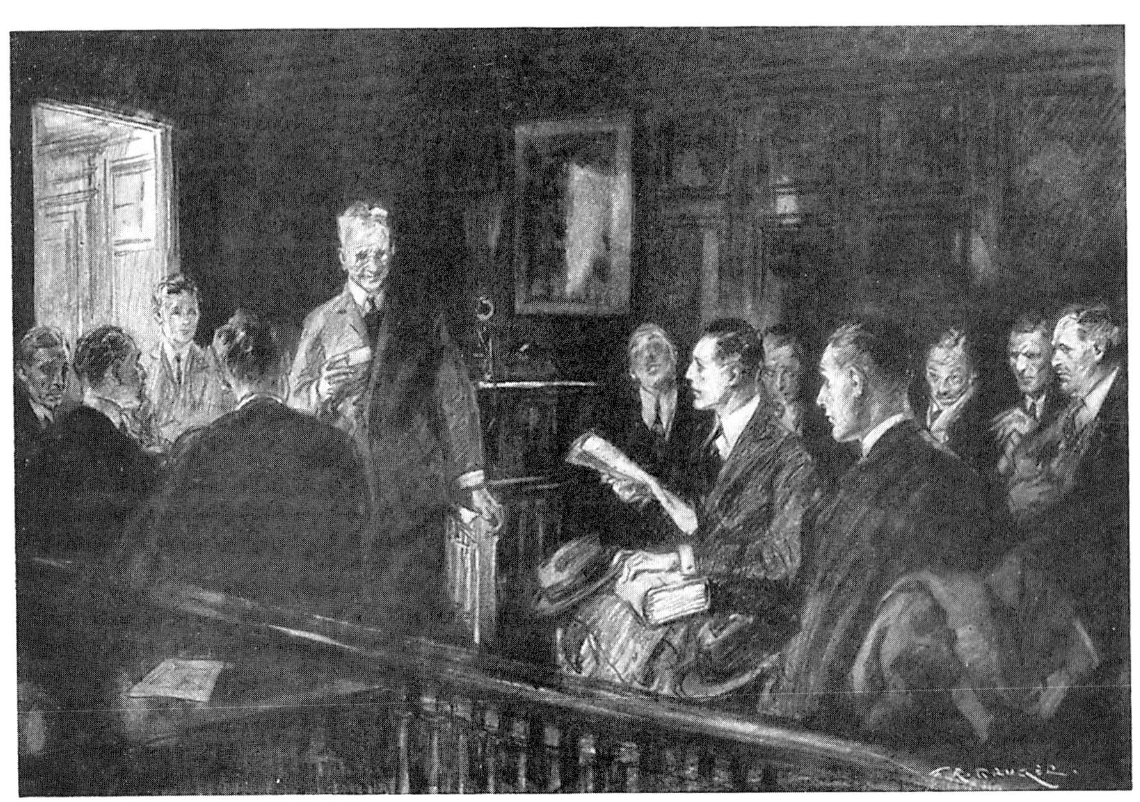

82   ASBESTOS—*F. R. Gruger*
Loaned by the Johns-Manville Co.
Exhibited by Newell-Emmett Co., Inc.

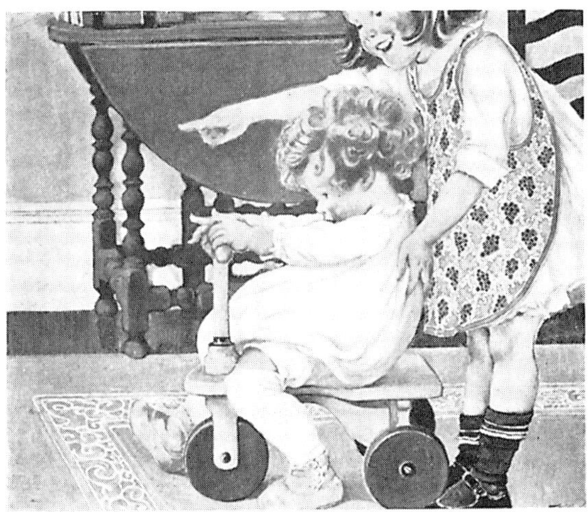

83 KIDDIE KARS—*Sarah Stilwell Weber*
Loaned by the H. C. White Co.
Exhibited by Barrows & Richardson

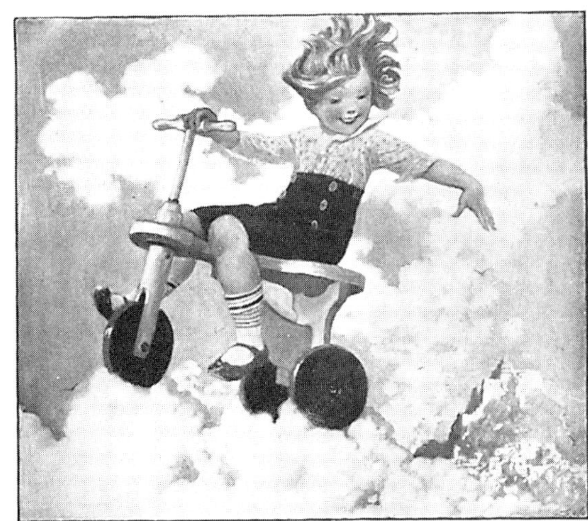

84 KIDDIE KARS—*Sarah Stilwell Weber*
Loaned by the H. C. White Co.
Exhibited by Barrows & Richardson

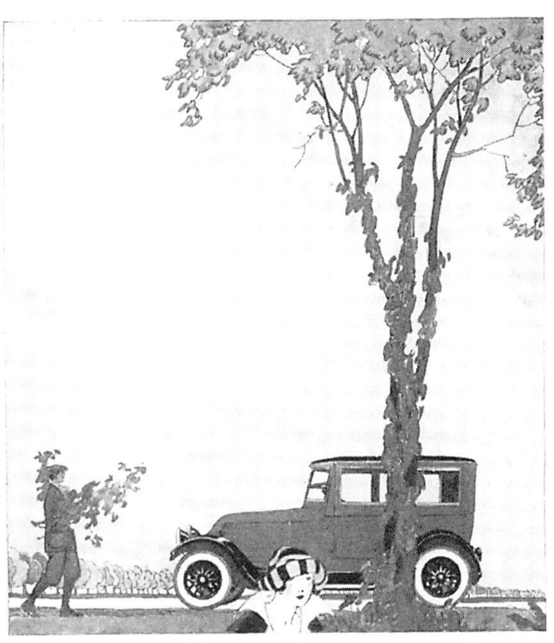

85 FRANKLIN MOTOR CARS—*F. T. Chapman*
Loaned by the Franklin Automobile Company
Exhibited by Patterson-Andress Co., Inc.

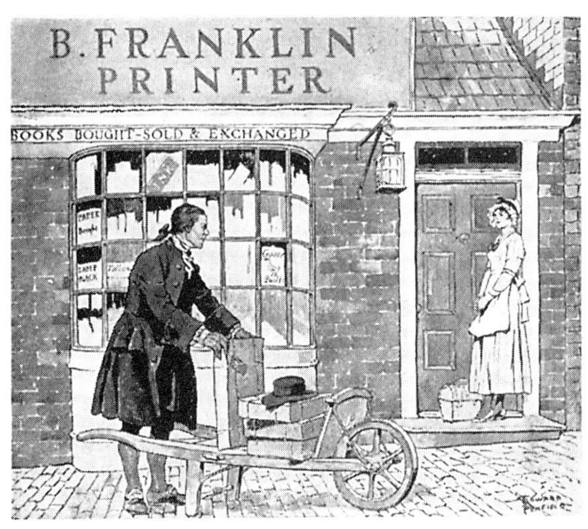

86 FRANKLIN PRINTING CO.—*Edward Penfield*
Loaned and exhibited by the Franklin Printing Co.

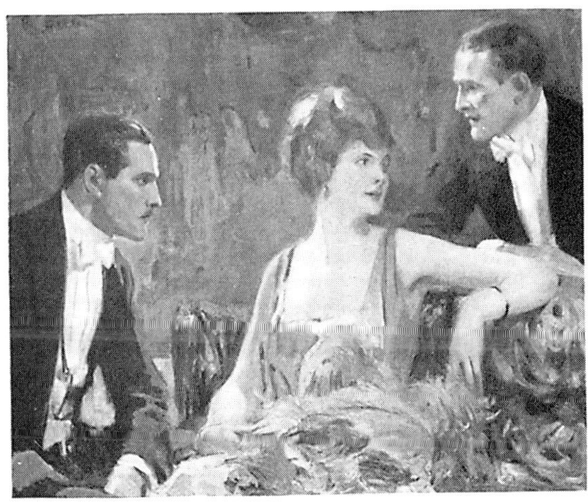

87 WOODBURY'S FACIAL SOAP—*Walter Biggs*
Loaned by The Andrew Jergens Company
Exhibited by J. Walter Thompson Co.

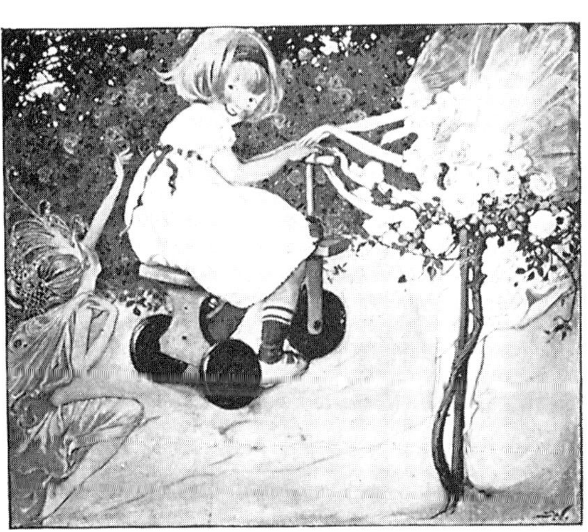

88 KIDDIE KARS—*Sarah Stilwell Weber*
Loaned by the H. C. White Co.
Exhibited by Barrows & Richardson

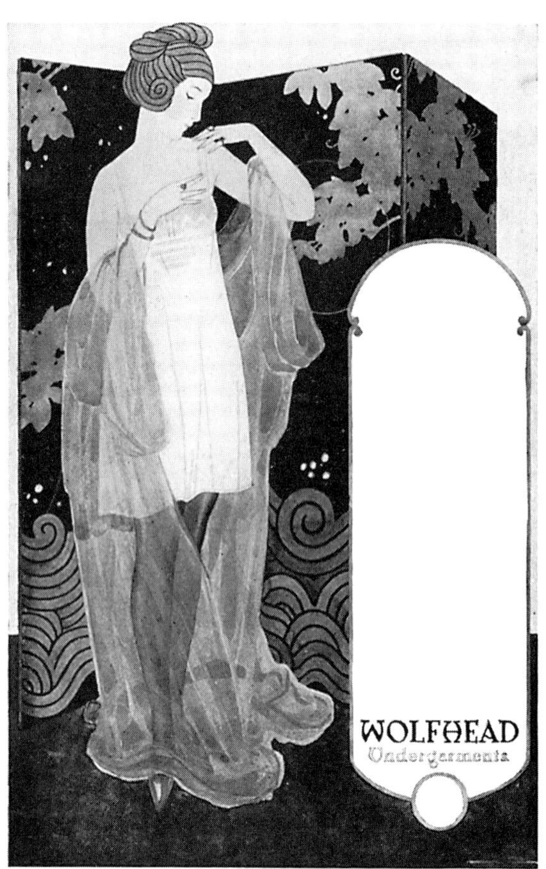

89   WOLFHEAD UNDERWEAR—*The Reeses*
Loaned by The Wolf Co.
Exhibited by Barrows & Richardson

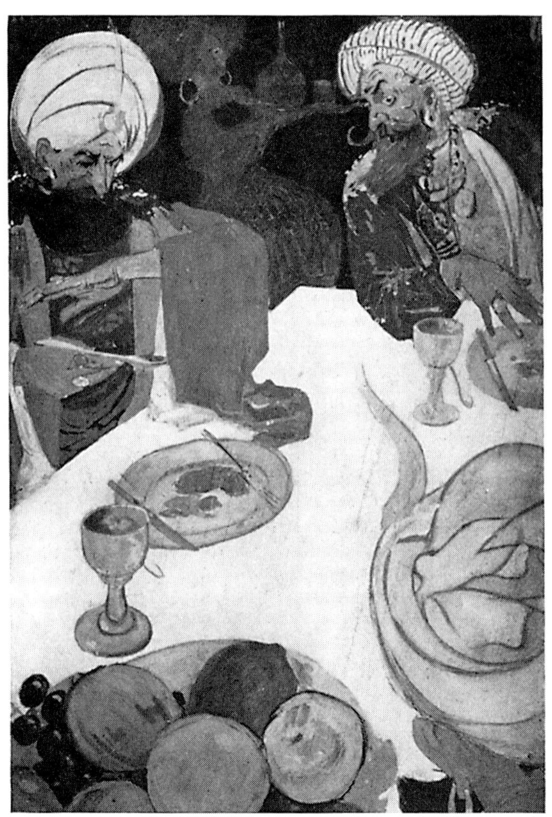

90   MURAL POSTER—*George J. Illian*]
Loaned and exhibited by M. Rusling Wood

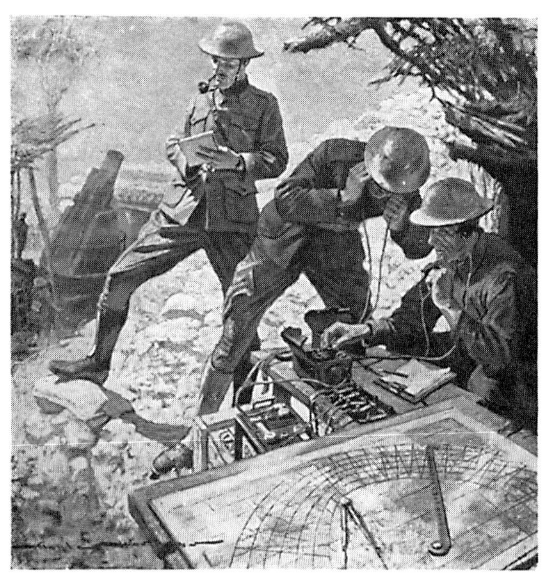

91   STORAGE BATTERIES—*Gail Porter Hoskins*
Loaned and exhibited by Gould Storage Battery Co.

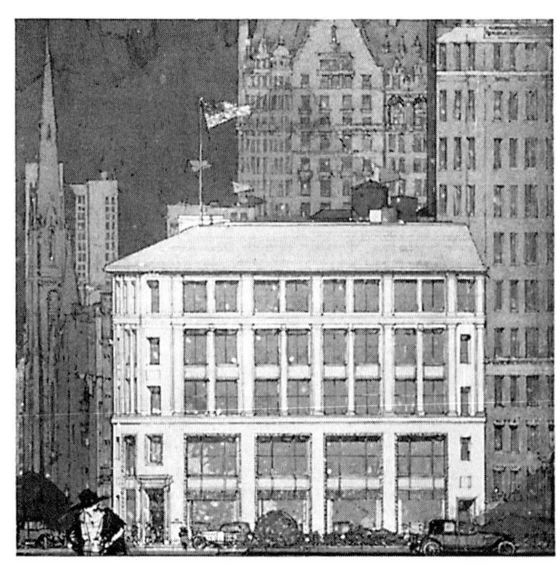

92   —*E. G. Teale*
Loaned and exhibited by the Caxton Company

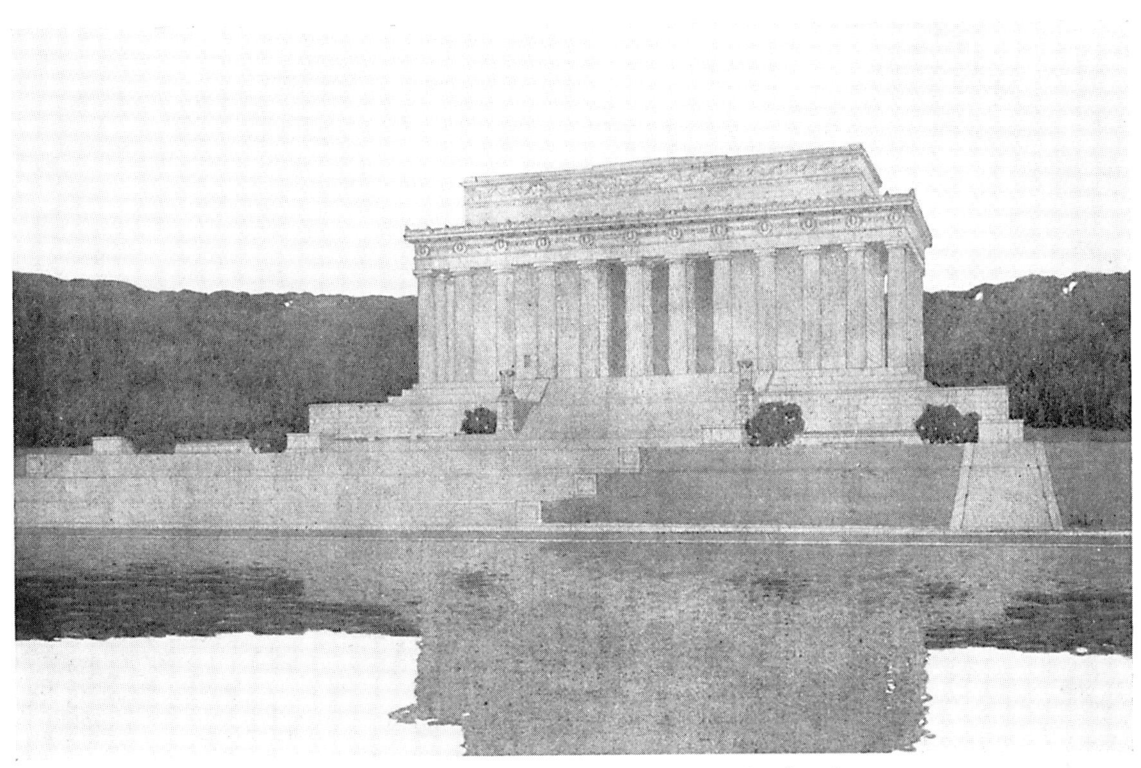

93 LINCOLN MEMORIAL BUILDING—*Jules Guerin*
Loaned by the George A. Fuller Co.
Exhibited by the Critchfield Co.

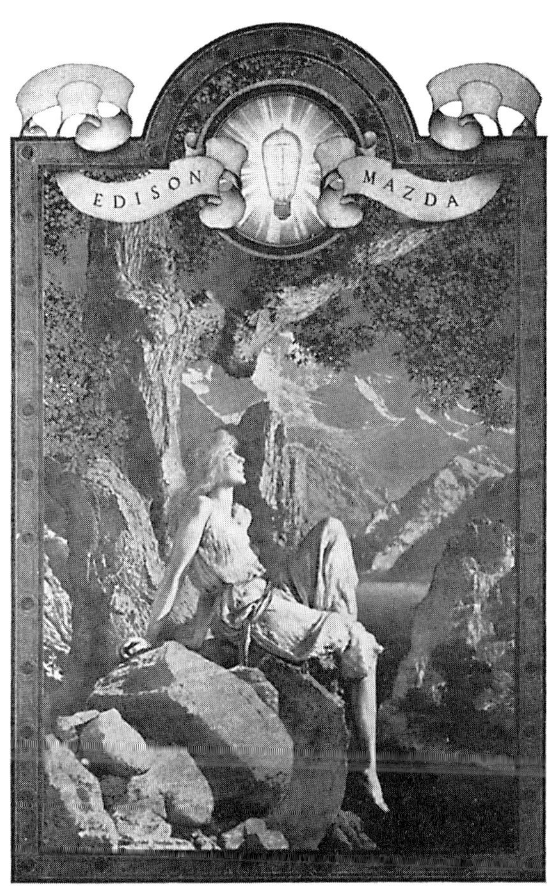

94 EDISON MAZDA LAMPS—*Maxfield Parrish*
Loaned by the Edison Lamp Works of General Electric Co.
Exhibited by Barton, Durstine & Osborn, Inc.

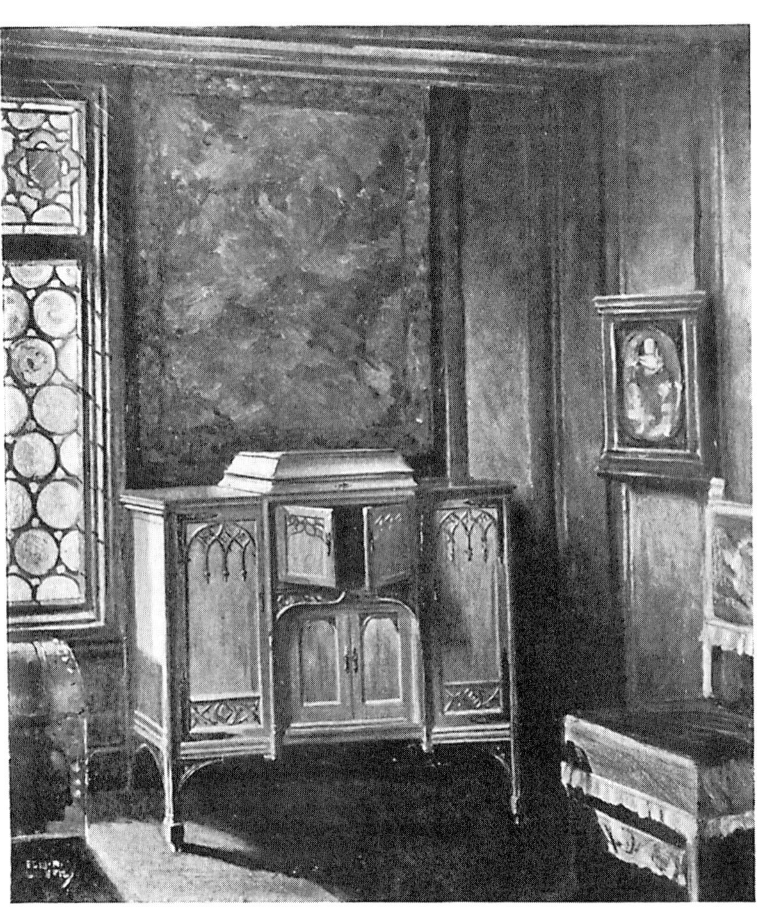

95 VICTOR TALKING MACHINES—*Edward A. Wilson*
Loaned by the Victor Talking Machine Co.
Exhibited by the Franklin Printing Co.

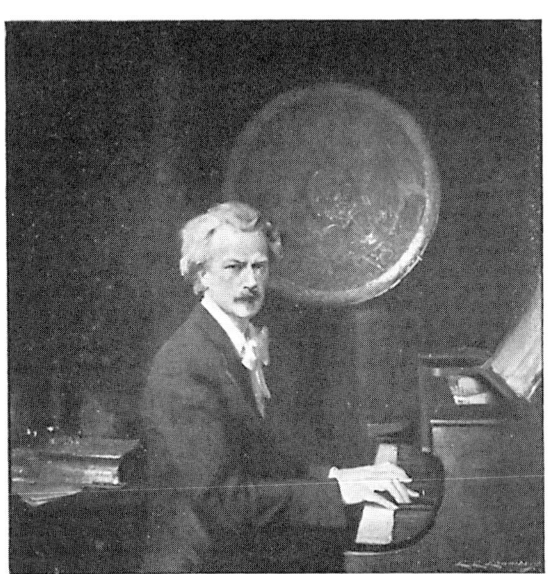

96 STEINWAY PIANOS—*Charles E. Chambers*
Loaned by Steinway & Sons
Exhibited by N. W. Ayer & Son

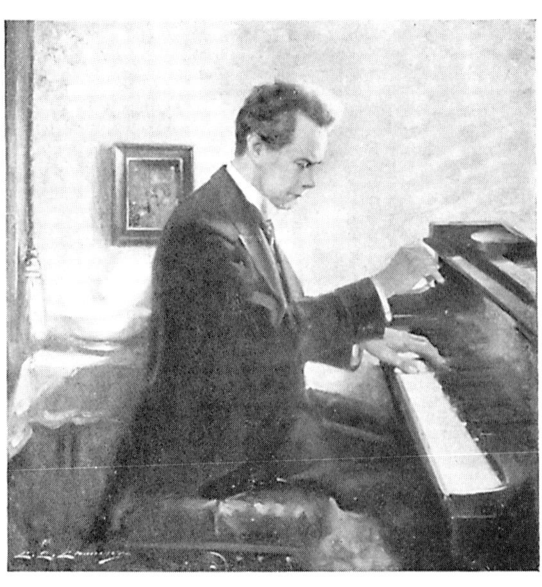

97 STEINWAY PIANOS—*Charles E. Chambers*
Loaned by Steinway & Sons
Exhibited by N. W. Ayer & Son

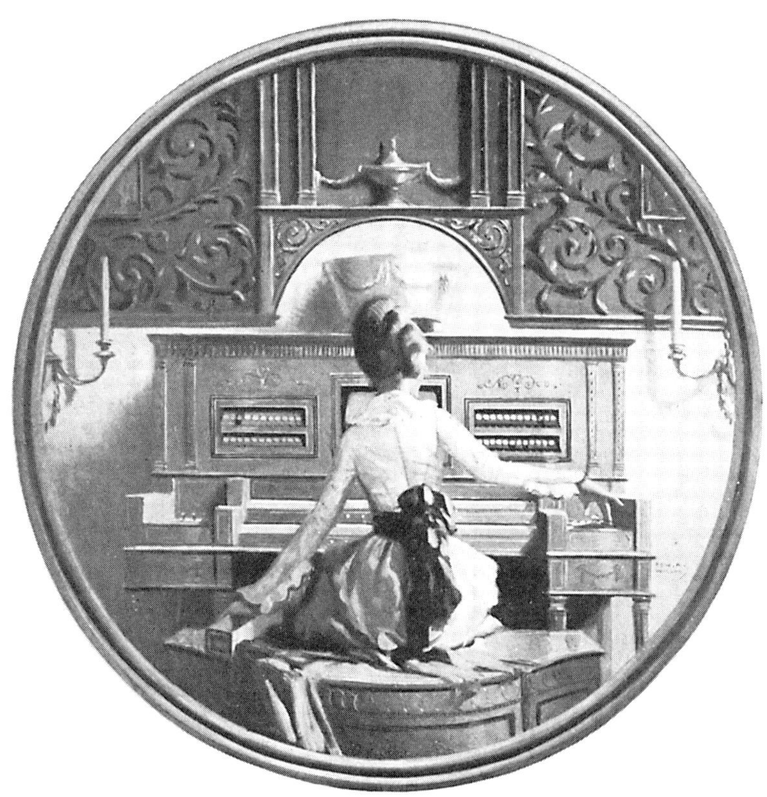

98 ESTEY ORGAN—*Edward A. Wilson*
Loaned by The Estey Organ Company
Exhibited by Calkins & Holden, Inc.

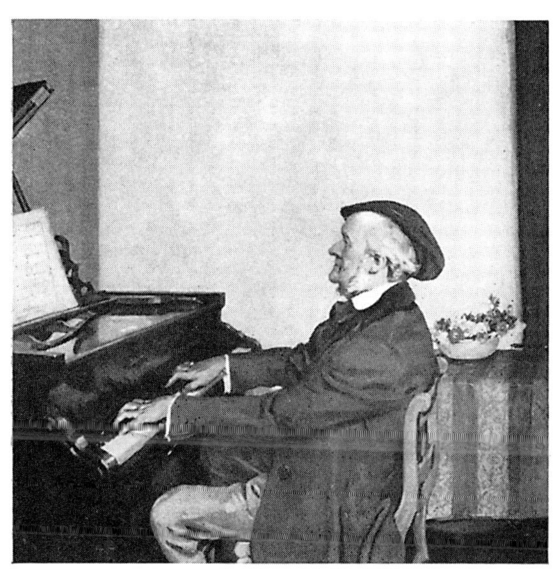

99 STEINWAY PIANOS—*Harry Townsend*
Loaned by Steinway & Sons
Exhibited by N. W. Ayer & Son

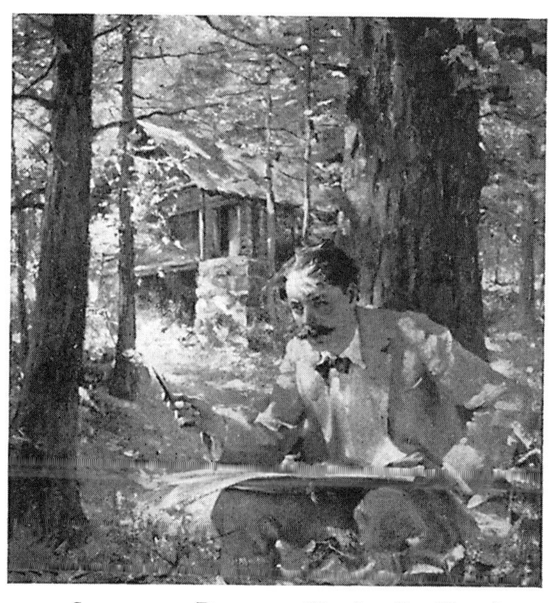

100 STEINWAY PIANOS—*Charles E. Chambers*
Loaned by Steinway & Sons
Exhibited by N. W. Ayer & Son

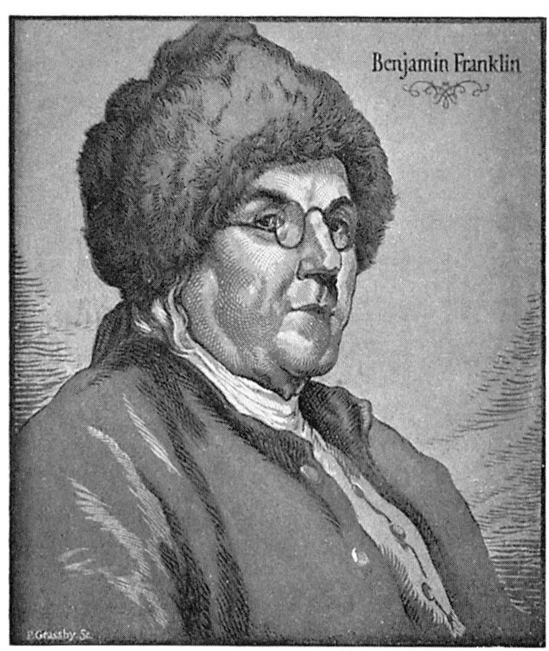

101   BENJAMIN FRANKLIN—*Percy Grassby*
Loaned and exhibited by the Franklin Printing Company

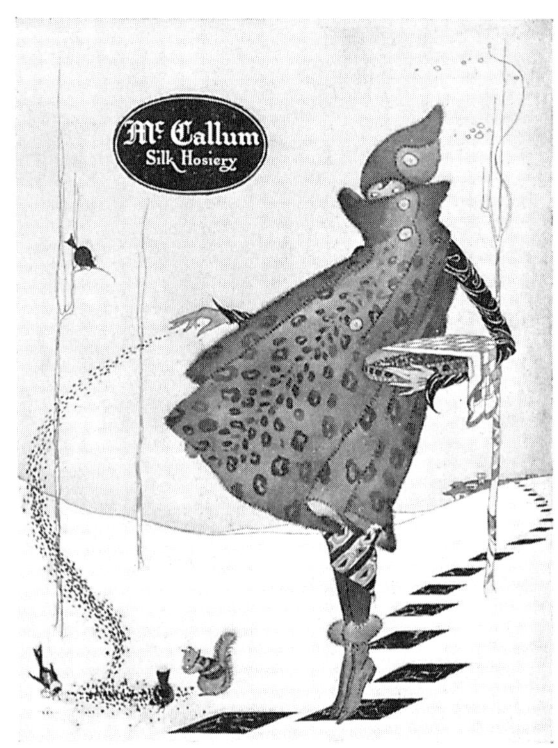

102   SILK HOSIERY—*Marjory C. Woodbury*
Loaned by the McCallum Hosiery Co.
Exhibited by George Batten Co., Inc.

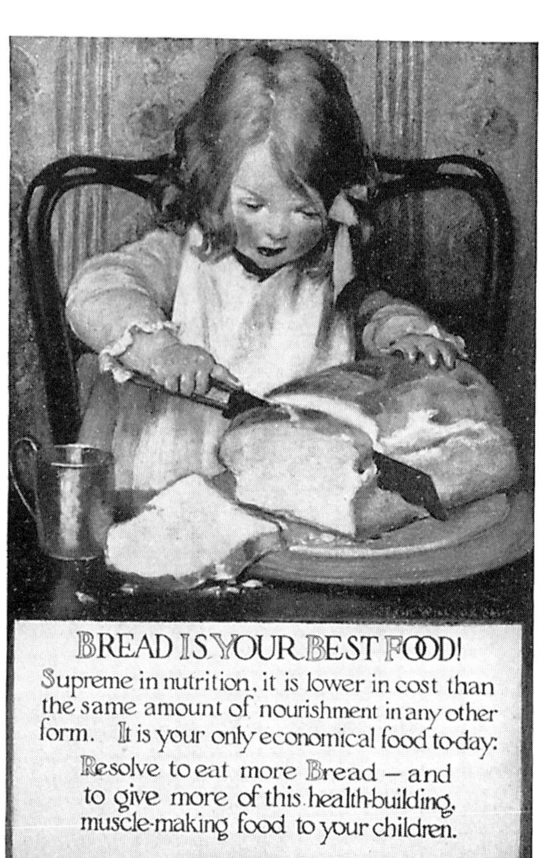

103   FLEISCHMANN'S YEAST—*Jessie Willcox Smith*
Loaned by The Fleischmann Co.
Exhibited by Donovan & Armstrong

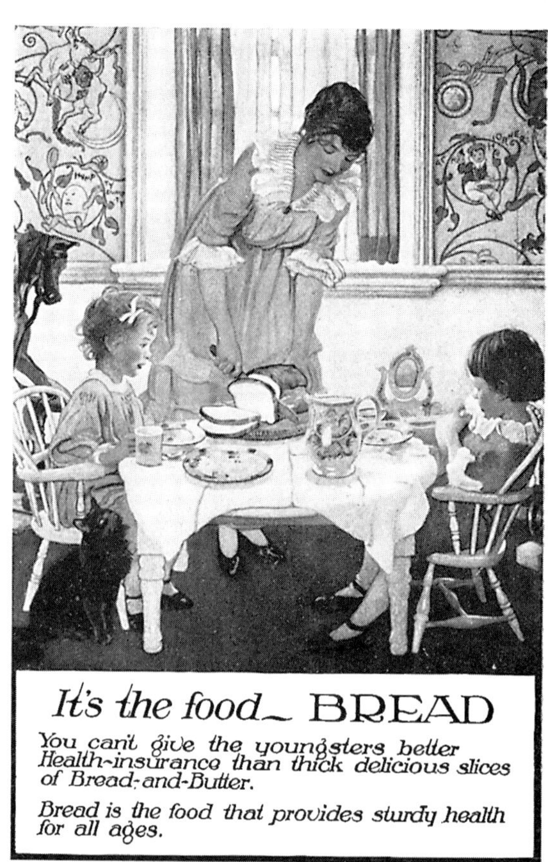

104   FLEISCHMANN'S YEAST
Elizabeth S. G. Elliott
Loaned by The Fleischmann Co.
Exhibited by Donovan & Armstrong

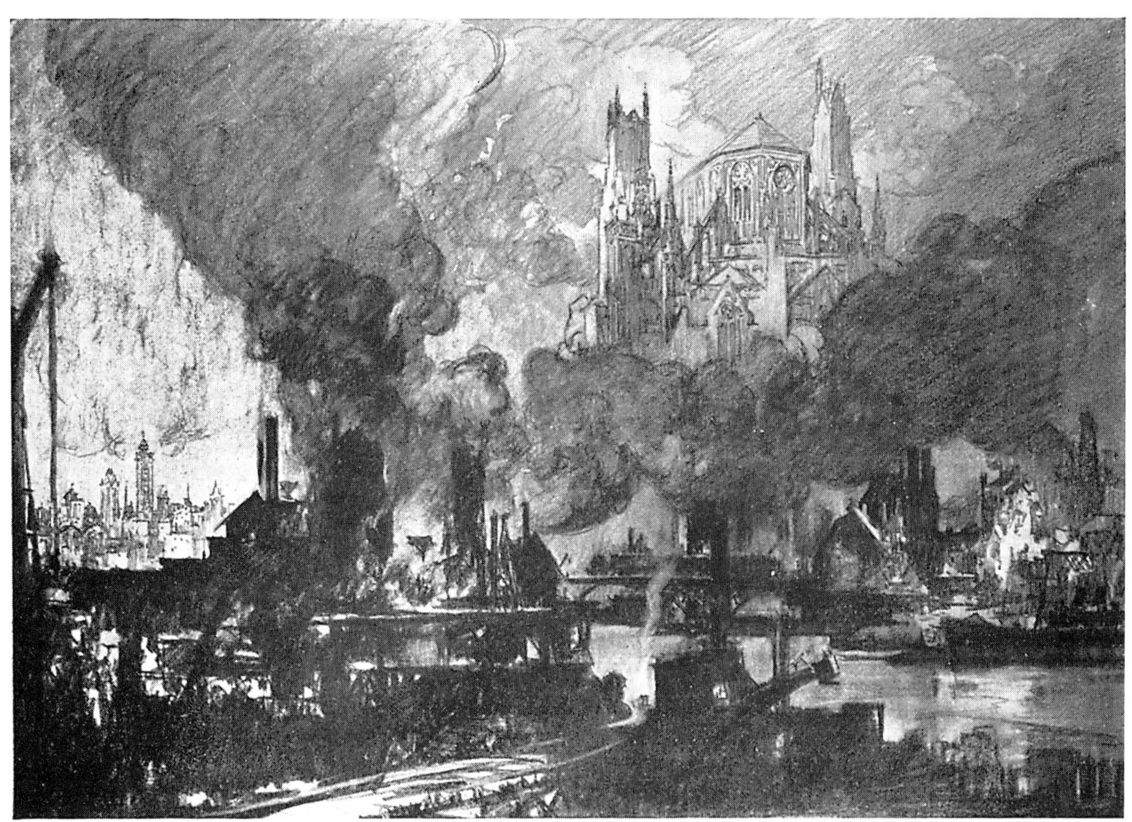

105 INTERCHURCH WORLD MOVEMENT—*F. R. Gruger*
Loaned by the Interchurch World Movement of North America
Exhibited by Barton, Durstine & Osborn, Inc.

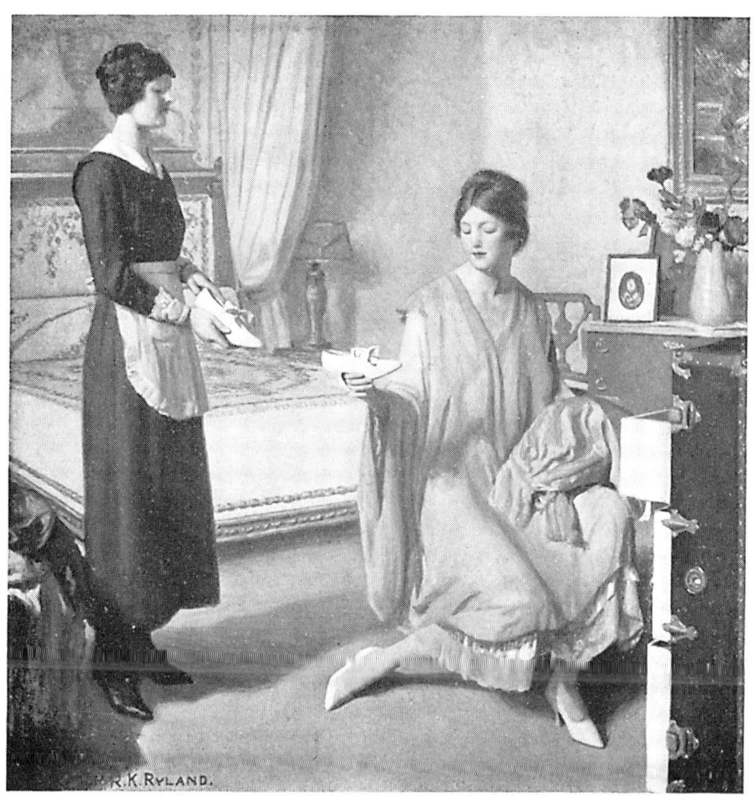

106 VODE KID—*R. K. Ryland*
Loaned by the Standard Kid Manufacturing Co.
Exhibited by George Batten Co., Inc.

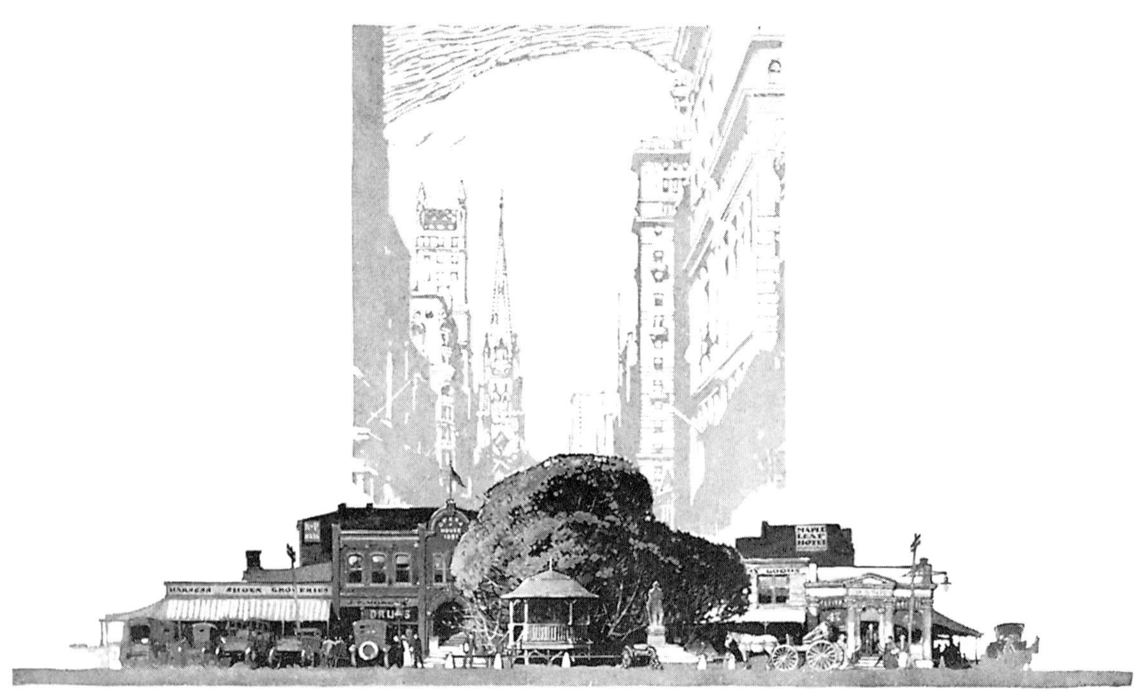

107   ADDING MACHINES—*Harry Lees*
Loaned and exhibited by the Burroughs Adding Machine Co.

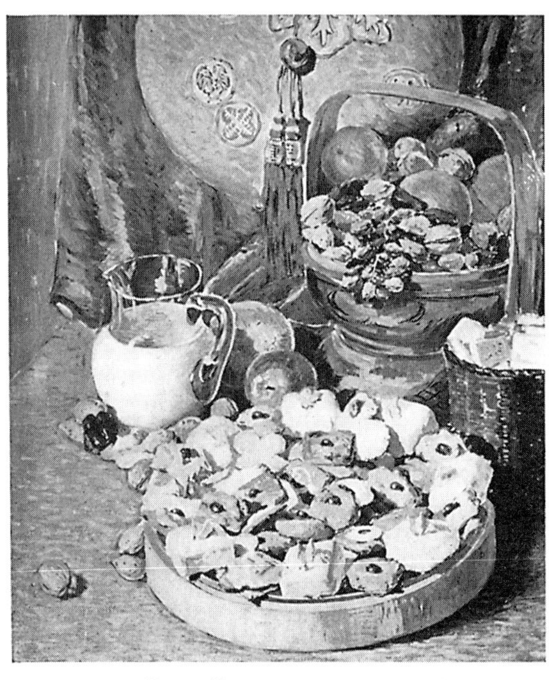

108   SWIFT FOOD PRODUCTS—*Sigmund Schou*
Loaned by Swift & Co.
Exhibited by J. Walter Thompson Co.

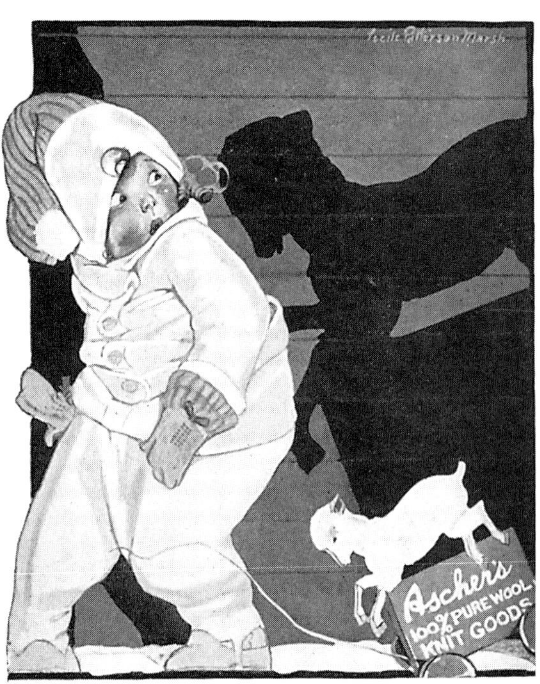

109 ASCHER'S KNIT GOODS—*Lucile Patterson Marsh*
Loaned by Simon Ascher & Co., Inc.
Exhibited by Biow Co., Inc.

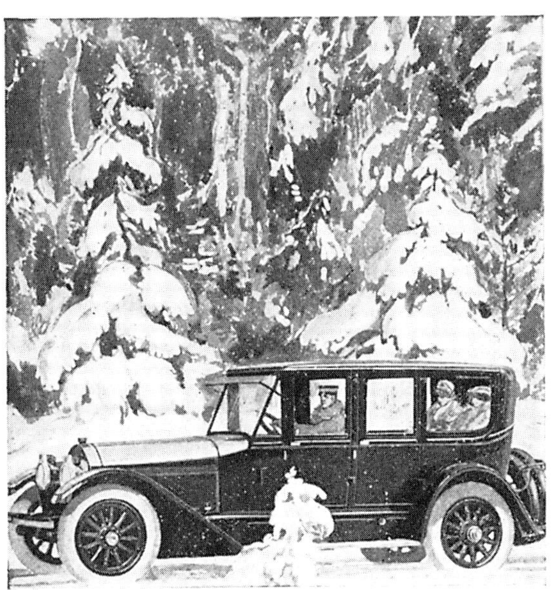

110   HARES MOTORS—*C. B. Falls*
Loaned by Hares Motors, Inc.
Exhibited by Hanff-Metzger, Inc.

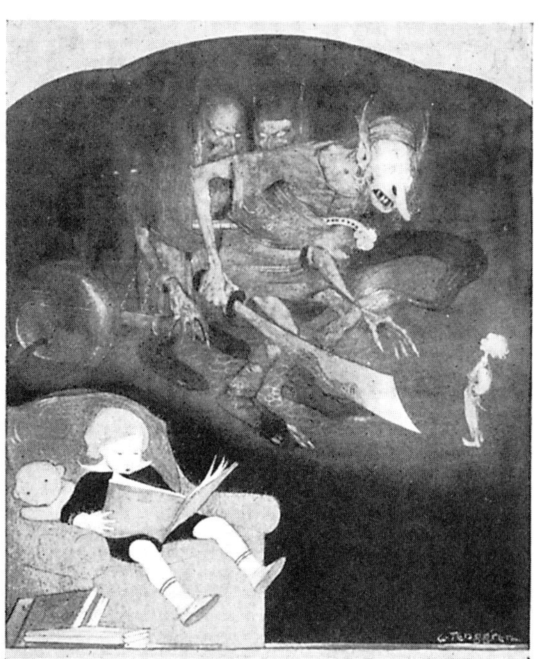

111   —*C. Tenggren*
Loaned by The Amsden Studios Co.

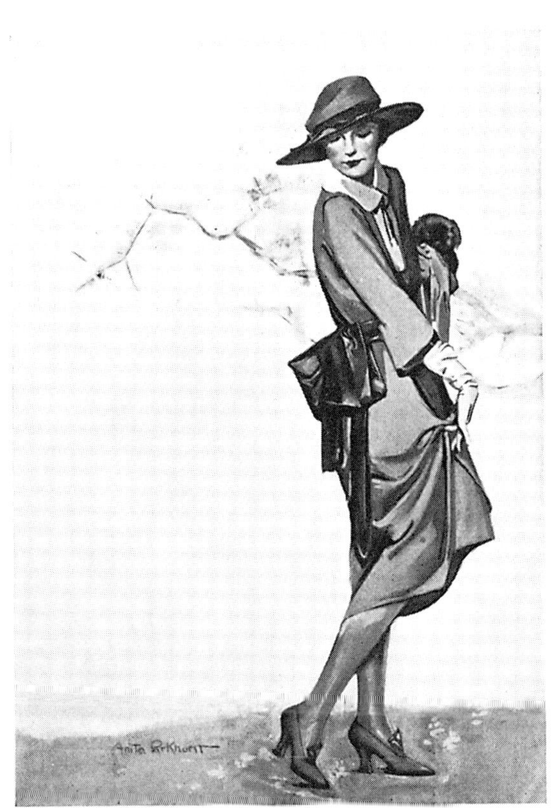

112   QUEEN QUALITY SHOES—*Anita Parkhurst*
Loaned by Thomas G. Plant Co.
Exhibited by Frank Seaman, Inc.

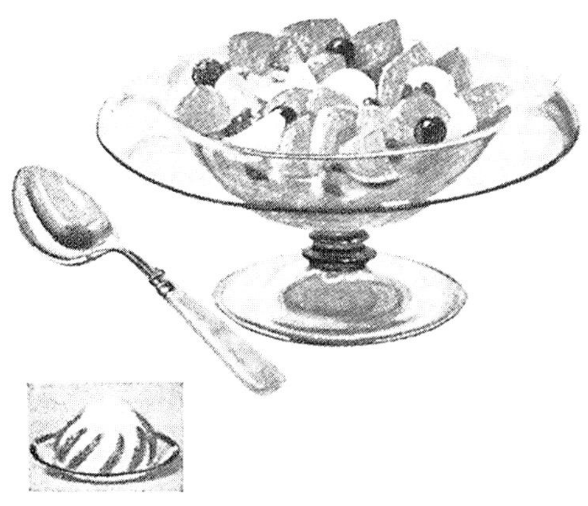
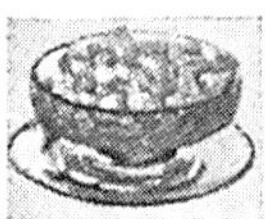
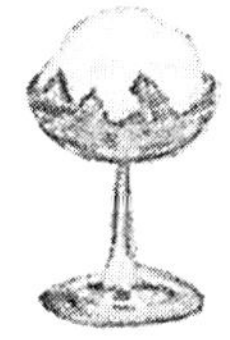
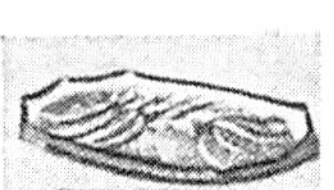

113   SUNKIST ORANGES
Charles Everett Johnson
Loaned by the California Fruit Growers Exchange
Exhibited by Lord & Thomas

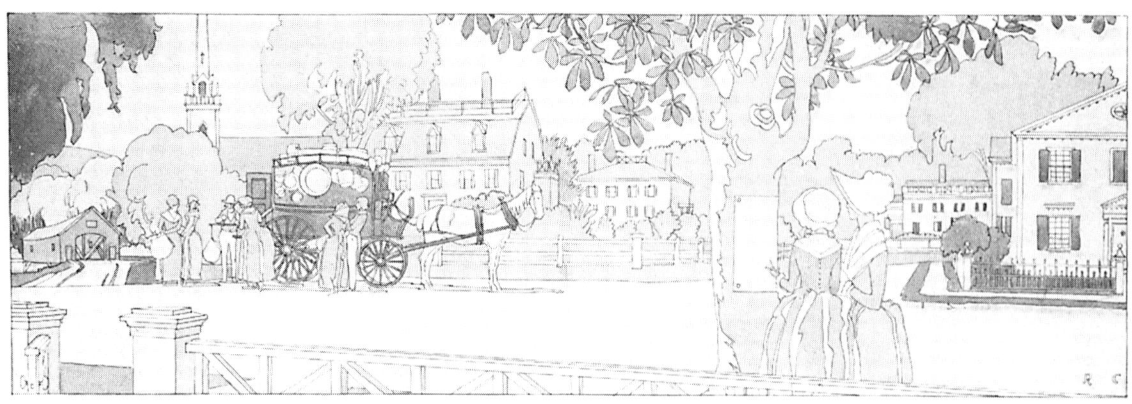

The First Award in Section III for Posters of all sizes including Car Cards
114   CRANE PAPERS—THE FIRST ADVERTISEMENT—*René Clarke*
Loaned by Crane & Co.
Exhibited by Calkins & Holden, Inc.

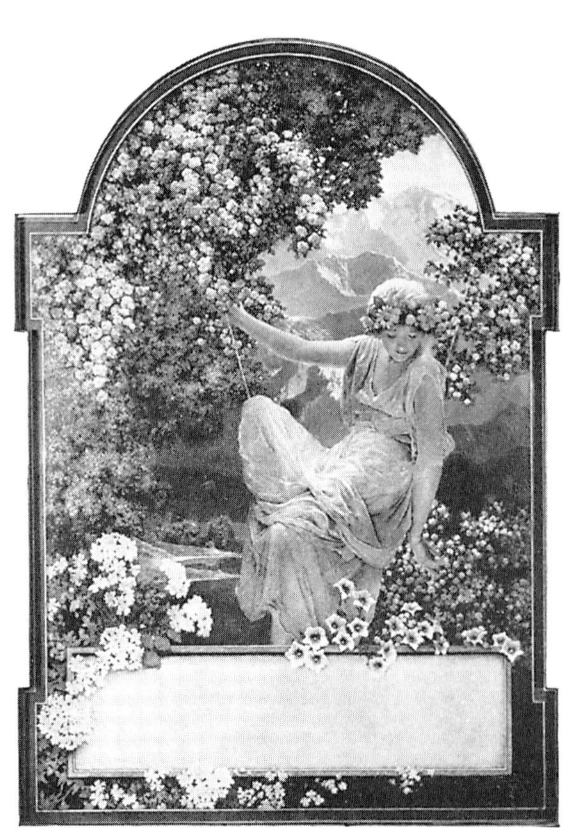

115   DJER-KISS—*Maxfield Parrish*
Loaned by the Alfred H. Smith Co.
Exhibited by The Blackman Co.

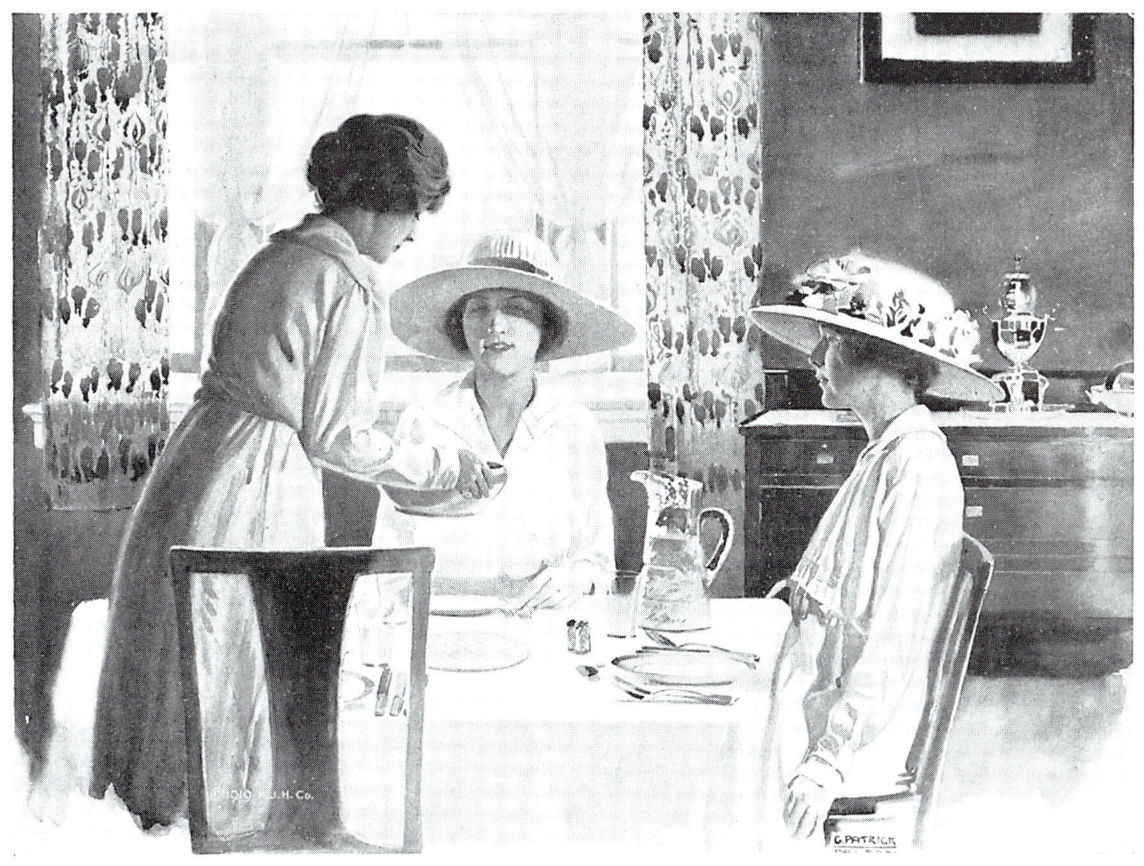

116 HEINZ SPAGHETTI—*G. Patrick Nelson*
Loaned by The H. J. Heinz Company
Exhibited by Calkins & Holden, Inc.

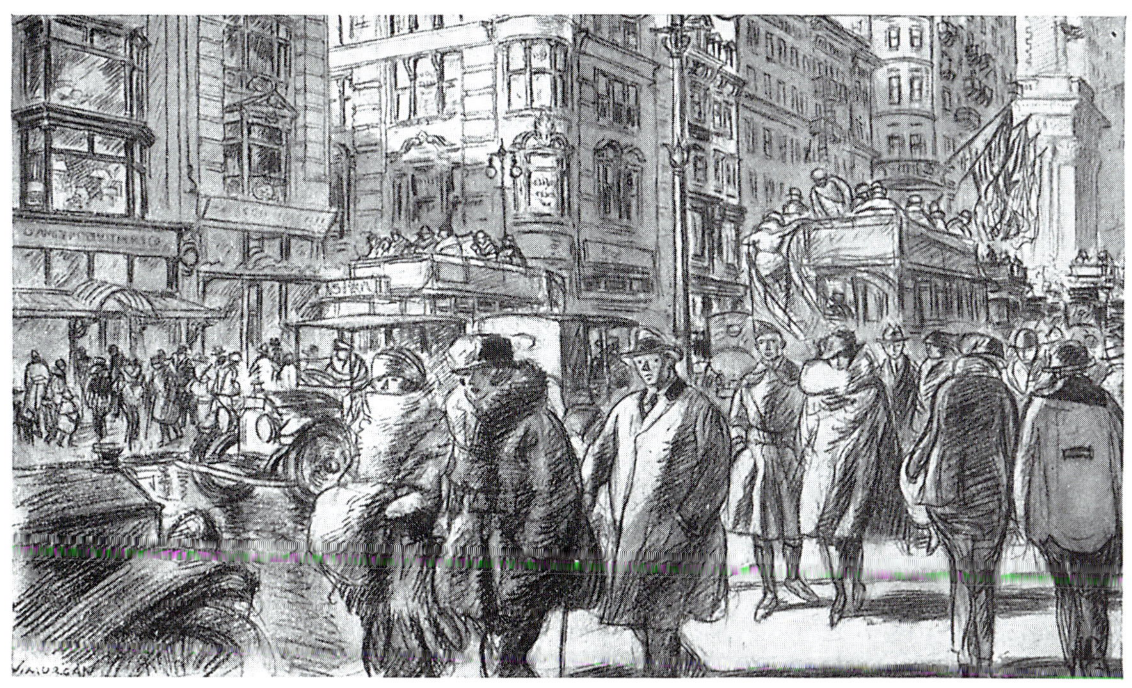

117 OVINGTON'S—*Wallace Morgan*
Loaned by Ovington Bros. Co.
Exhibited by Barton, Durstine & Osborn, Inc.

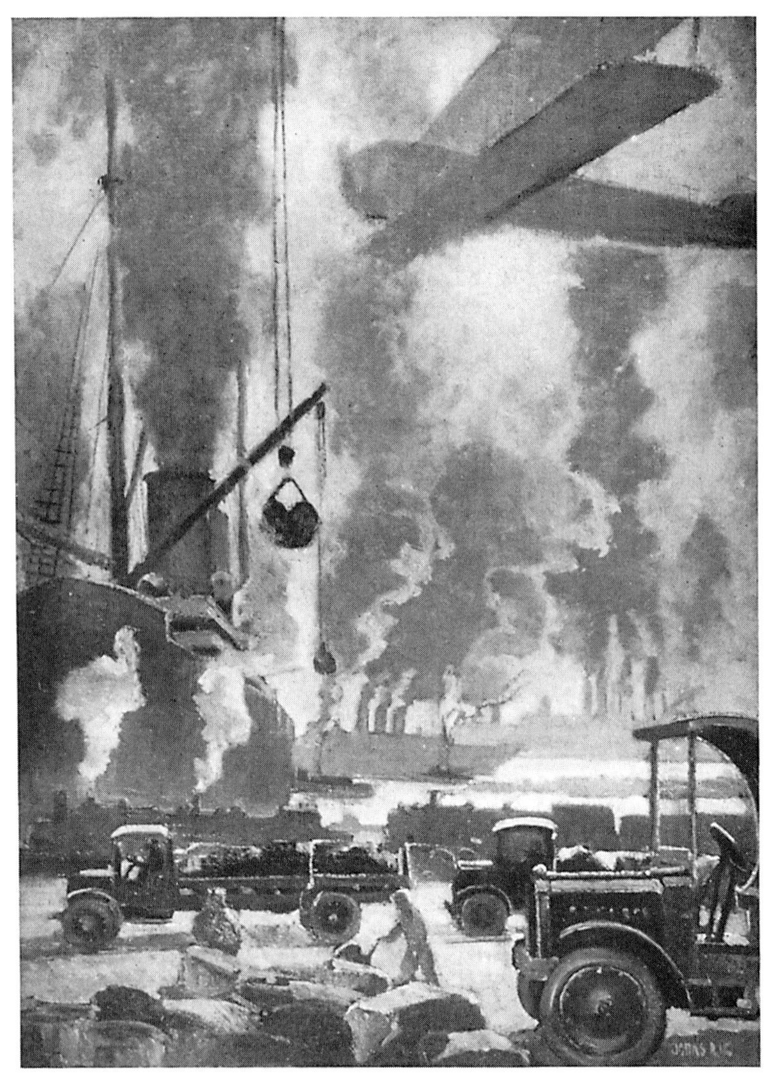

118 SPIRIT OF TRANSPORTATION—*Jonas Lie*
Loaned and exhibited by The Clark Equipment Co.

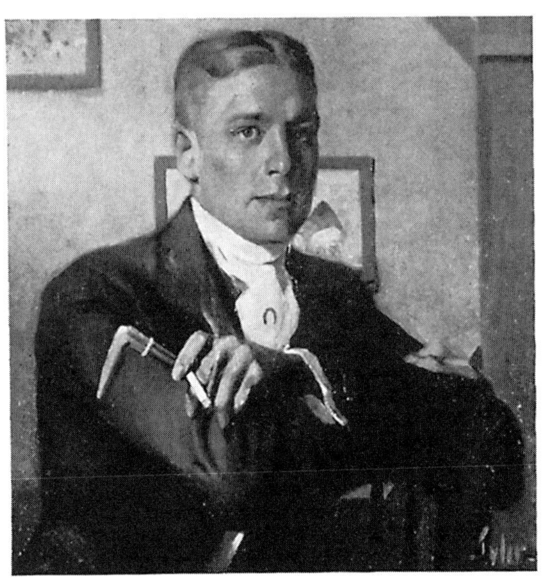

119 FATIMA CIGARETTES—*Audubon Tyler*
Loaned by the Liggett & Myers Tobacco Co.
Exhibited by Newell-Emmett Co., Inc.

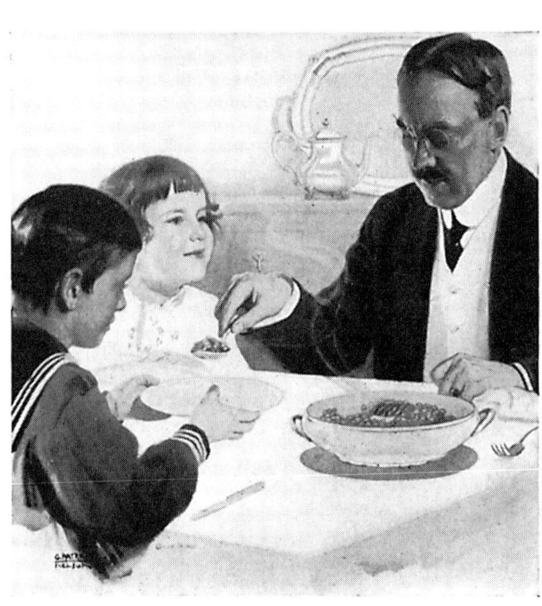

120 HEINZ BAKED BEANS—*G. Patrick Nelson*
Loaned by The H. J. Heinz Company
Exhibited by Calkins & Holden, Inc.

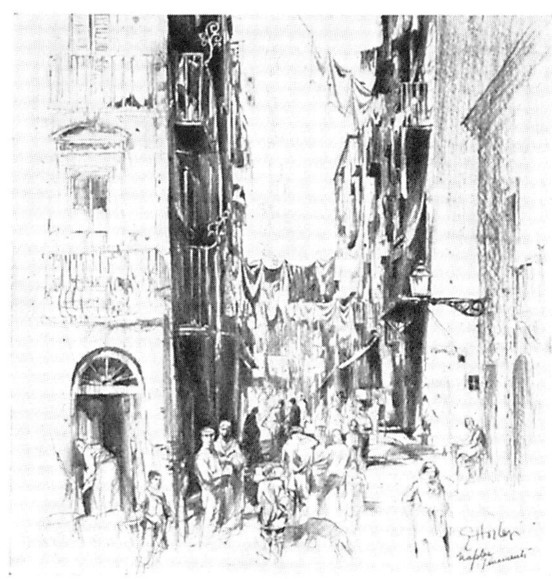

121   ELDORADO LEAD PENCILS—*Earl Horter*
Loaned by the Joseph Dixon Crucible Co.
Exhibited by N. W. Ayer & Son

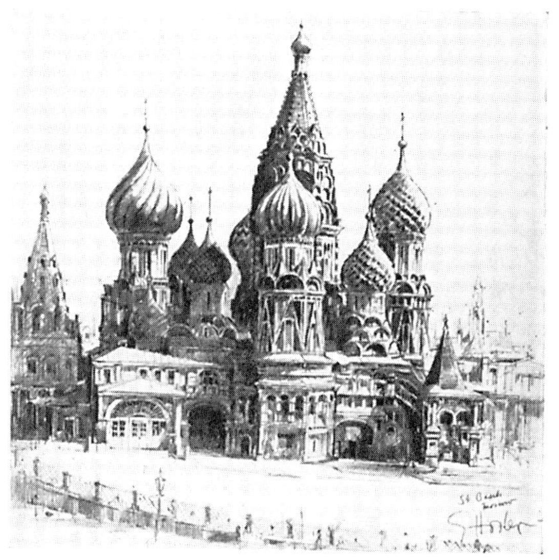

122   ELDORADO LEAD PENCILS—*Earl Horter*
Loaned by the Joseph Dixon Crucible Co.
Exhibited by N. W. Ayer & Son

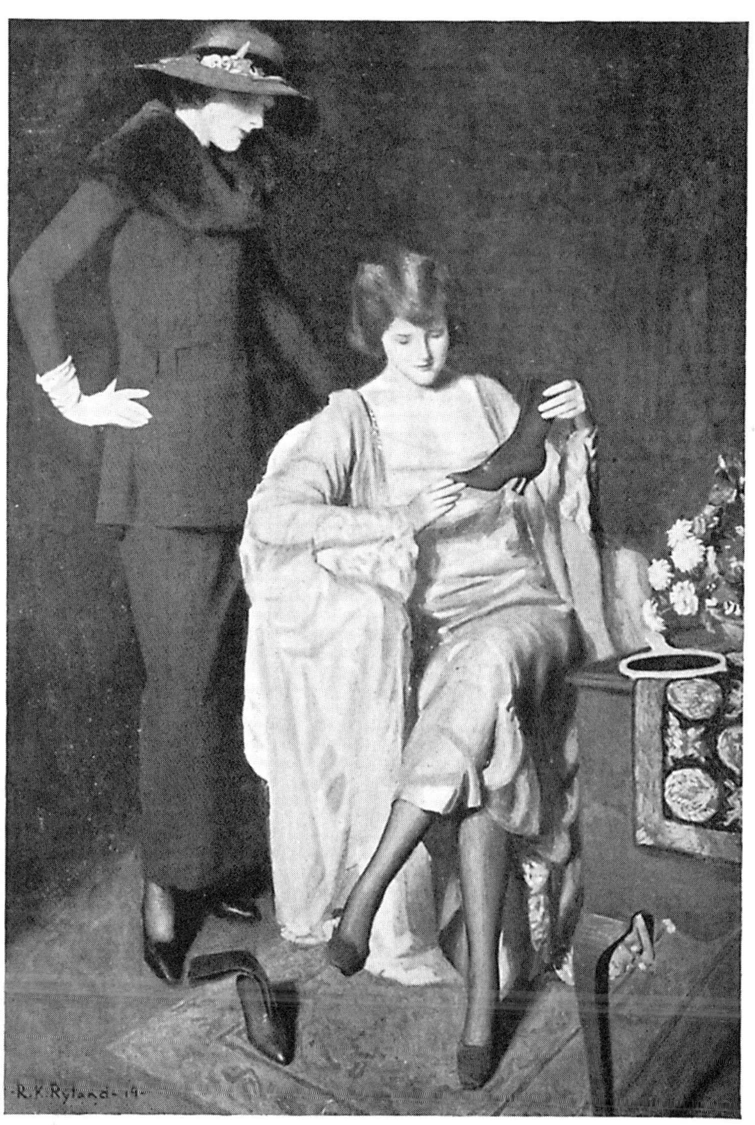

123   VODE KID—*R. K. Ryland*
Loaned by the Standard Kid Mfg. Co.
Exhibited by George Batten Co., Inc.

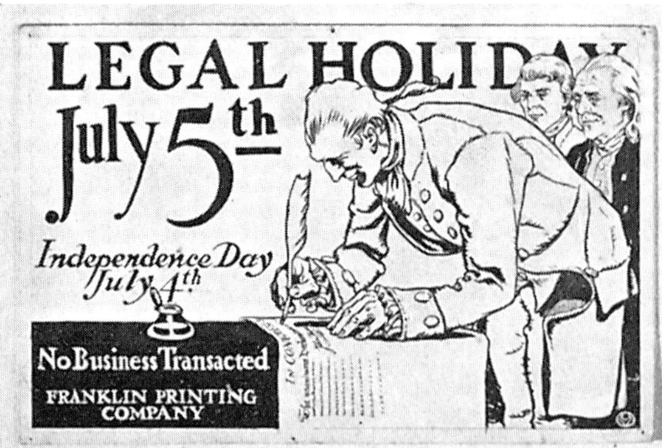

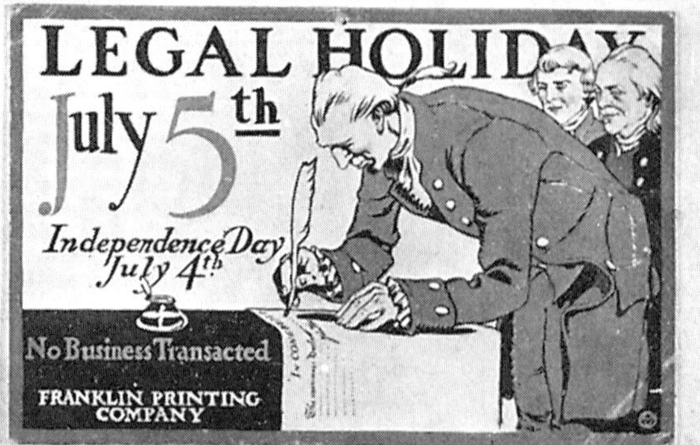

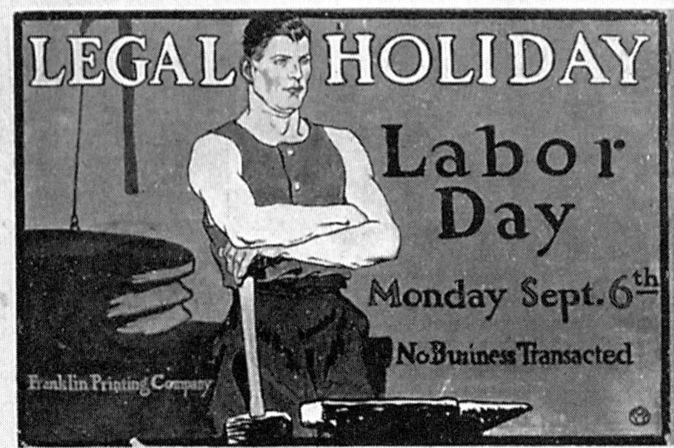

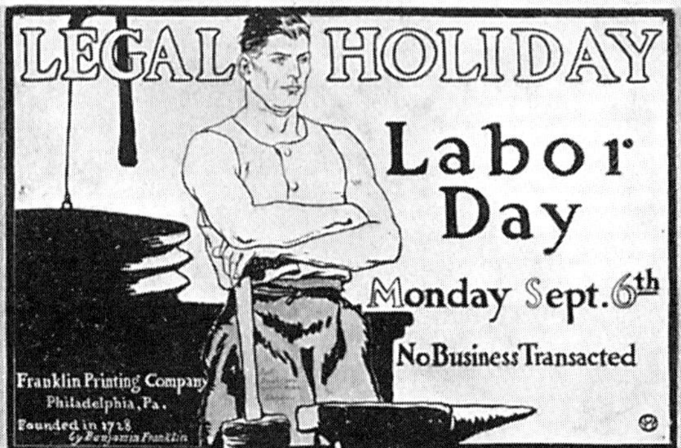

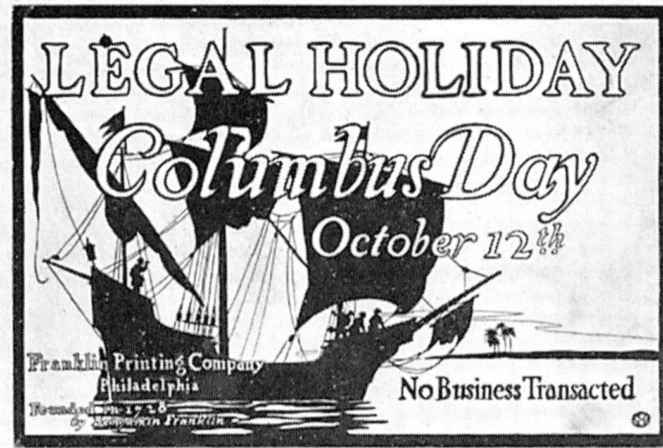

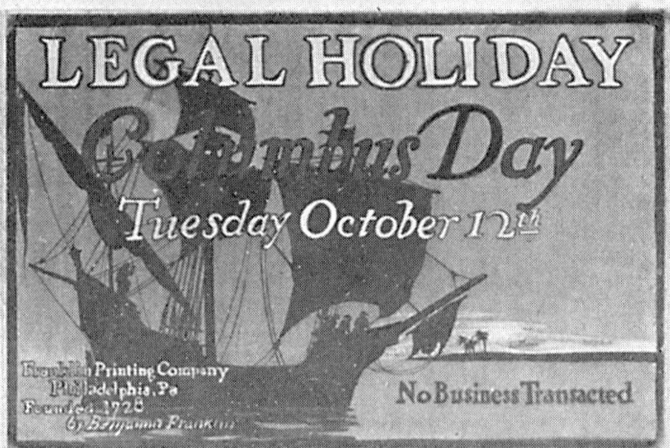

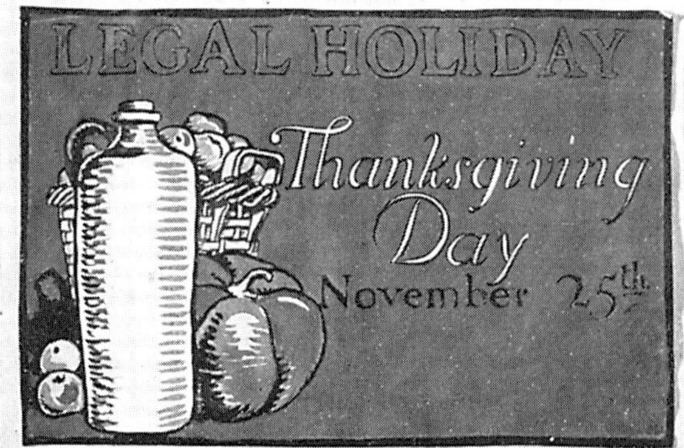

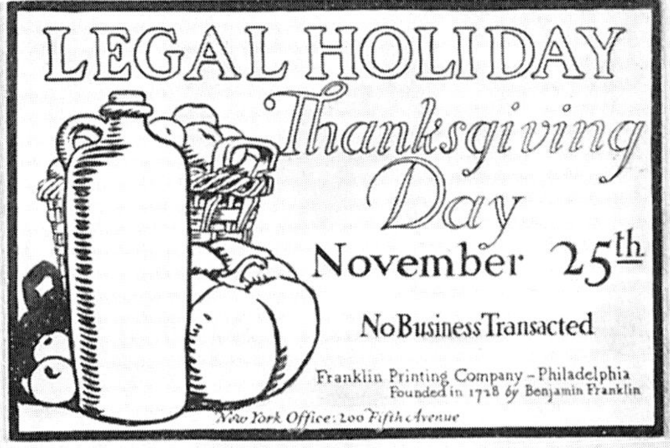

124 FRANKLIN PRINTING COMPANY—*Edward Penfield*
Loaned and exhibited by the Franklin Printing Company

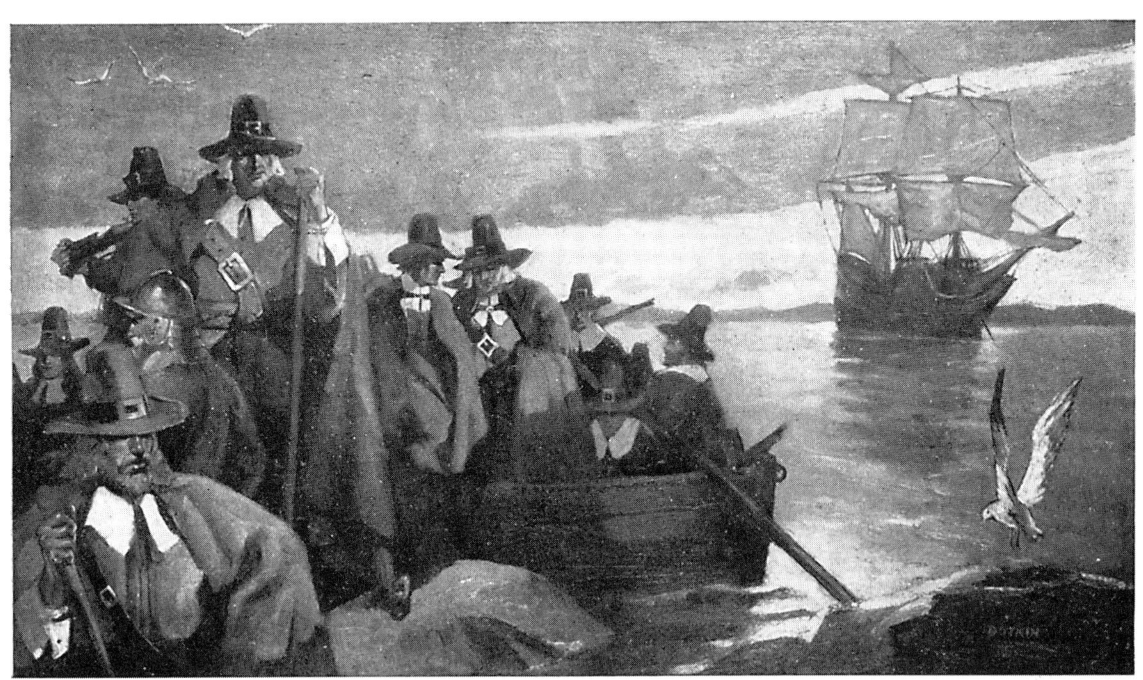

125 OLD COLONY TRUST CO.—*Henry A. Botkin*
Loaned by the Old Colony Trust Co.
Exhibited by The H. K. McCann Co.

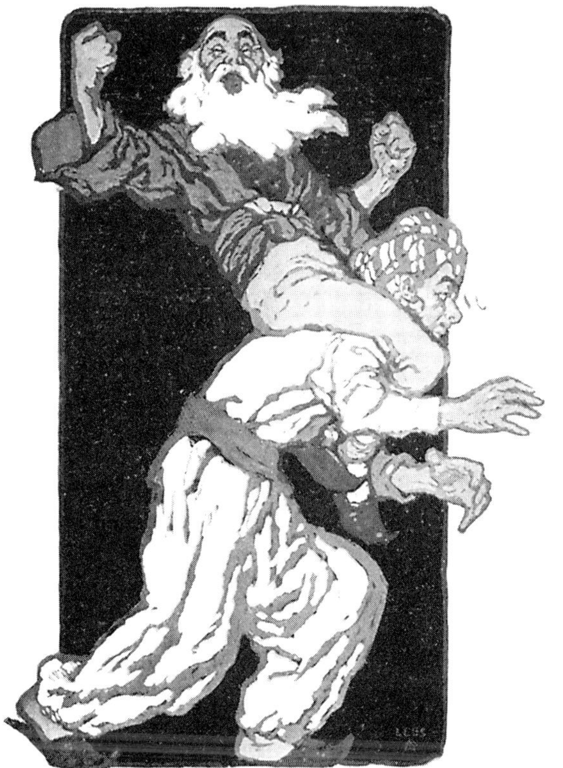

126 MULTIGRAPH—*Harry Lees*
Loaned and exhibited by the Multigraph Co.

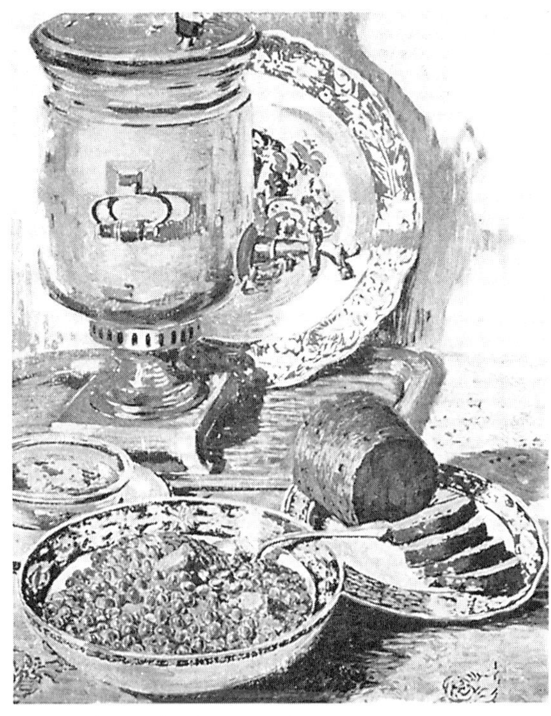

127 LIBBY'S BAKED BEANS—*Sigmund Schou*
Loaned by Libby, McNeill & Libby
Exhibited by J. Walter Thompson Co.

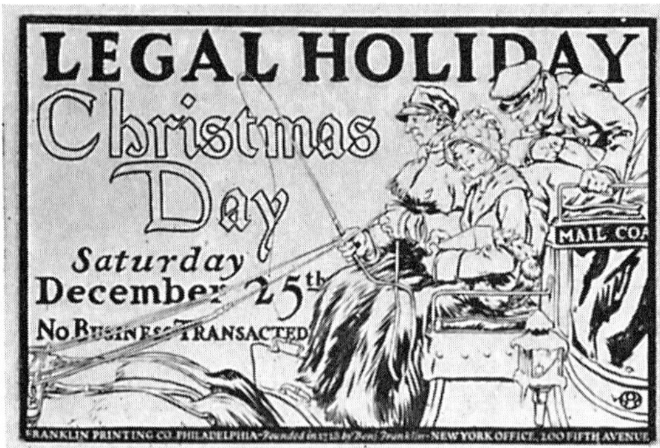

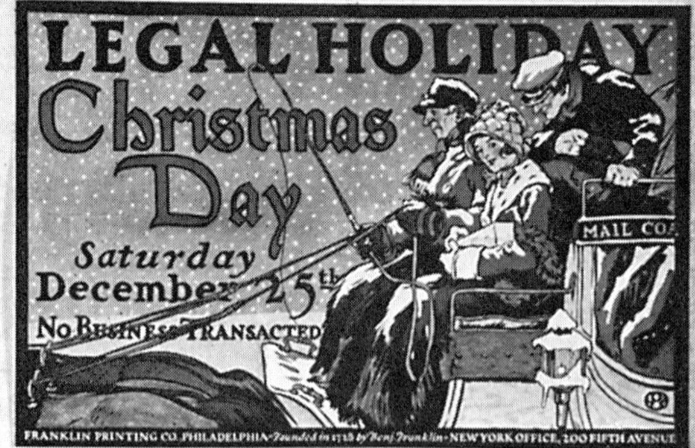

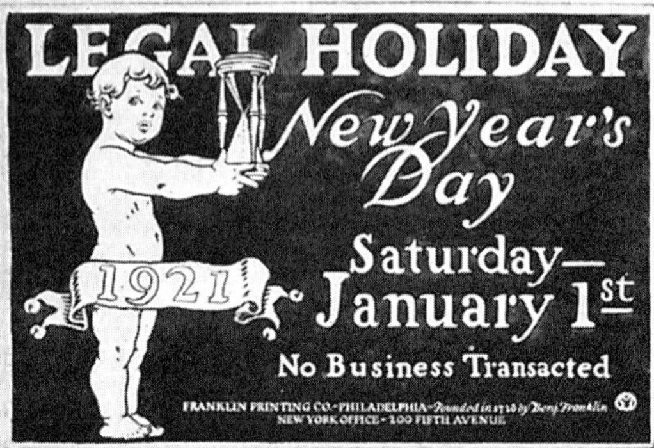

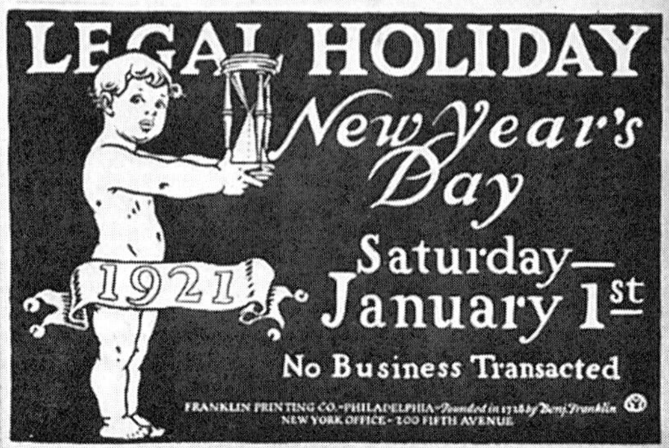

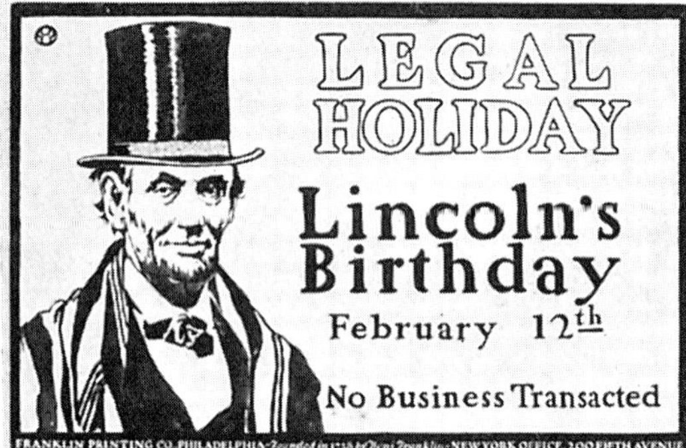

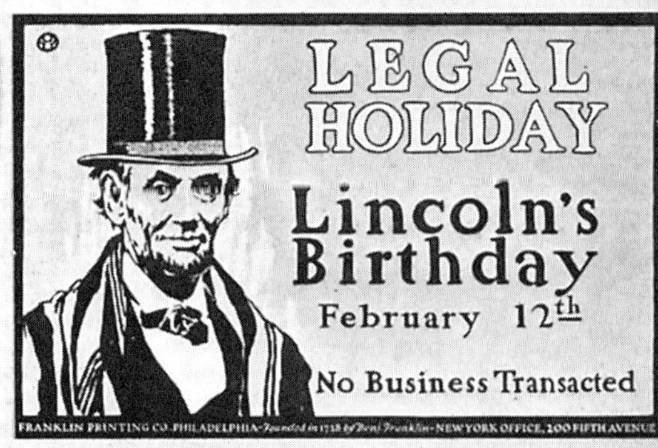

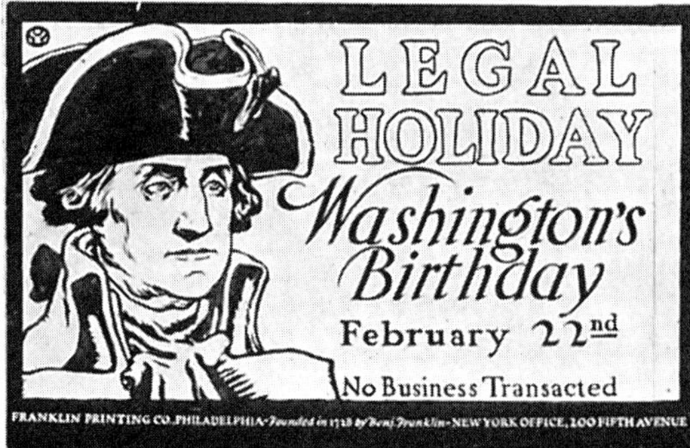

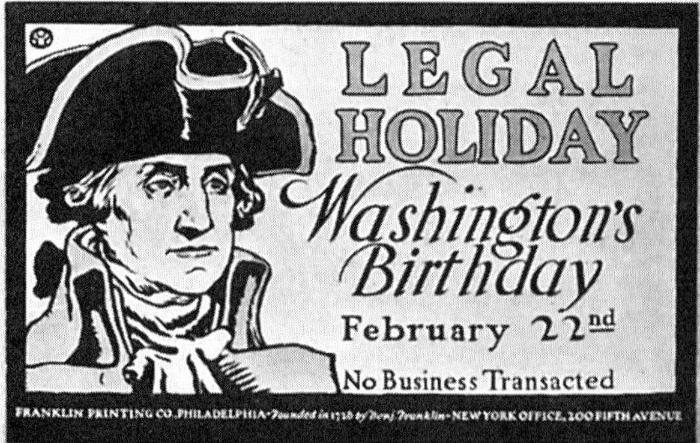

128 FRANKLIN PRINTING COMPANY—*Edward Penfield*
Loaned and exhibited by the Franklin Printing Company

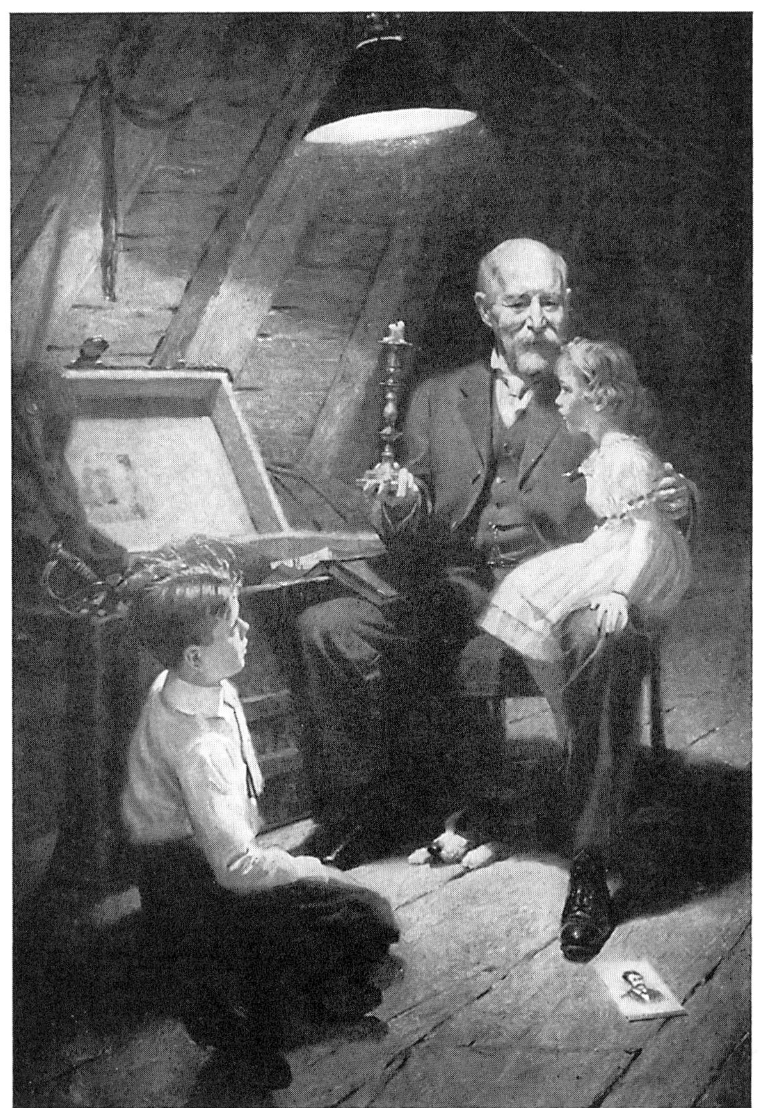

129 Edison Mazda Lamps—*Norman Rockwell*
Loaned by the Edison Lamp Works of General Electric Co.
Exhibited by Barton, Durstine & Osborn, Inc.

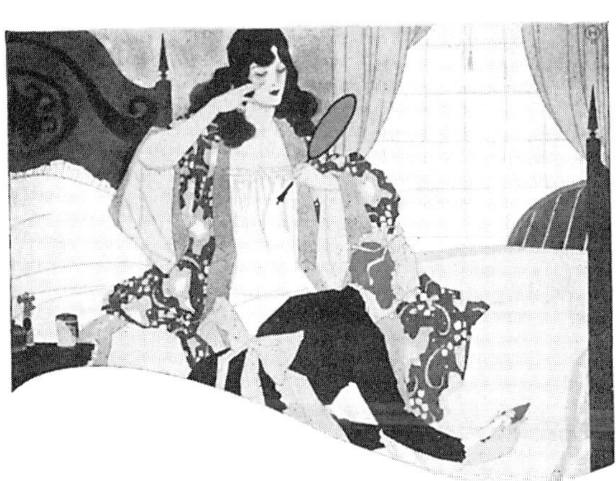

130 Pompeian Cream—*W. F. Heitland*
Loaned by the Pompeian Mfg. Co.
Exhibited by George Batten Co., Inc.

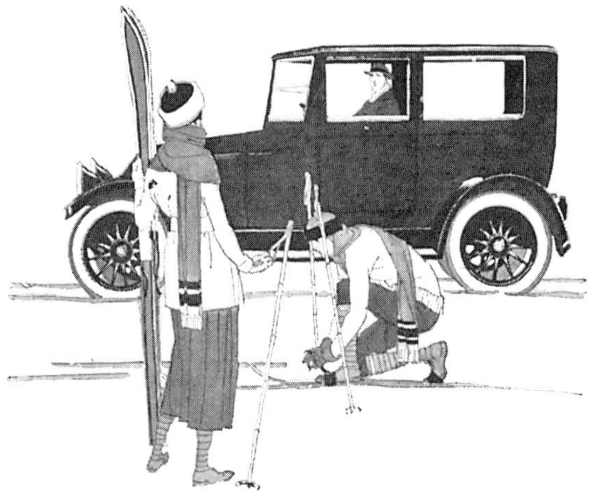

131 Franklin Motor Cars—*F. T. Chapman*
Loaned by the Franklin Automobile Company
Exhibited by Patterson-Andress Co., Inc.

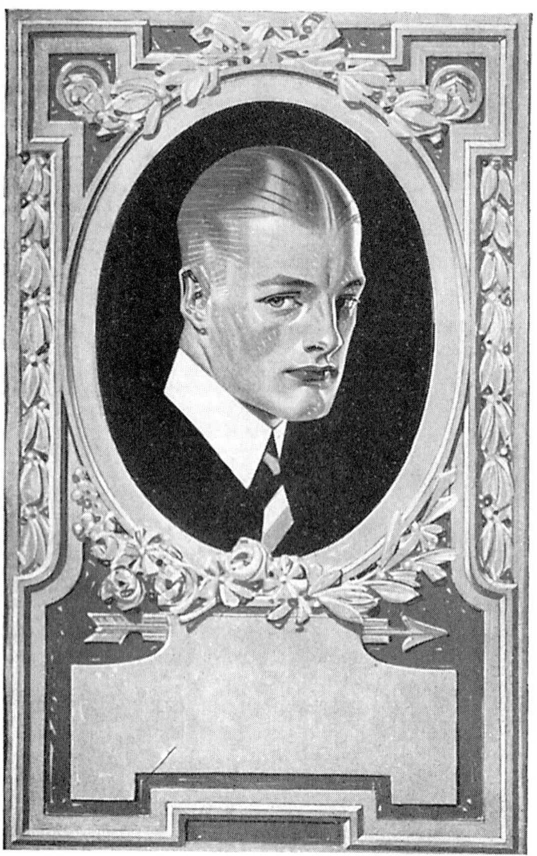

132 ARROW COLLARS—*J. C. Leyendecker*
Loaned and exhibited by Cluett, Peabody & Co., Inc.

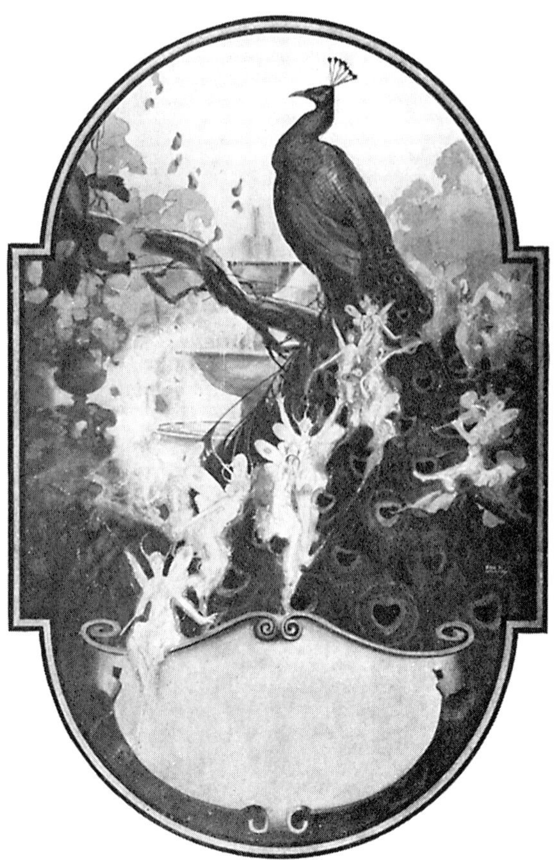

133 DJER-KISS—*Edward A. Wilson*
Loaned by the Alfred H. Smith Co.
Exhibited by The Blackman Co.

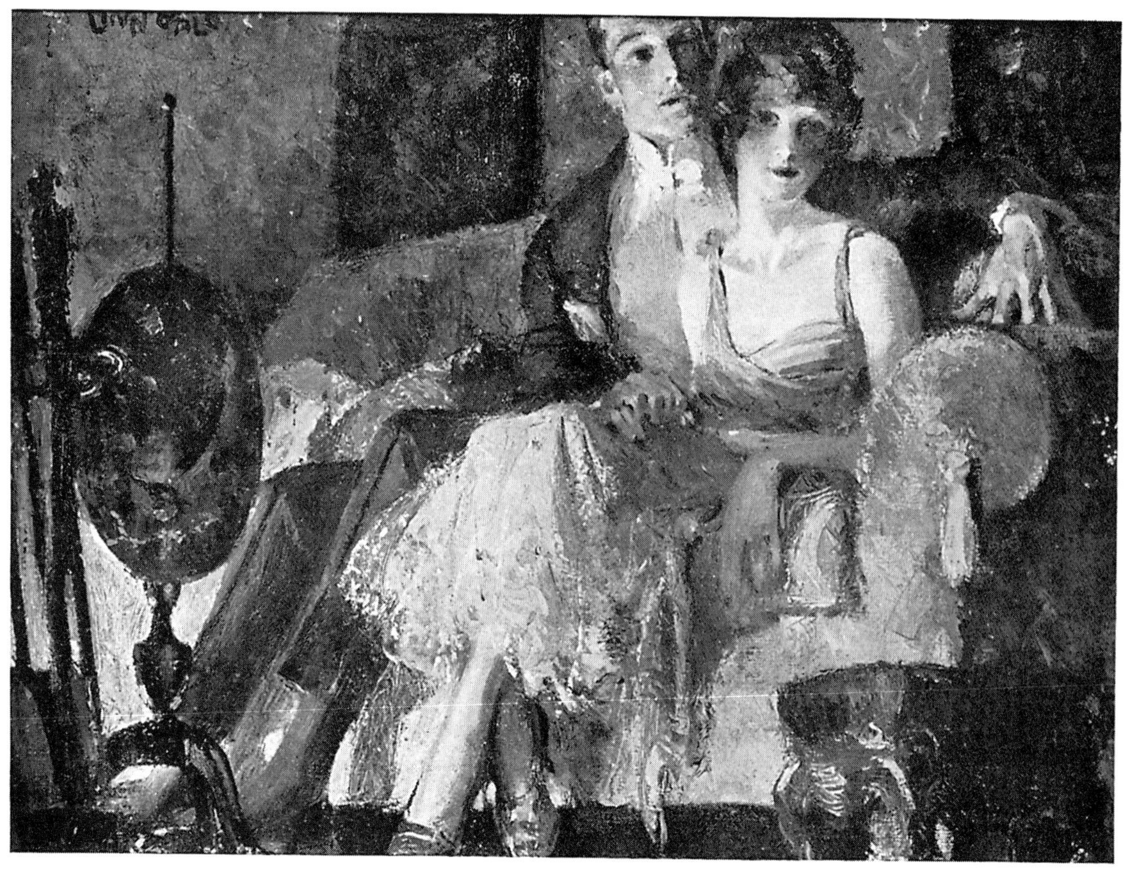

134 MUM—*Linn Ball*
Loaned by George B. Evans
Exhibited by John O. Powers Company

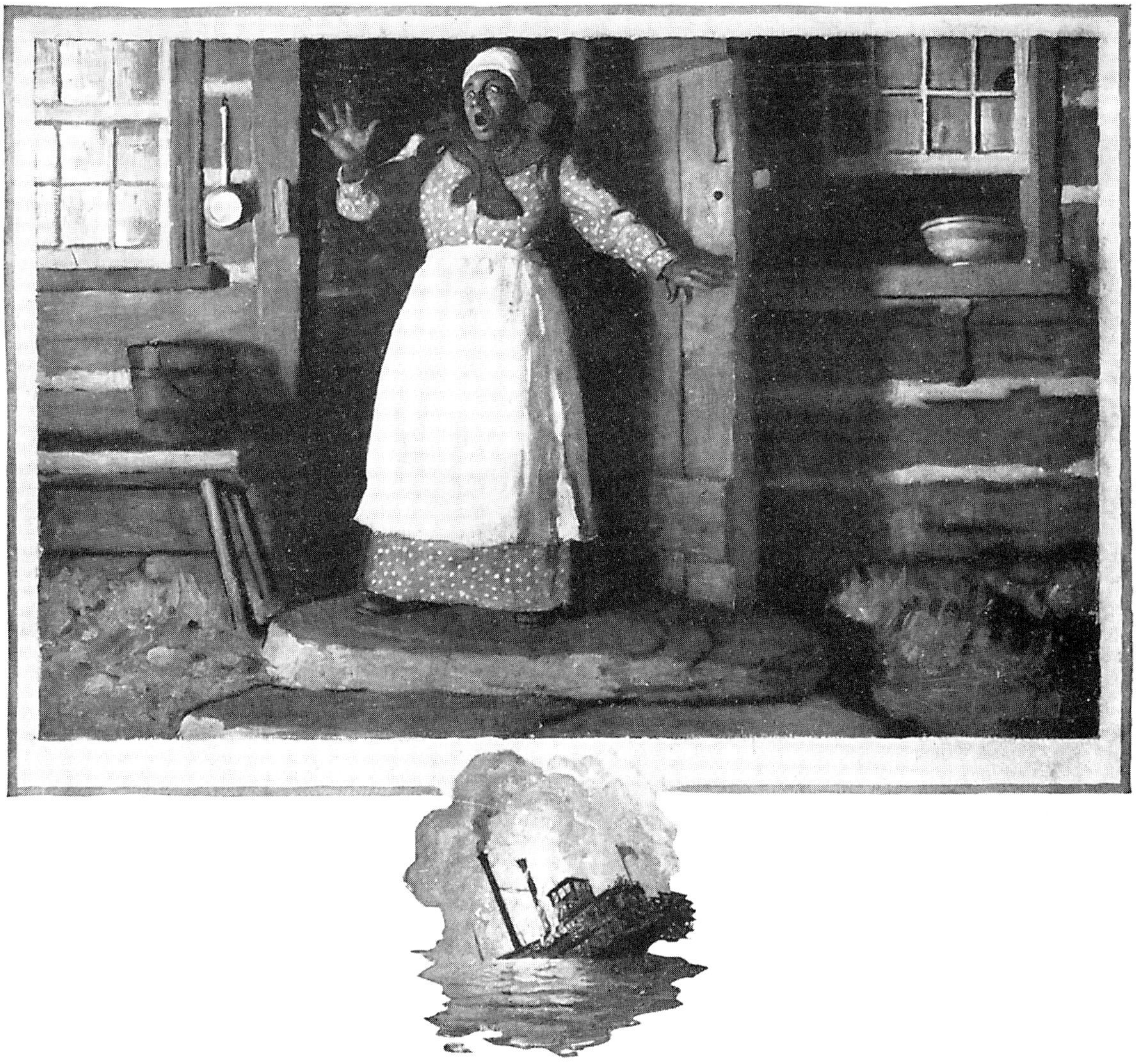

135 Aunt Jemima's Pancake Flour—*N. C. Wyeth*
Loaned by the Aunt Jemima Mills Co.
Exhibited by J. Walter Thompson Co.

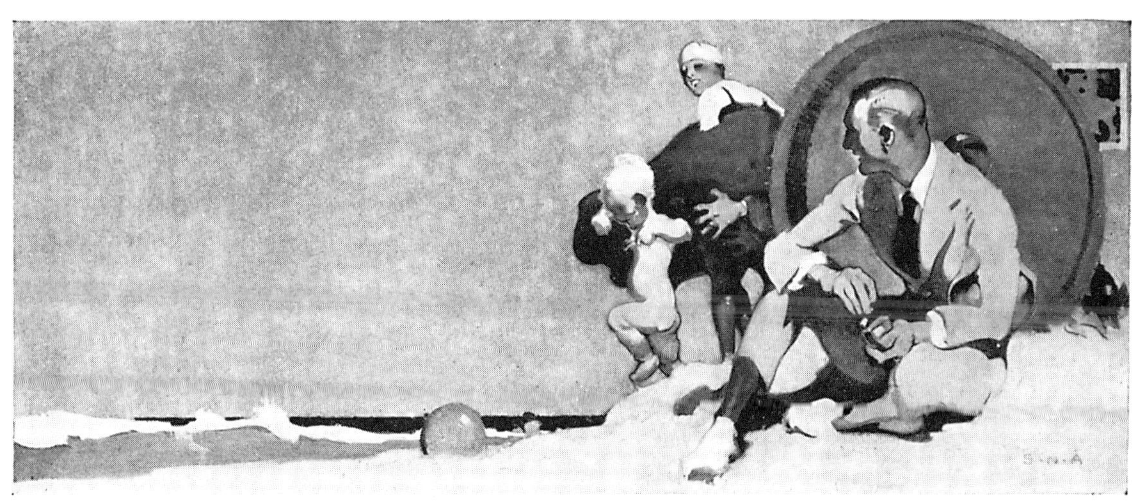

136 Men's Clothing—*S. N. Abbott*
Loaned and exhibited by Hart Schaffner & Marx

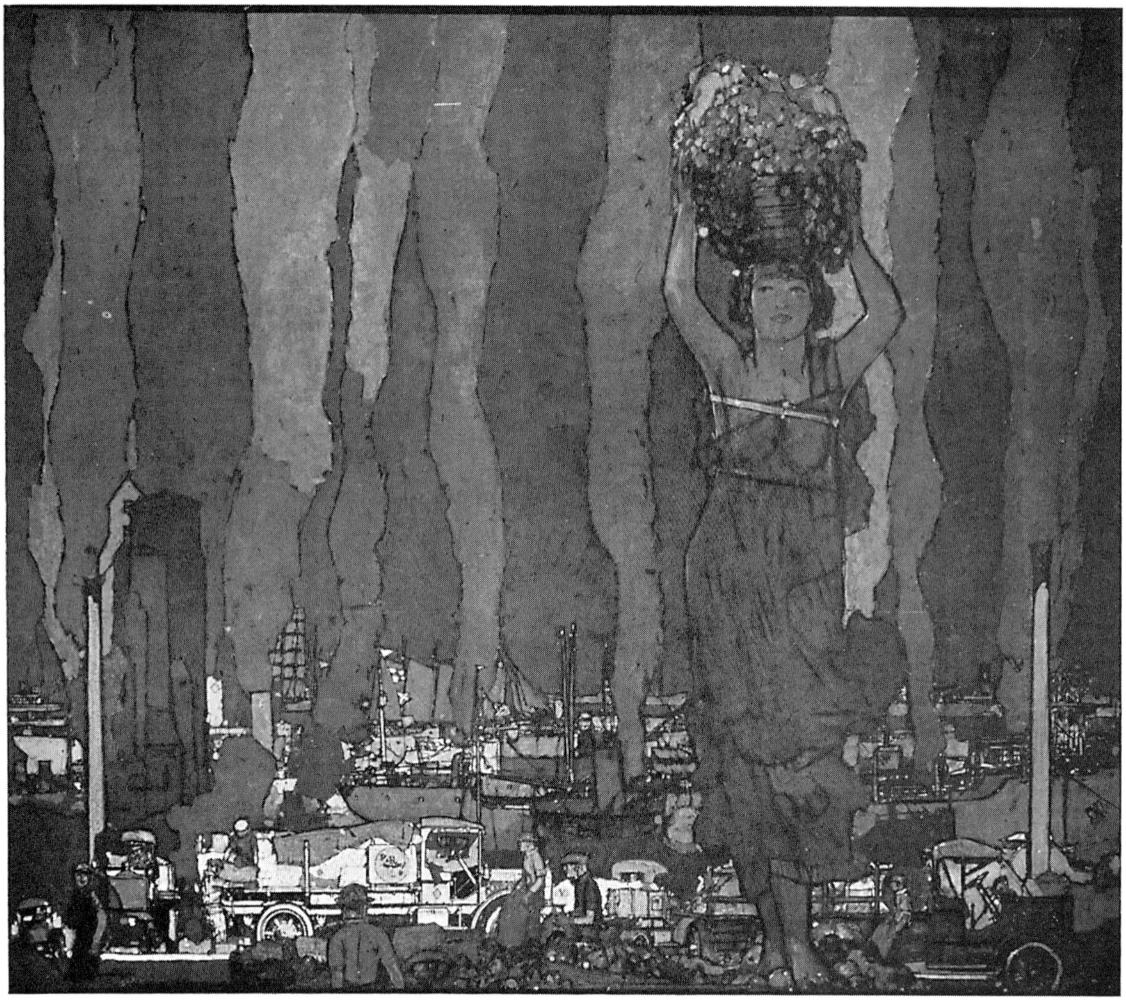

137 THE WHITE MOTOR TRUCK—*E. G. Teale*
Loaned and exhibited by the Caxton Company

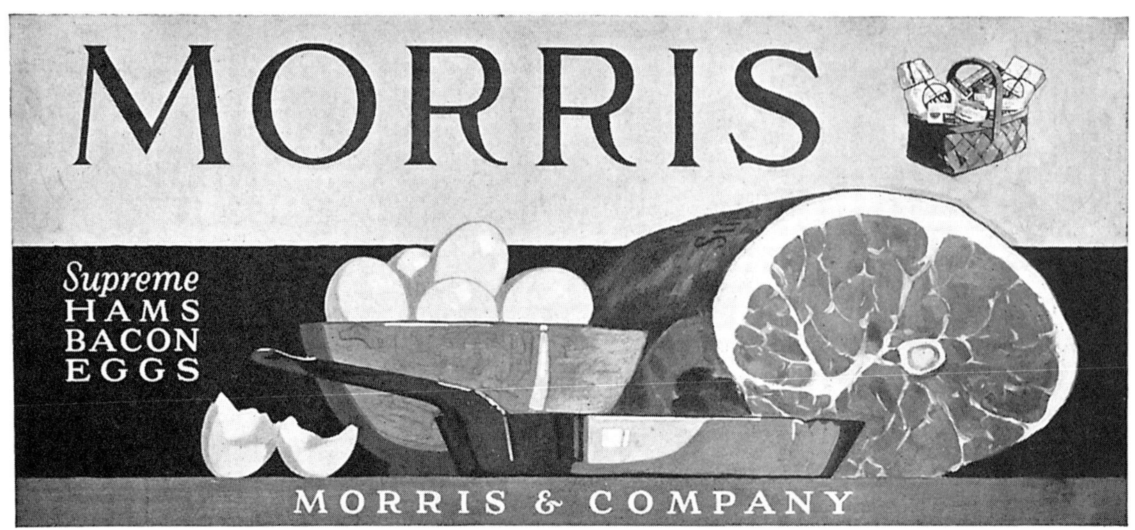

138 MORRIS' HAM AND BACON—*Maurice Logan*
Loaned and exhibited by Morris & Company

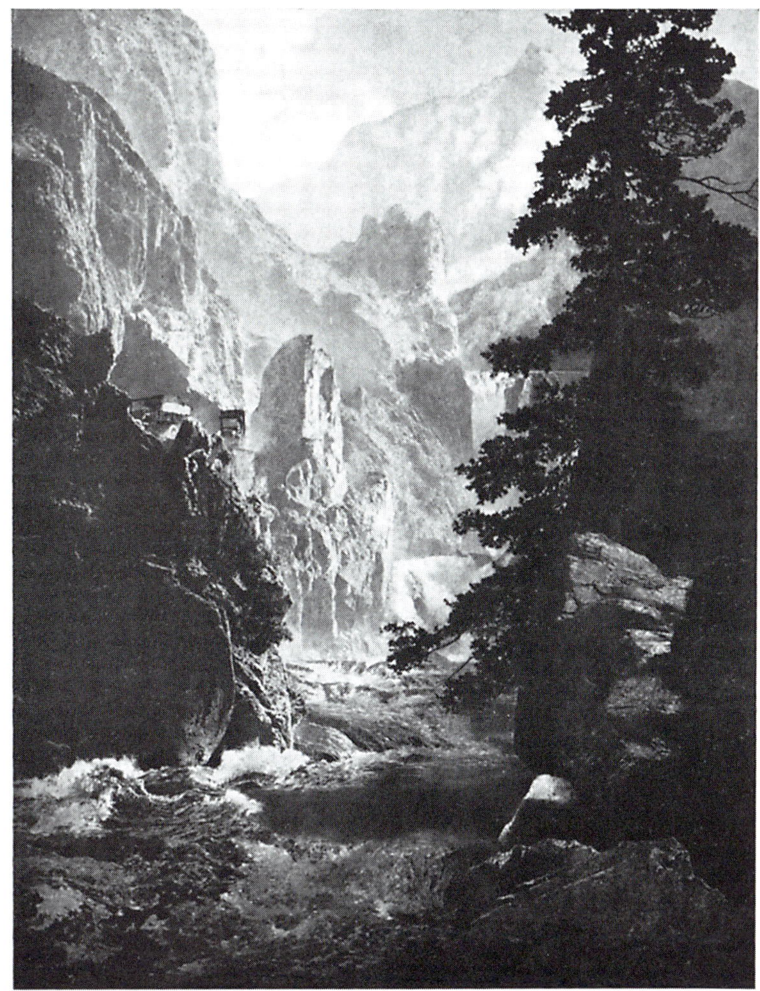

139   THE SPIRIT OF TRANSPORTATION—*Maxfield Parrish*
Loaned and exhibited by The Clark Equipment Co.

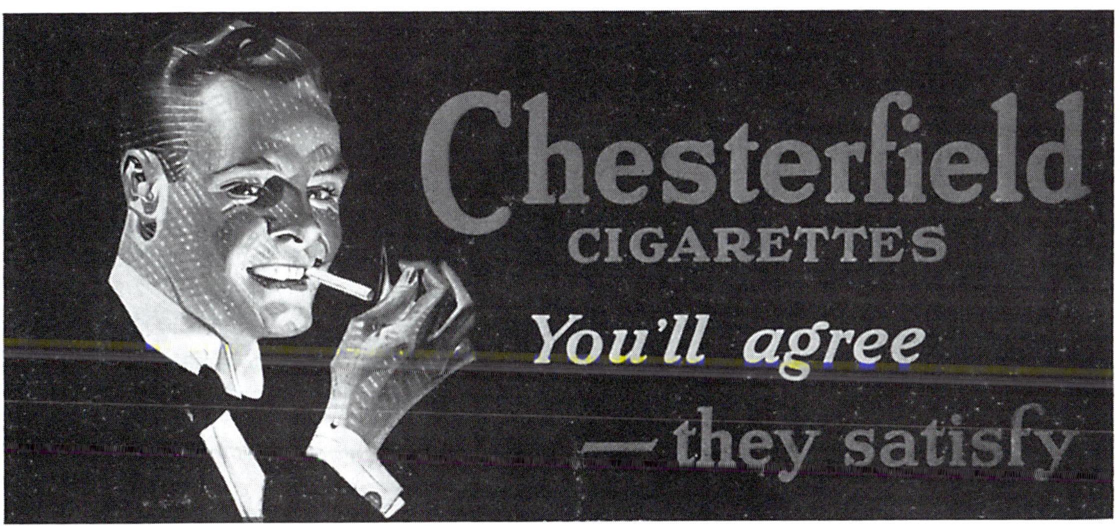

140   CHESTERFIELD CIGARETTES—*J. C. Leyendecker*
Loaned and exhibited by the Liggett & Myers Tobacco Co.

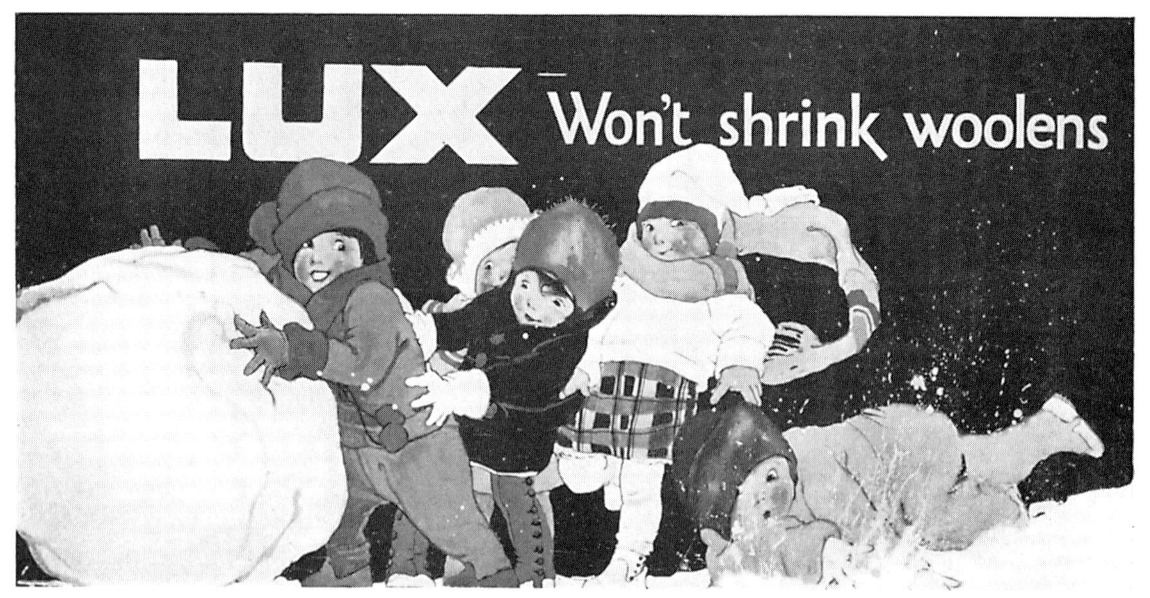

141   LUX—*Lucile Patterson Marsh*
Loaned by the Lever Bros. Co.
Exhibited by J. Walter Thompson Co.

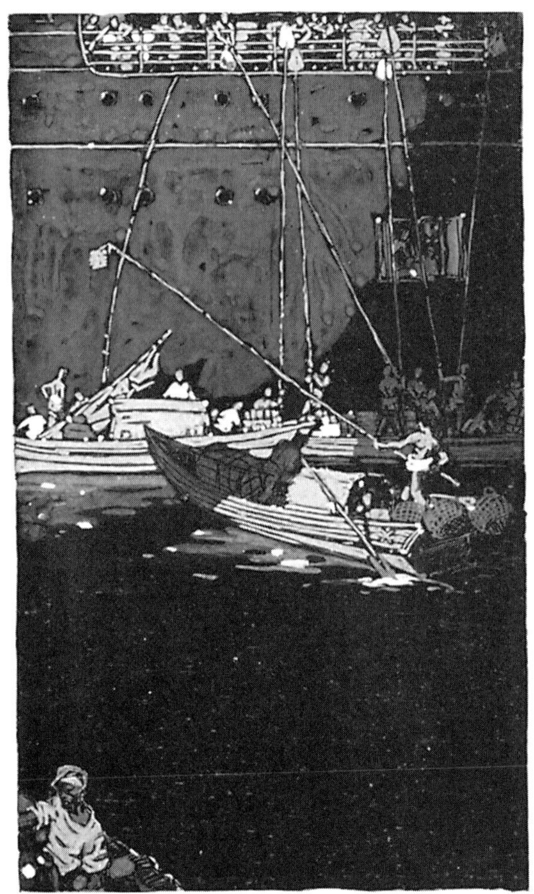

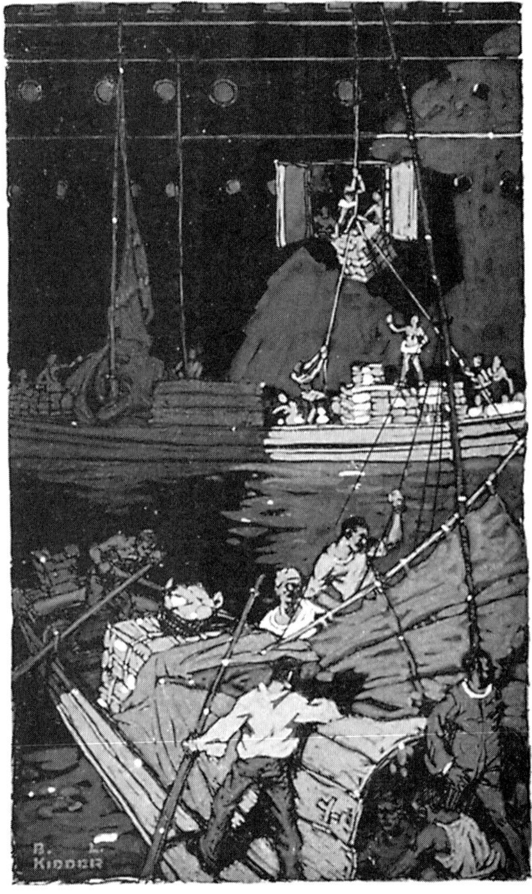

142   CARGO CARRIERS AT AN ORIENTAL PORT   143
Ben. L. Kidder

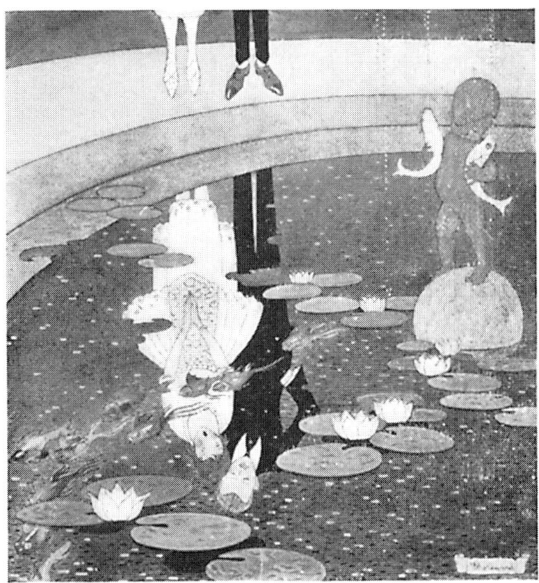

144 CATALOG COVER—*Joseph Bolegard*
Loaned by Marshall Field & Co.
Exhibited by the Wm. H. Rankin Co.

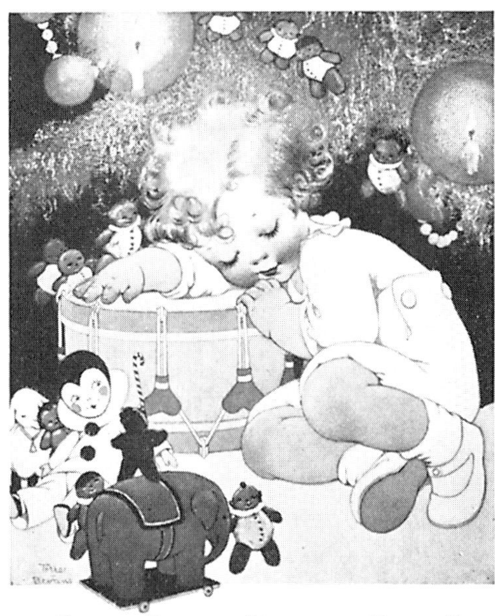

145 ROYAL BAKING POWDER—*Torre Bevans*
Loaned by the Royal Baking Powder Co.
Exhibited by the Federal Advertising Agency, Inc.

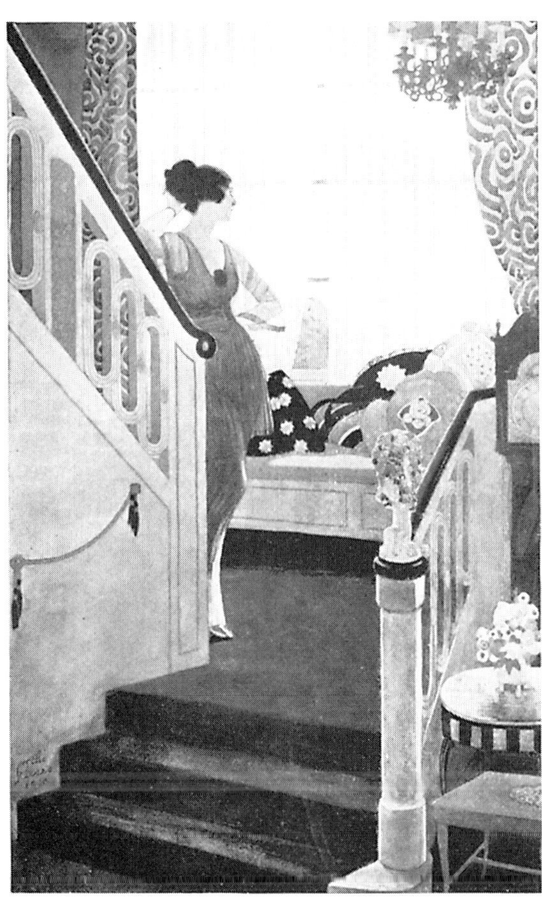

146 LACE CURTAINS—*The Reeses*
Loaned by the Scranton Lace Co.
Exhibited by Barrows & Richardson

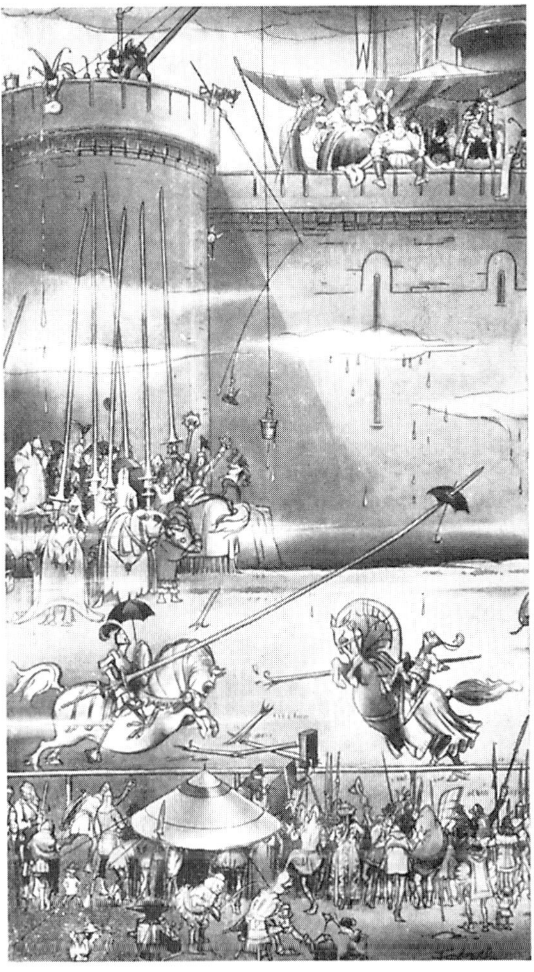

147 MEN'S CLOTHING—*Charles H. Forbell*
Loaned and exhibited by Rogers Peet Co.

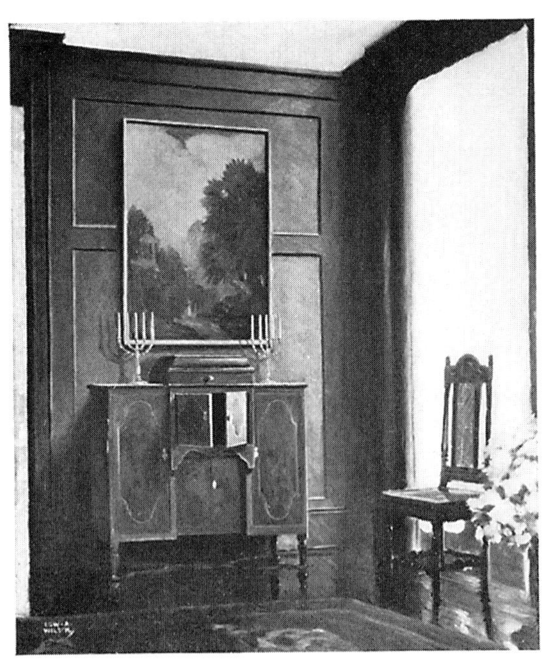

148 VICTOR TALKING MACHINES
Edward A. Wilson
Loaned by the Victor Talking Machine Co.
Exhibited by the Franklin Printing Company

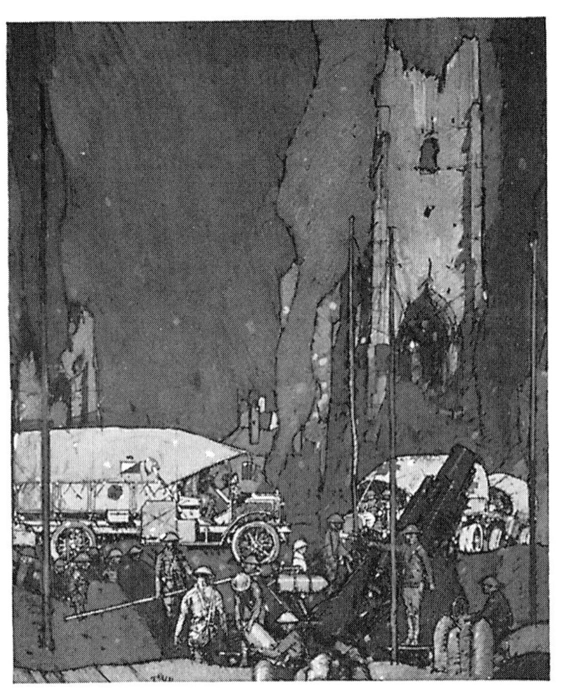

149 WHITE MOTOR TRUCK—*E. G. Teale*
Loaned and exhibited by the Caxton Company

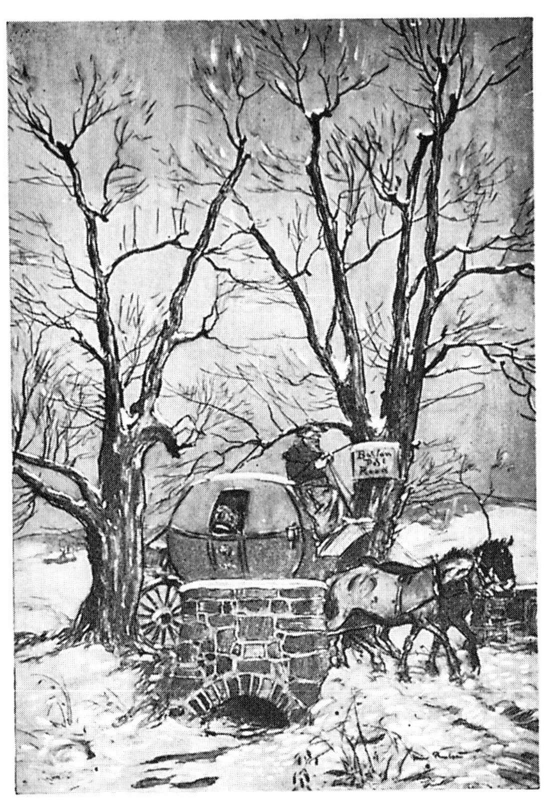

150 CALENDAR ILLUSTRATION—*James Preston*
Loaned and exhibited by the Beck Engraving Co.

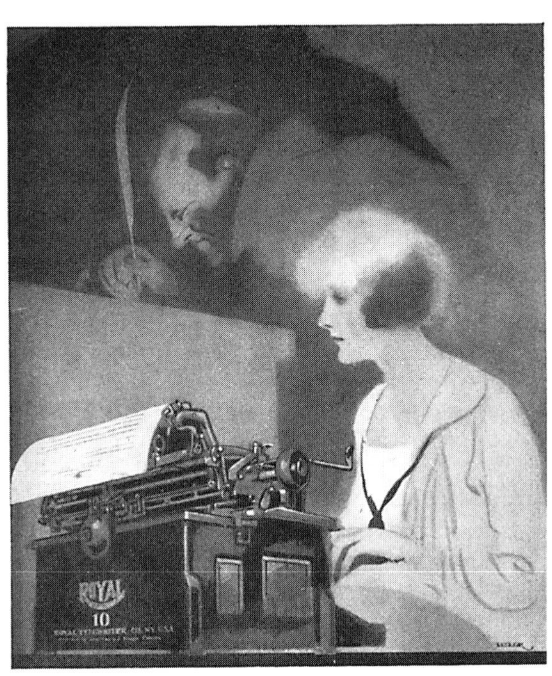

151 ROYAL TYPEWRITERS—*Clarence Helck*
Loaned by the Royal Typewriter Co.
Exhibited by The H. K. McCann Co.

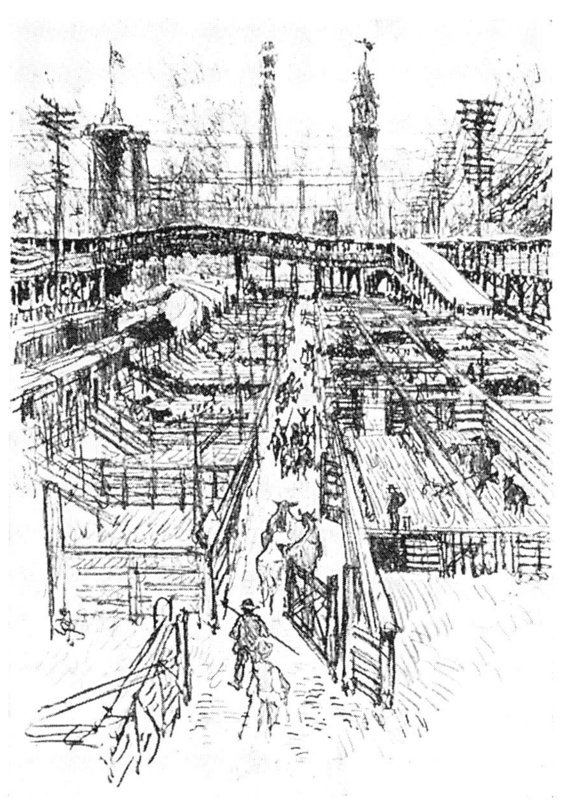

152 Union Stock Yards
Charcoal Study by Joseph Pennell
Loaned and exhibited by Armour & Co.

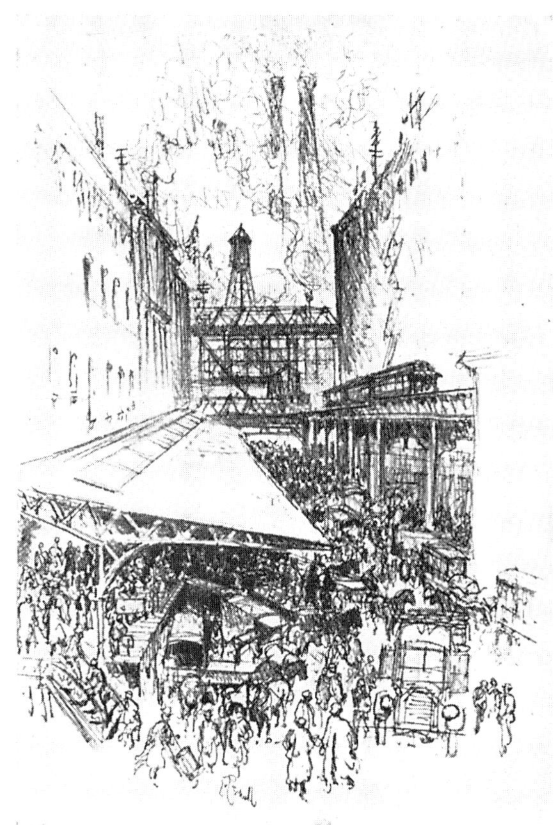

153 Union Stock Yards
Charcoal Study by Joseph Pennell
Loaned and exhibited by Armour & Co.

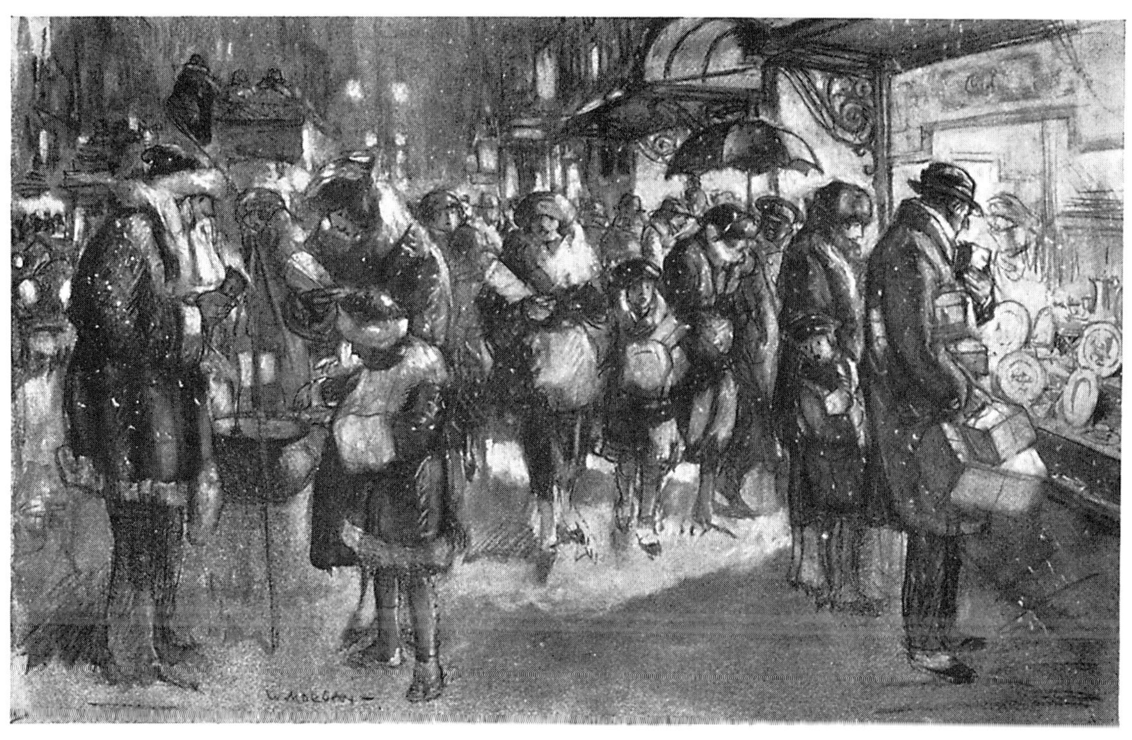

154 Ovington's—*Wallace Morgan*
Loaned by the Ovington Bros. Co.
Exhibited by Barton, Durstine & Osborn, Inc.

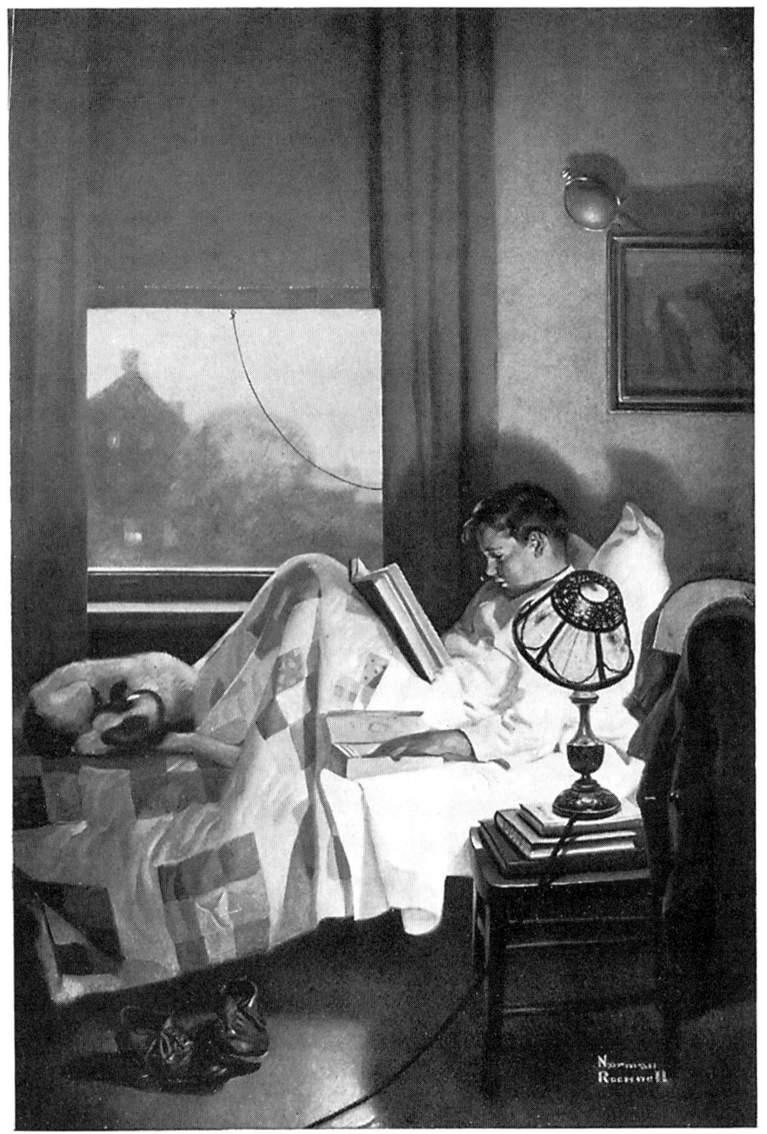

155　Edison Mazda Lamps—*Norman Rockwell*
Loaned by the Edison Lamp Works of General Electric Co.
Exhibited by Barton, Durstine & Osborn, Inc.

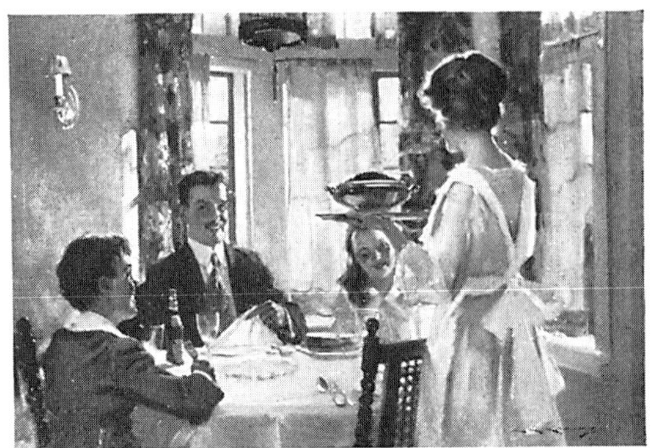

156　Heinz Baked Beans—*Charles E. Chambers*
Loaned by The H. J. Heinz Company
Exhibited by Calkins & Holden, Inc.

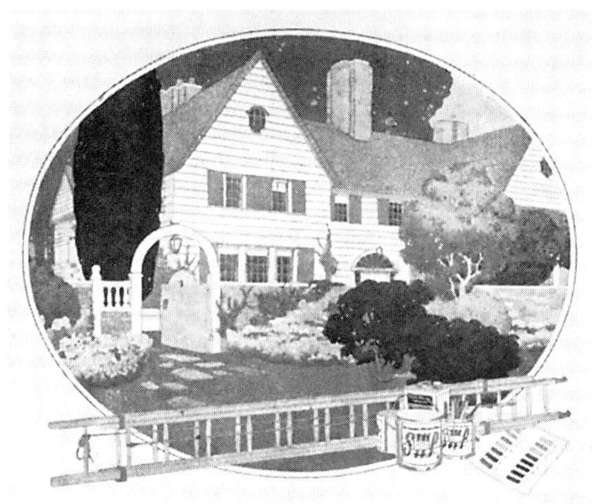

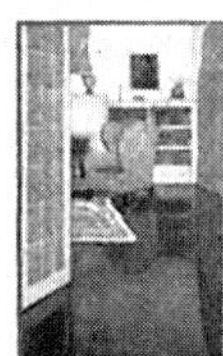

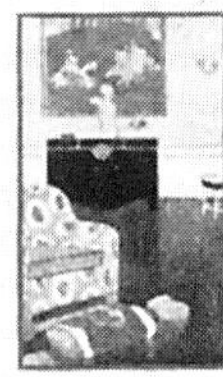

157 SHERWIN-WILLIAMS PAINTS AND VARNISHES
The Reeses
Loaned by The Sherwin-Williams Co.
Exhibited by Calkins & Holden, Inc.

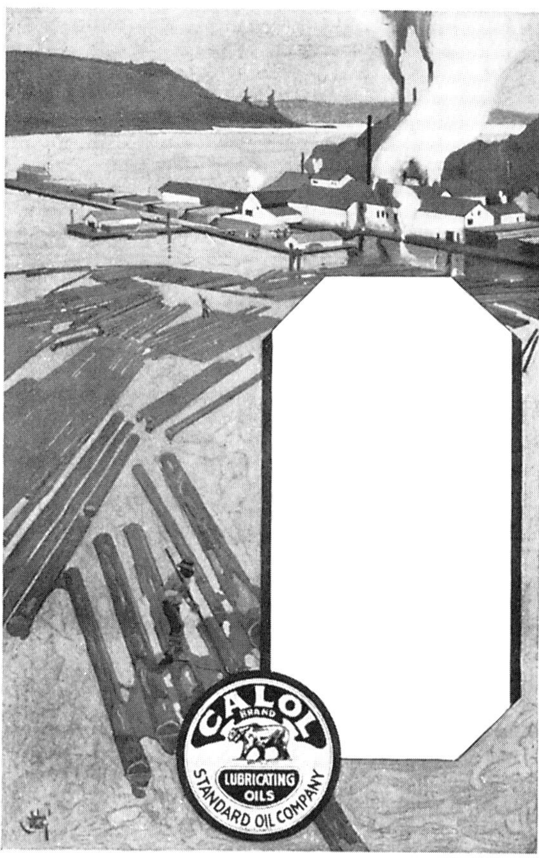

158 CALOL LUBRICATING OILS—*John Kelly*
Loaned by the Standard Oil Company of Calif.
Exhibited by The H. K. McCann Co.

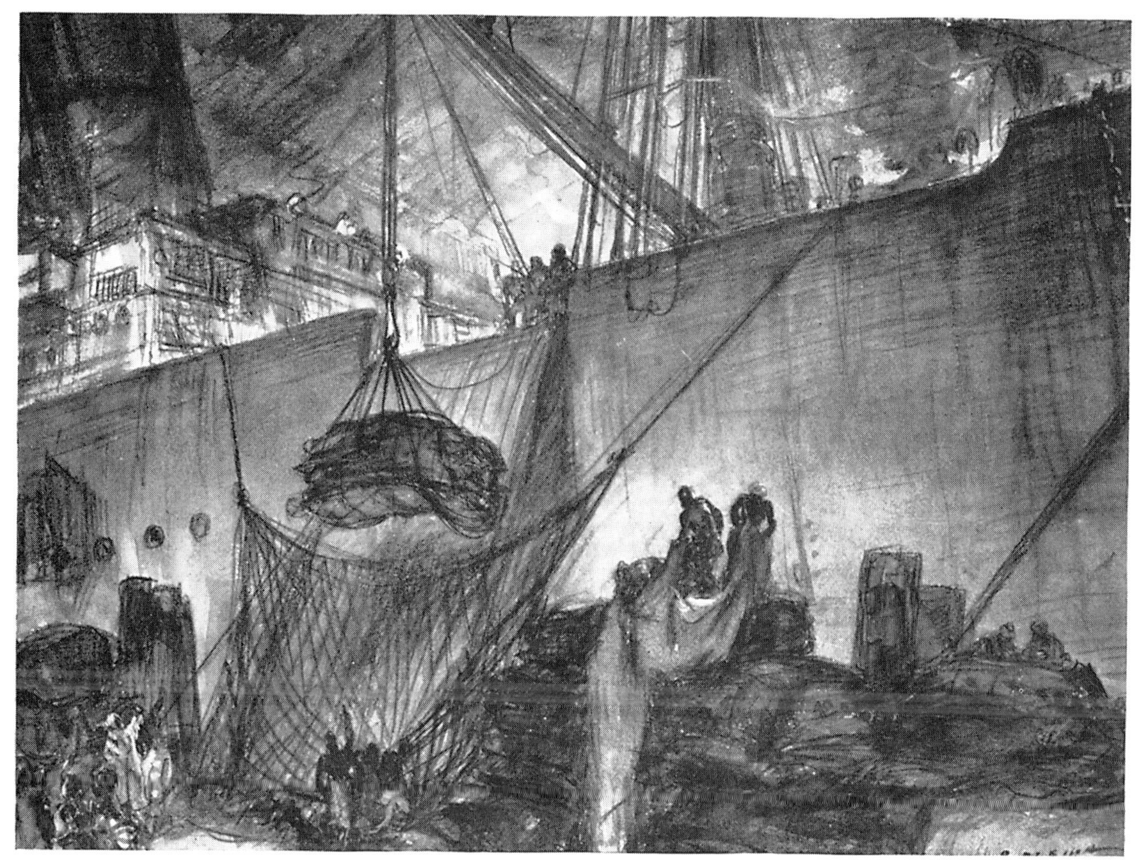

159 MCELWAIN SHOES—*Henry Raleigh*
Loaned by W. H. McElwain Co.
Exhibited by Barton, Durstine & Osborn, Inc.

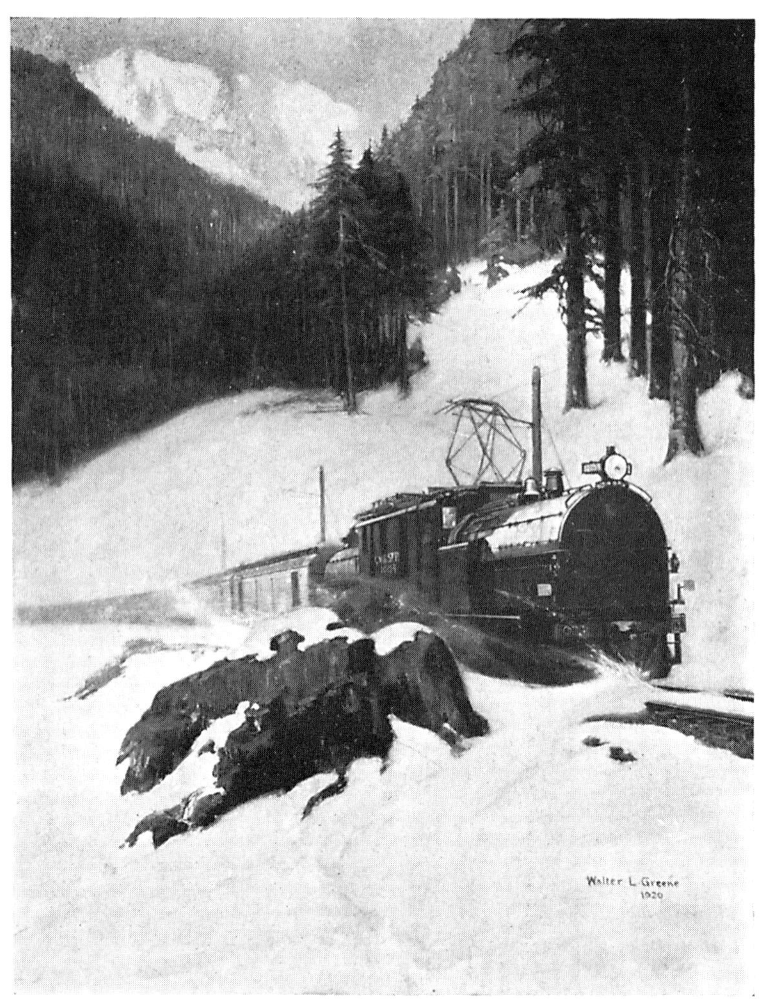

160 ELECTRIC LOCOMOTIVE—*Walter Greene*
Loaned and exhibited by the General Electric Co.

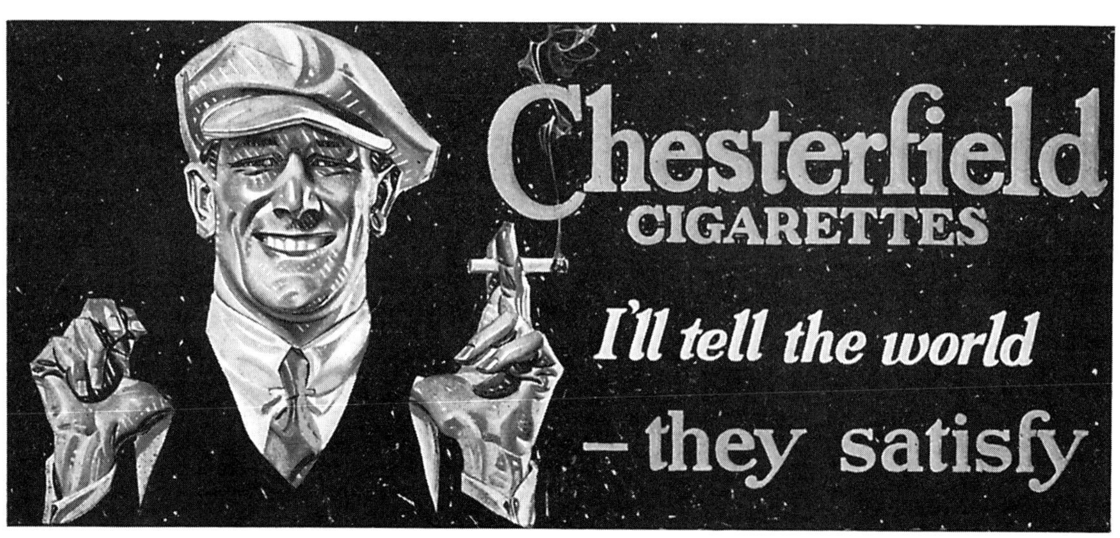

161 CHESTERFIELD CIGARETTES—*J. C. Leyendecker*
Loaned and exhibited by the Liggett & Myers Tobacco Co.

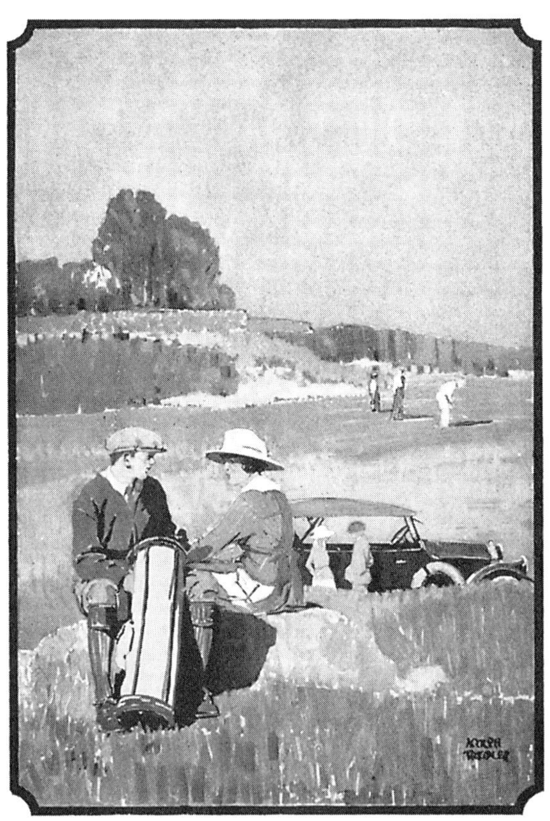

162   THE PIERCE-ARROW MOTOR CAR
Adolph Treidler
Loaned by The Pierce-Arrow Motor Car Co.
Exhibited by the Bartlett-Orr Press

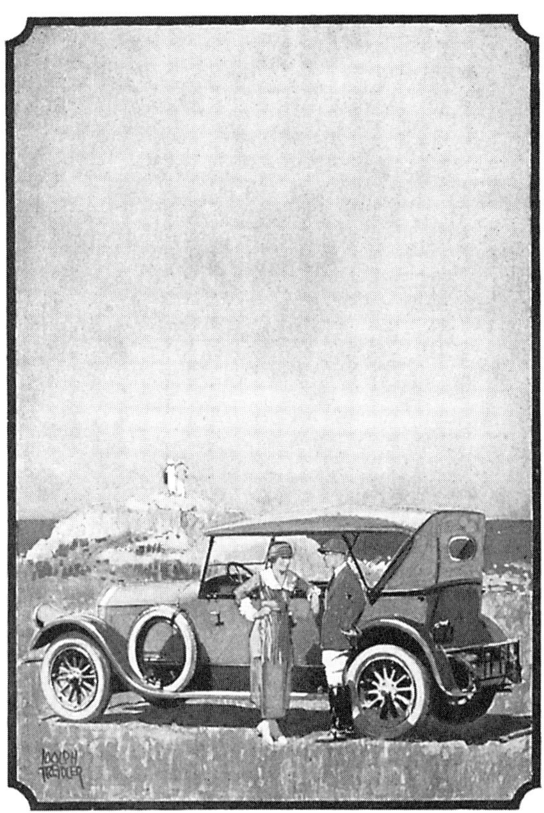

163   THE PIERCE-ARROW MOTOR CAR
Adolph Treidler
Loaned by The Pierce-Arrow Motor Car Co.
Exhibited by the Bartlett-Orr Press

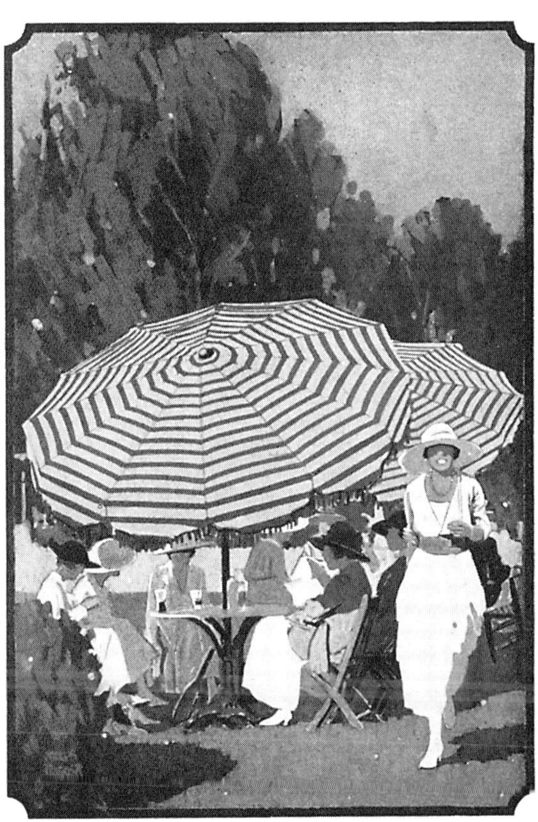

164   THE PIERCE-ARROW MOTOR CAR—*Adolph Treidler*
Loaned by The Pierce-Arrow Motor Car Co.
Exhibited by the Bartlett-Orr Press

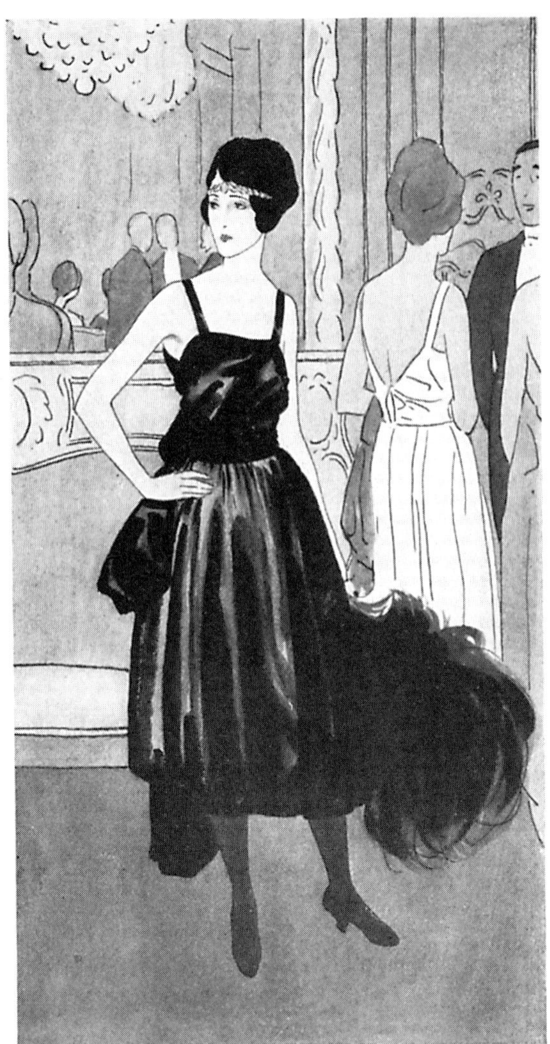

165 FRENCH SATIN—*Carl Erickson*
Loaned and exhibited by Pelgram & Myer

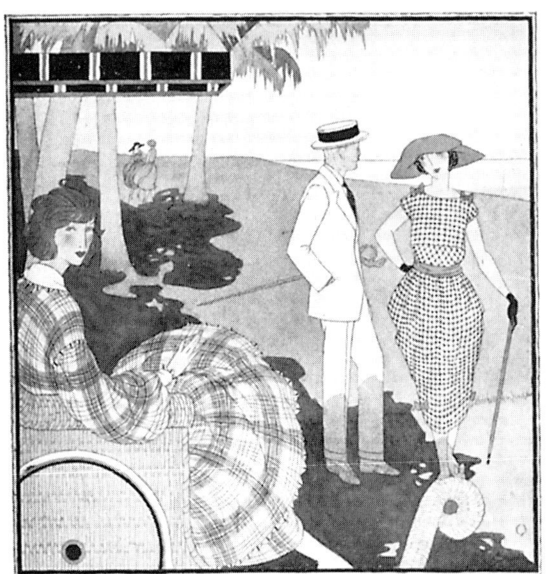

166 GILBRAE GINGHAM—*Margaret Montgomery*
Loaned by Amory, Browne & Co.
Exhibited by George Batten Co., Inc.

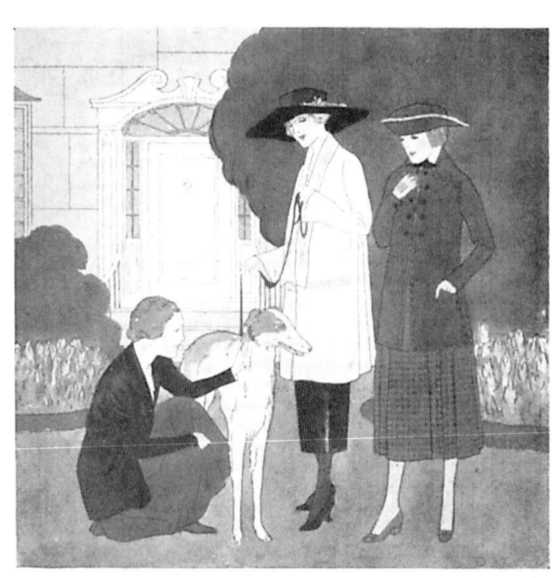

167 PORTABLE HOUSES—*Samuel Otis*
Loaned and exhibited by the R. L. Kenyon Co.

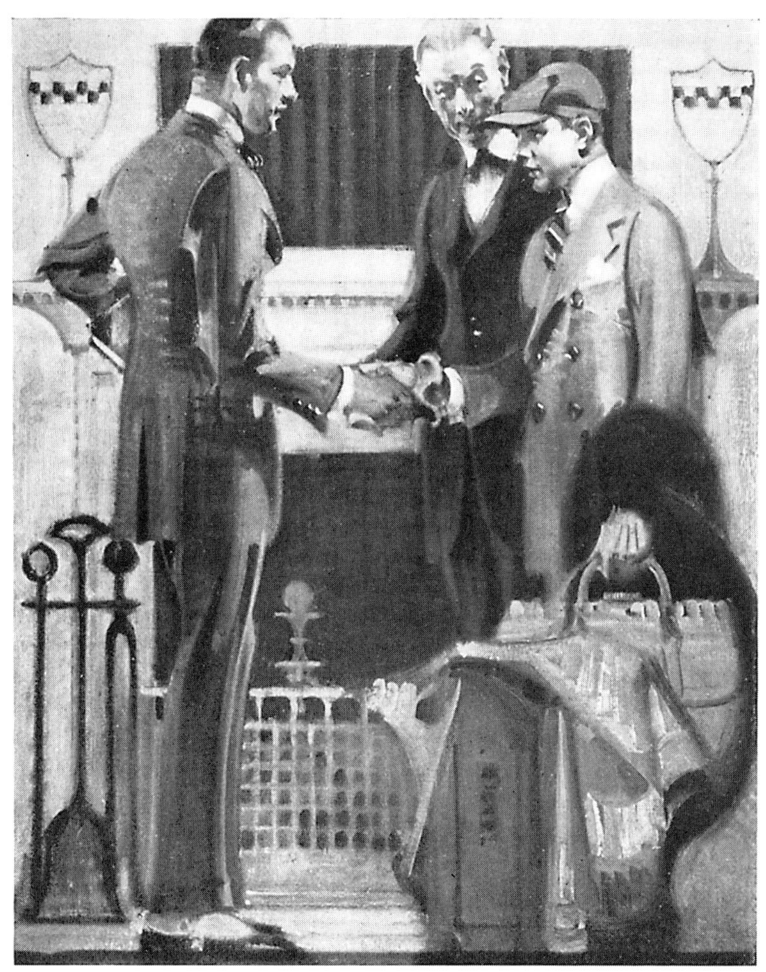

168　Society Brand Clothing—*Leon M. Gordon*
Loaned by Alfred Decker & Cohn
Exhibited by George Batten Co., Inc.

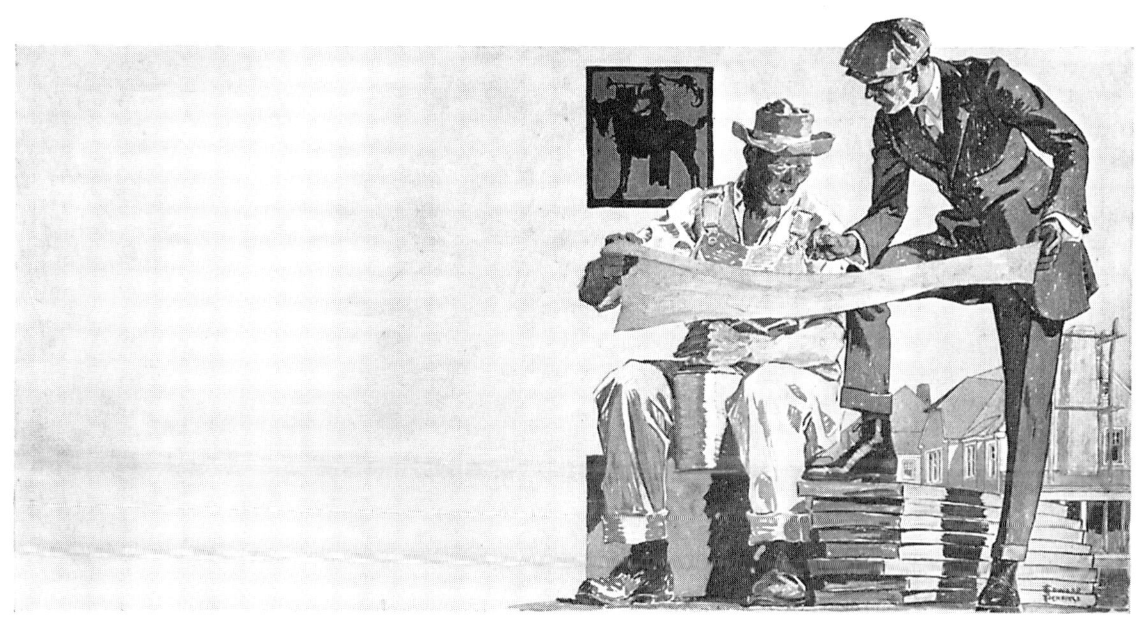

169　Men's Clothing—*Edward Penfield*
Loaned and exhibited by Hart Schaffner & Marx

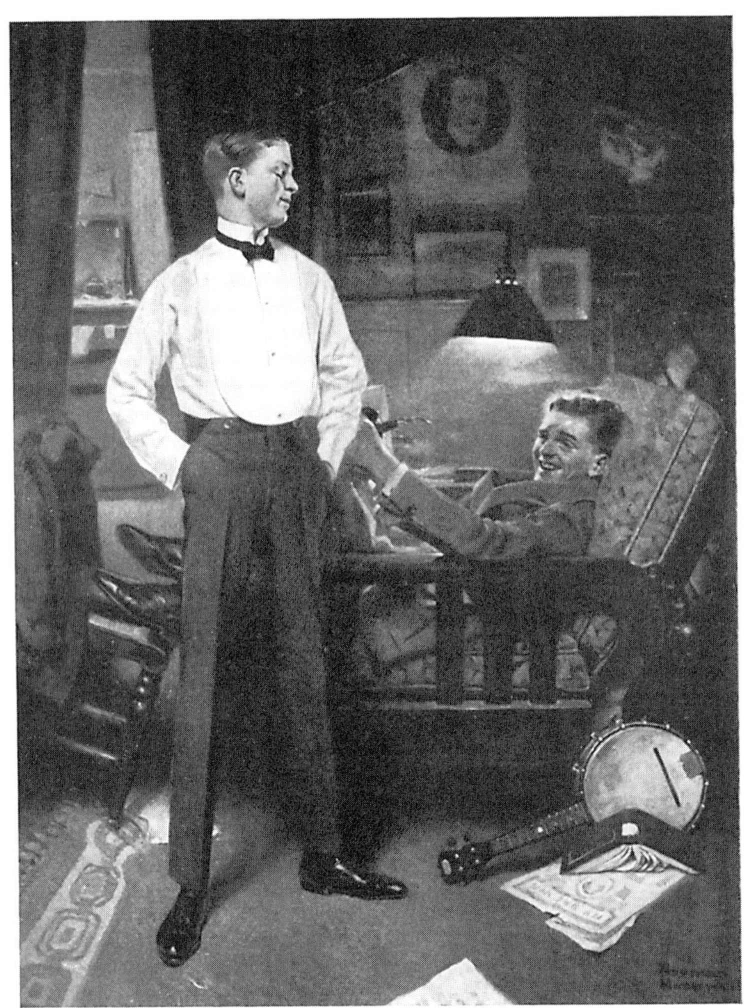

170 ARROW COLLARS—*Norman Rockwell*
Loaned and exhibited by Cluett, Peabody & Co., Inc.

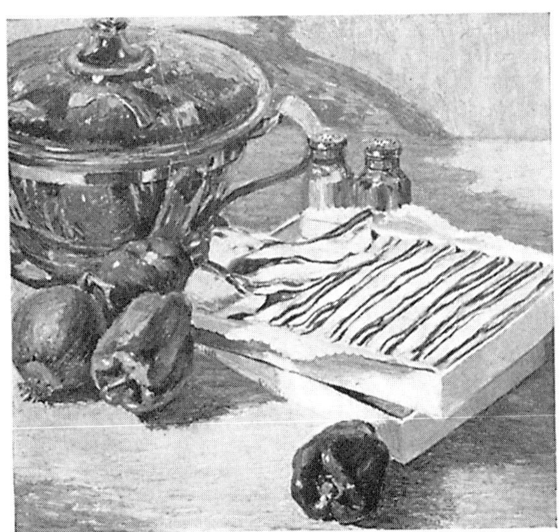

171 LIBBY'S BACON—*Sigmund Schou*
Loaned by Libby, McNeill & Libby
Exhibited by J. Walter Thompson Co.

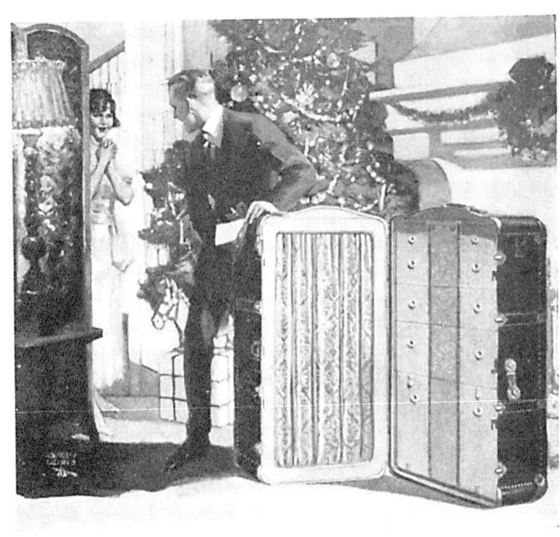

172 HARTMANN TRUNKS—*J. Chenoweth*
Loaned by the Hartmann Trunk Co.
Exhibited by the Wm. H. Rankin Co.

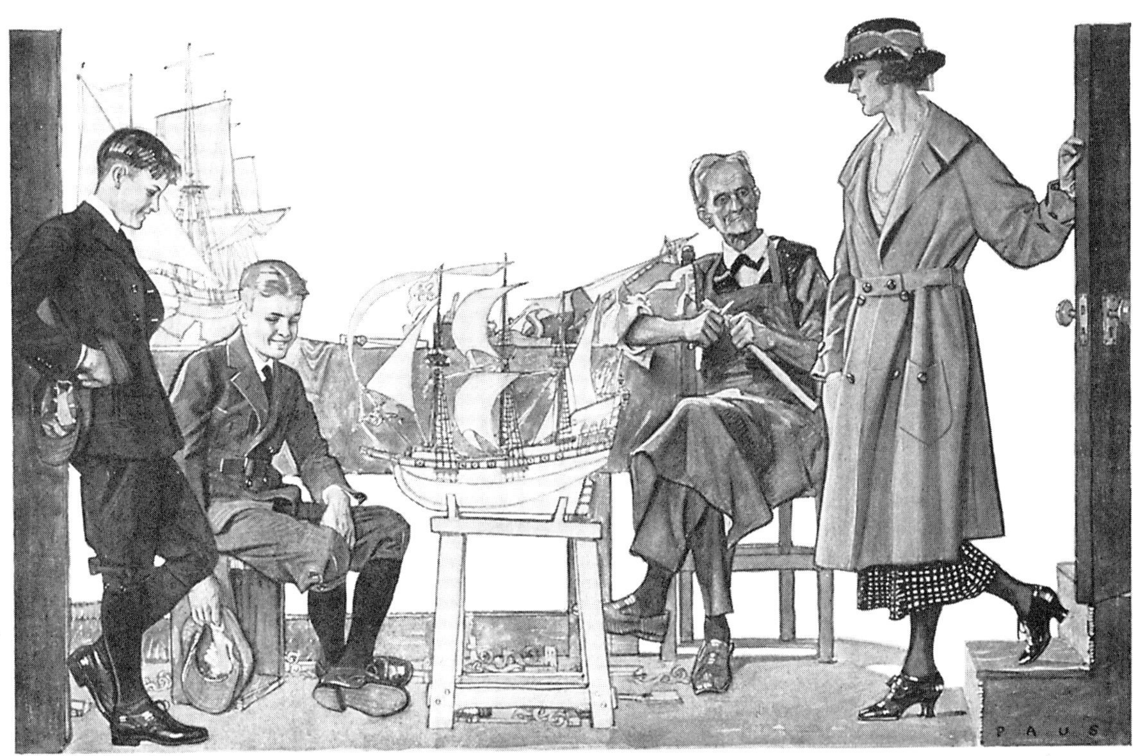

173 Men's Clothing—*Herbert Paus*
Loaned and exhibited by Hart Schaffner & Marx

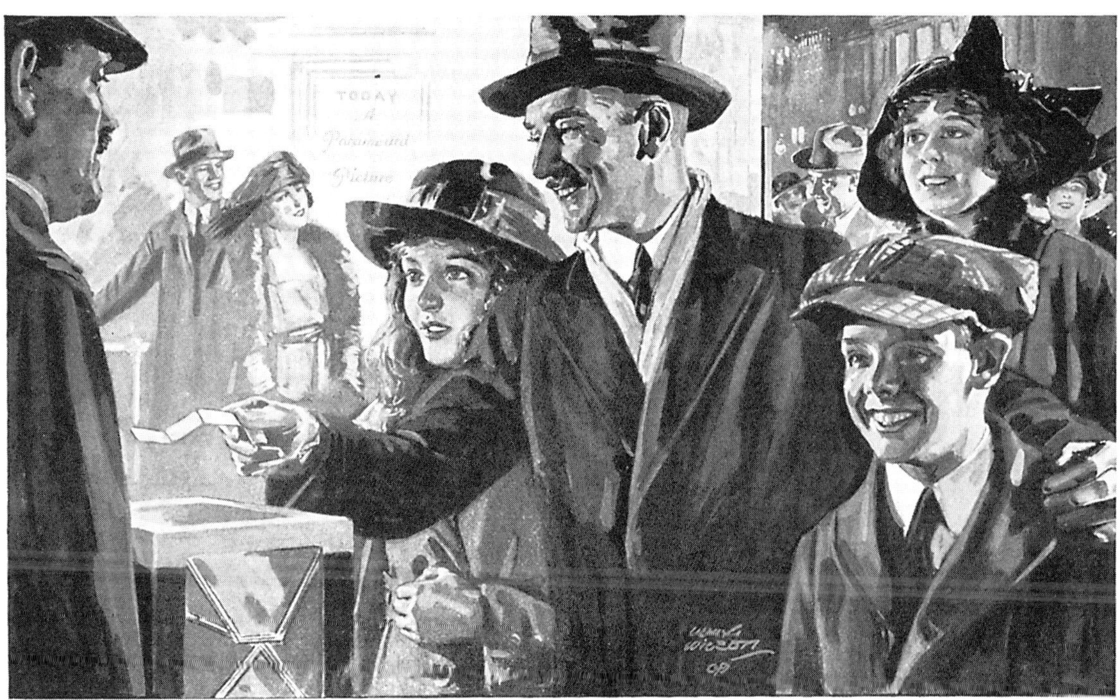

174 Paramount Pictures—*Vaux Wilson*
Loaned by the Famous Players-Lasky Corpn.
Exhibited by Hanff-Metzger, Inc.

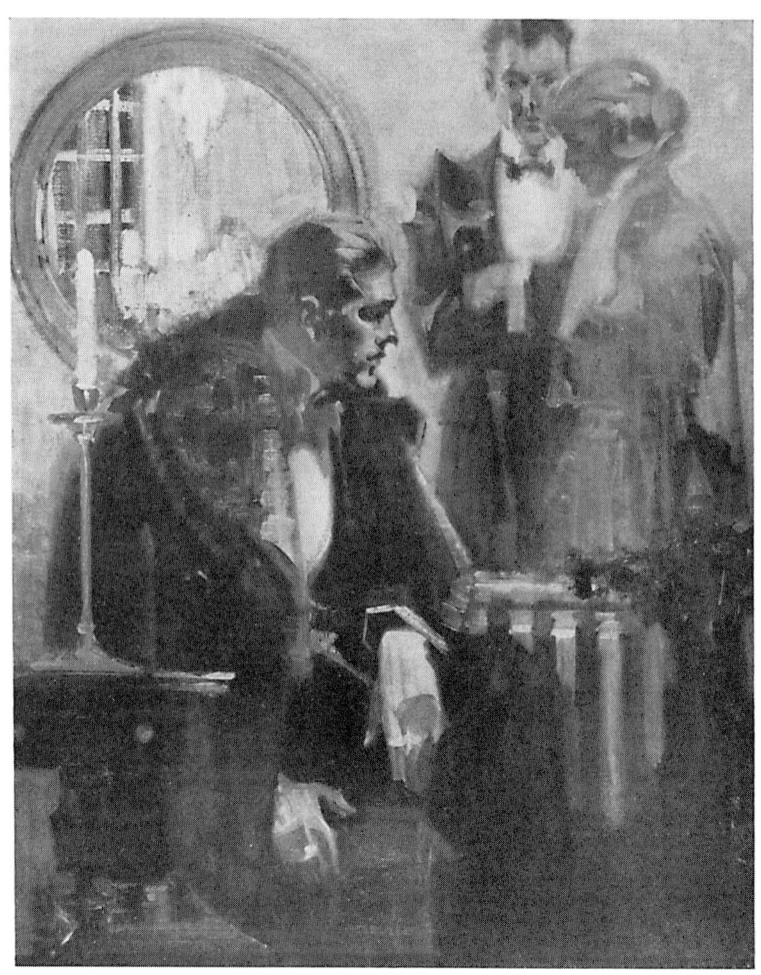

175　Society Brand Clothing—*Leon M. Gordon*
Loaned by Alfred Decker & Cohn
Exhibited by George Batten Co , Inc.

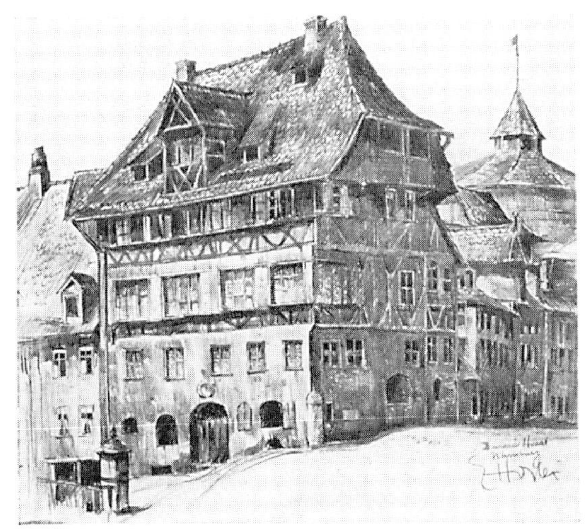

176　Eldorado Pencils—*Earl Horter*
Loaned by the Joseph Dixon Crucible Co.
Exhibited by N. W. Ayer & Son

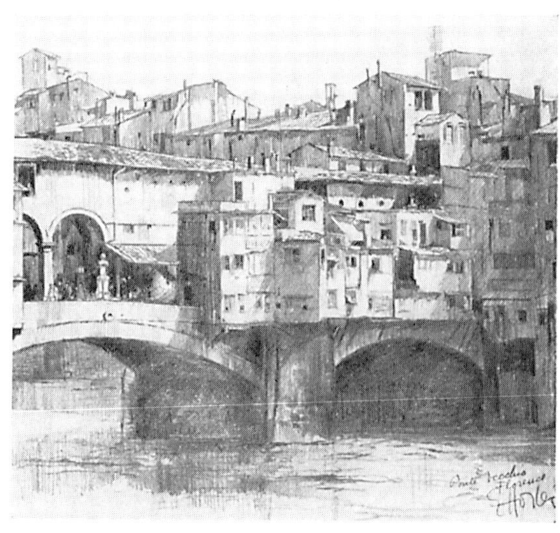

177　Eldorado Pencils—*Earl Horter*
Loaned by the Joseph Dixon Crucible Co.
Exhibited by N. W. Ayer & Son

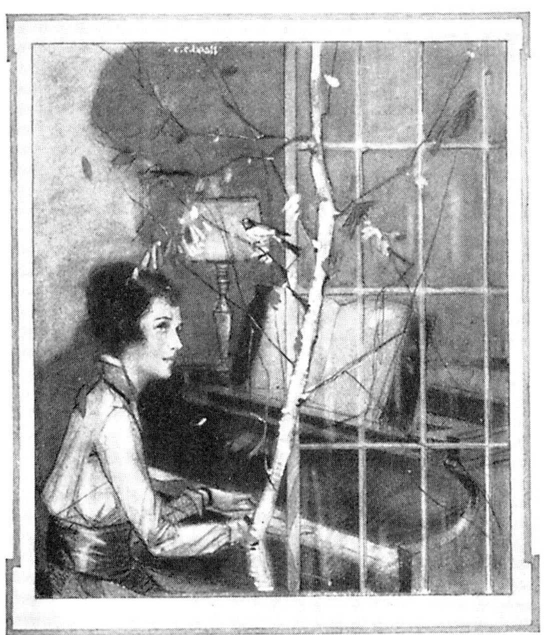

178 AMERICAN PIANOS—*C. C. Beall*
Loaned by the American Piano Co.
Exhibited by the Bricka-Ford Co.

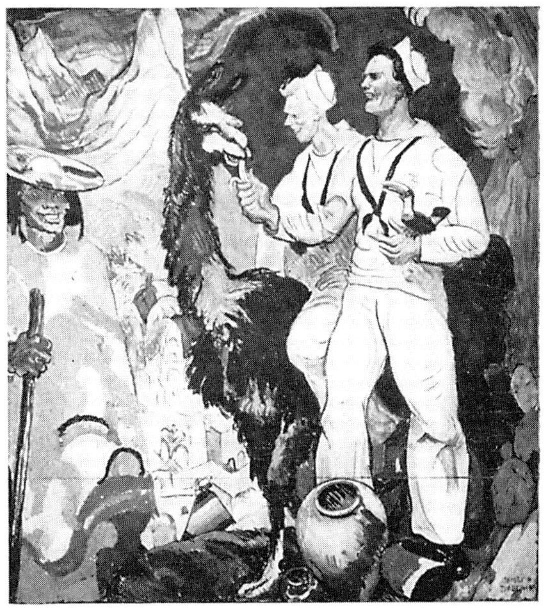

179 U. S. NAVY POSTER—*James H. Daugherty*
Loaned and exhibited by the U. S. Navy Publicity Bureau

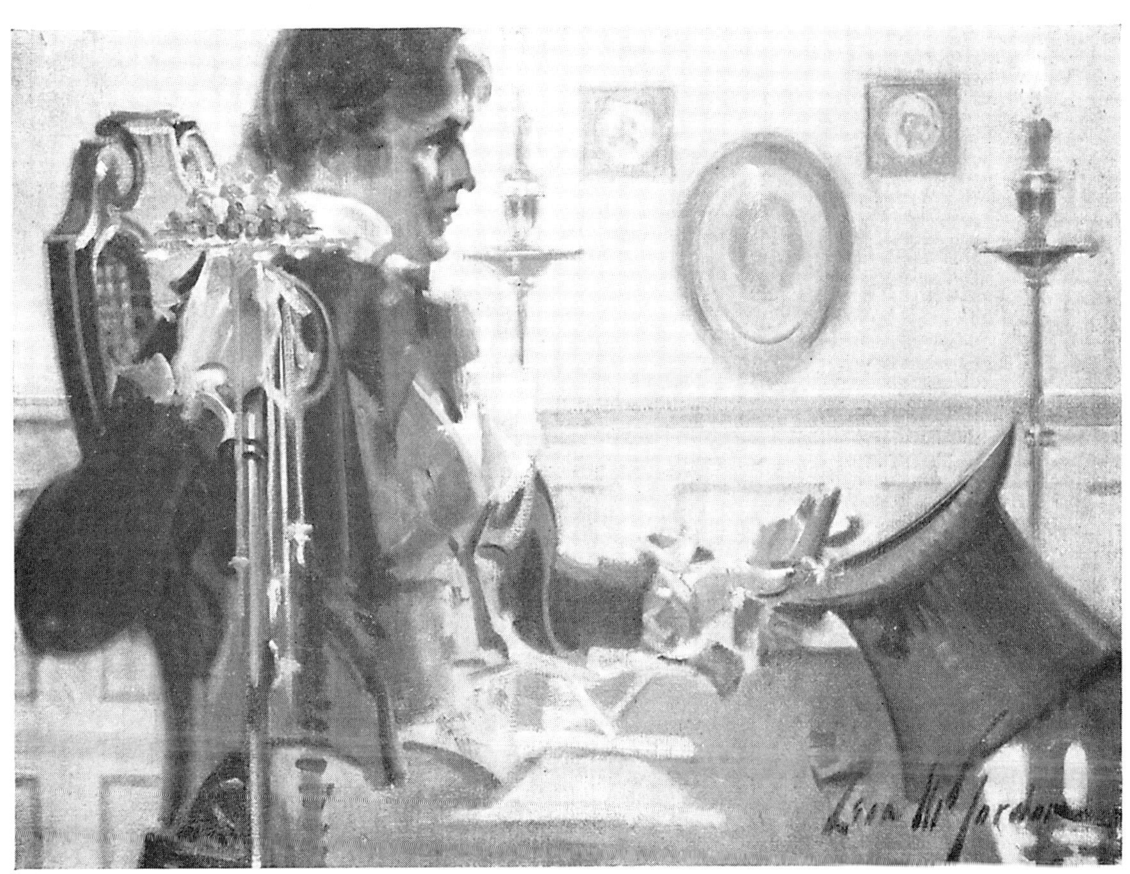

180 MALLORY HATS—*Leon M. Gordon*
Loaned by E. A. Mallory & Sons, Inc.
Exhibited by George Batten Co., Inc.

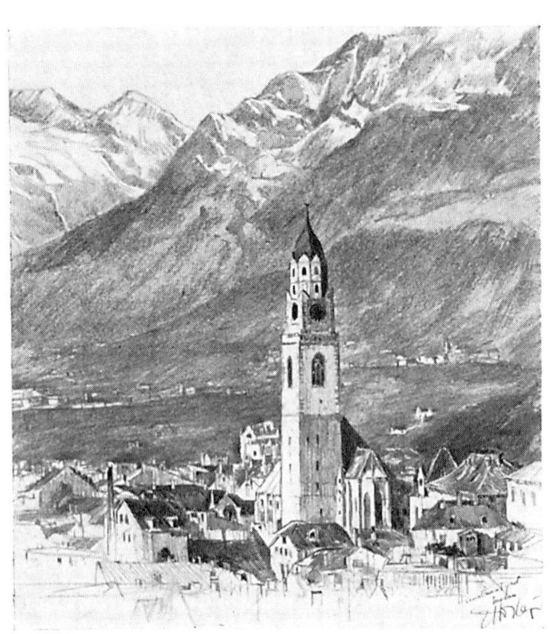

181   ELDORADO PENCILS—*Earl Horter*
Loaned by the Joseph Dixon Crucible Co.
Exhibited by N. W. Ayer & Son

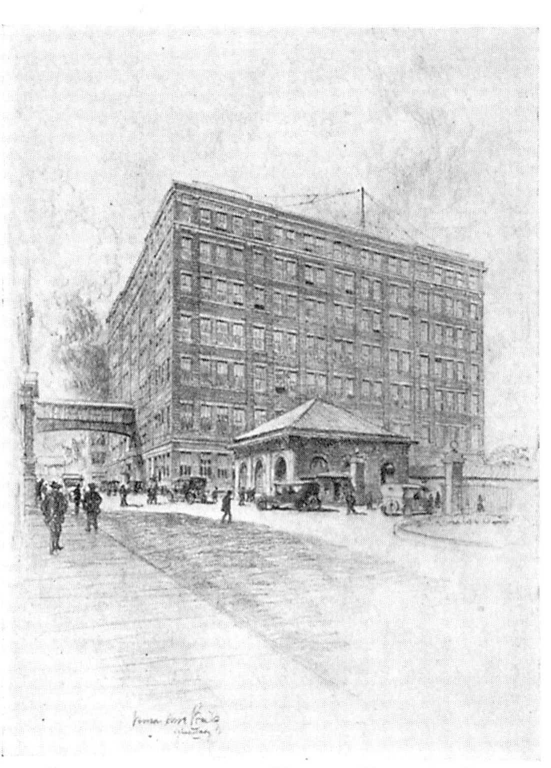

182   —*Vernon Howe Bailey*
Loaned and exhibited by the General Electric Co.

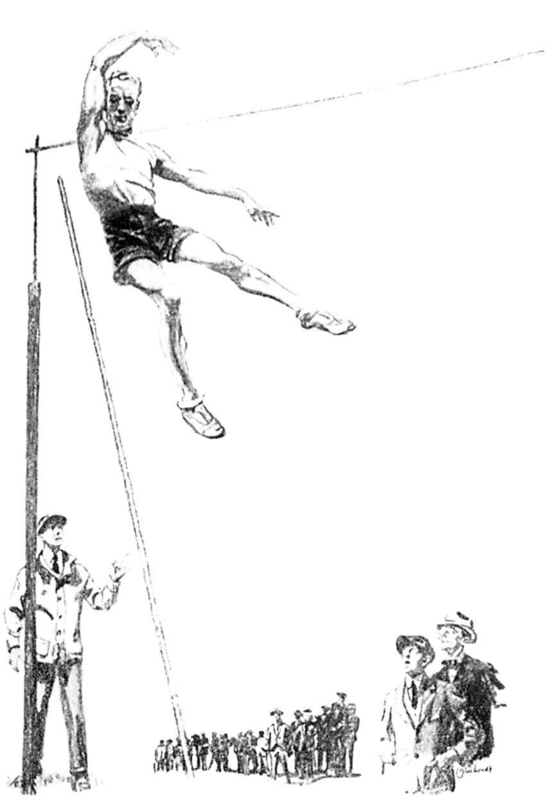

183   FATIMA CIGARETTES—*William Oberhardt*
Loaned by the Liggett & Myers Tobacco Co.
Exhibited by Newell-Emmett Co., Inc.

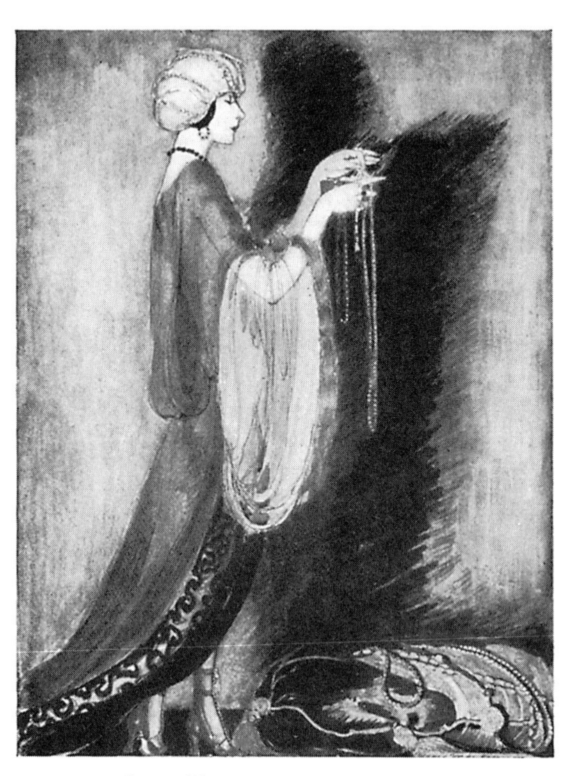

184   SILK HOSIERY—*Mary McKinnon*
Loaned by the McCallum Hosiery Co.
Exhibited by George Batten Co., Inc.

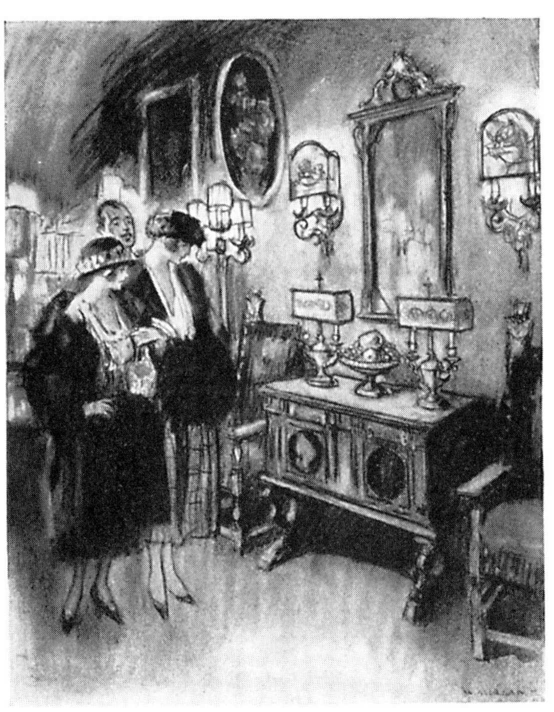

185 OVINGTON'S—*Wallace Morgan*
Loaned by Ovington Bros. Co.
Exhibited by Barton, Durstine & Osborn, Inc.

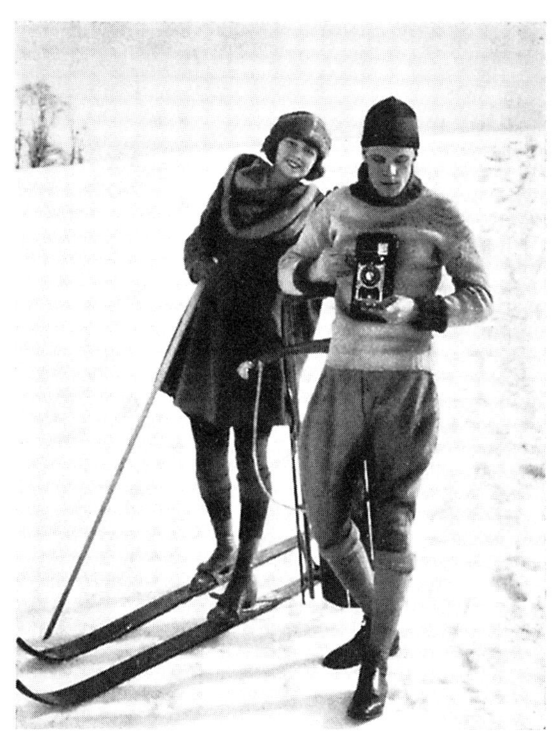

186 EASTMAN KODAKS—*William Smith*
Loaned by the Eastman Kodak Co.
Exhibited by Frank Seaman, Inc.

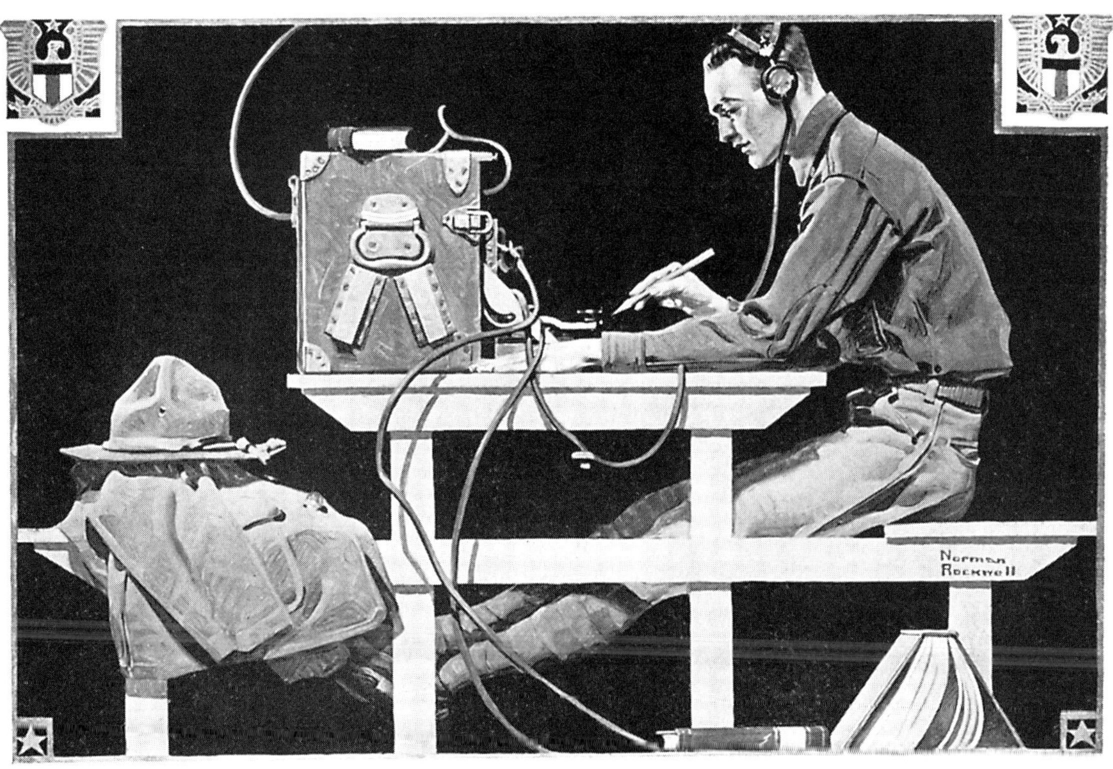

187 U. S. ARMY TEACHES TRADES—*Norman Rockwell*
Loaned by the U. S. Army
Exhibited by Calkins & Holden, Inc.

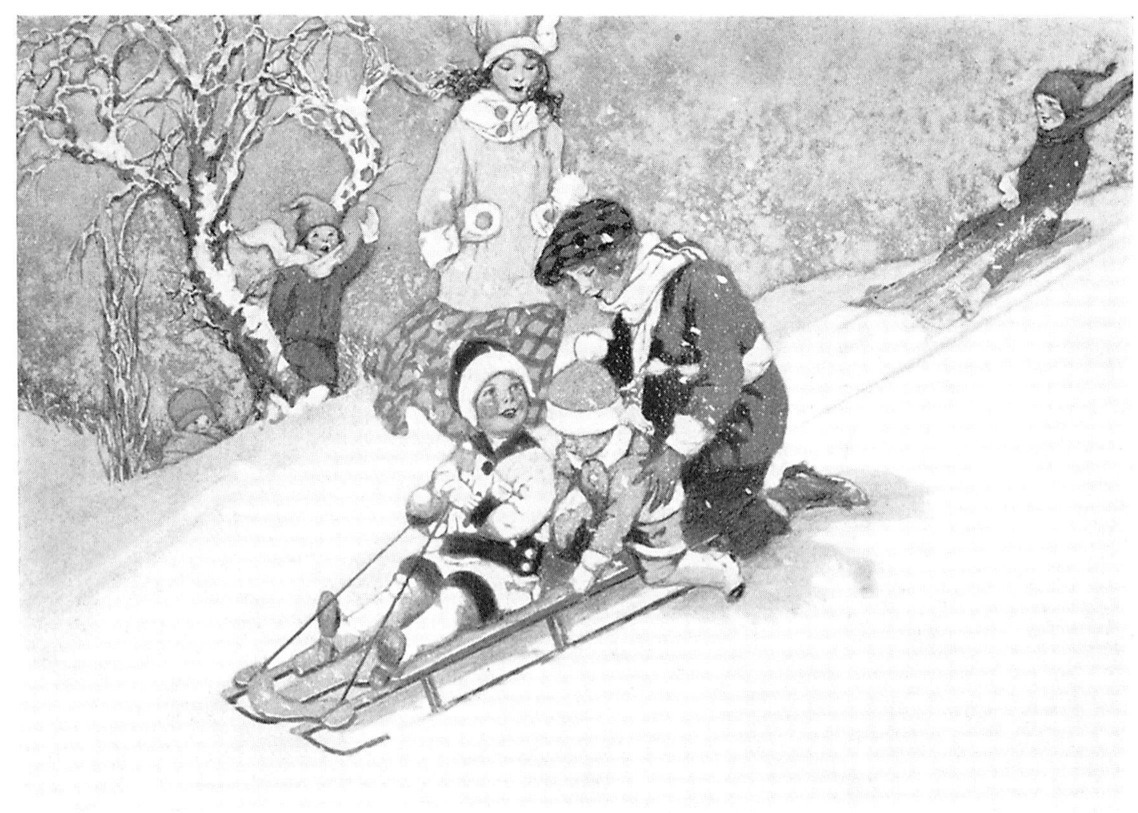

188 LUX—*Willy Pogany*
Loaned by Lever Bros. Co.
Exhibited by J. Walter Thompson Co.

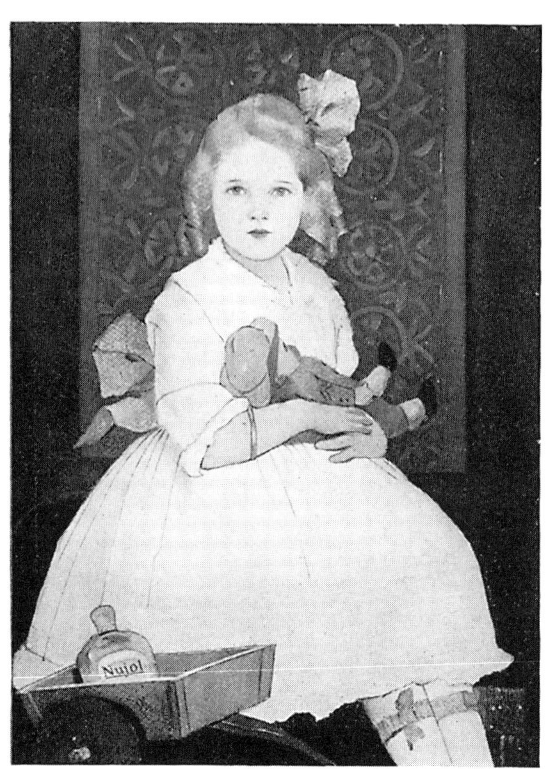

189 NUJOL—*Walter Dean Goldbeck*
Loaned by the Nujol Laboratories
Exhibited by The H. K. McCann Co.

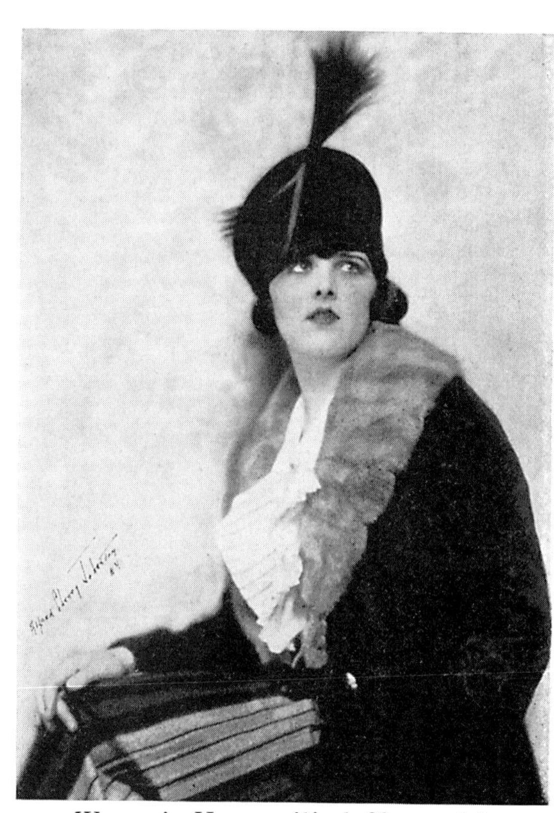

190 WOMEN'S HATS—*Alfred Cheney Johnston*
Loaned and exhibited by Dobbs & Co.

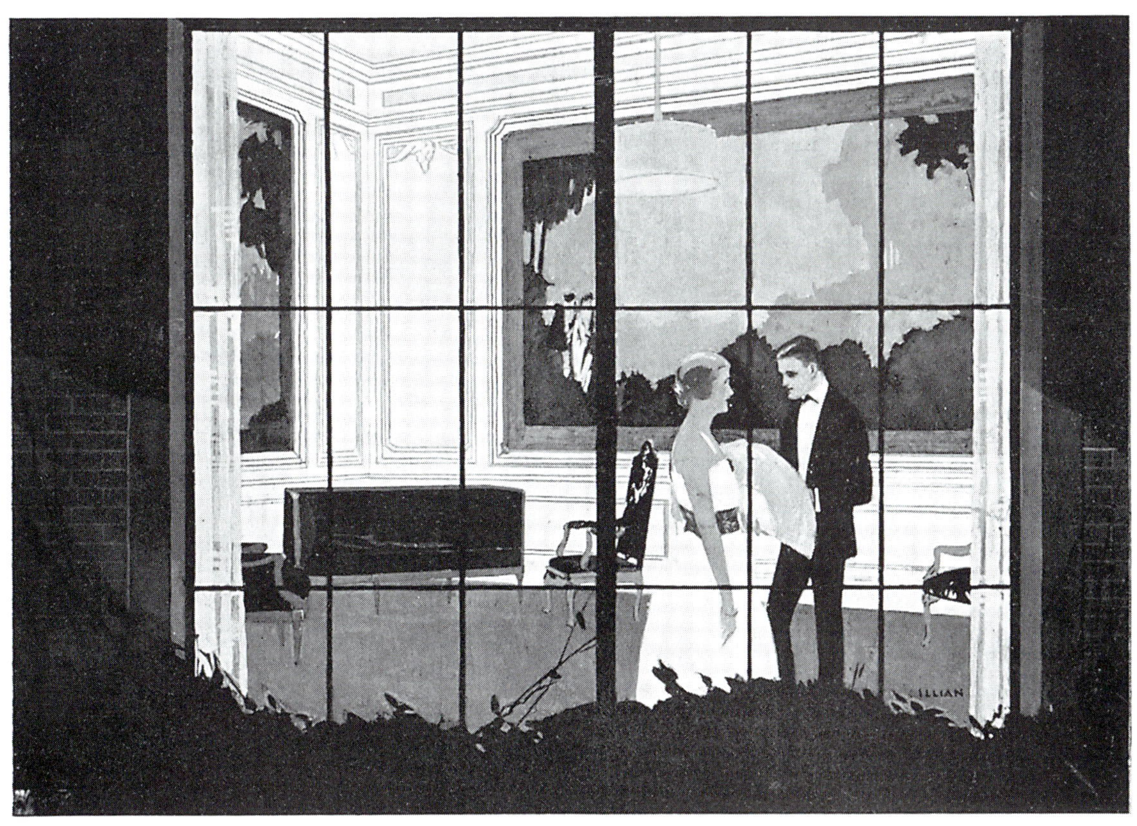

191 DUPLEX LIGHTING FIXTURES—*George J. Illian*
Loaned by the Duplex Lighting Works of General Electric Co.
Exhibited by Barrows & Richardson

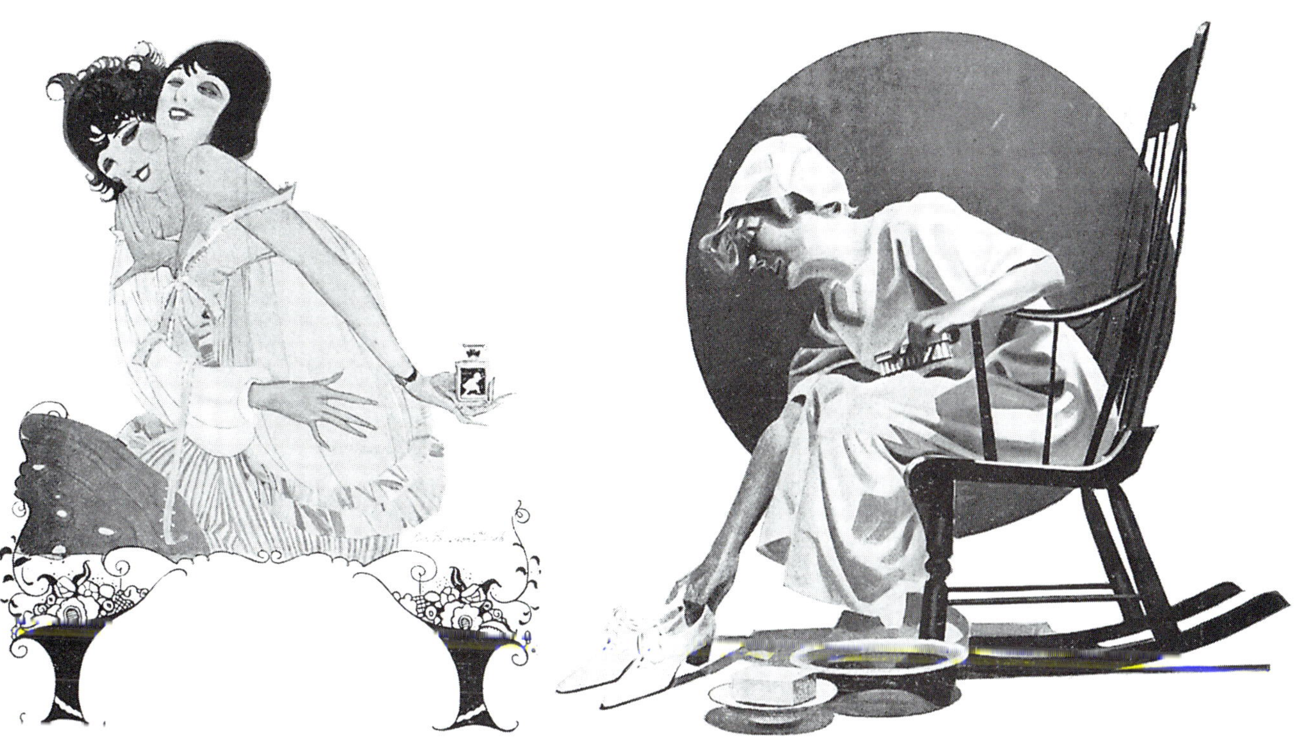

192 PERFUME L'AMUSETTE
Lucile Patterson Marsh
Loaned by Frederick Stearns & Co.
Exhibited by Sheridan, Shawhan & Sheridan, Inc.

193 BON AMI—*Cushman Parker*
Loaned by the Bon Ami Company
Exhibited by The Erickson Company

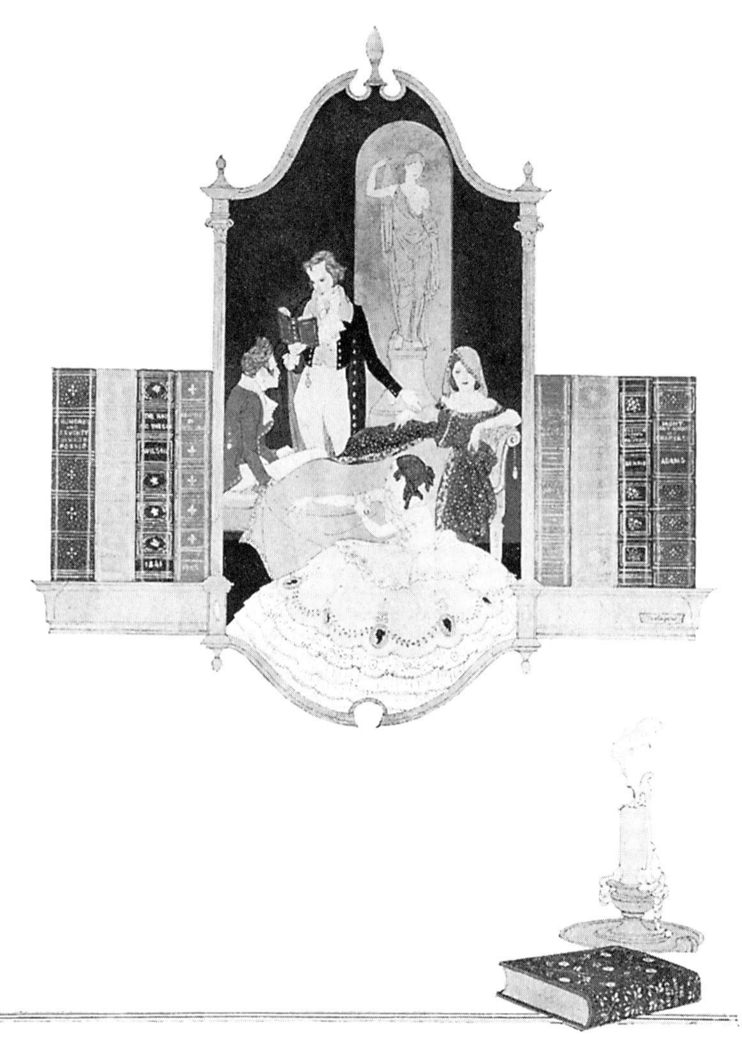

194 MARSHALL FIELD & CO.—*Joseph Bolegard*
Loaned by Marshall Field & Co.
Exhibited by the Wm. H. Rankin Co.

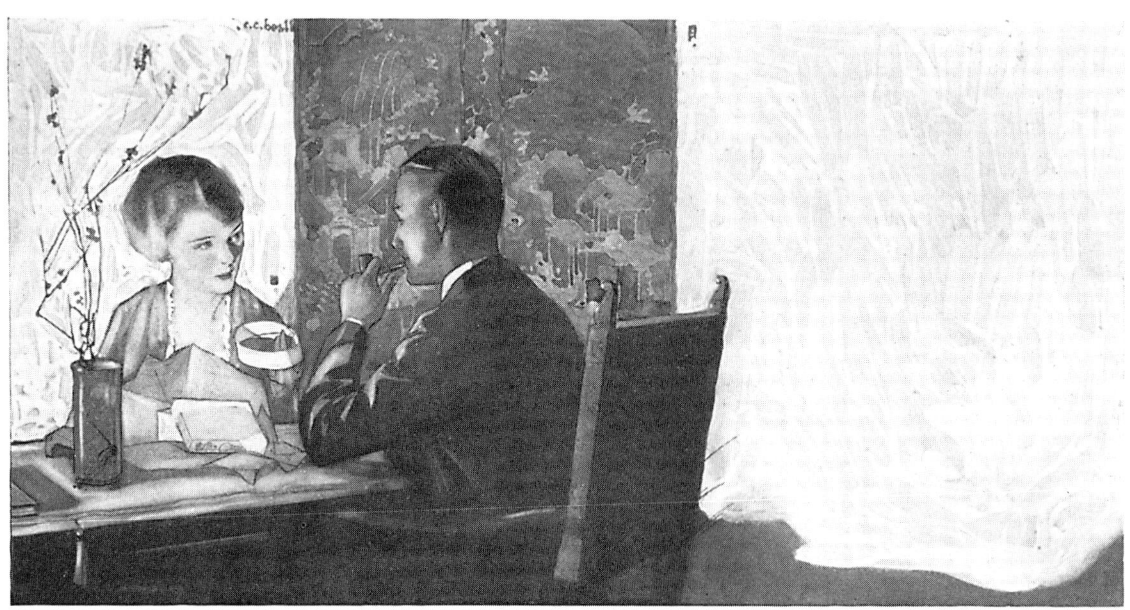

195 LION COLLARS—*C. C. Beall*
Loaned by the United Shirt & Collar Co.
Exhibited by Picard Company, Inc.

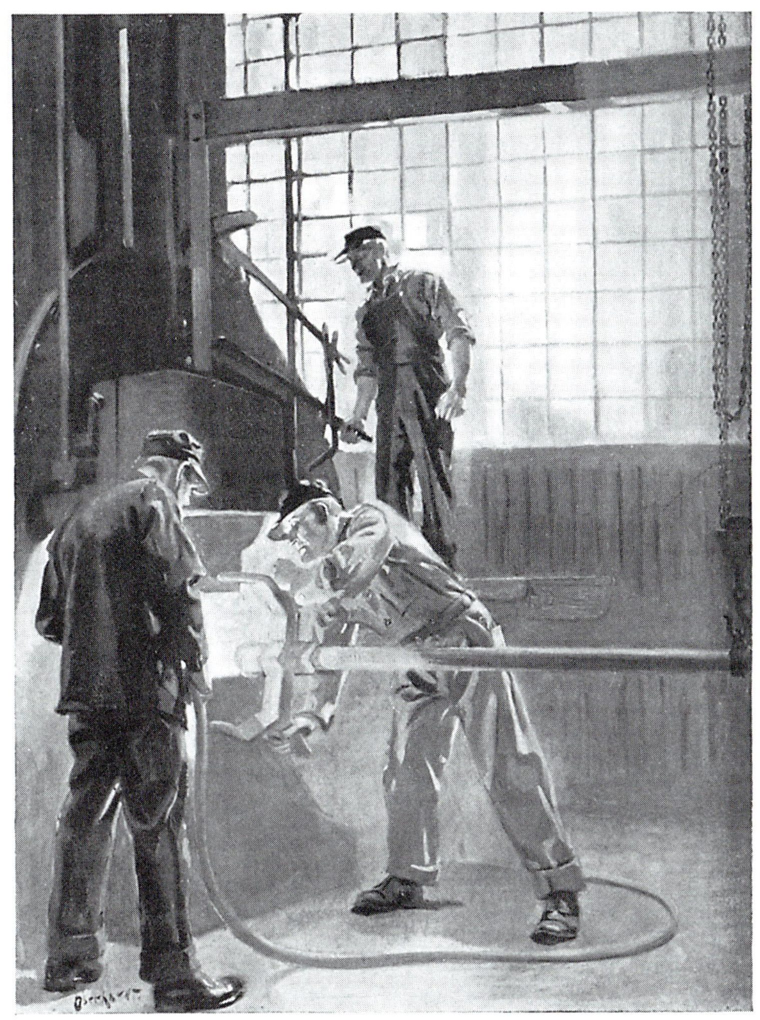

196 Blue Buckle Overalls—*William Oberhardt*
Loaned and exhibited by the Jobbers Overall Co.

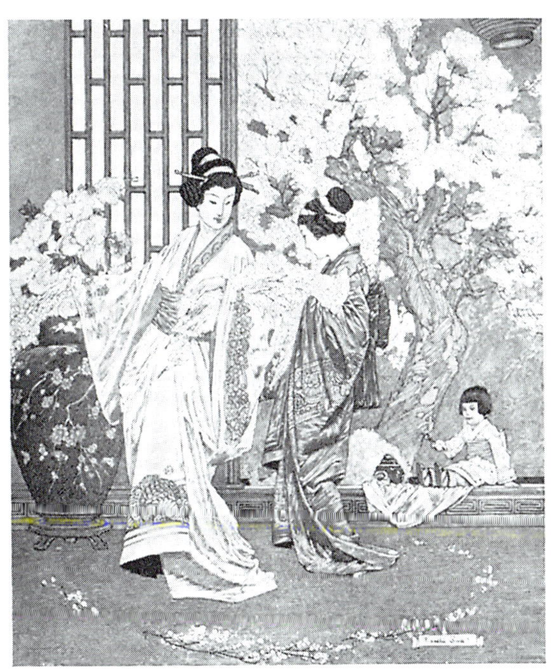

197 Madam Butterfly—*Franklin Booth*
Loaned by the Victor Talking Machine Co.
Exhibited by the Franklin Printing Company

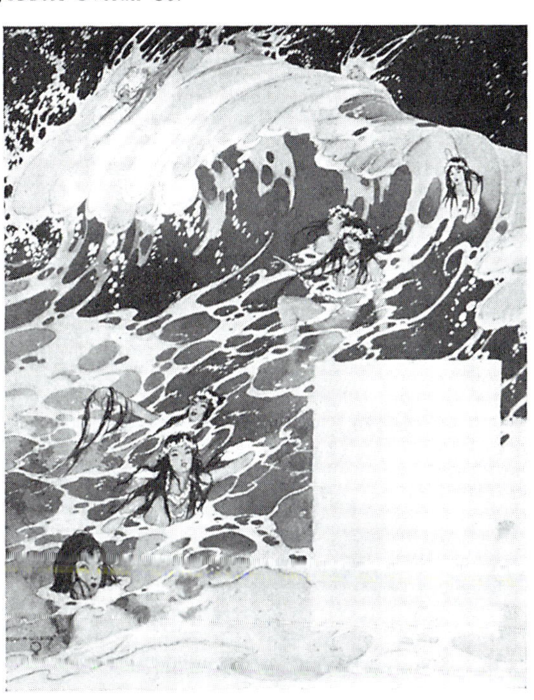

198 Djer-Kiss—*Edward A. Wilson*
Loaned by the Alfred H. Smith Co.
Exhibited by The Blackman Company

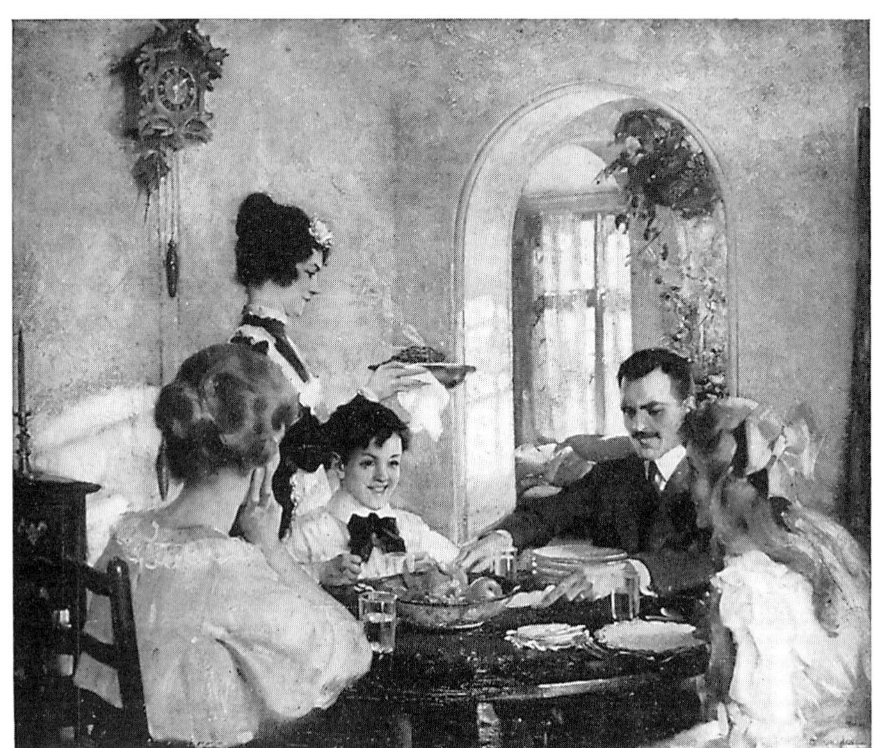

199   HEINZ BAKED BEANS—*Charles E. Chambers*
Loaned by The H. J. Heinz Company
Exhibited by Calkins & Holden, Inc.

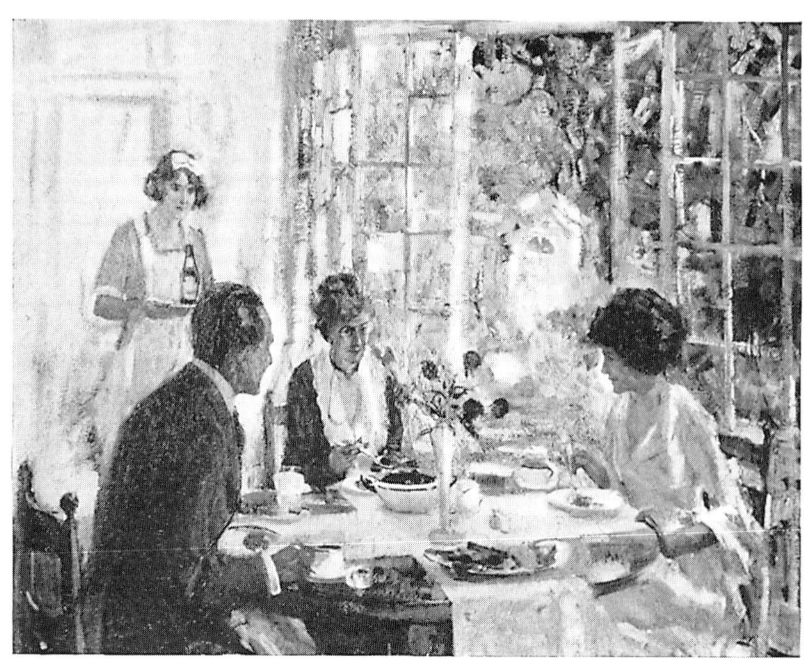

200   HEINZ BAKED BEANS—*Walter Biggs*
Loaned by The H. J. Heinz Company
Exhibited by Calkins & Holden, Inc.

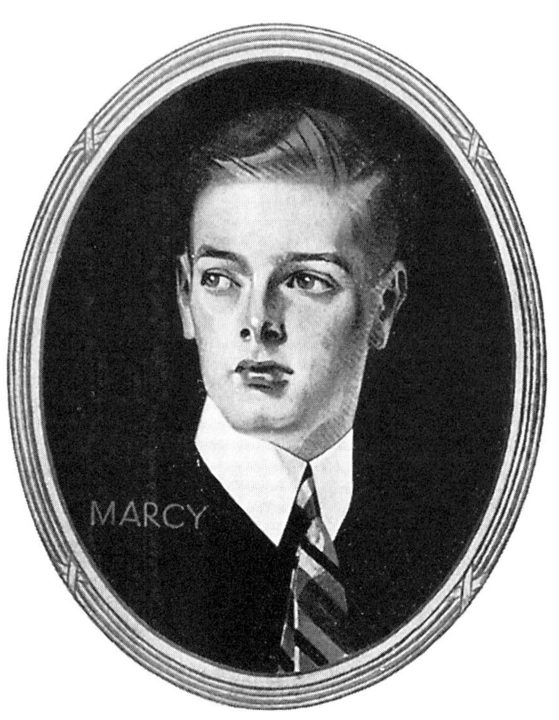

201   ARROW COLLARS—*J. C. Leyendecker*
Loaned and exhibited by Cluett, Peabody & Co., Inc.

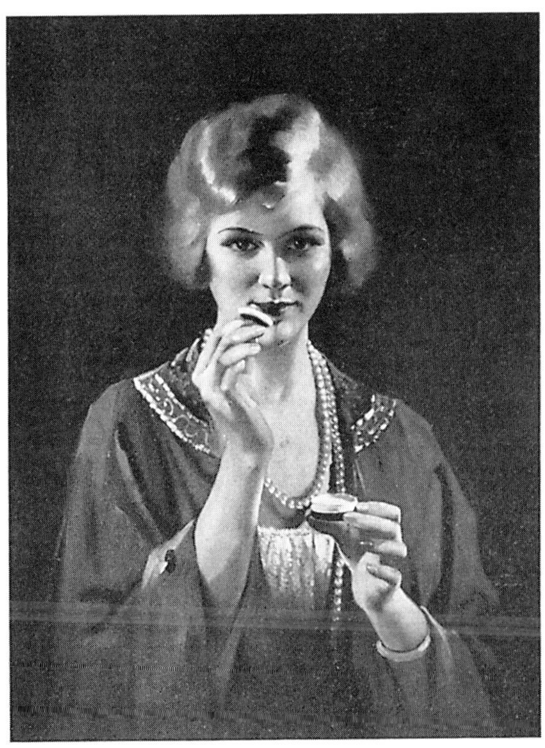

202   TALC JONTEEL—*Walter Dean Goldbeck*
The United Drug Co.
Loaned and exhibited by Street & Finney, Inc.

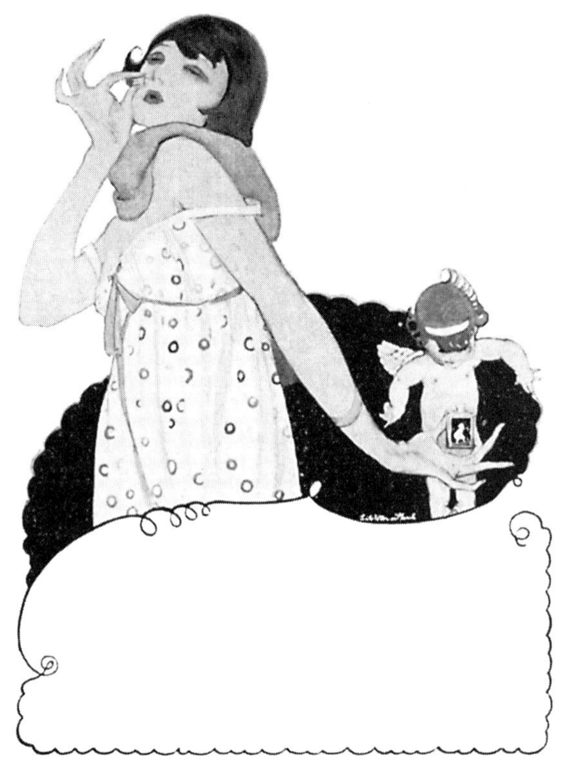

203 PERFUME L'AMUSETTE—*Lucile Patterson Marsh*
Loaned by Frederick Stearns & Co.
Exhibited by Sheridan, Shawhan & Sheridan

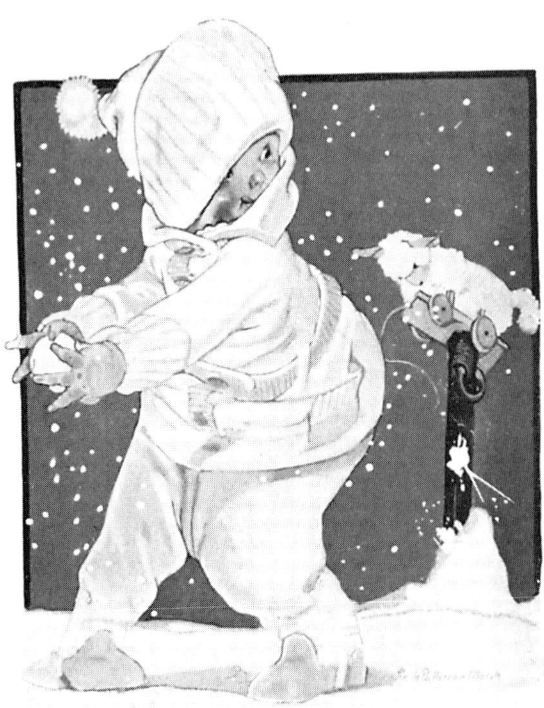

204 ASCHER'S KNIT GOODS—*Lucile Patterson Marsh*
Loaned by Simon Ascher & Co., Inc.
Exhibited by Biow Co., Inc.

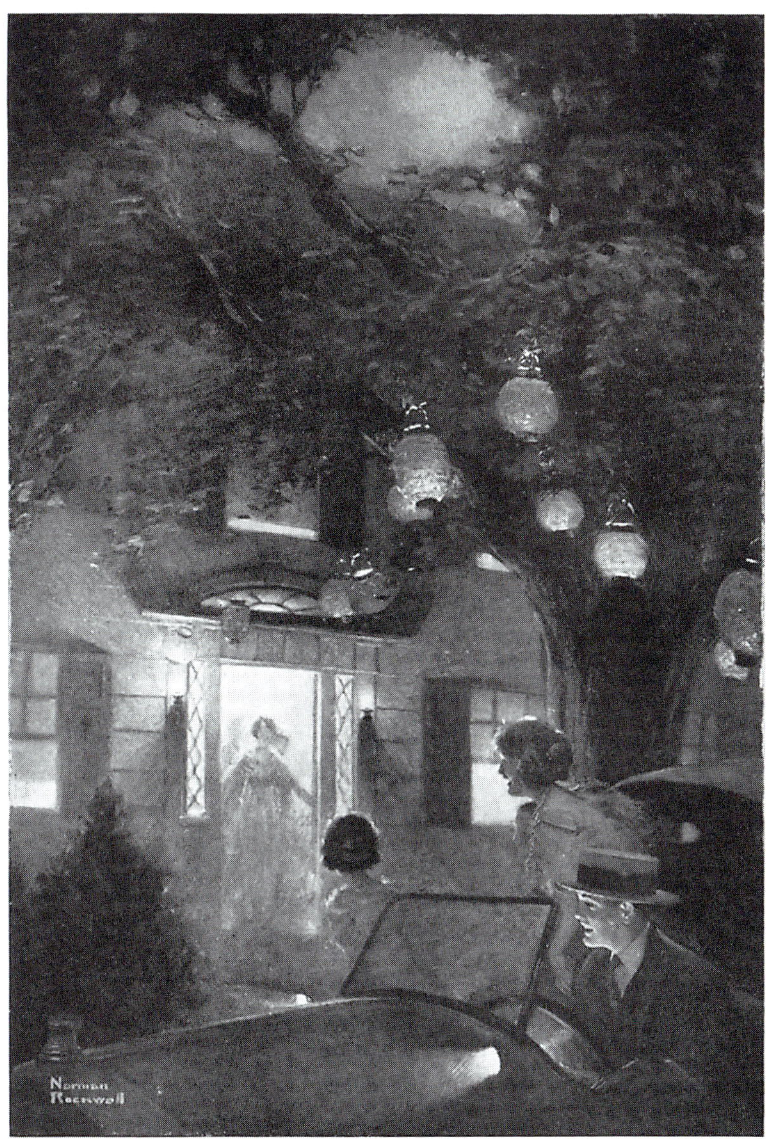

205   EDISON MAZDA LAMPS—*Norman Rockwell*
Loaned by the Edison Lamp Works of General Electric Co.
Exhibited by Barton, Durstine & Osborn, Inc.

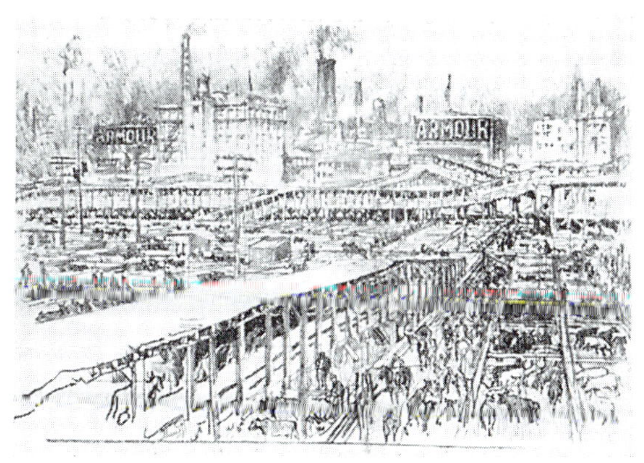

206   UNION STOCK YARDS
Charcoal Sketch by Joseph Pennell
Loaned and exhibited by Armour & Co

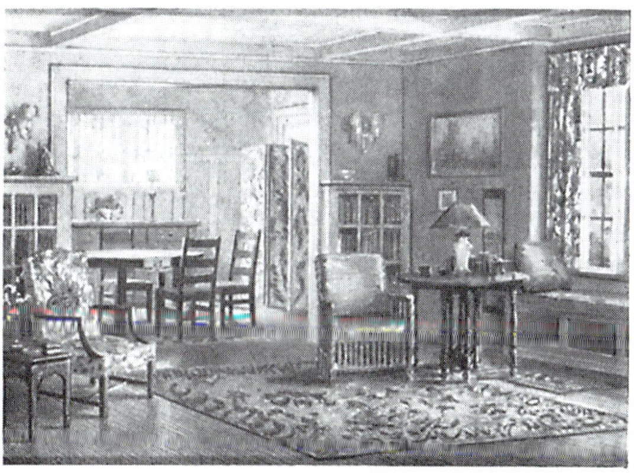

207   LINOLEUM—*George W. Blake*
Loaned by the Armstrong Cork Co.
Exhibited by George Batten Co., Inc.

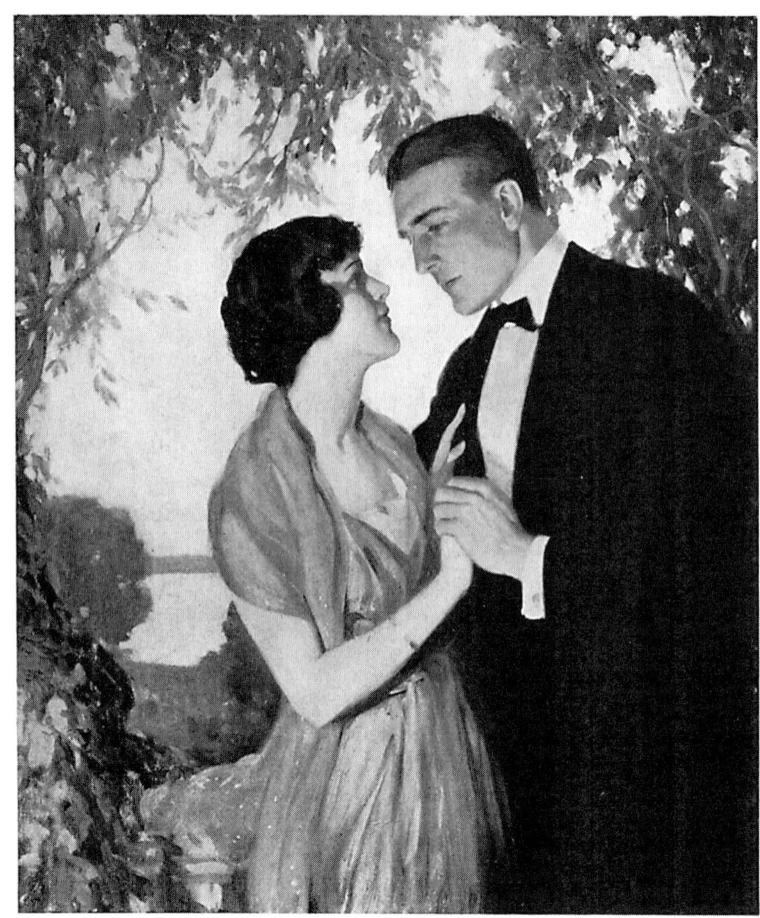

208 WOODBURY'S FACIAL SOAP—*John Newton Howitt*
Loaned by The Andrew Jergens Company
Exhibited by the J. Walter Thompson Co.

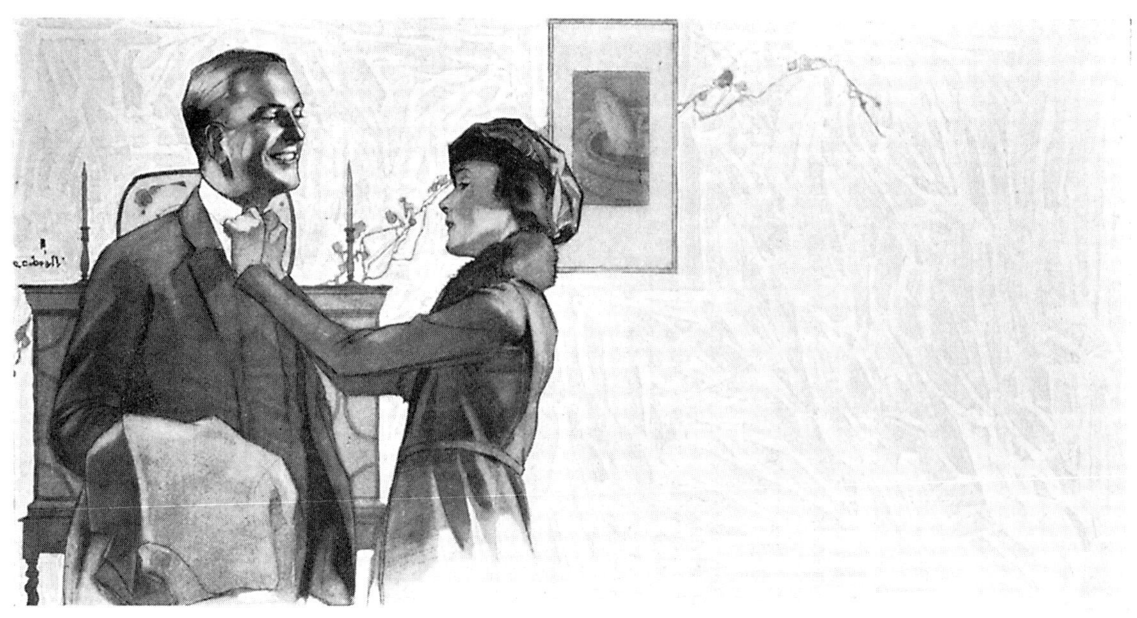

209 LION COLLARS—*C. C. Beall*
Loaned by the United Shirt & Collar Co.
Exhibited by the Picard Company, Inc.

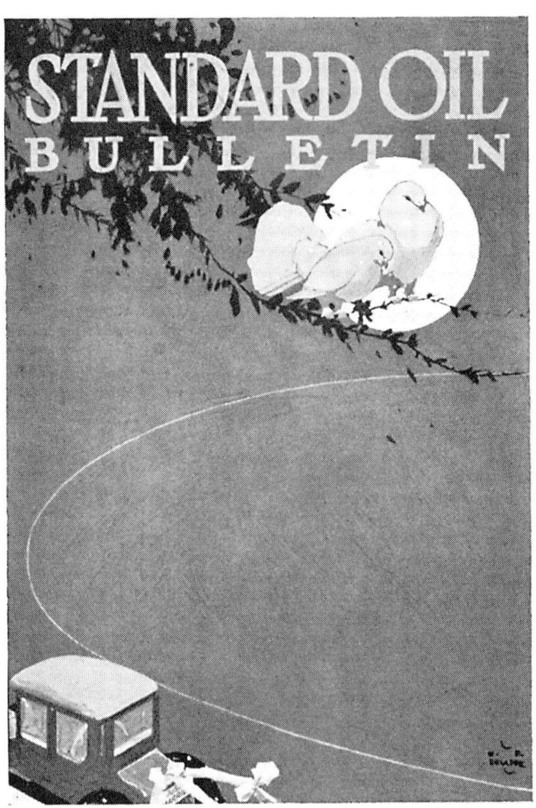

210   HOUSE ORGAN—*W. R. DeLappe*
Loaned by the Standard Oil Co. of California
Exhibited by The H. K. McCann Co.

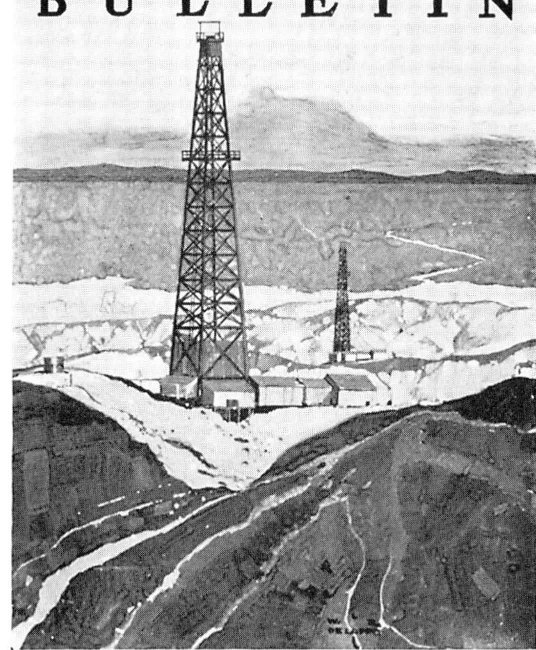

211   HOUSE ORGAN—*W. R. DeLappe*
Loaned by the Standard Oil Co. of California
Exhibited by The H. K. McCann Co.

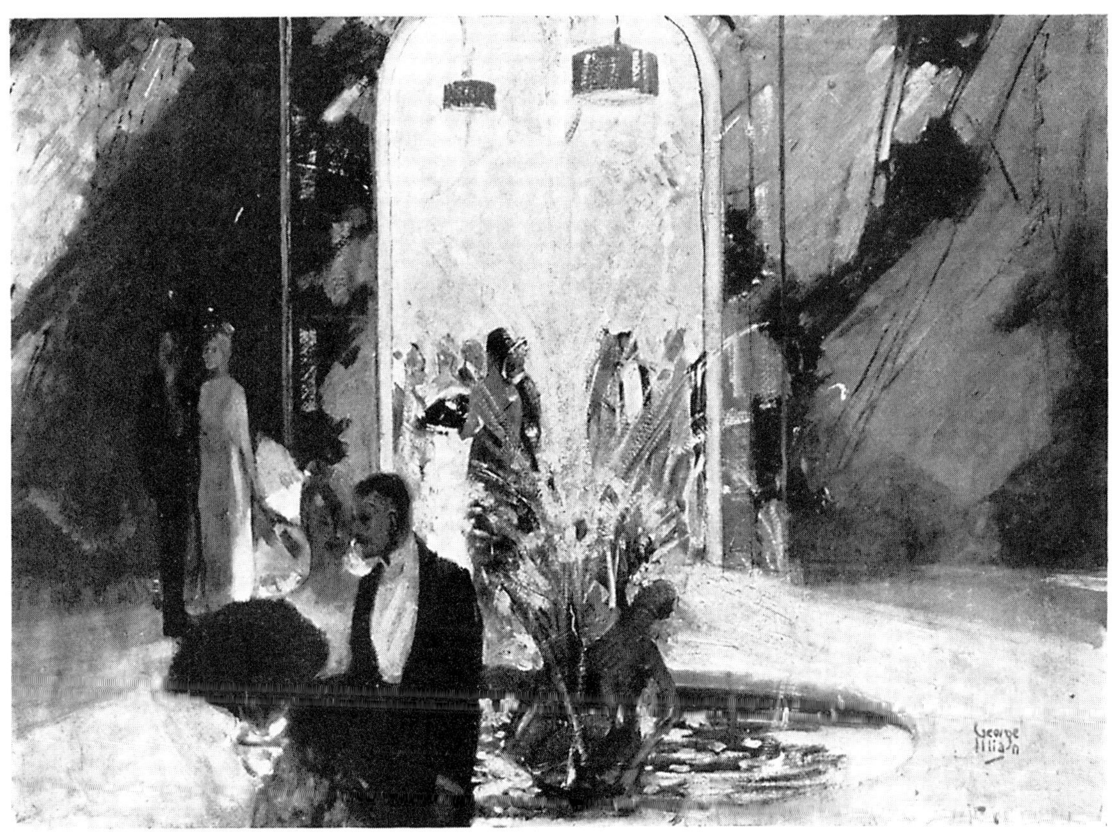

212   DUPLEX LIGHTING FIXTURES—*George J. Illian*
Loaned by the Duplex Lighting Works of General Electric Co.
Exhibited by Barrows & Richardson

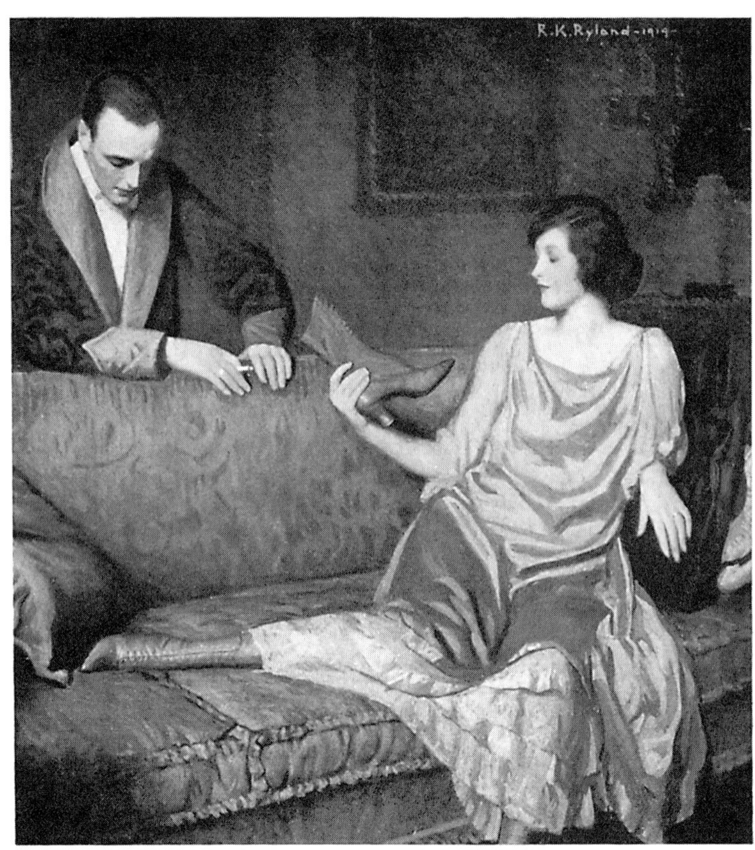

213   VODE KID—*R. K. Ryland*
Loaned by the Standard Kid Manufacturing Co.
Exhibited by George Batten Co., Inc.

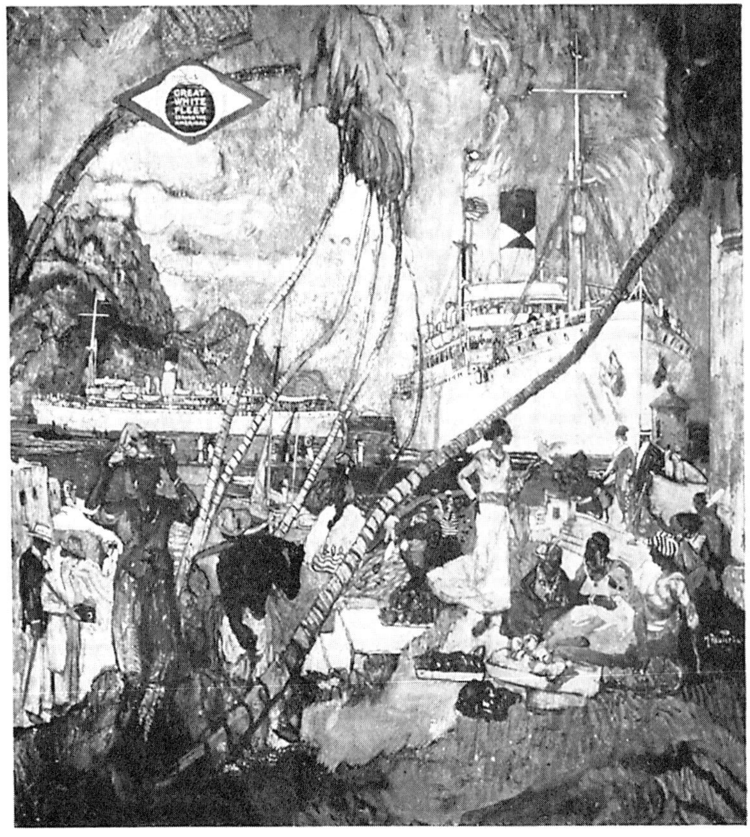

214   GREAT WHITE FLEET—*Henry Reuterdahl*
Loaned and exhibited by the United Fruit Co.

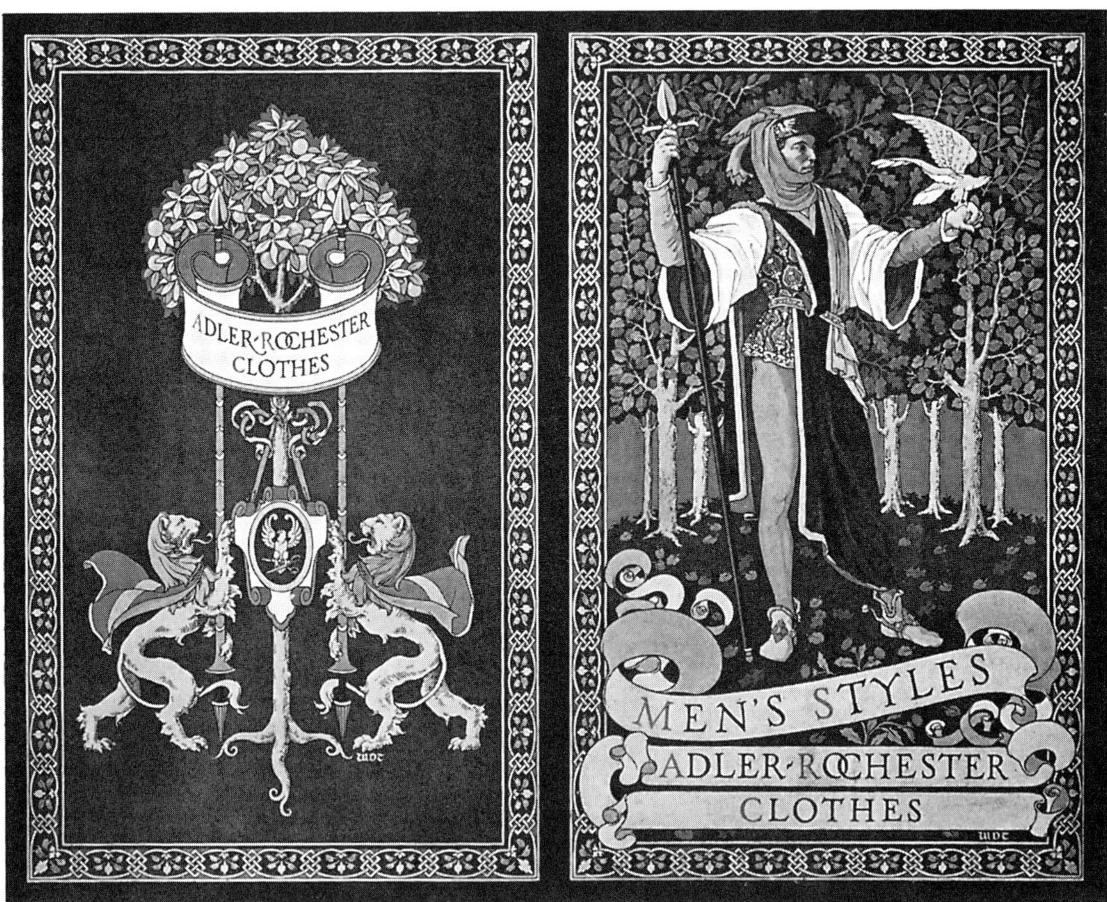

215   ADLER-ROCHESTER CLOTHES—*Walter Dorwin Teague*
Loaned by L. Adler, Bros. & Co.
Exhibited by Berrien Co., Inc.

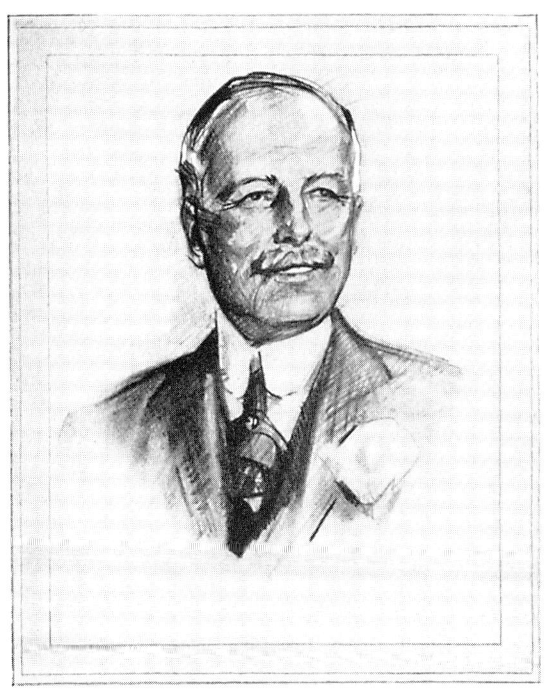

216   LYON'S TOOTH PASTE—*O. F. Howard*
Loaned by I. W. Lyon & Sons
Exhibited by Patterson-Andress Co., Inc.

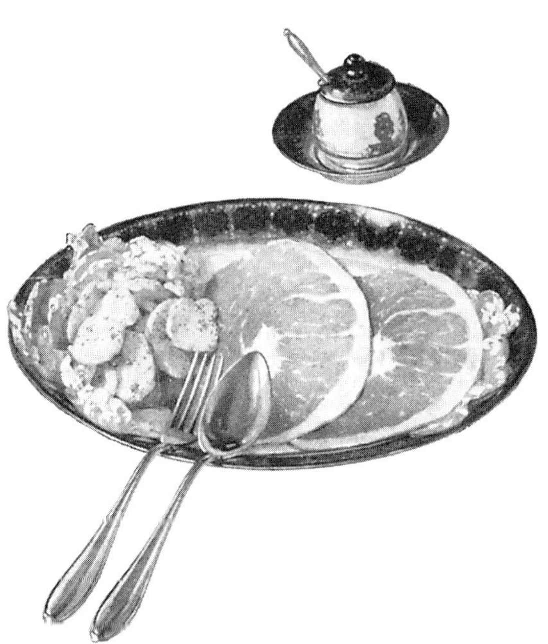

217   MORRIS' HAM—*Charles Everett Johnson*
Loaned by Morris & Company
Exhibited by Williams & Cunningham

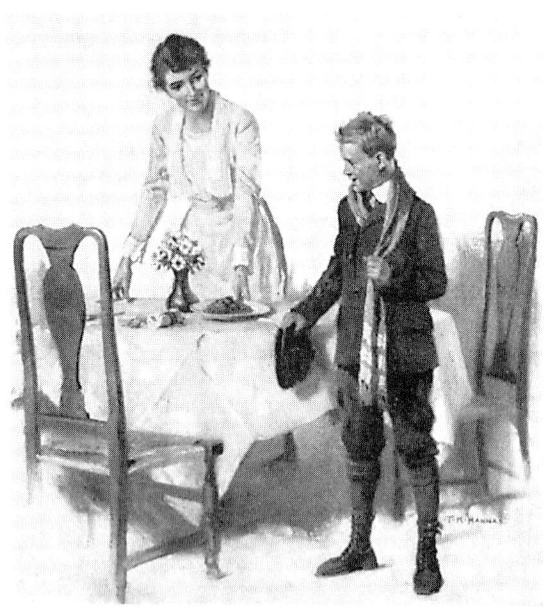

219 HEINZ BAKED BEANS—*T. K. Hanna*
Loaned by The H. J. Heinz Company
Exhibited by Calkins & Holden, Inc.

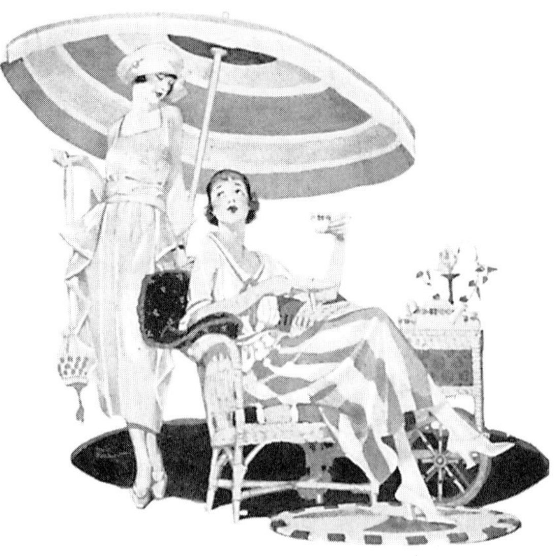

220 FRENCH SATIN—*Anita Parkhurst*
Loaned by Pelgram & Myer
Exhibited by the Federal Advertising Agency, Inc.

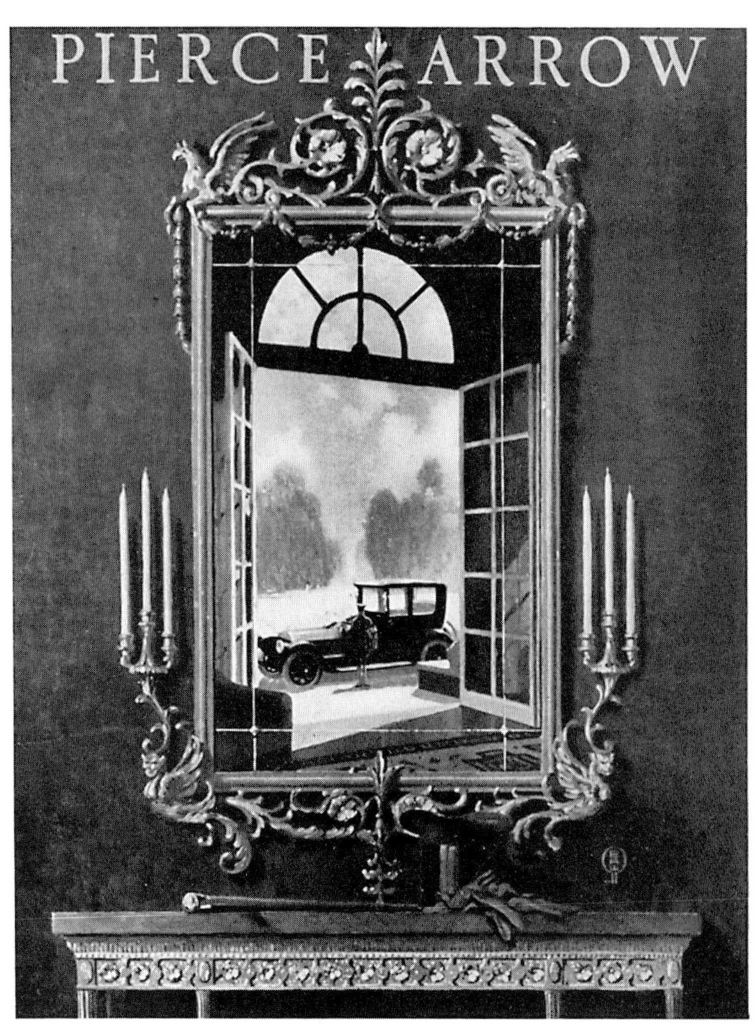

218   PIERCE-ARROW MOTOR CAR—*Edward A. Wilson*
Loaned by The Pierce-Arrow Motor Car Company
Exhibited by Calkins & Holden, Inc.

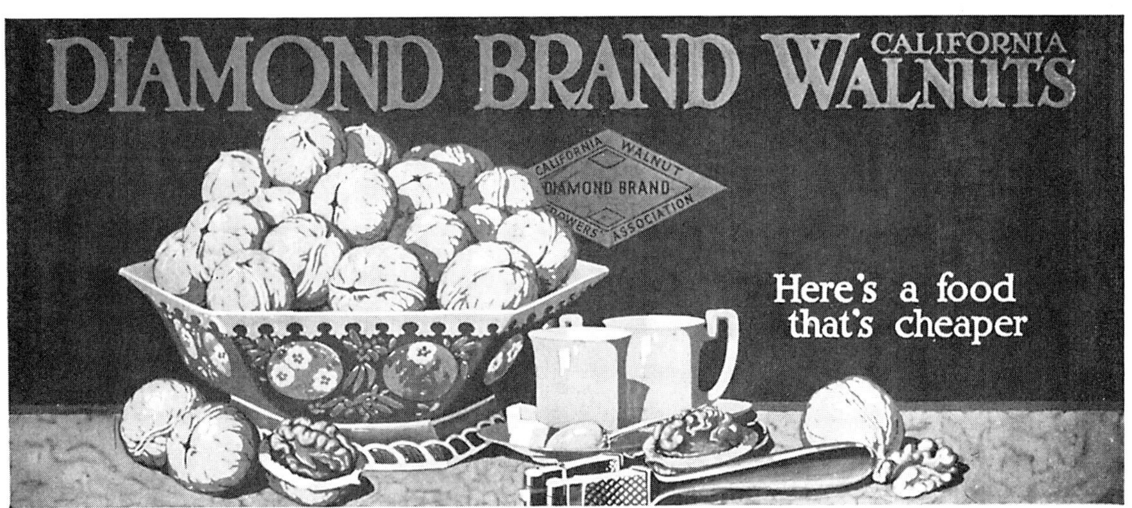

221   DIAMOND BRAND WALNUTS—*Robert Kerfoot*
Loaned by the California Walnut Growers Association
Exhibited by The H. K. McCann Co.

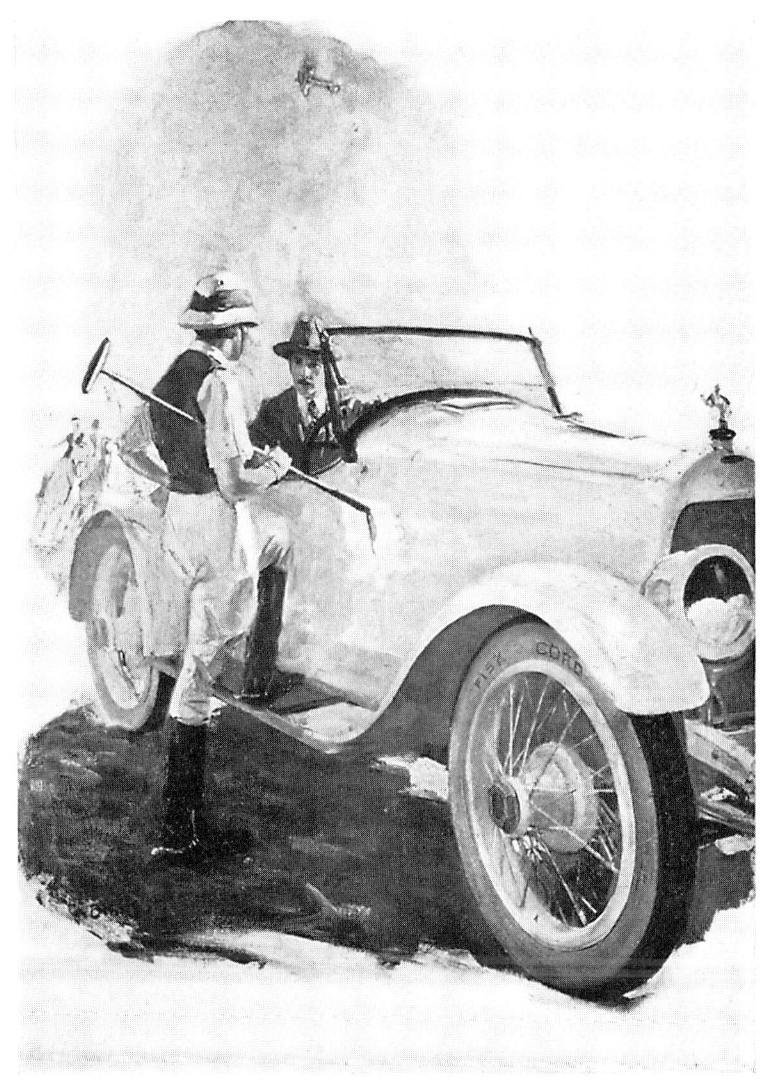

222   FISK TIRES—*Walter Biggs*
Loaned by The Fisk Rubber Co.
Exhibited by the Martin V. Kelley Co.

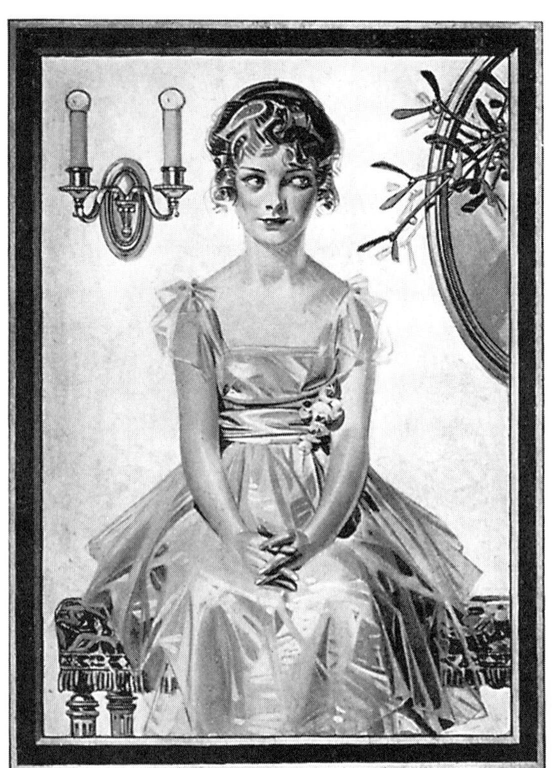

223 MEN'S CLOTHING—*J. C. Leyendecker*
Loaned by B. Kuppenheimer & Company
Exhibited by The George L. Dyer Co.

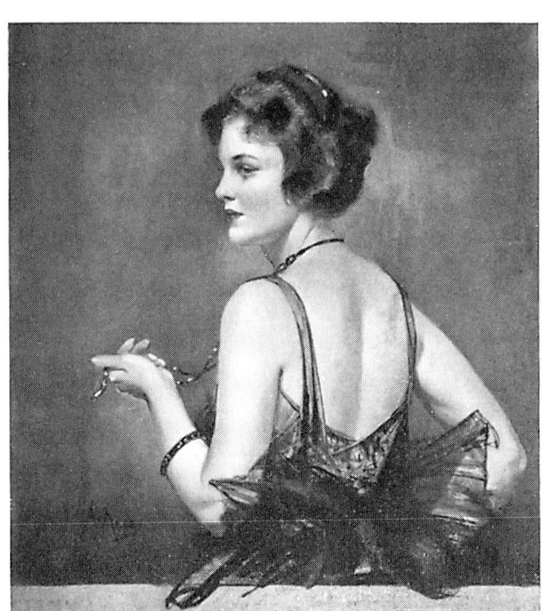

225 WALLACE SILVER—*Neysa McMein*
Loaned by R. Wallace & Sons Mfg. Co.
Exhibited by The Erickson Company

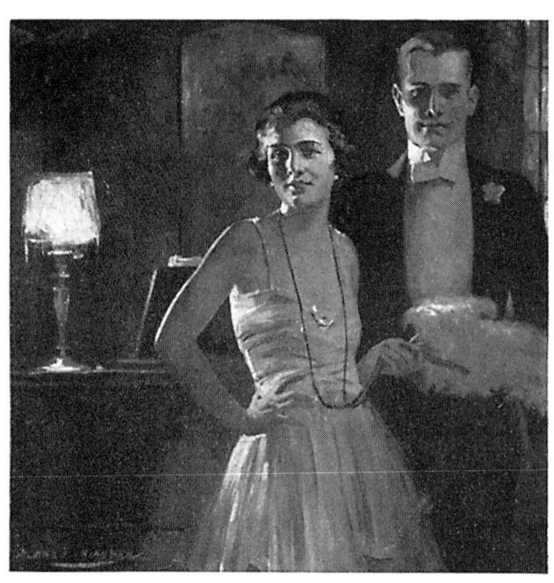

224   *—Alonzo Kimball*
The Amsden Studios Co.

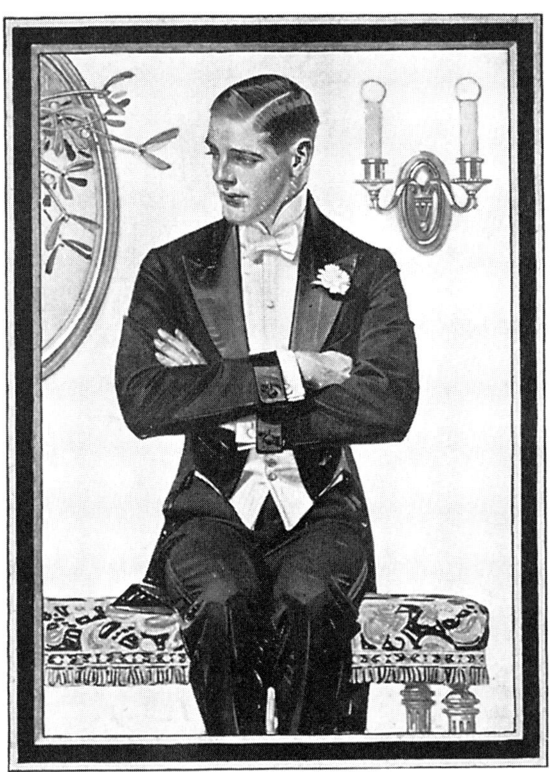

226 Men's Clothing—*J. C. Leyendecker*
Loaned by B. Kuppenheimer & Company
Exhibited by The George L. Dyer Co.

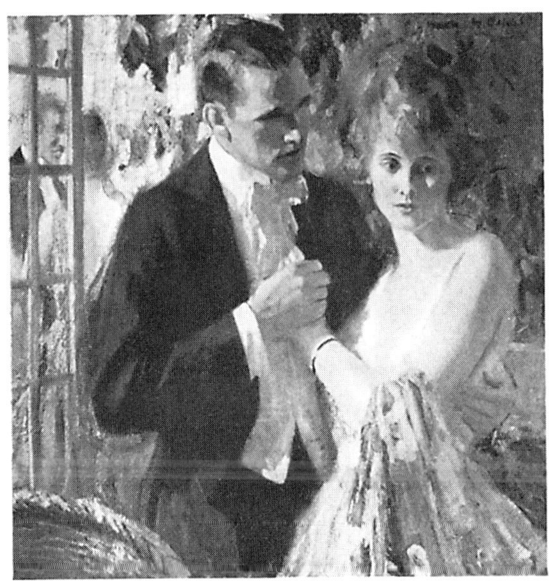

227 Woodbury's Facial Soap—*Walter Biggs*
Loaned by The Andrew Jergens Company
Exhibited by J. Walter Thompson Co.

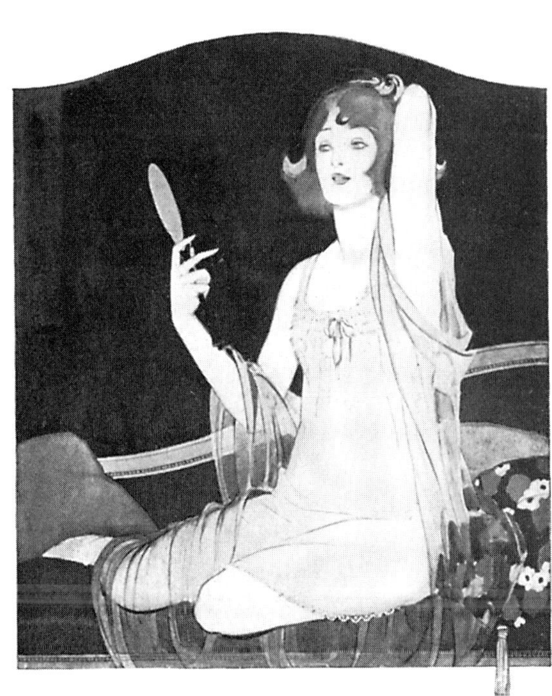

228 La Grecque Underwear—*W. E. Heitland*
Loaned by the La Grecque Underwear Co.
Exhibited by the Redfield Advertising Agency

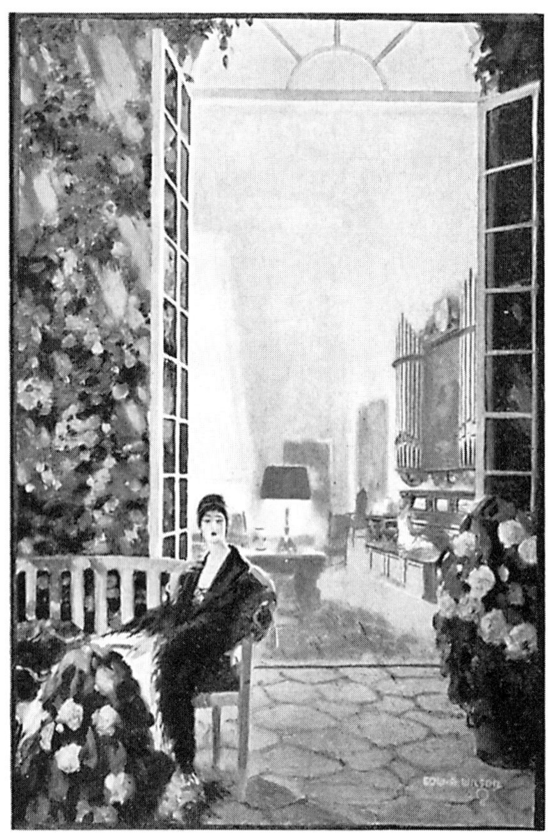

229

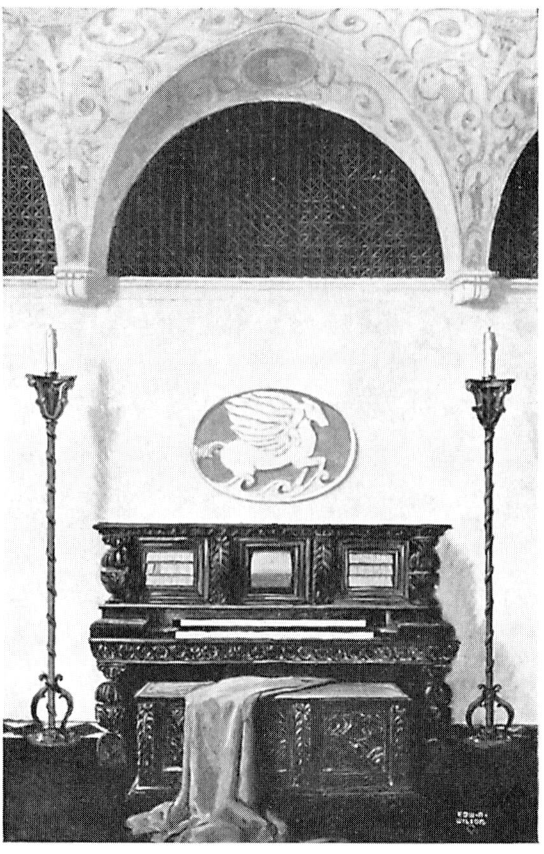

230

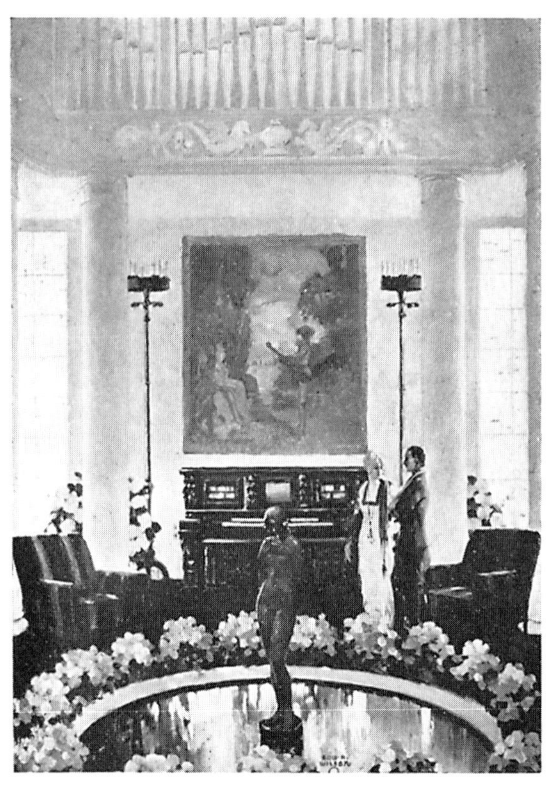

231

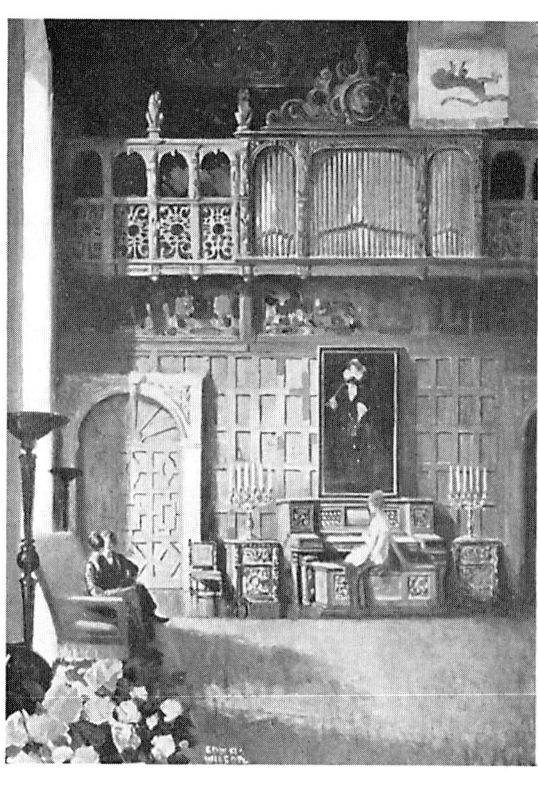

232

ESTEY ORGAN—*Designs by Edward A. Wilson*
Loaned by The Estey Organ Company
Exhibited by Calkins & Holden, Inc.

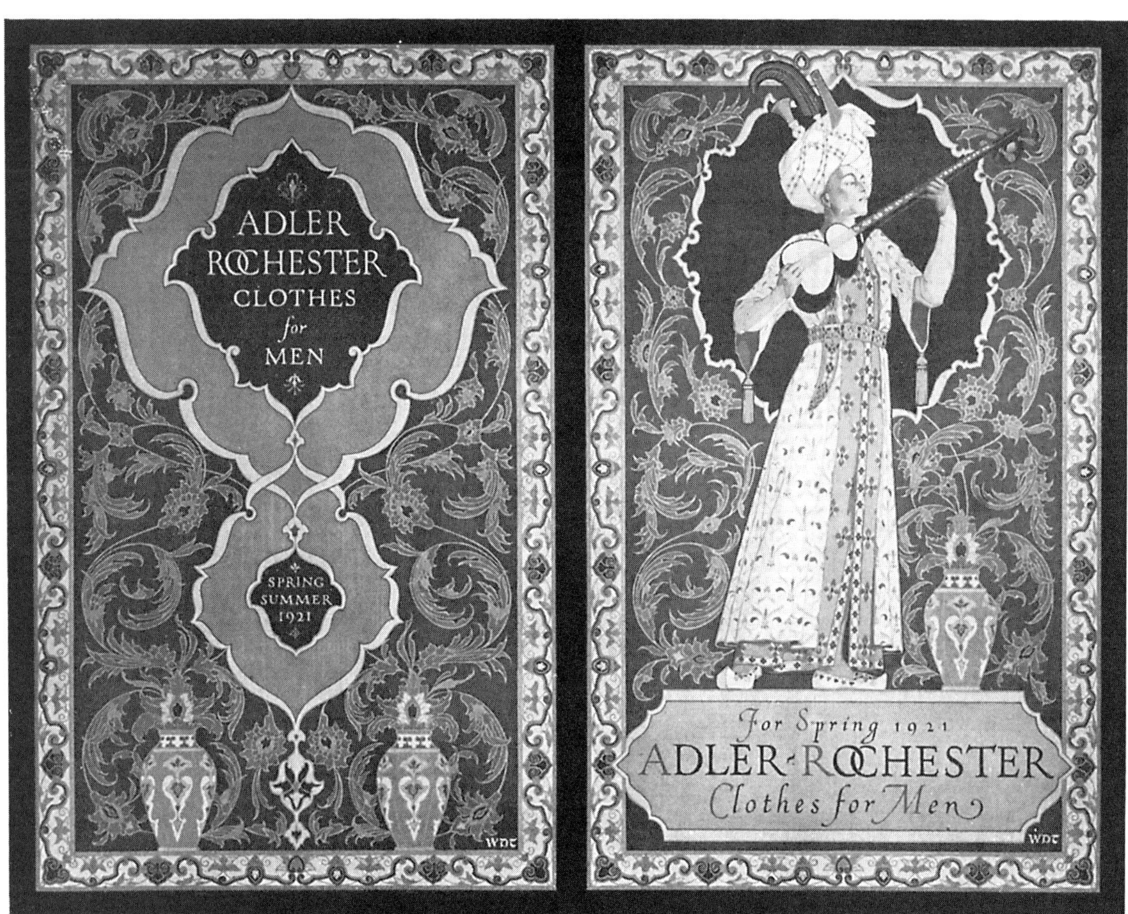

251   ADLER-ROCHESTER CLOTHES—*Walter Dorwin Teague*
Loaned by L. Adler, Bros. & Co.
Exhibited by Berrien Co , Inc.

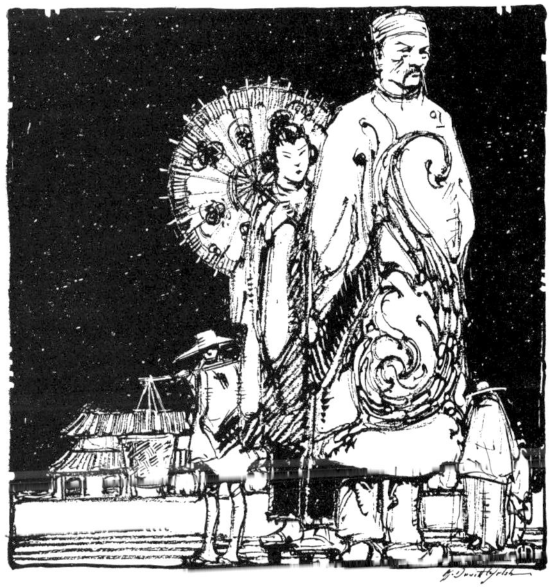

252 EQUITABLE TRUST COMPANY—*H. Devitt Welsh*
Loaned by The Equitable Trust Company
Exhibited by Albert Frank & Company

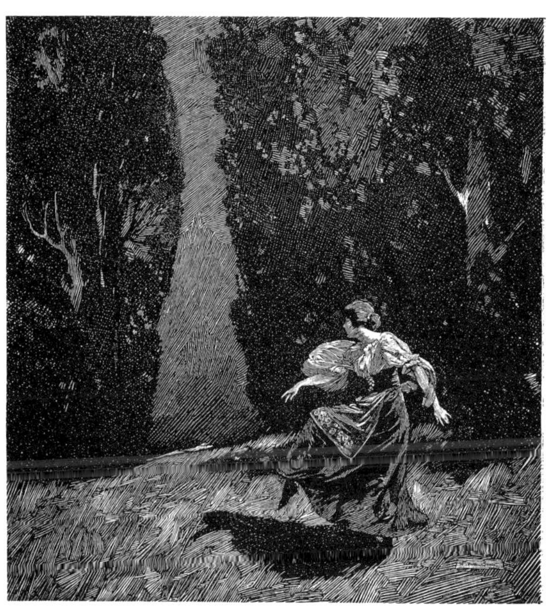

253   VICTOR RECORDS—*Franklin Booth*
Loaned by the Victor Talking Machine Co.
Exhibited by the Franklin Printing Company

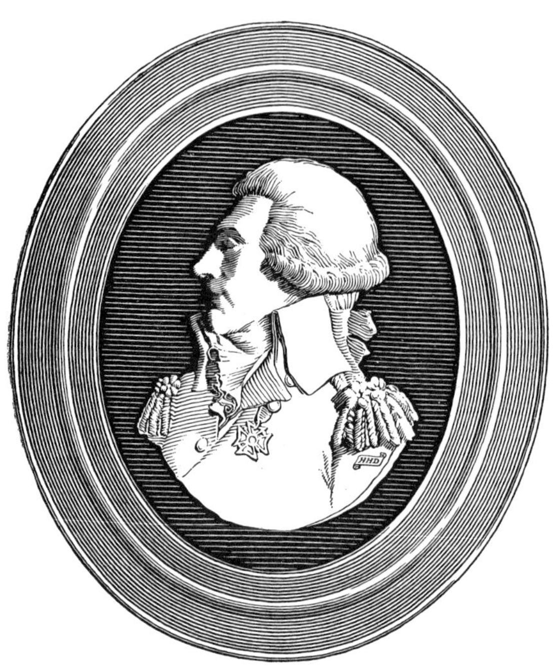

247 LAFAYETTE MOTOR CAR
Harvey Hopkins Dunn
Loaned by the Lafayette Motors Co.
Exhibited by Erwin, Wasey & Co.

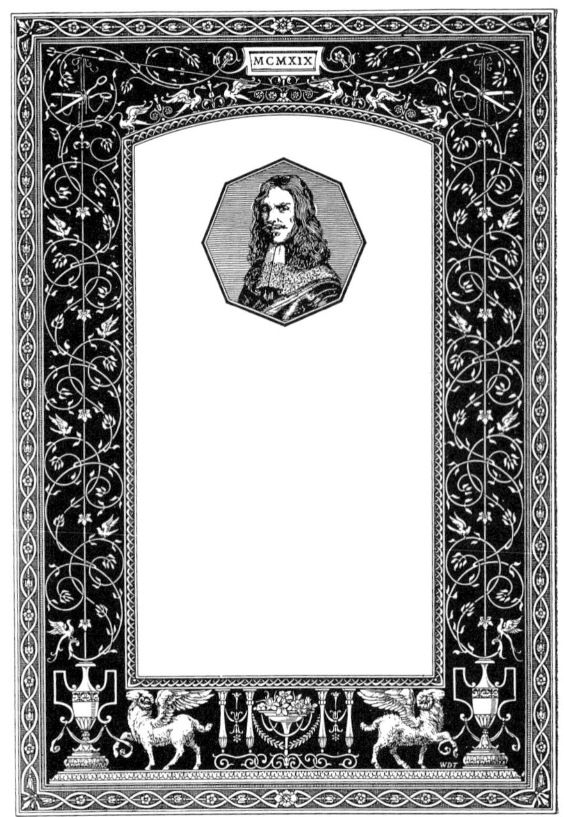

248 ADLER-ROCHESTER CLOTHES
Walter Dorwin Teague
Loaned by L. Adler, Bros. & Co.
Exhibited by Berrien Co., Inc.

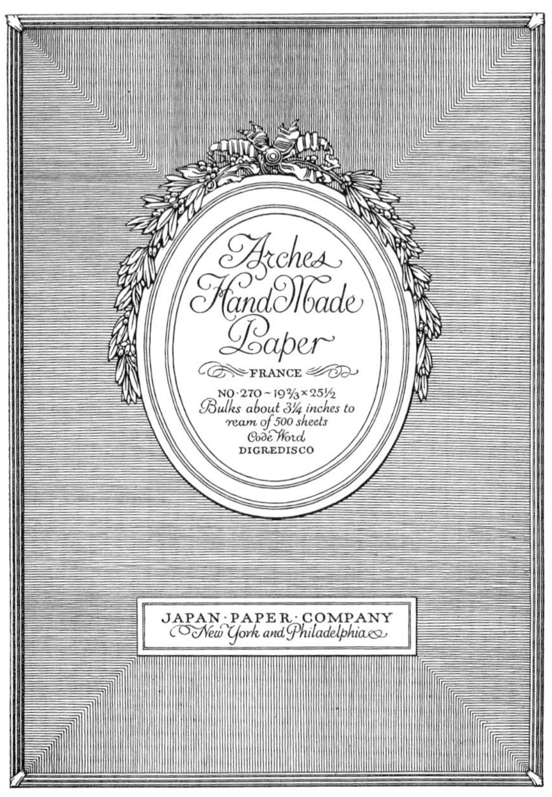

249 ARCHES HAND MADE PAPER
Harvey Hopkins Dunn
Loaned and exhibited by the Japan Paper Company

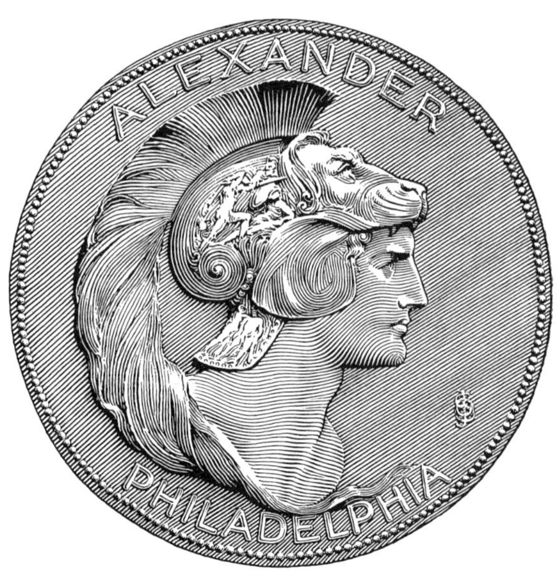

250 LEATHER BELTING—*Harvey Hopkins Dunn*
Loaned and exhibited by Alexander Bros.

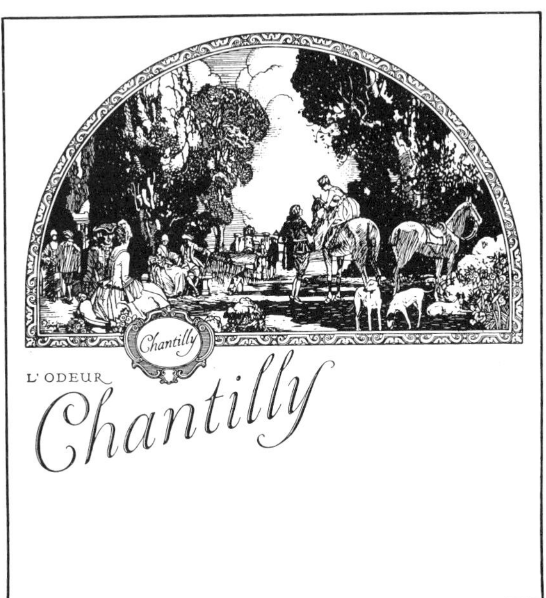

243　CHANTILLY TOILET GOODS
Harry L. Timmins
Loaned by Chantilly Toilet Goods
Exhibited by the D'Arcy Advertising Agency

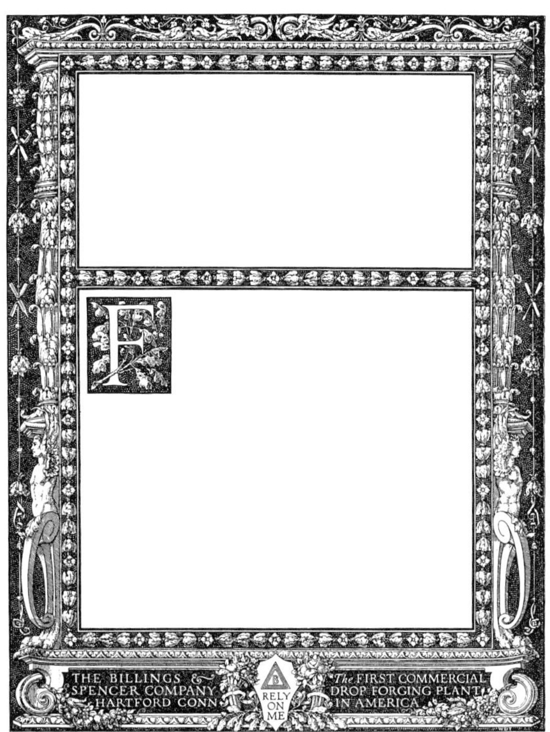

244　BORDER DESIGN—*Walter Dorwin Teague*
Loaned by The Billings & Spencer Co.
Exhibited by the Harry Porter Co.

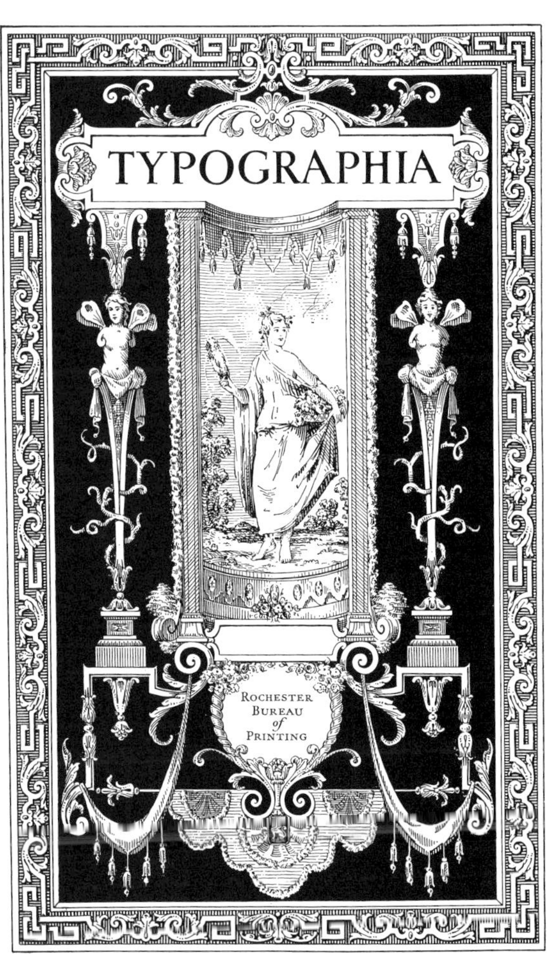

245　COVER DESIGN—*O. W. Jaquish, Jr.*
Loaned and exhibited by the Rochester Bureau of Printing

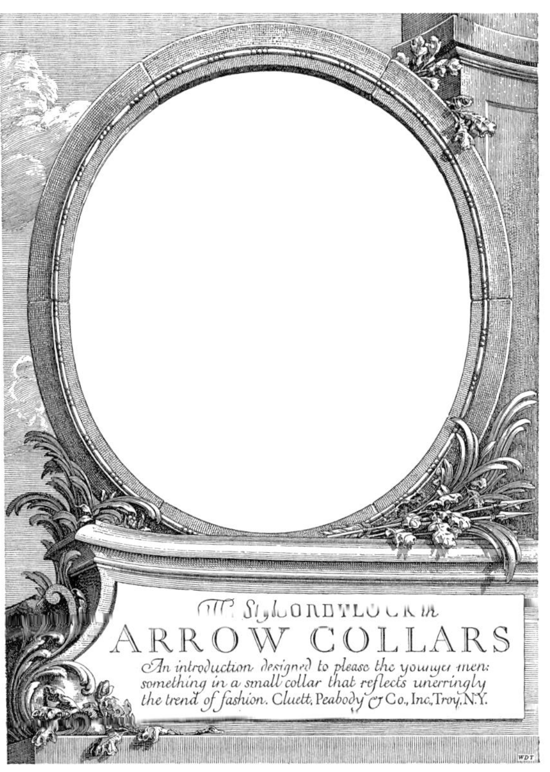

246　ARROW COLLARS—*Walter Dorwin Teague*
Loaned by Cluett, Peabody & Co., Inc.
Exhibited by Smith, Sturgis & Moore, Inc.

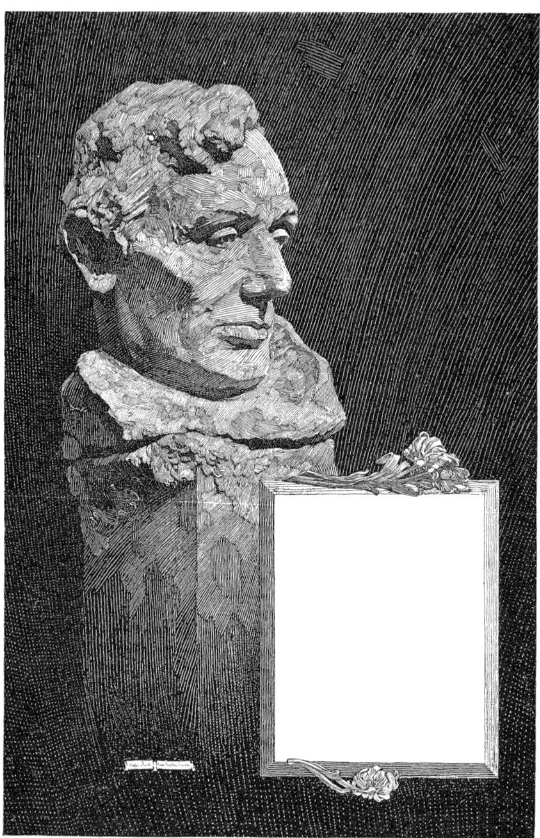

240 BILLINGS & SPENCER—*Franklin Booth*
Loaned by The Billings & Spencer Co.
Exhibited by the Harry Porter Co.

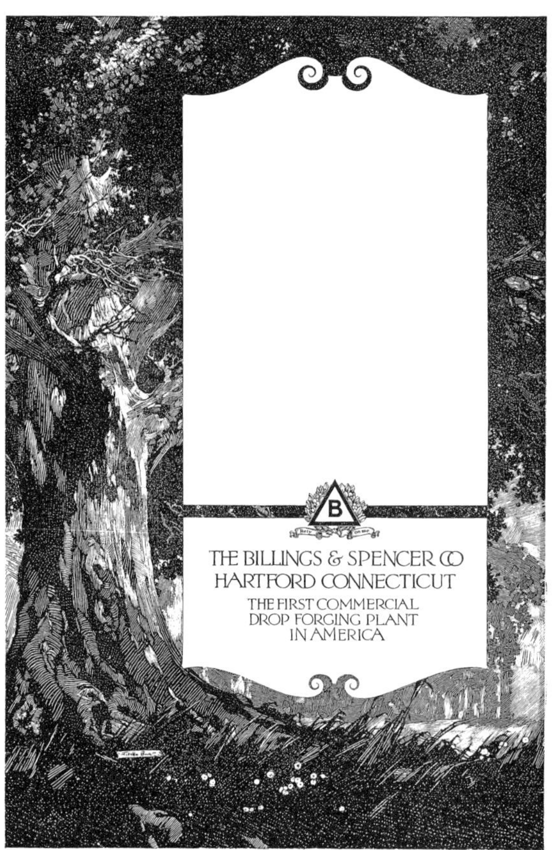

241 BILLINGS & SPENCER—*Franklin Booth*
Loaned by The Billings & Spencer Co.
Exhibited by the Harry Porter Co.

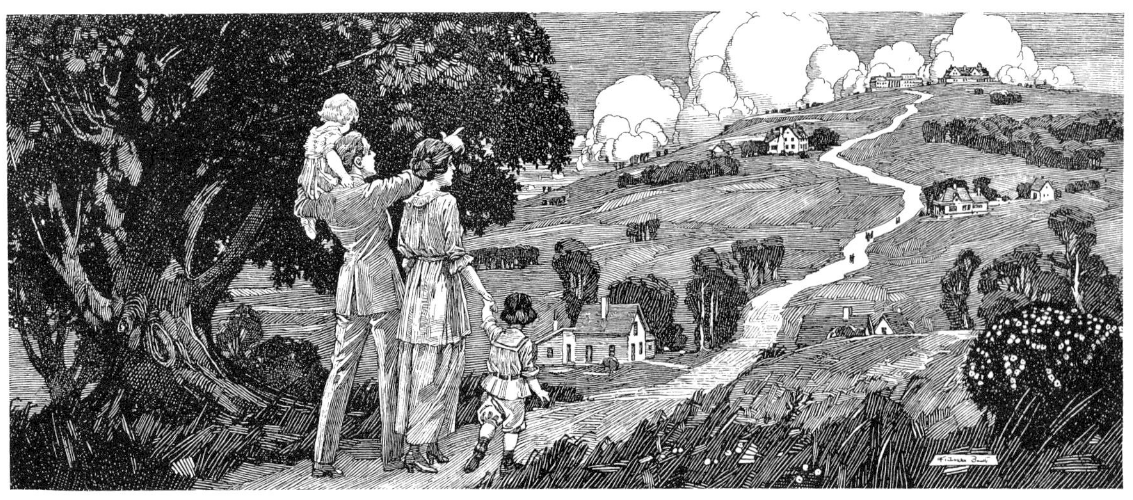

242 ALEXANDER HAMILTON INSTITUTE—*Franklin Booth*
Loaned by the Alexander Hamilton Institute
Exhibited by Barton, Durstine & Osborn, Inc.

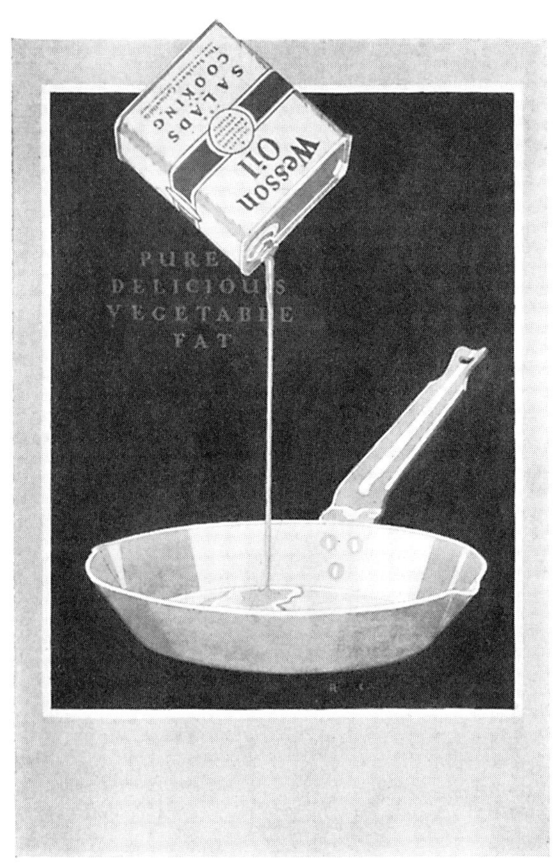

236

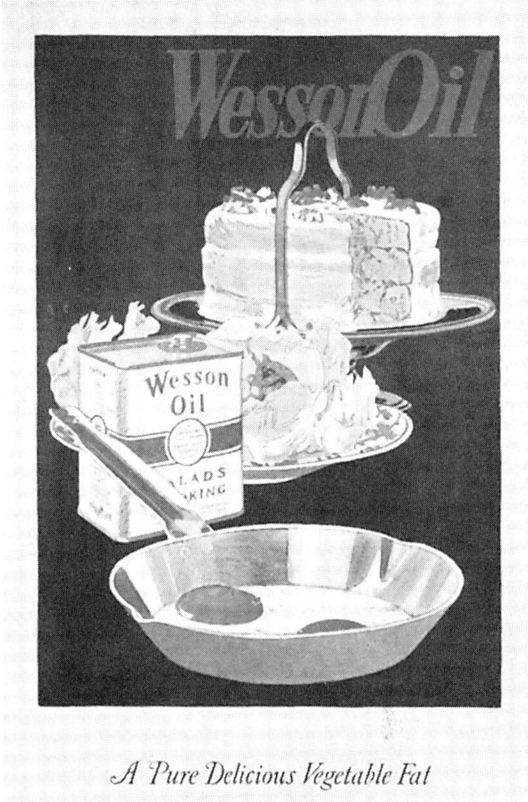

A Pure Delicious Vegetable Fat

237

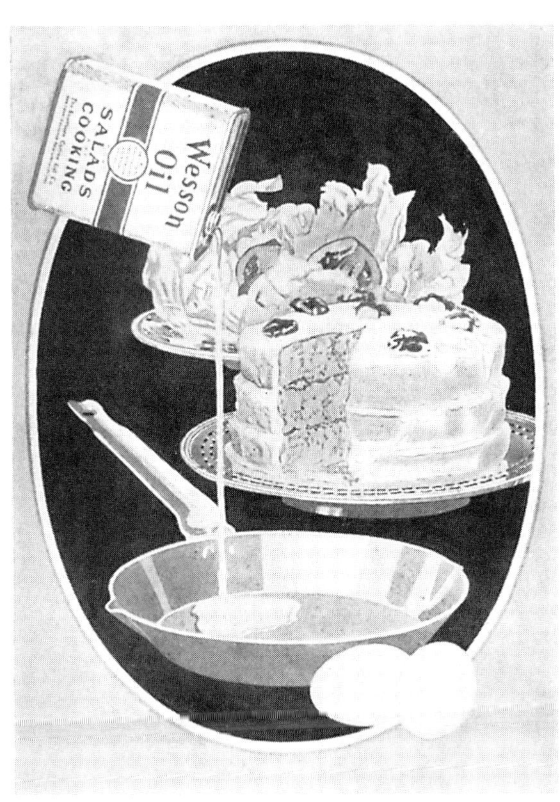

238

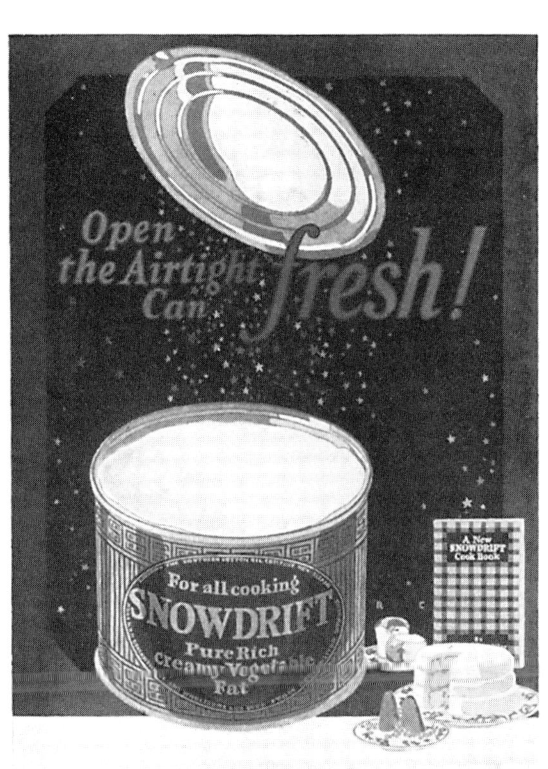

239

WESSON OIL AND SNOWDRIFT—*Designs by René Clarke*
Loaned by The Southern Cotton Oil Co.
Exhibited by Calkins & Holden, Inc.

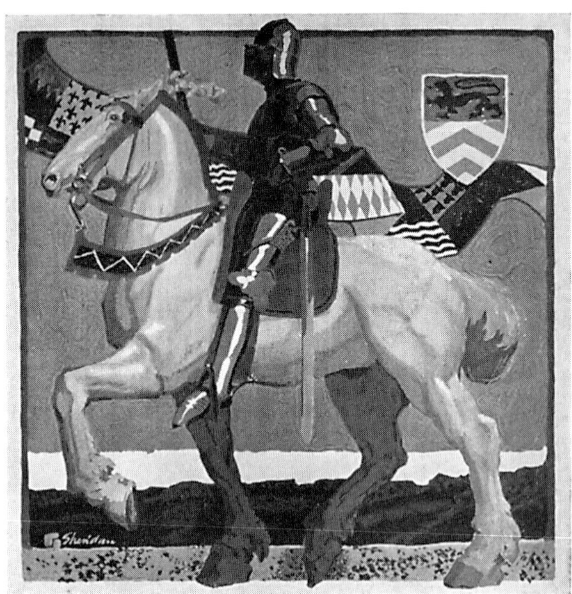

233 MEN'S CLOTHING—*John E. Sheridan*
Loaned and exhibited by Hart Schaffner & Marx

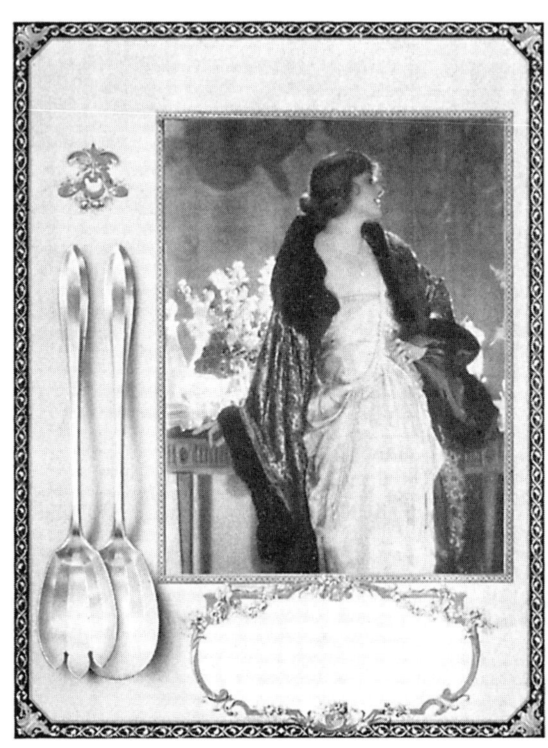

234 COMMUNITY SILVERWARE—*Baron de Meyer*
Loaned and exhibited by Oneida Community, Ltd.

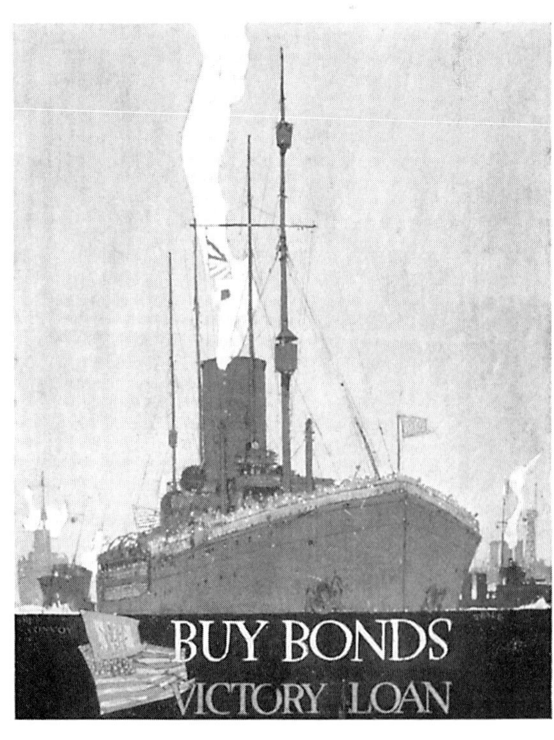

235 U. S. VICTORY LOAN—*E. G. Teale*
Loaned and exhibited by the Caxton Company

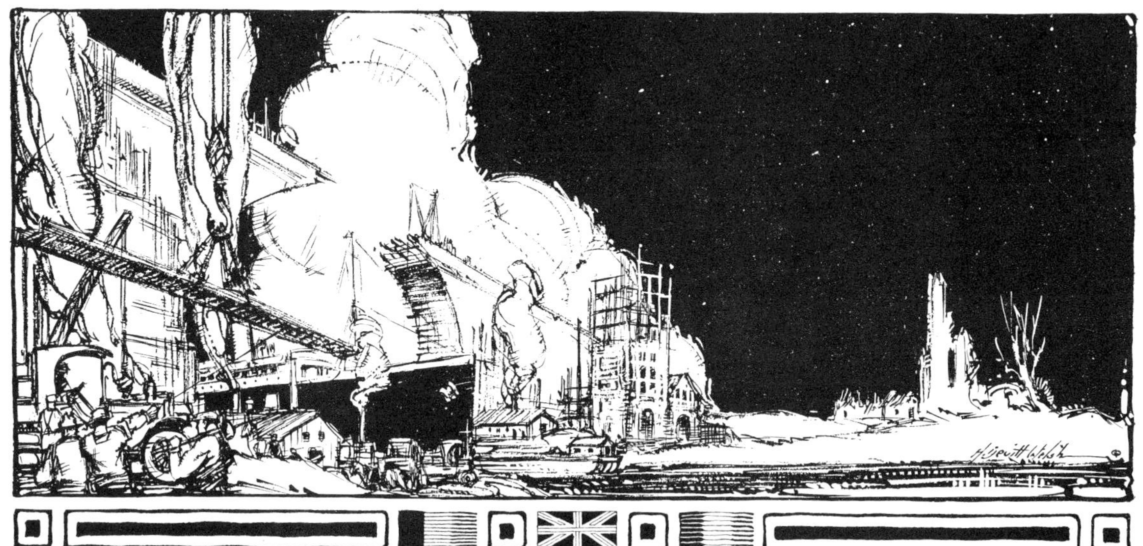

254 BONDS—*H. Devitt Welsh*
Loaned by Halsey, Stuart & Company
Exhibited by Albert Frank & Company

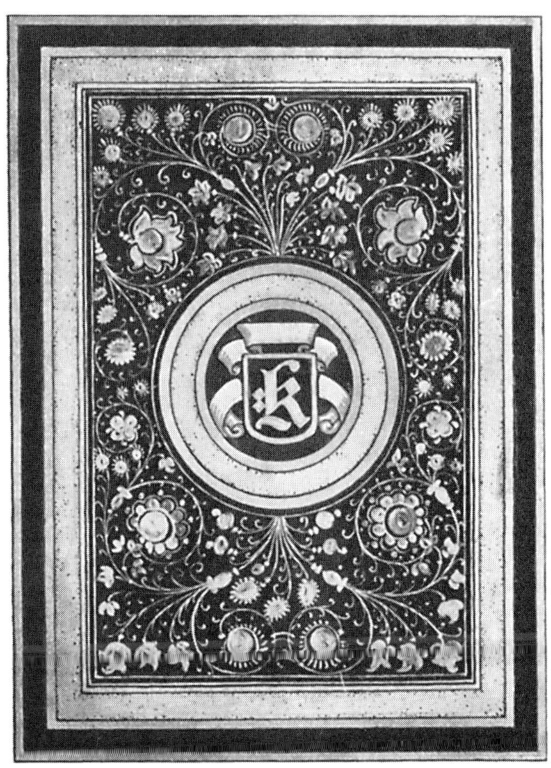

255 MEN'S CLOTHING—*J. C. Leyendecker*
Loaned by B. Kuppenheimer & Company
Exhibited by The George L. Dyer Co.

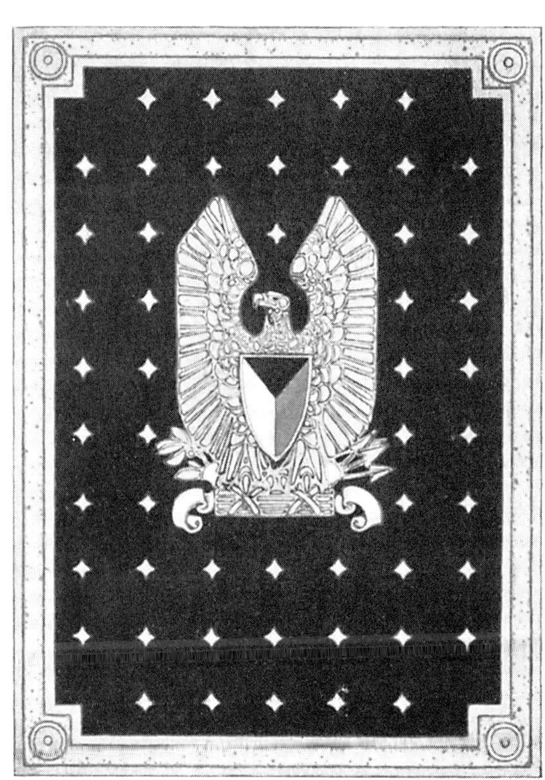

256 MEN'S CLOTHING—*J. C. Leyendecker*
Loaned by B. Kuppenheimer & Company
Exhibited by The George L. Dyer Co.

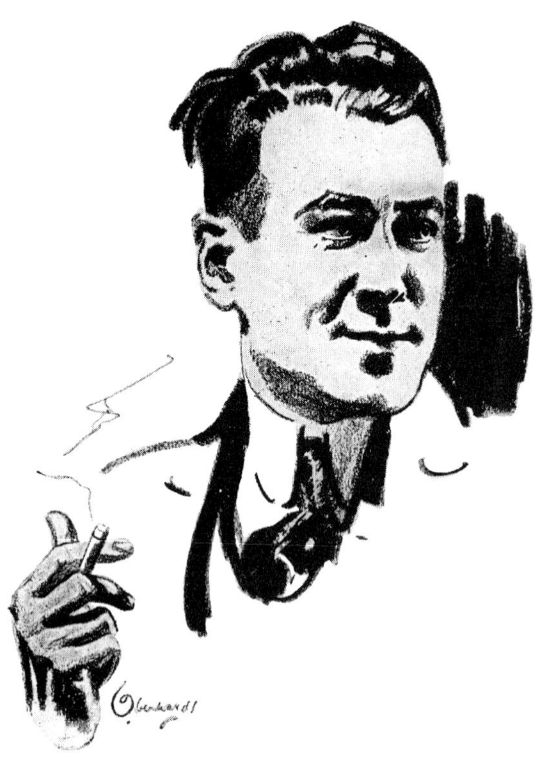

257 FATIMA CIGARETTES—*William Oberhardt*
Loaned by the Liggett & Myers Tobacco Co.
Exhibited by Newell-Emmett Co., Inc.

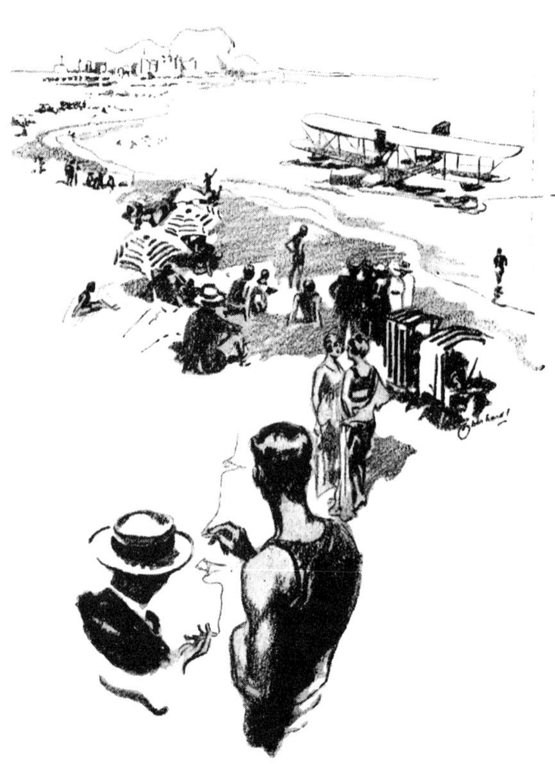

258 FATIMA CIGARETTES—*William Oberhardt*
Loaned by the Liggett & Myers Tobacco Co.
Exhibited by Newell-Emmett Co., Inc.

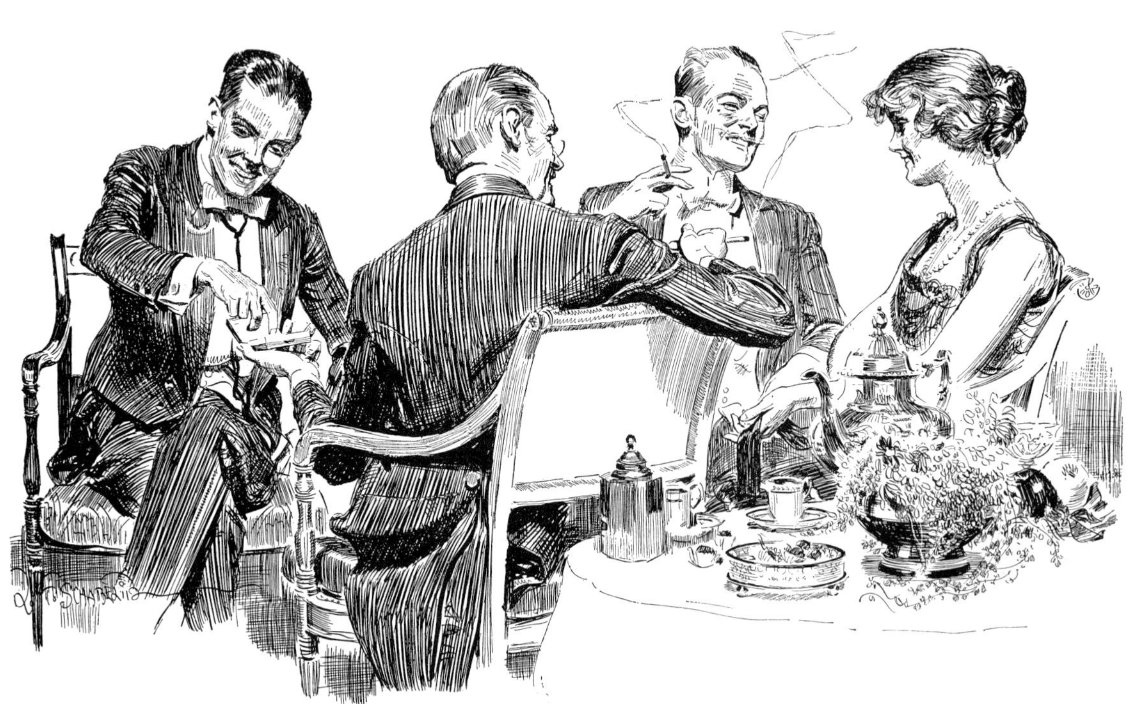

259 PHILIP MORRIS CIGARETTES—*R. F. Schabelitz*
Loaned by Philip Morris & Co., Ltd.
Exhibited by Albert Frank & Company

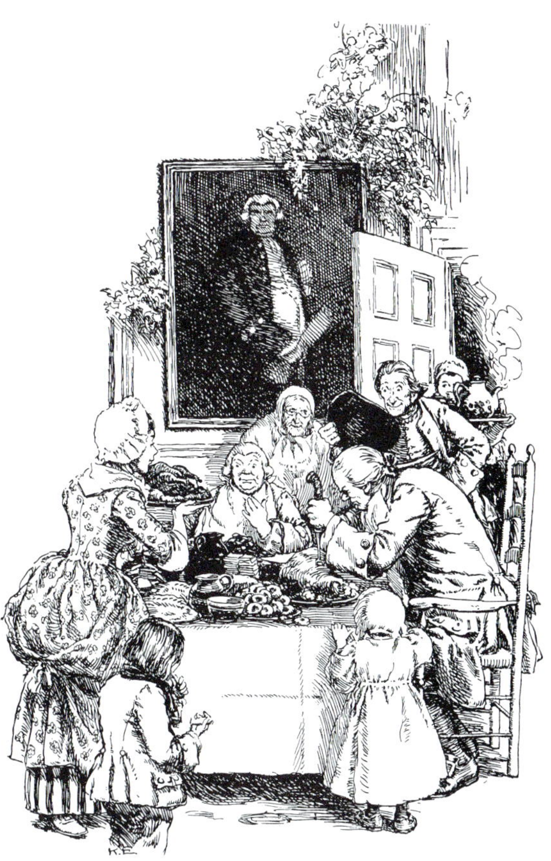

260 YUBAN COFFEE—*Kerr Eby*
Loaned by Arbuckle Bros.
Exhibited by J. Walter Thompson Co.

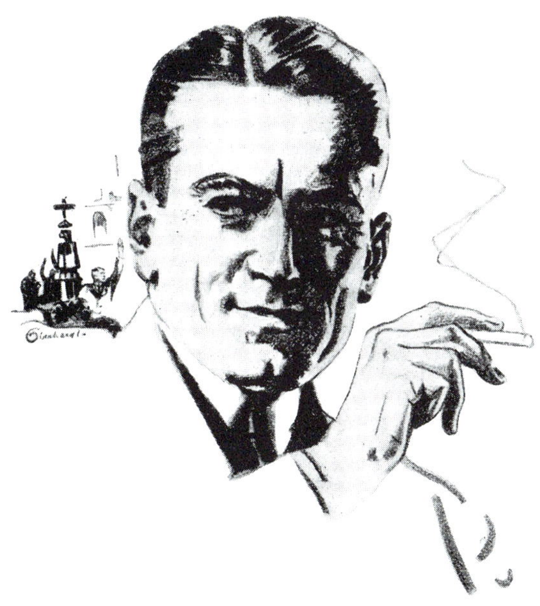

261 FATIMA CIGARETTES—*William Oberhardt*
Loaned by the Liggett & Myers Tobacco Co.
Exhibited by Frank Seaman, Inc.

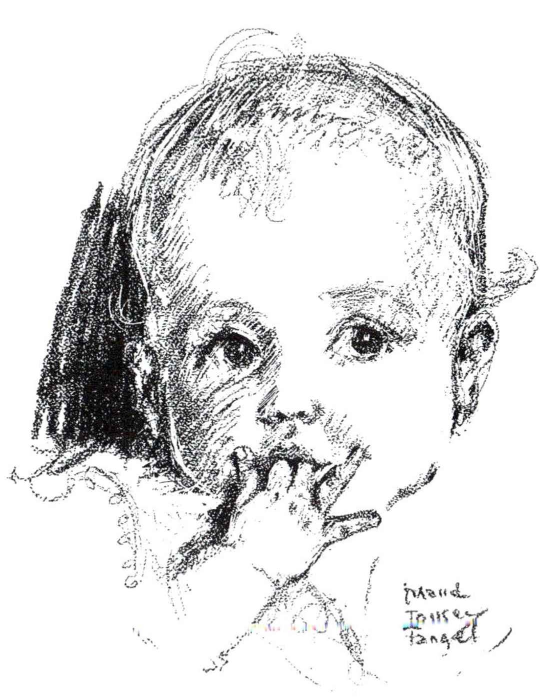

262 WOMAN'S HOME COMPANION
Maud Tousey Fangel
Loaned by The Crowell Publishing Company
Exhibited by Calkins & Holden, Inc.

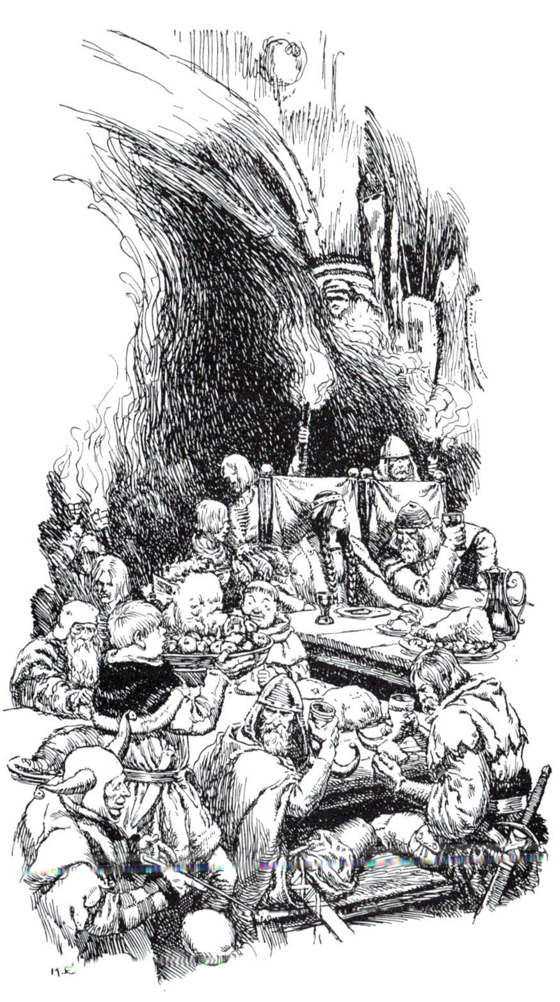

263 YUBAN COFFEE—*Kerr Eby*
Loaned by Arbuckle Bros.
Exhibited by J. Walter Thompson Co.

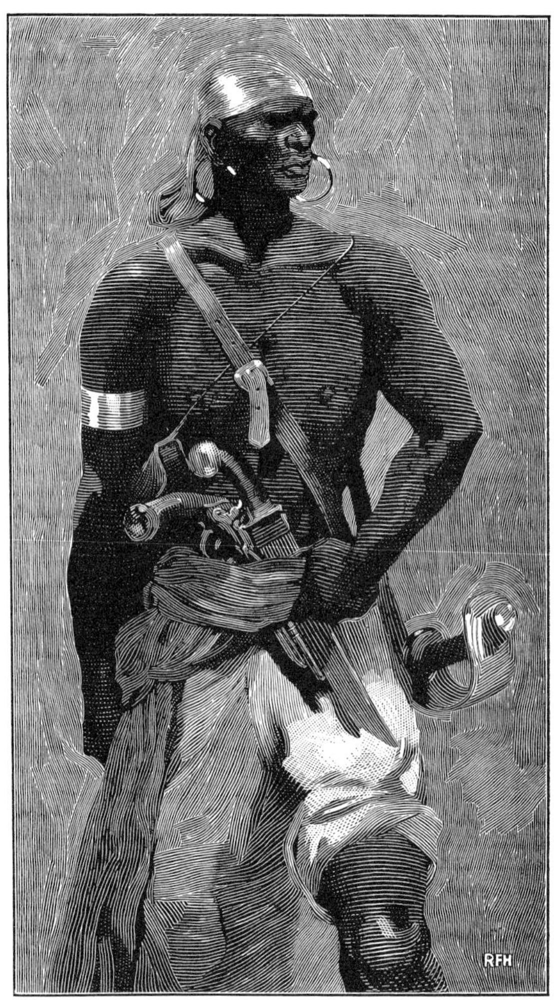

264   PEN DRAWING—*R. F. Heinrich*
Exhibited by R. F. Heinrich

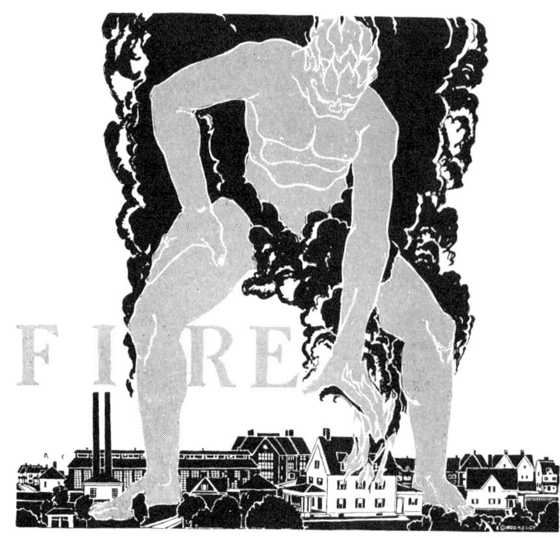

265   HARTFORD FIRE INSURANCE—*René Clarke*
Loaned by The Hartford Fire Insurance Co.
Exhibited by Calkins & Holden, Inc.

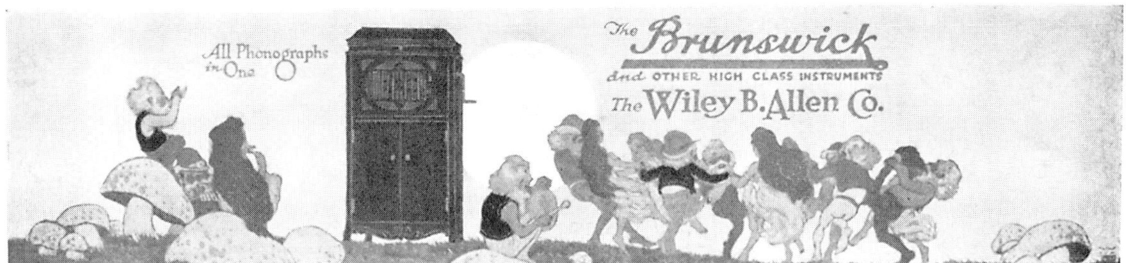

266 THE BRUNSWICK PHONOGRAPH
Loaned by The Wiley B. Allen Co.
Exhibited by Foster & Kleiser

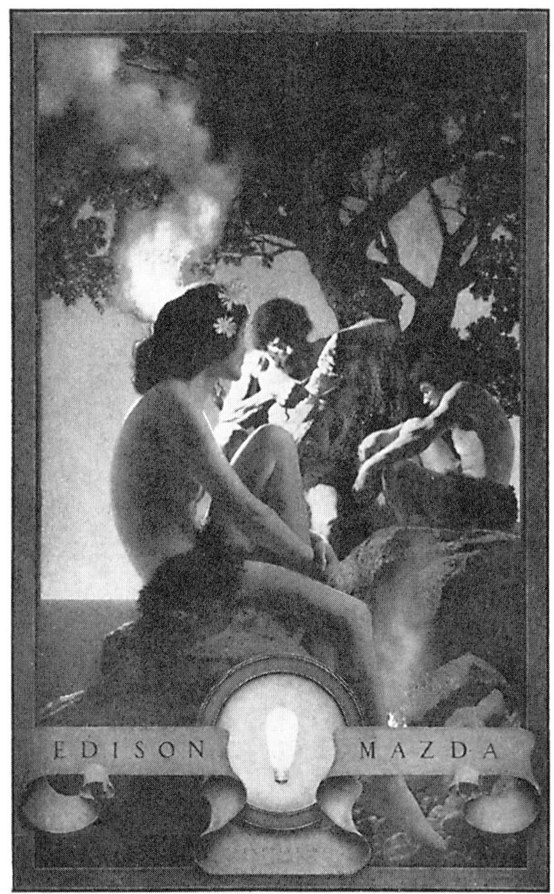

267 EDISON MAZDA LAMPS—*Maxfield Parrish*
Loaned by the Edison Lamp Works of General Electric Co.
Exhibited by Barton, Durstine & Osborn, Inc.

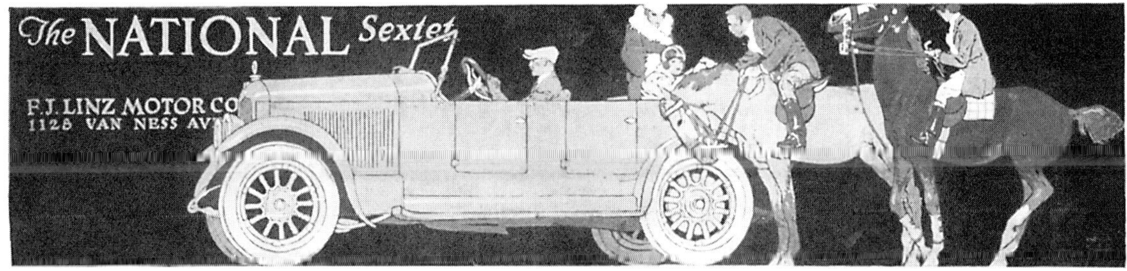

268 THE NATIONAL SEXTET
Loaned by the F. J. Linz Motor Co.
Exhibited by Foster & Kleiser

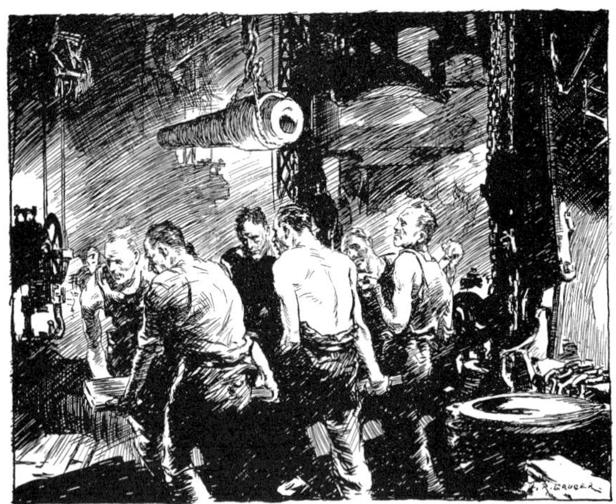

269 O'SULLIVAN'S HEELS—*F. R. Gruger*
Loaned by the Lamont Corliss Co.
Exhibited by J. Walter Thompson Co.

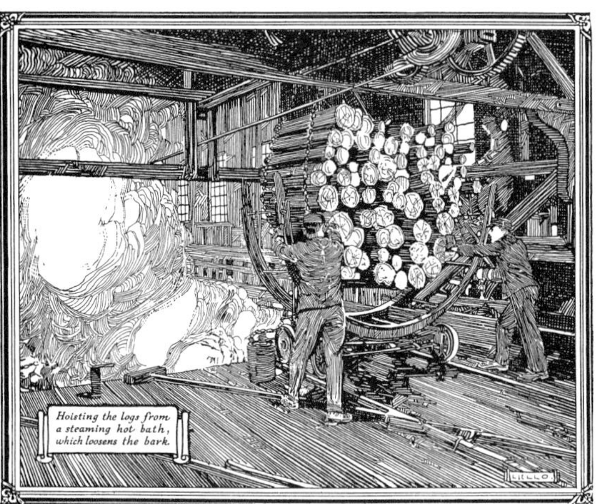

270 WRITING PAPER—*John Liello*
Loaned by the Eastern Mfg. Co.
Exhibited by The H. K. McCann Co.

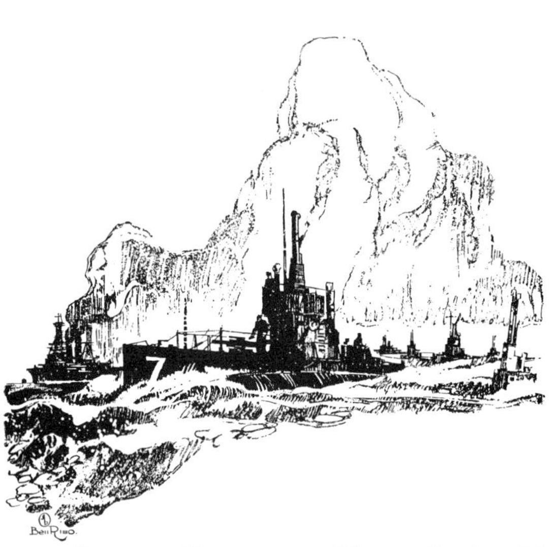

271 STORAGE BATTERIES—*Thomas D. Ben Rimo*
Loaned by the Electric Storage Battery Co.
Exhibited by George Batten Co., Inc.

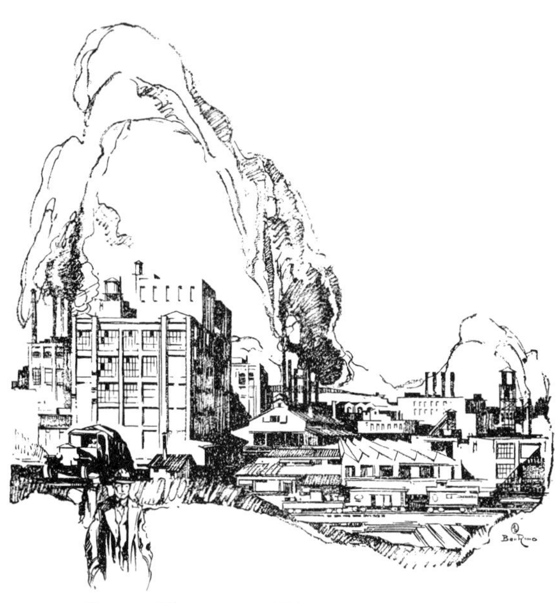

272 REAL ESTATE—*Thomas D. Ben Rimo*
Loaned by Louis Schlesinger, Inc.
Exhibited by Albert Frank & Company

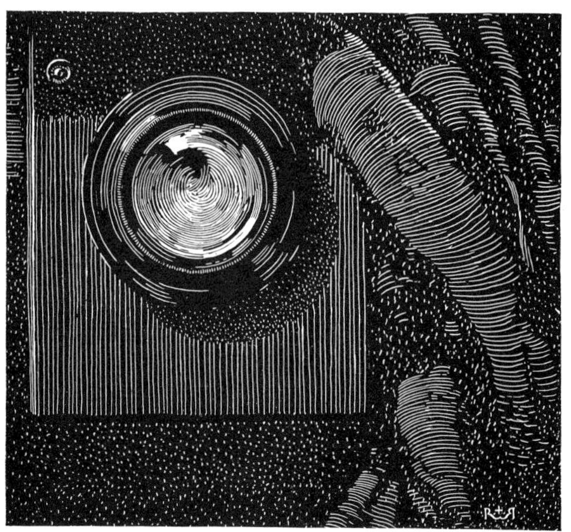

273 OPTICAL LENSES—*Guido & Lawrence Rosa*
Loaned by the Bausch and Lomb Optical Co.
Exhibited by Frank Seaman, Inc.

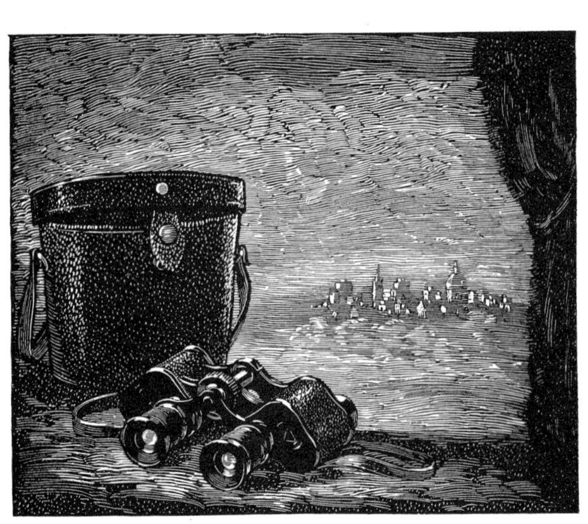

274 OPTICAL LENSES—*Guido & Lawrence Rosa*
Loaned by the Bausch and Lomb Optical Co.
Exhibited by Frank Seaman, Inc.

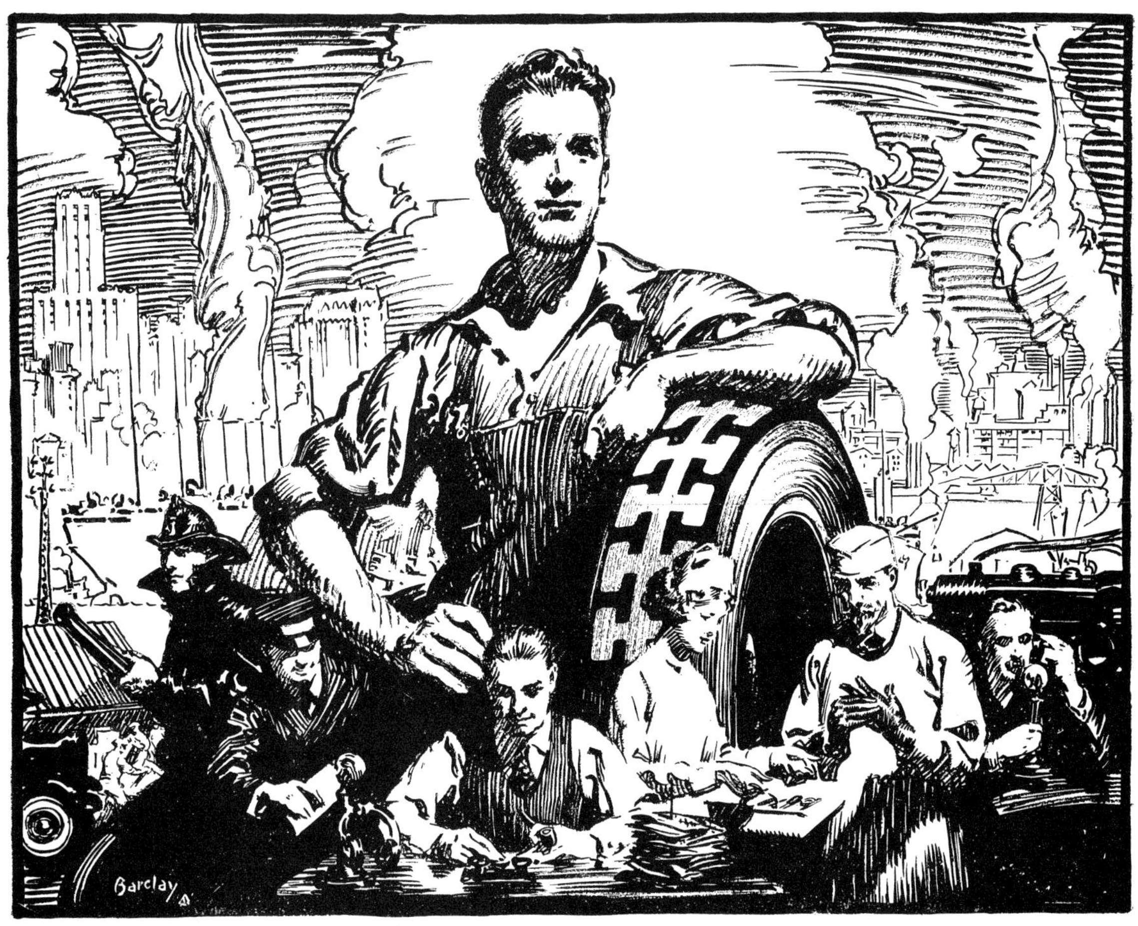

275 GOODRICH TIRES—*MacClelland Barclay*
Loaned by The B. F. Goodrich Company

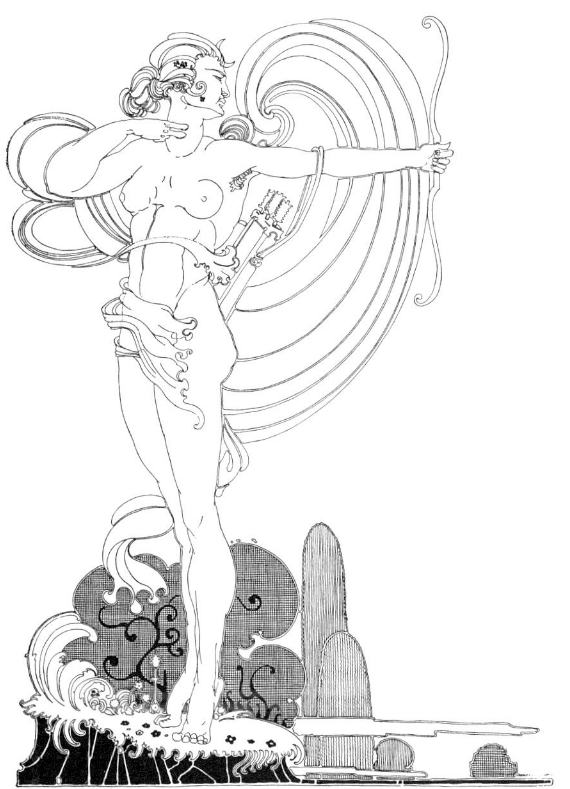

276 THE SPIRIT OF TRANSPORTATION
James Cady Ewell
Loaned by The Clark Equipment Co.
Exhibited by the McKinney Co.

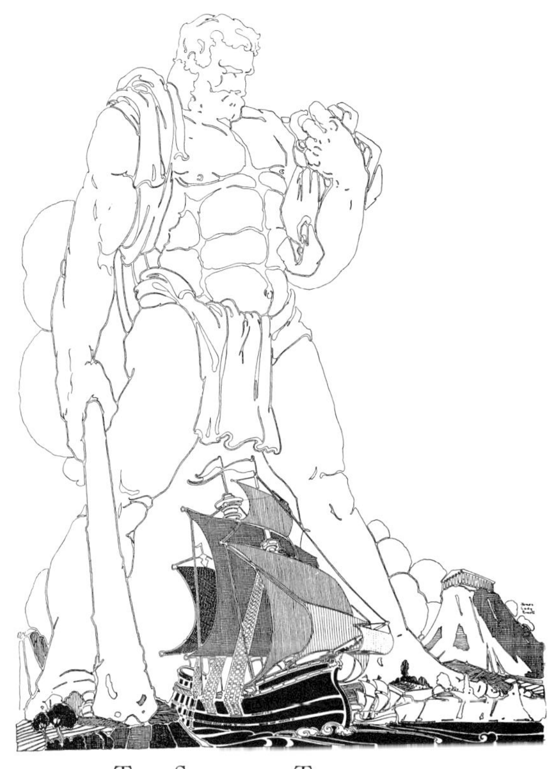

277 THE SPIRIT OF TRANSPORTATION
James Cady Ewell
Loaned by The Clark Equipment Co.
Exhibited by the McKinney Co.

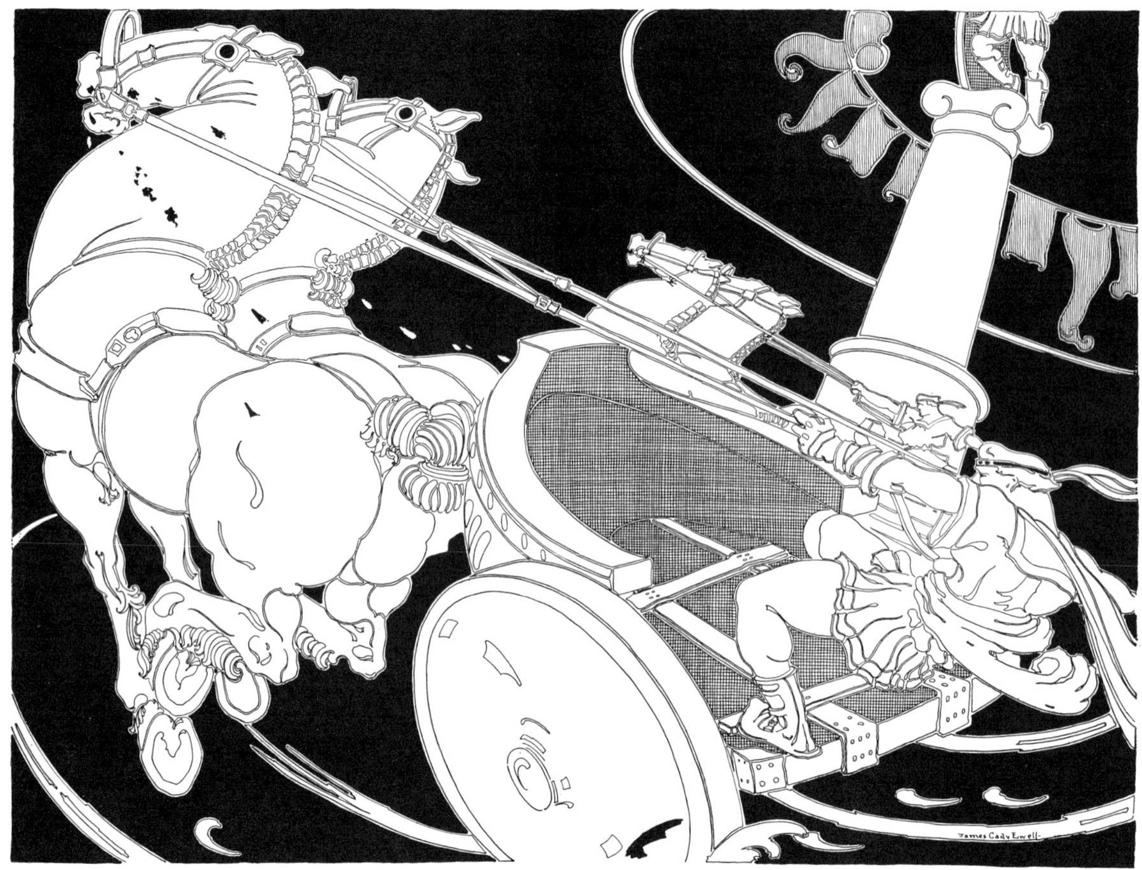

278   THE SPIRIT OF TRANSPORTATION—*James Cady Ewell*
Loaned by The Clark Equipment Co.
Exhibited by the McKinney Co.

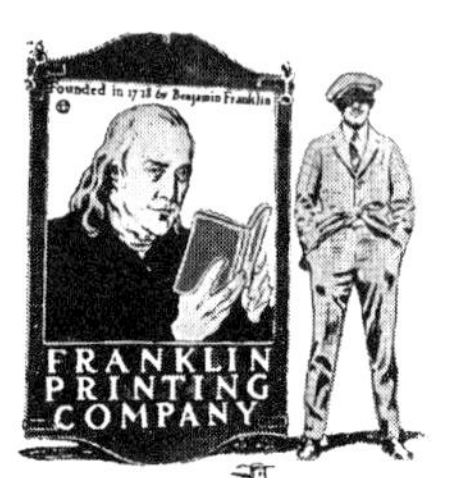

279   FRANKLIN SIGN
Edward Penfield
Loaned and exhibited by the
Franklin Printing Company

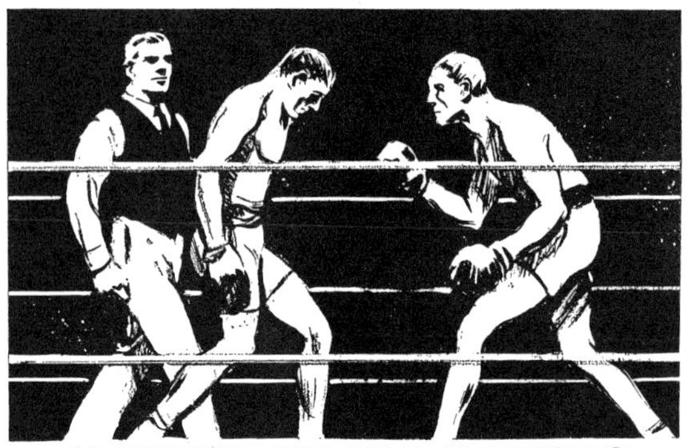

280   NUJOL—*C. B. Falls*
Loaned by the Nujol Laboratories
Exhibited by The H. K. McCann Co

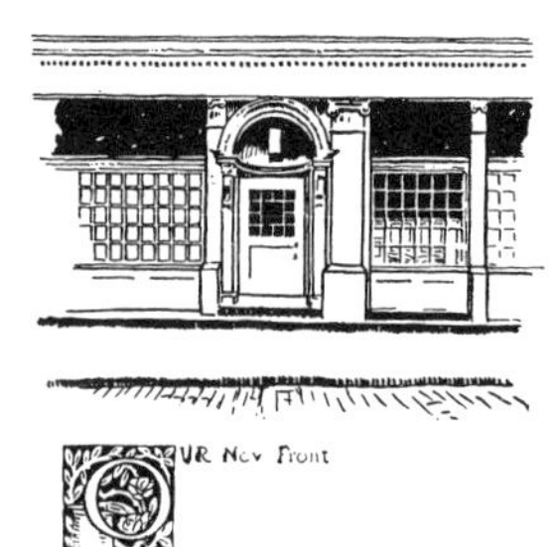

281   DOORWAY & INITIAL
Edward Penfield
Loaned and exhibited by the
Franklin Printing Company

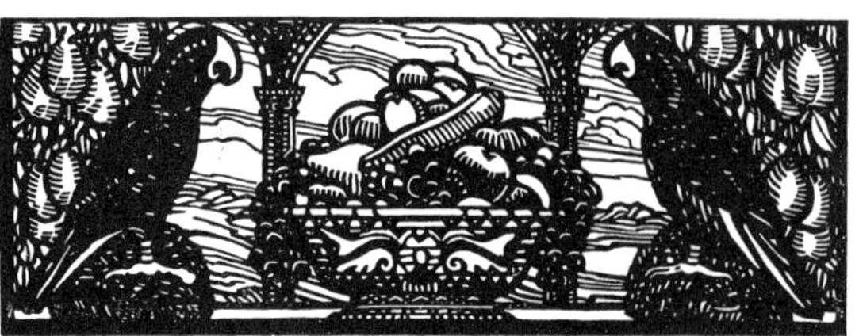

282   RITZ-CARLTON HOTEL—*John J. A. Murphy*
Loaned by the Ritz-Carlton Hotel
Exhibited by The Irving Press

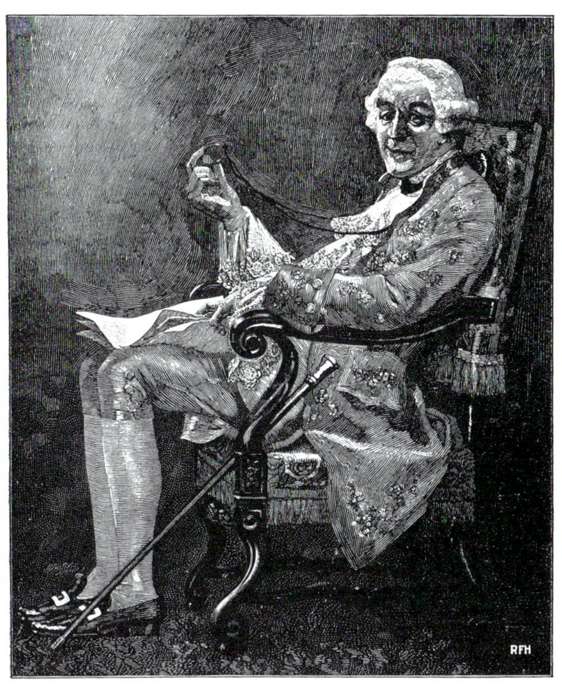

283 Pen Drawing—*R. F. Heinrich*
Exhibited by R. F. Heinrich

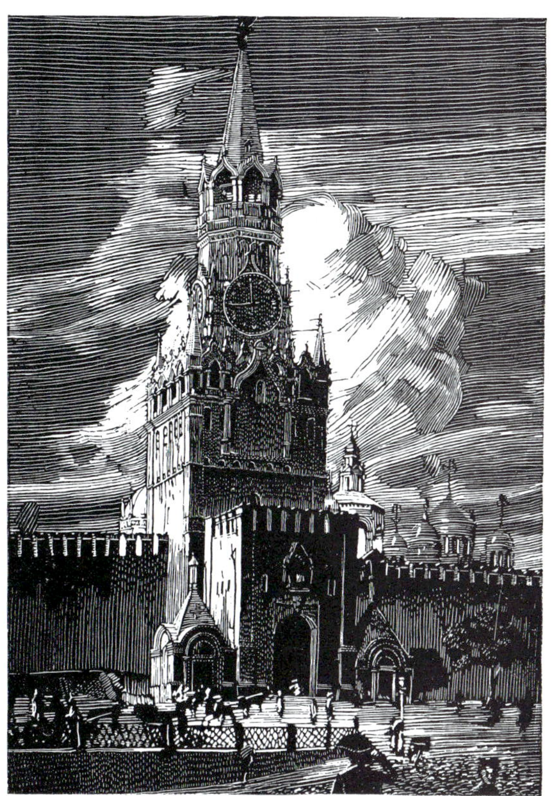

284 The Kremlin—*Louis H. Reid*
Loaned by Otis Elevator Co.
Exhibited by Reid, Fletcher & Hart

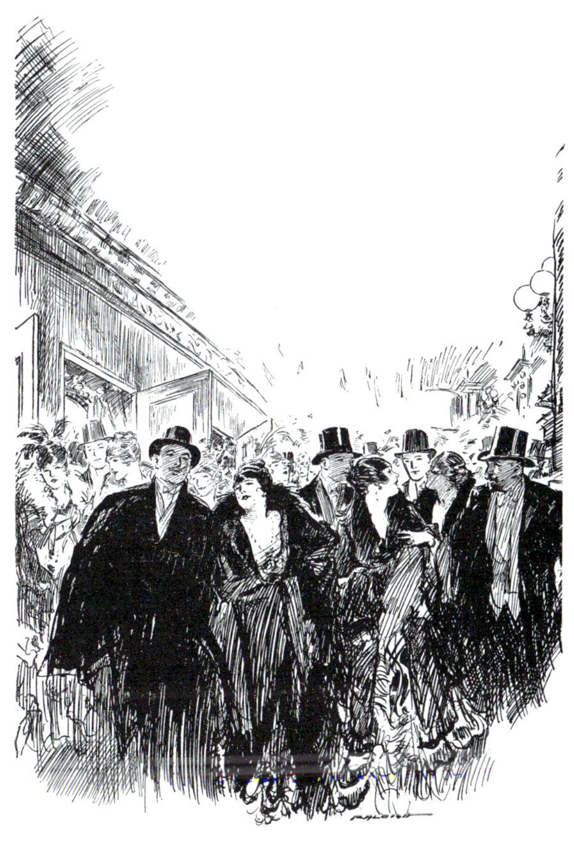

285 Fatima Cigarettes *Henry Raleigh*
Loaned by the Liggett & Myers Tobacco Co.
Exhibited by Newell-Emmett Co., Inc.

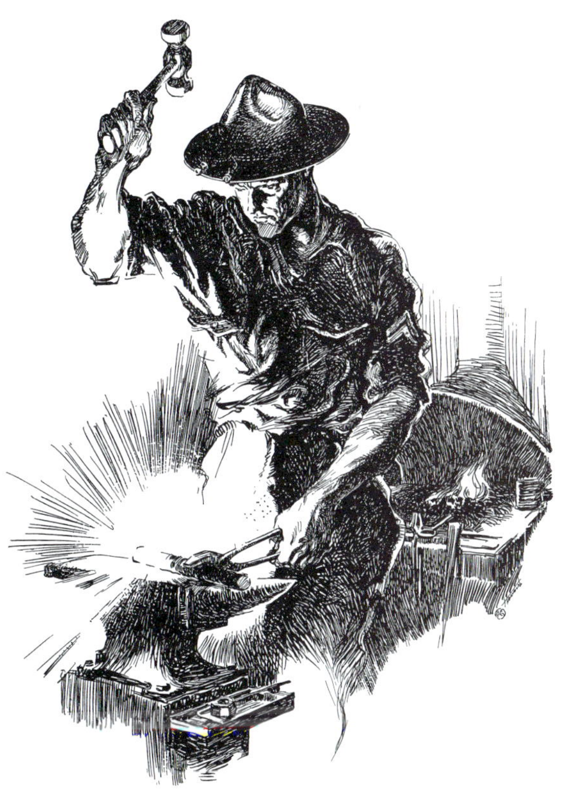

286 U. S. Army Teaches Trades
James H. Hammon
Loaned by the U. S. Army
Exhibited by Calkins & Holden, Inc.

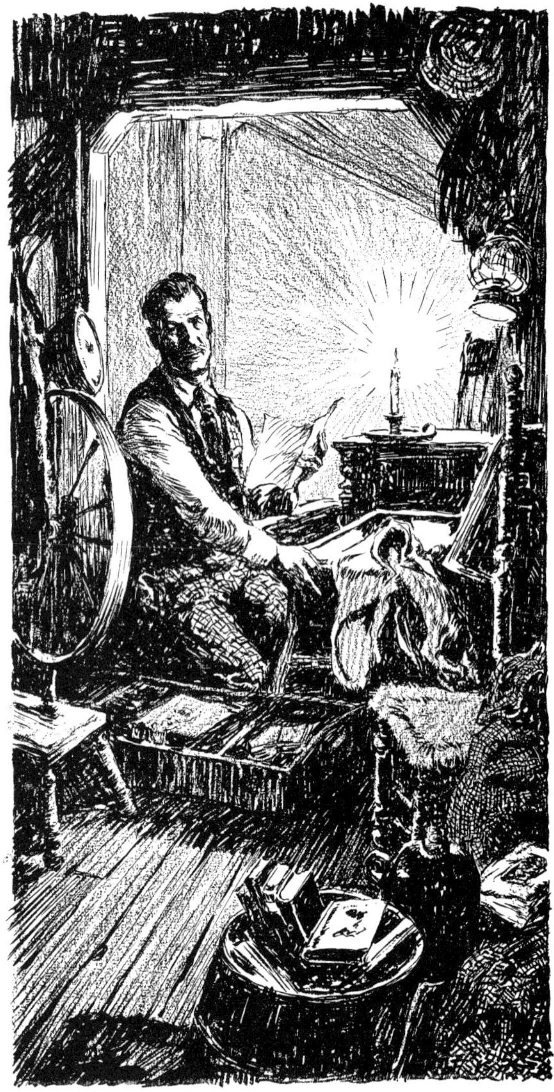

287   FARM & FIRESIDE—*Bob Williams*
Loaned by the Crowell Publishing Company
Exhibited by J. Walter Thompson Co.

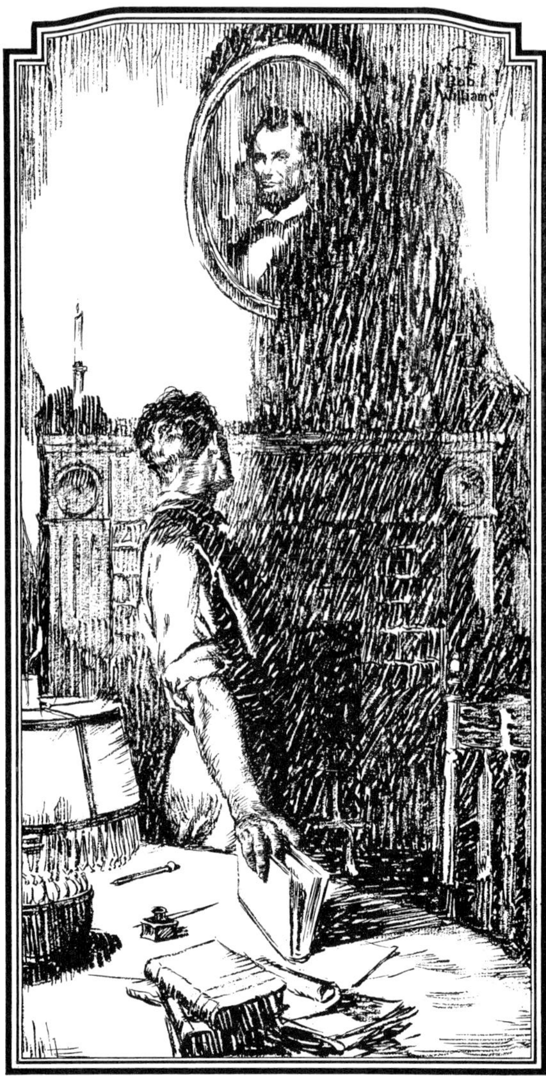

288   FARM & FIRESIDE—*Bob Williams*
Loaned by the Crowell Publishing Company
Exhibited by J. Walter Thompson Co.

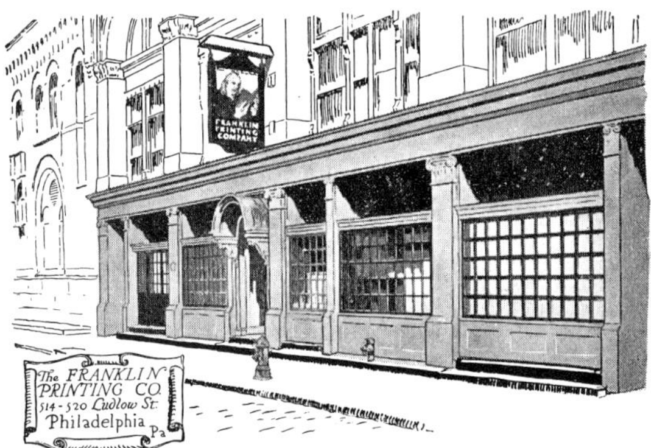

289   SHOP FRONT—*Edward Penfield*
Loaned and exhibited by the Franklin Printing Company

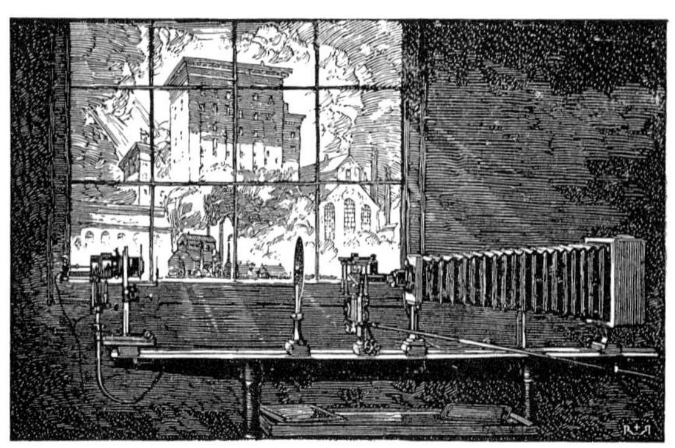

290   OPTICAL LENSES—*Guido & Lawrence Rosa*
Loaned by the Bausch and Lomb Optical Co.
Exhibited by Frank Seaman, Inc.

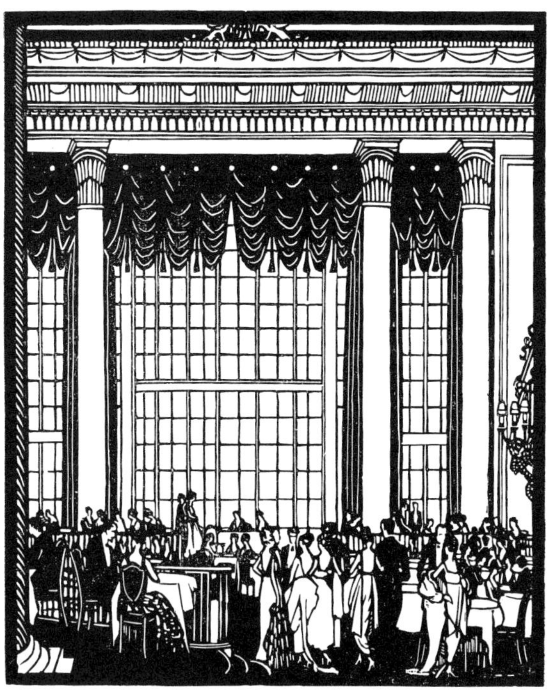

291 RITZ-CARLTON HOTEL—*John J. A. Murphy*
Loaned by the Ritz-Carlton Hotel
Exhibited by The Irving Press

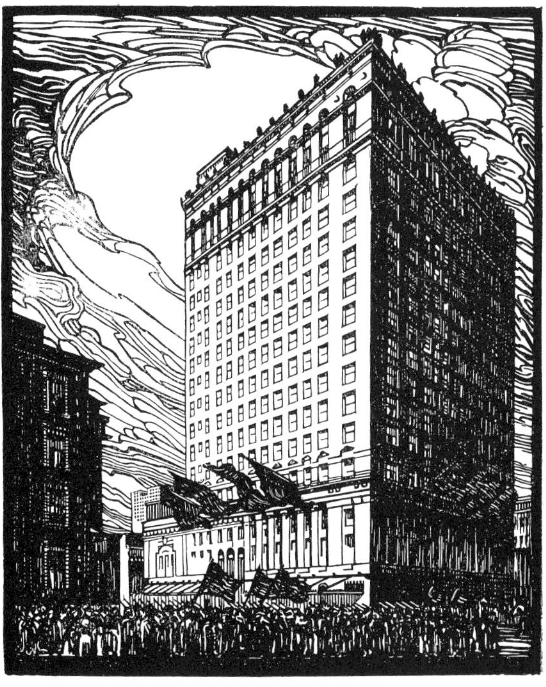

292 RITZ-CARLTON HOTEL—*John J. A. Murphy*
Loaned by the Ritz-Carlton Hotel
Exhibited by The Irving Press

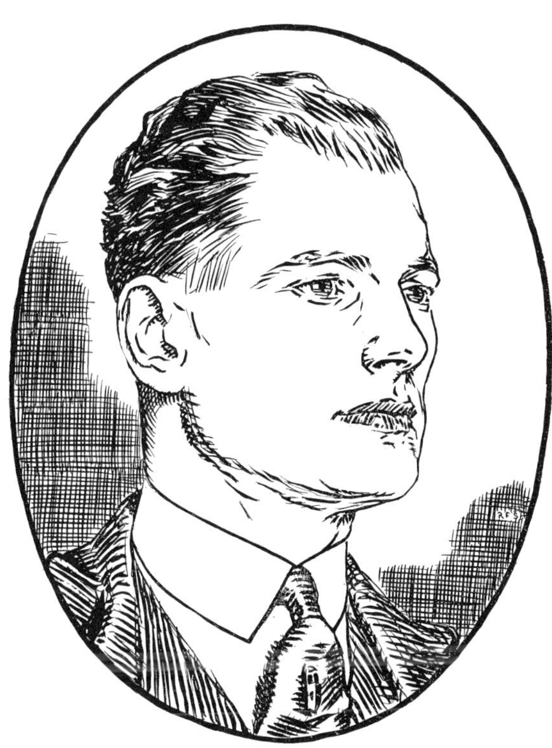

293 E. & W. COLLARS—*R. F. Schabelitz*
Loaned by Earl & Wilson, Inc.
Exhibited by Barton, Durstine & Osborn, Inc.

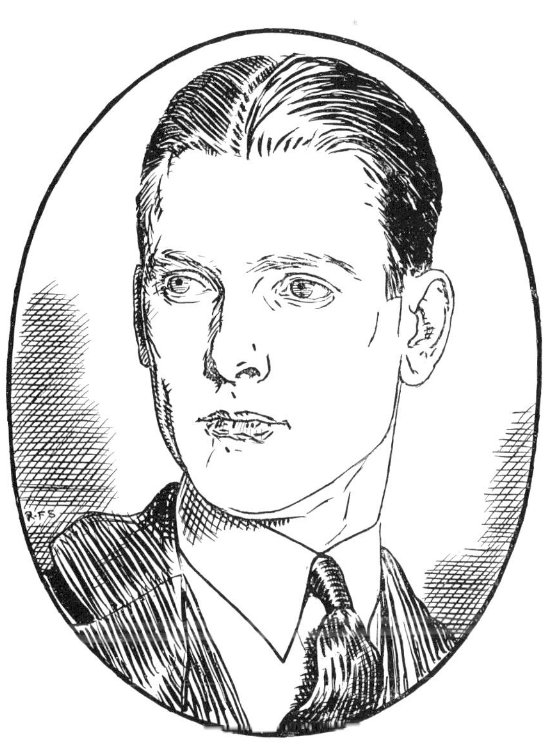

294 E. & W. COLLARS—*R. F. Schabelitz*
Loaned by Earl & Wilson, Inc.
Exhibited by Barton, Durstine & Osborn, Inc.

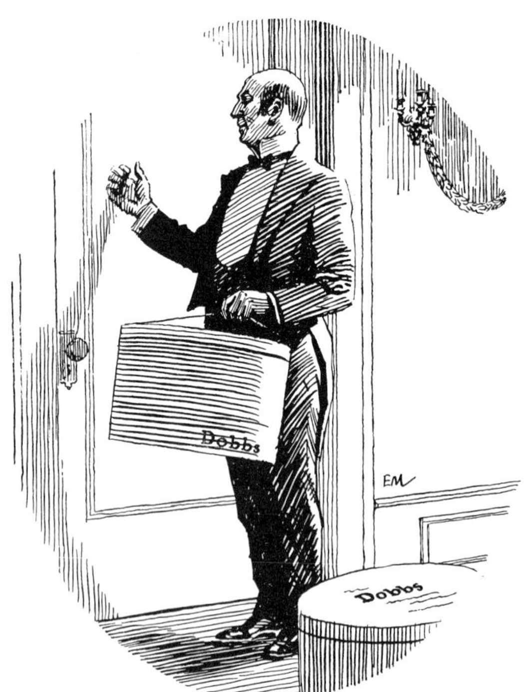

295 WOMEN'S HATS—*Edward Monks*
Loaned by Dobbs & Co.
Exhibited by Dobbs & Co.

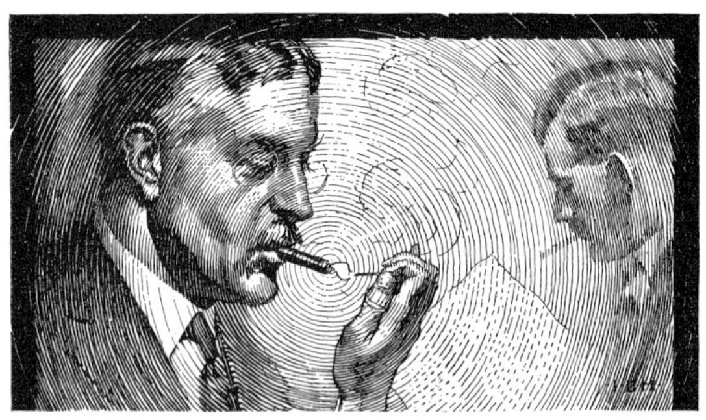

297 BLACKSTONE CIGARS—*I. B. Hazelton*
Loaned by Waite & Bond
Exhibited by George Batten Co., Inc.

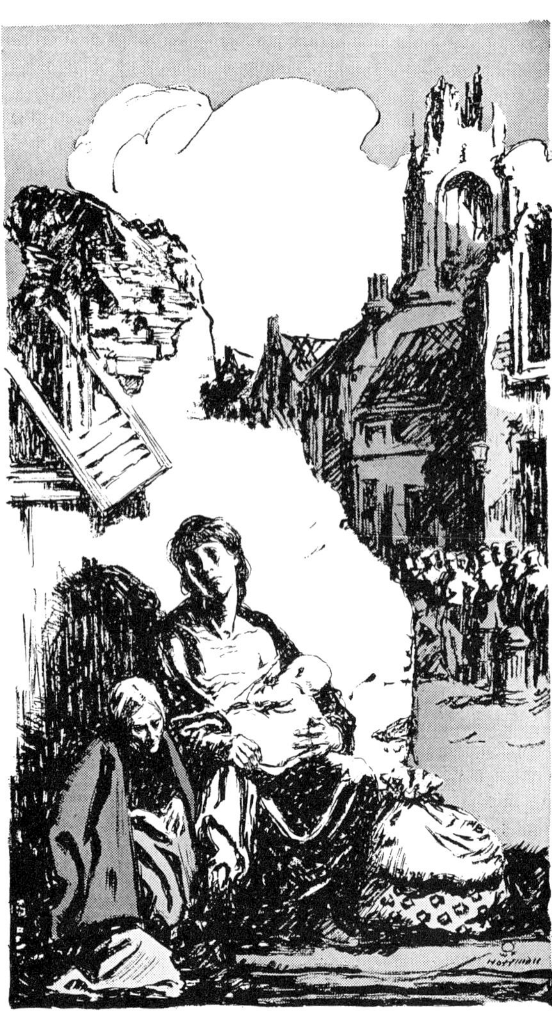

296 FARM & FIRESIDE—*Frank B. Hoffman*
Loaned by the Crowell Publishing Company
Exhibited by J. Walter Thompson Co.

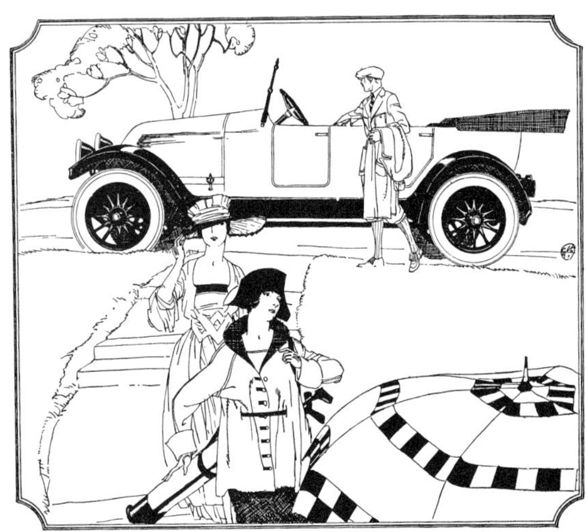

298 FRANKLIN MOTOR CARS—*F. T. Chapman*
Loaned by the Franklin Automobile Company
Exhibited by Patterson-Andress Co., Inc.

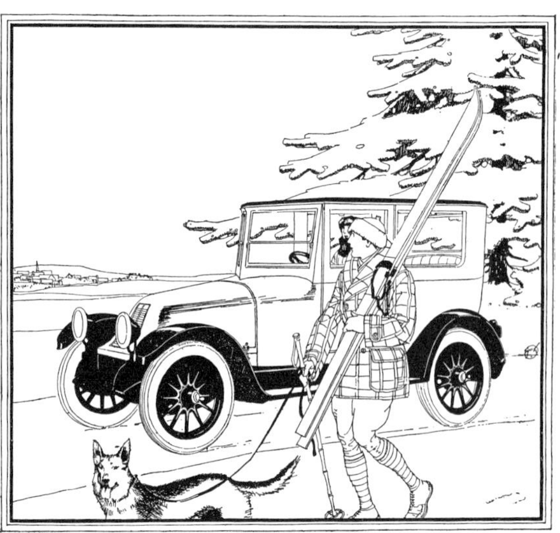

299 FRANKLIN MOTOR CARS—*F. T. Chapman*
Loaned by the Franklin Automobile Company
Exhibited by Patterson-Andress Co., Inc.

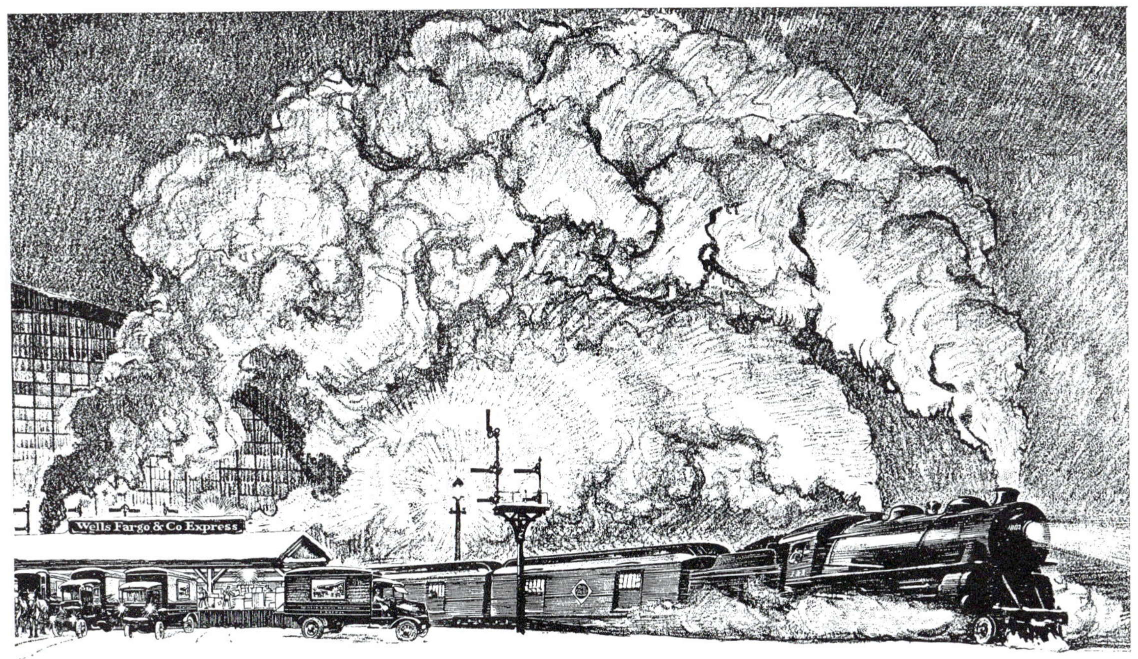

300 WELLS FARGO EXPRESS—*F. B. Masters*
Loaned and exhibited by Wells Fargo & Co.

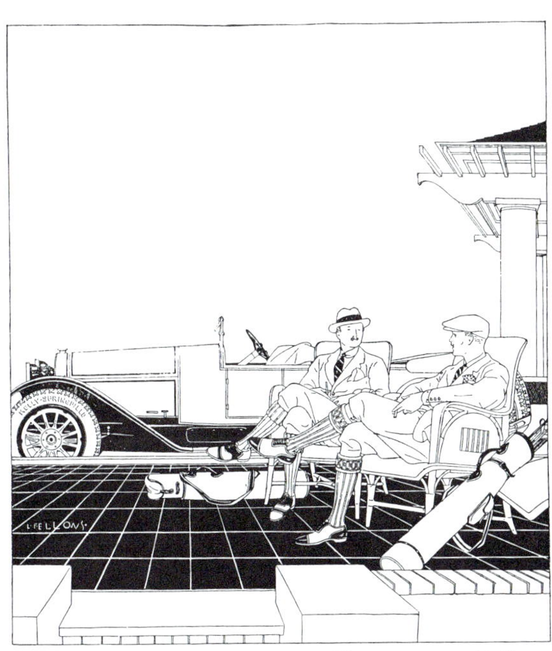

301 KELLY-SPRINGFIELD TIRES—*L. Fellows*
Loaned and exhibited by the Kelly-Springfield Tire Co.

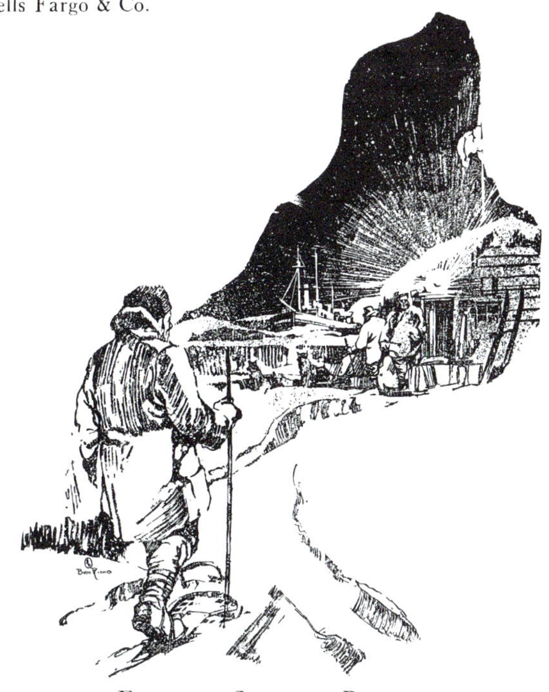

302 ELECTRIC STORAGE BATTERIES
Thomas D. Ben Rimo
Loaned by the Electric Storage Battery Co.
Exhibited by George Batten Co., Inc.

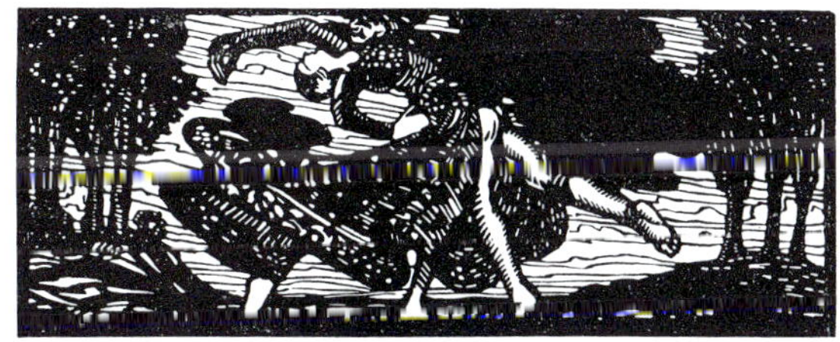

303 RITZ-CARLTON HOTEL—*John J. A. Murphy*
Loaned by the Ritz-Carlton Hotel
Exhibited by The Irving Press

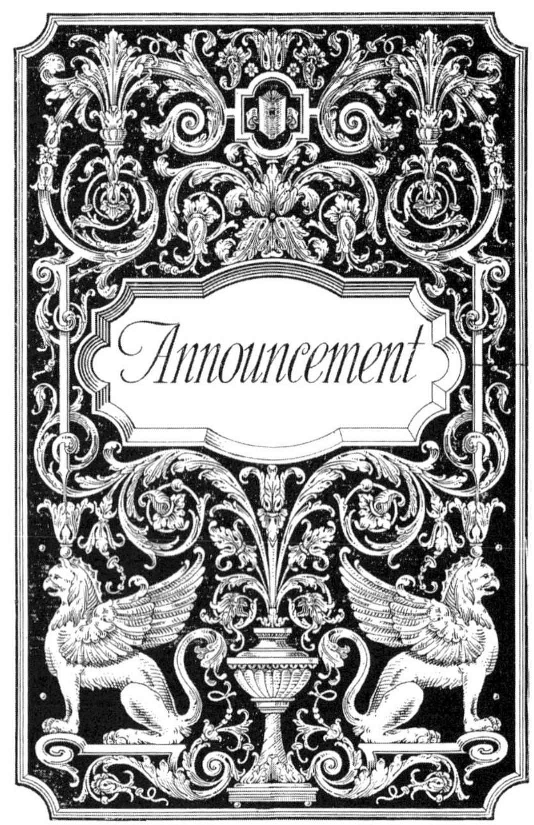

304 BOOK COVER

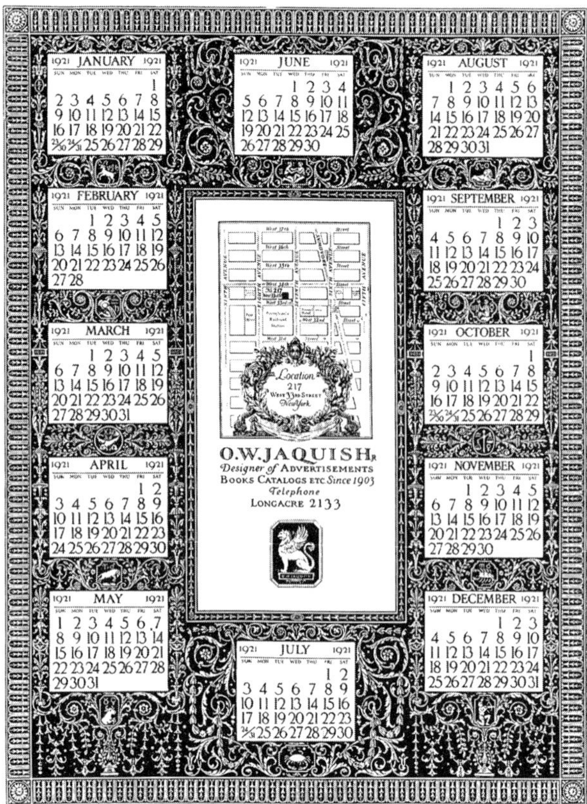

305 CALENDAR

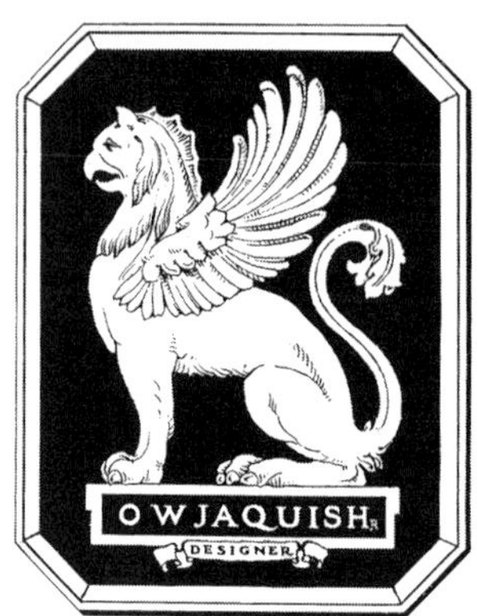

306 SEAL

Designs by O. W. Jaquish, Jr.
Loaned by O. W. Jaquish, Jr.

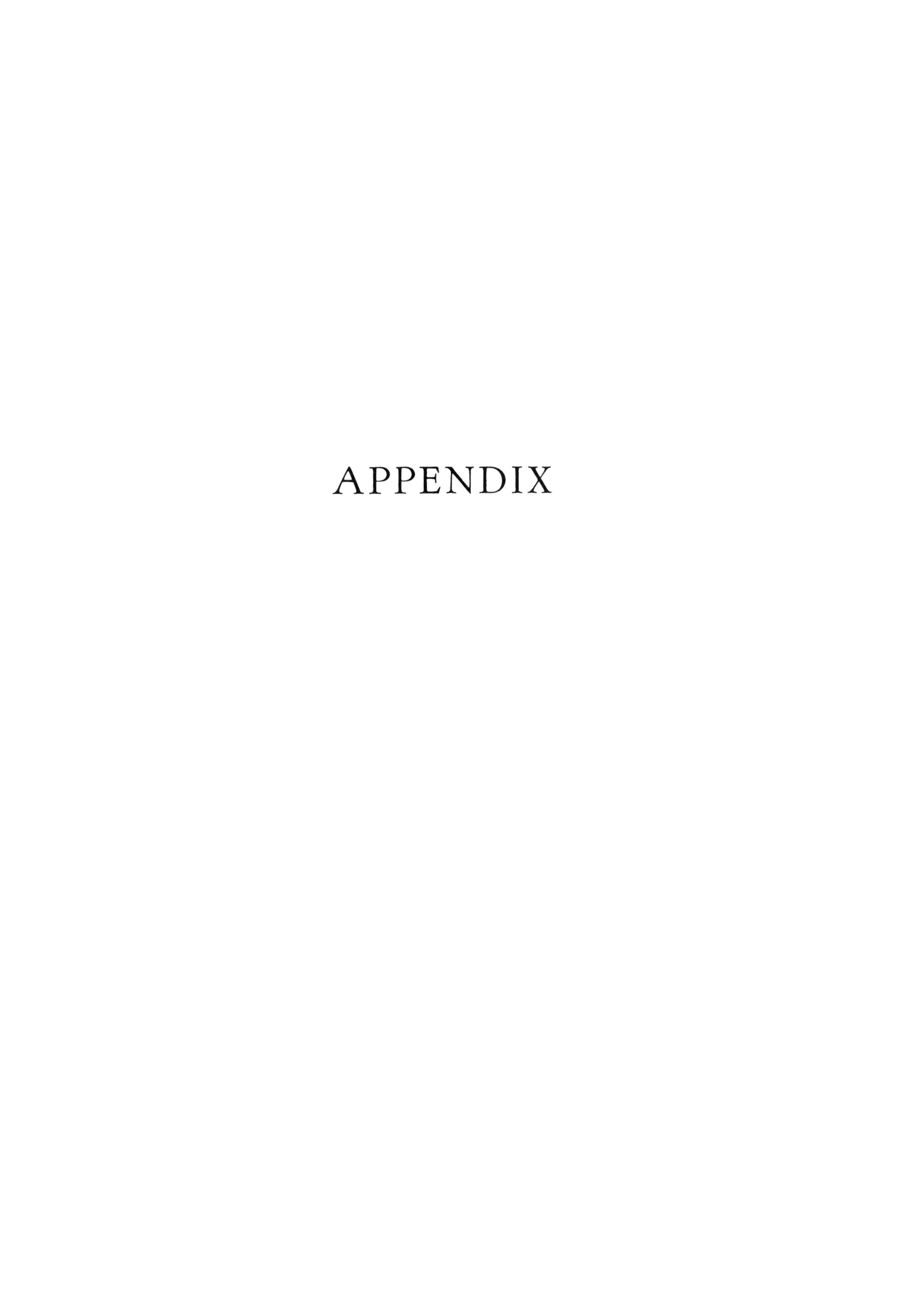

APPENDIX

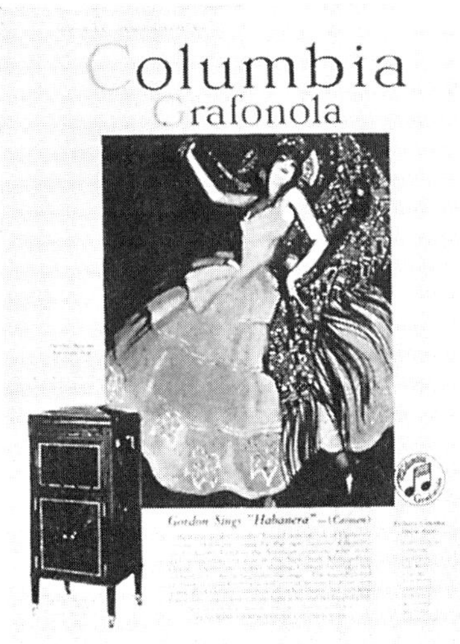

A

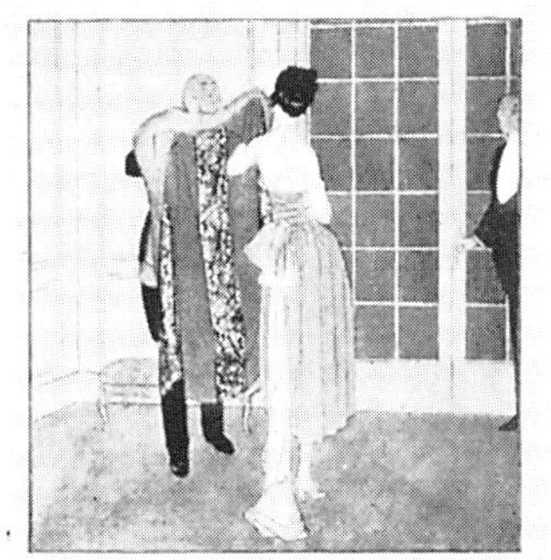

2

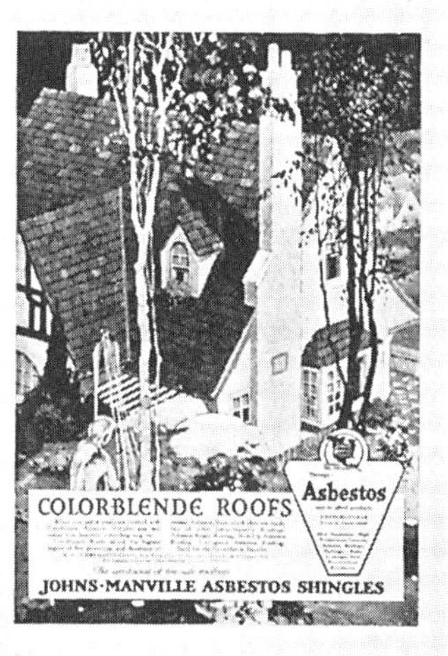

9

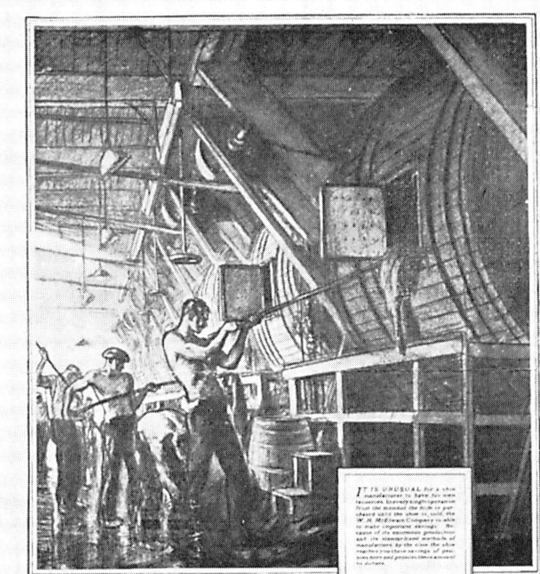

Mc Elwain tanneries make your McElwain shoes cost less

WHY should you be interested in the fact that the McElwain Company—unlike most shoe manufacturers—owns and operates its own tanneries?

Because these tanneries are one added reason why McElwain Shoes come to you at a substantial saving in price.

Just as McElwain men in the hide markets of three continents are able to buy the best at the lowest cost; just as a little saving is made in the manufacture of each separate part of the shoe; so the tanneries, also, have their part in giving you—dollar for dollar—the utmost in beauty and in value and wear.

THIRTY-FIVE thousand pairs of shoes a day are required to meet the demand of American men and boys for the McElwain product. And the demand grows greater year by year as more and more men form the money-saving habit of turning over the shoe before they buy to find the McElwain mark on the sole.

You can buy McElwain Shoes at the stores of 25,000 leading independent shoe merchants throughout the country.

Send to us for the booklet, "How to Make Your Shoes Last." It will help you to make a definite reduction in your shoe bills, and it is free. A card will bring it to you.

W. H. McElwain Company
354 Congress St., Boston 3, Mass.
MEN'S AND BOYS' SHOES FOR DRESS AND EVERY-DAY WEAR

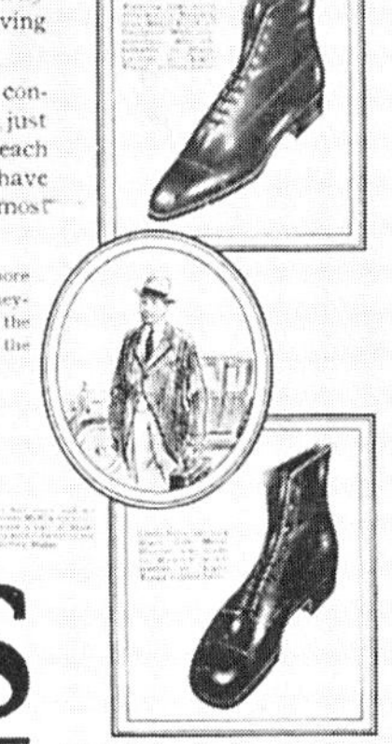

3

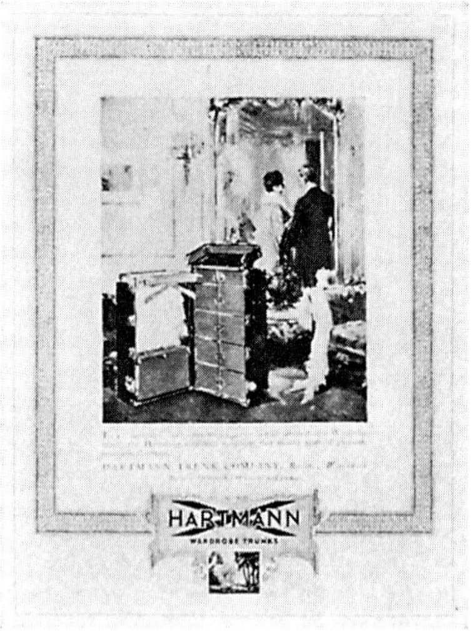

10

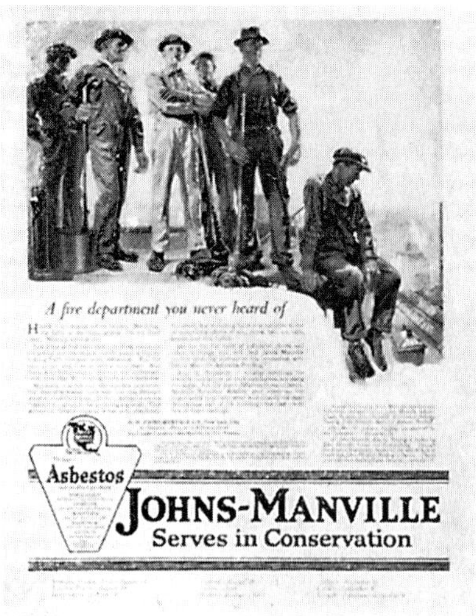

12

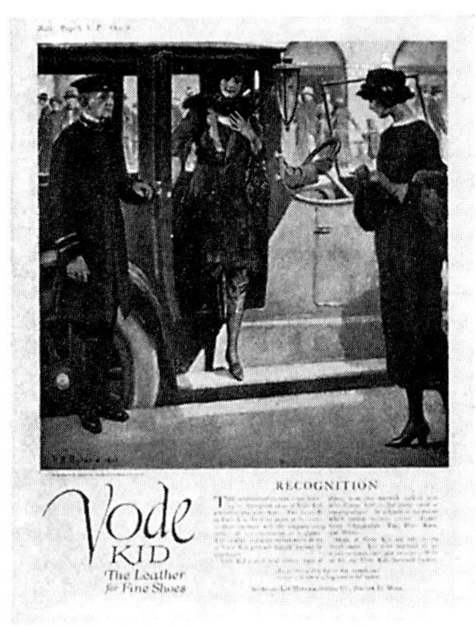

15

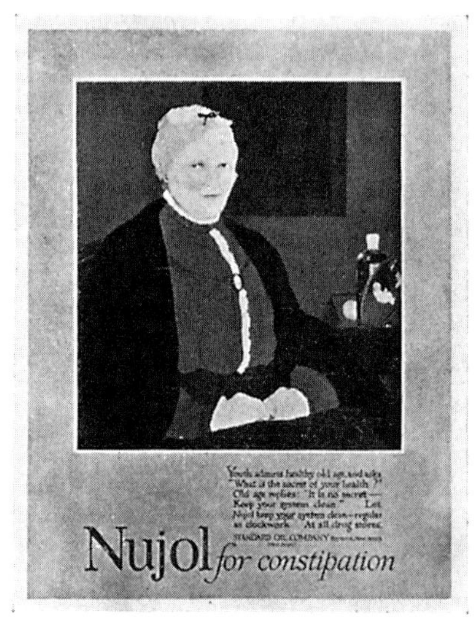

16

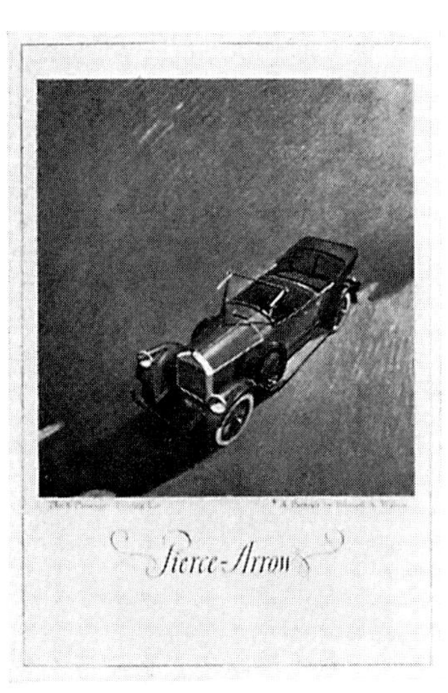

18

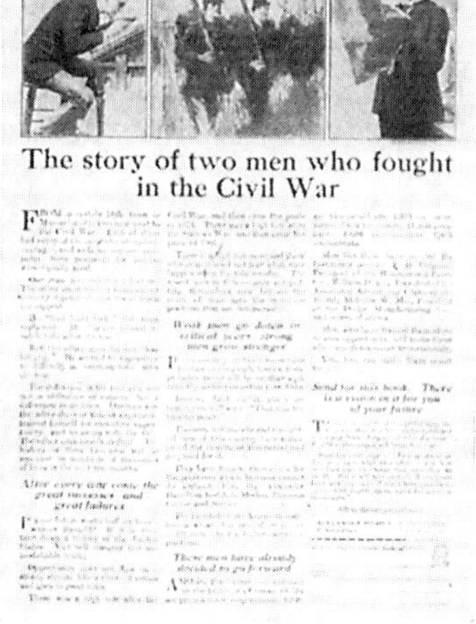

22

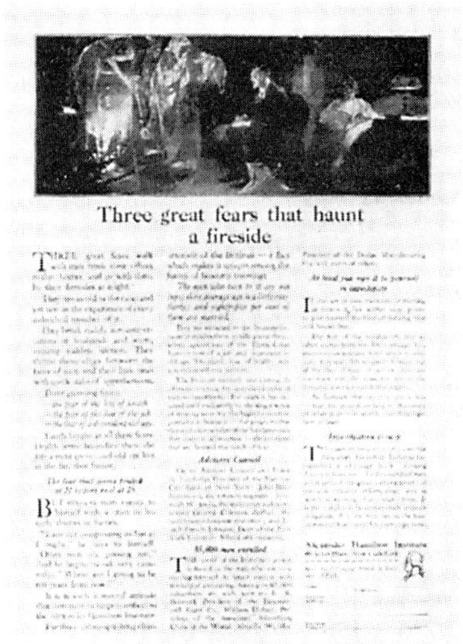

24

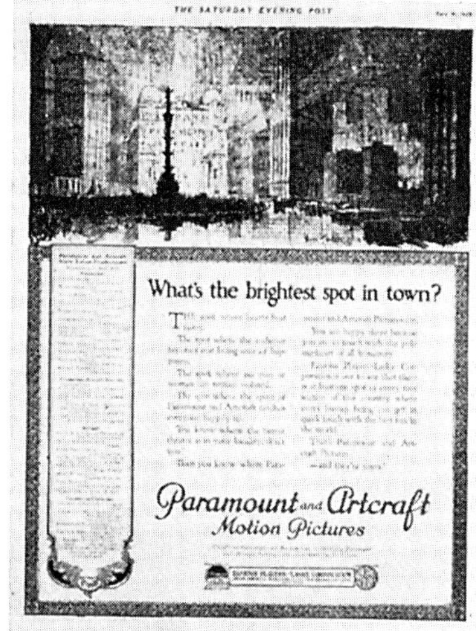

27

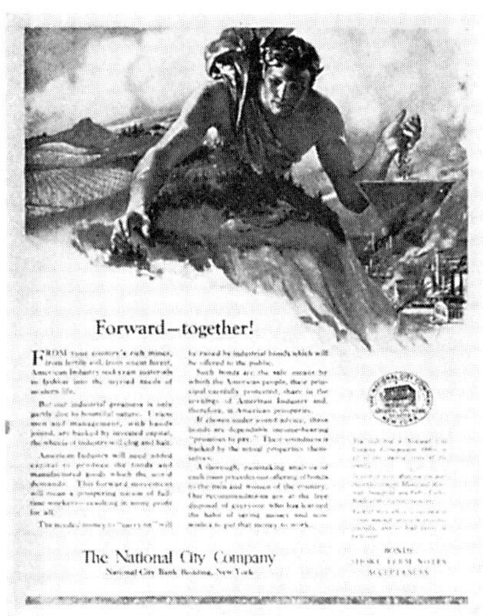

28

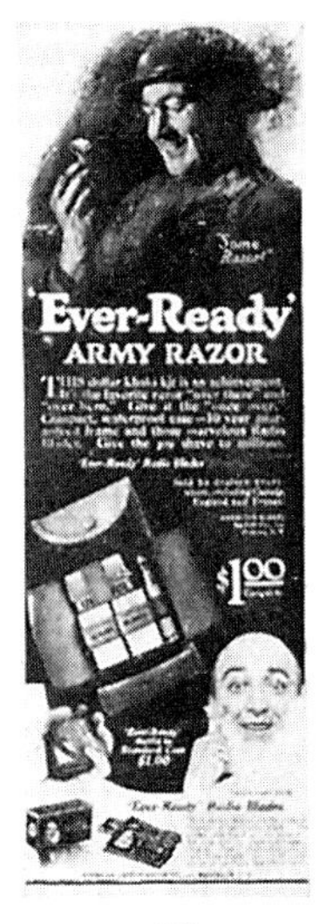

29

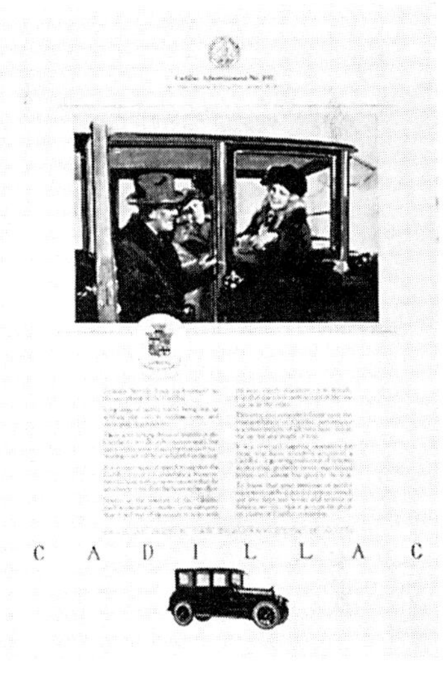

31

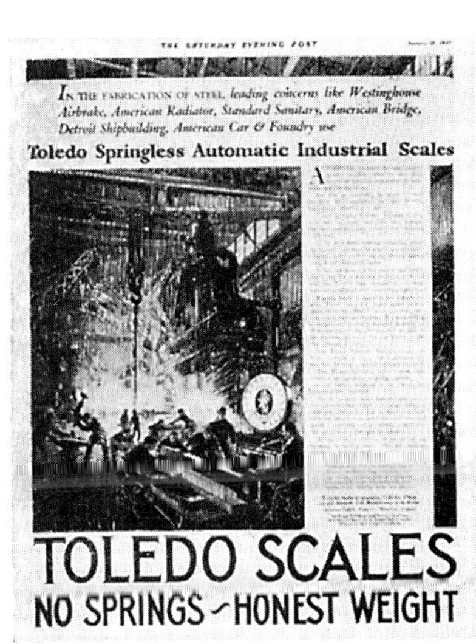

34

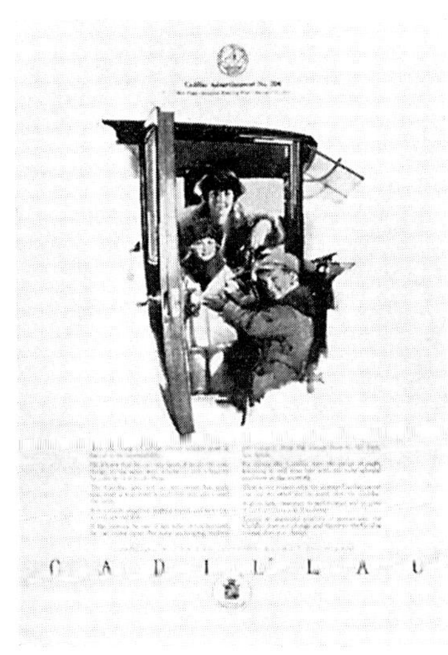

35

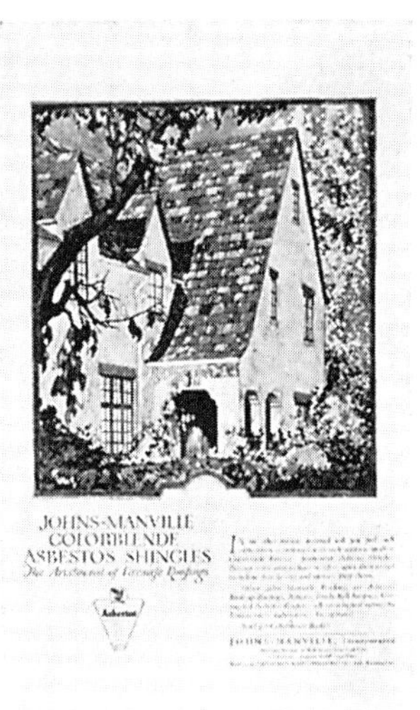

39

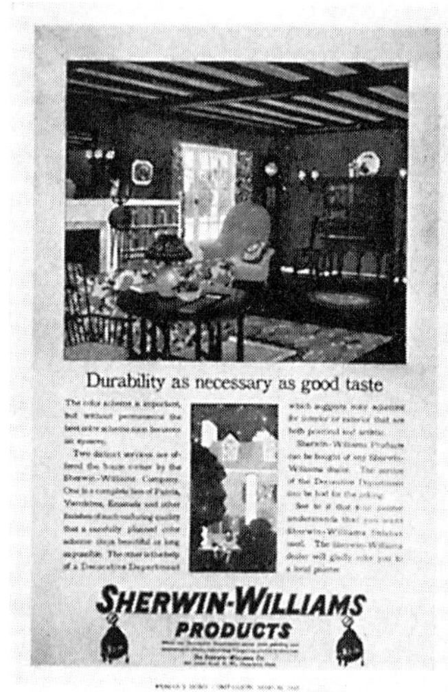

48

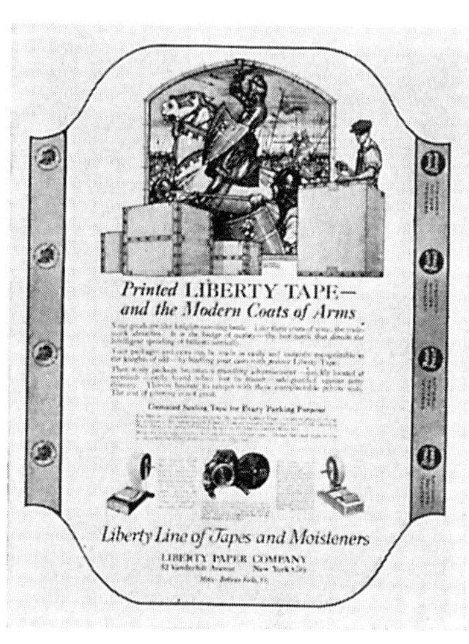

53

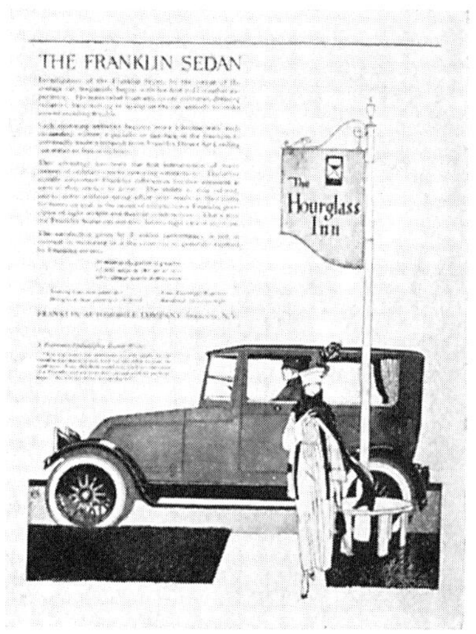

57

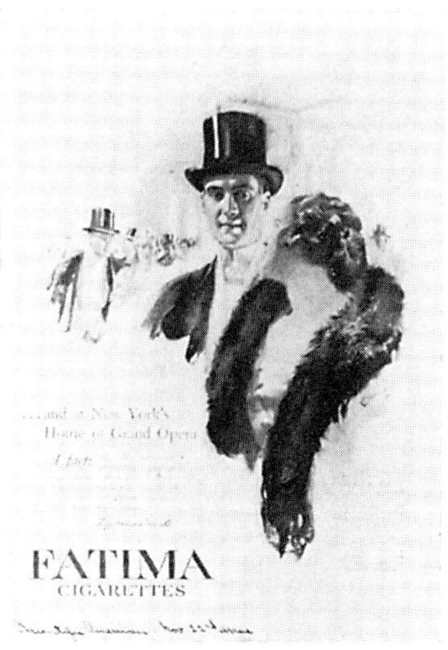

59

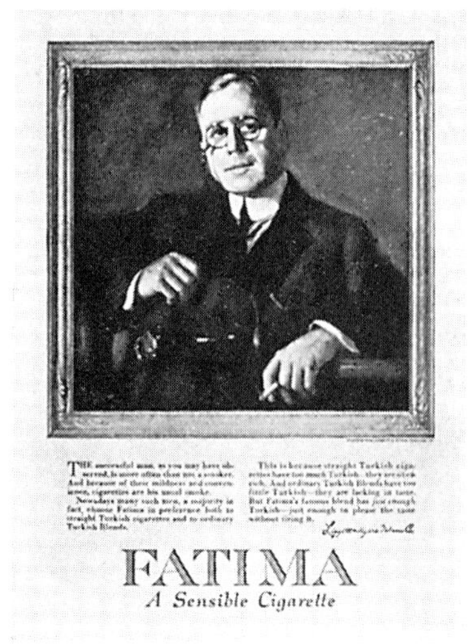

60

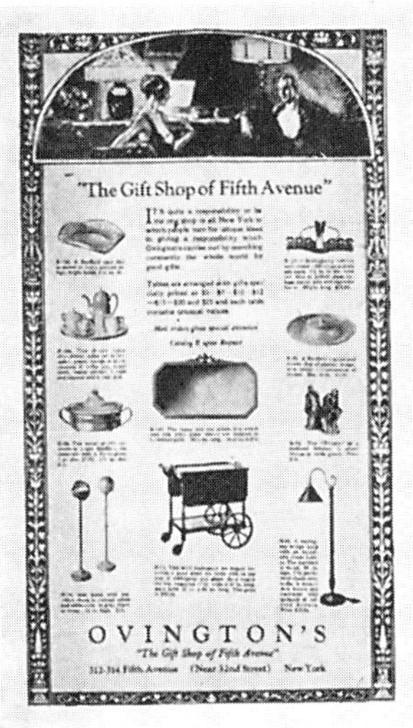

63

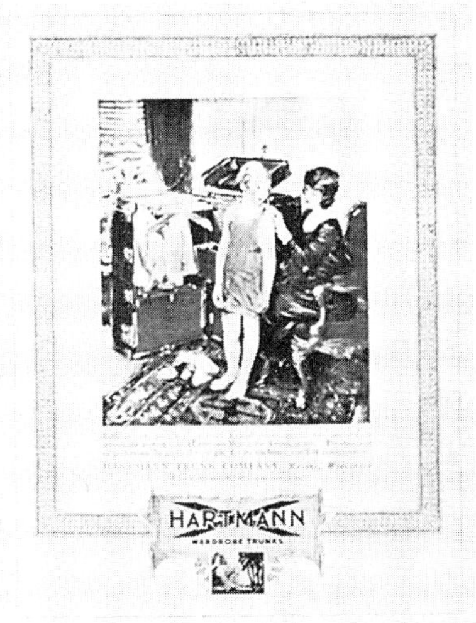

65

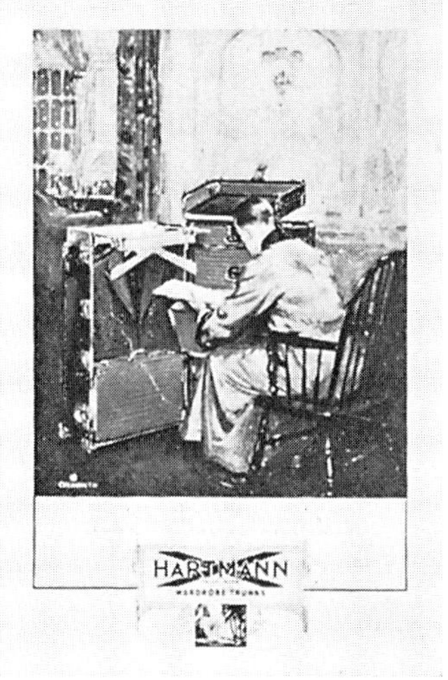

68

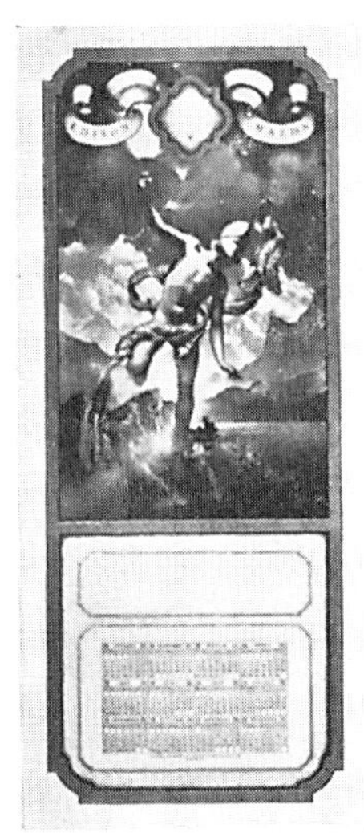

69

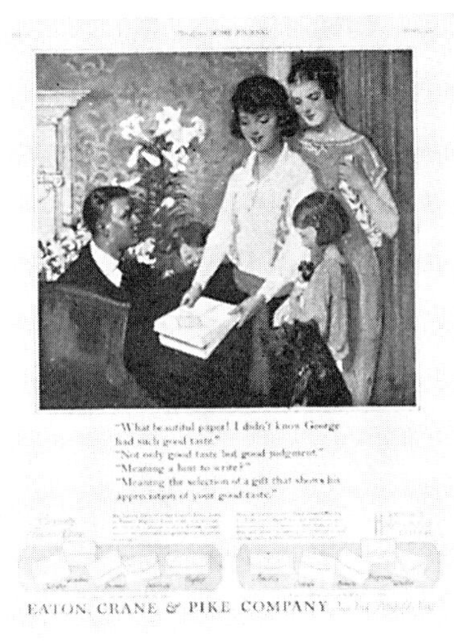

71

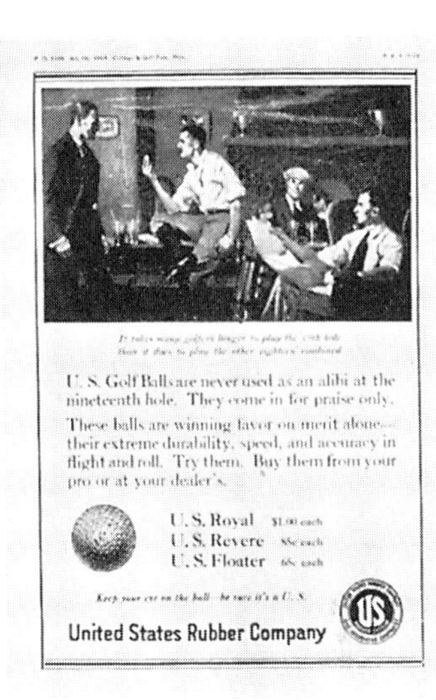

72

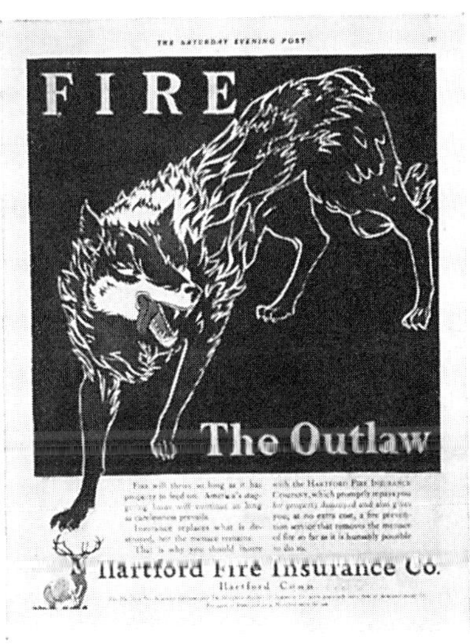

80

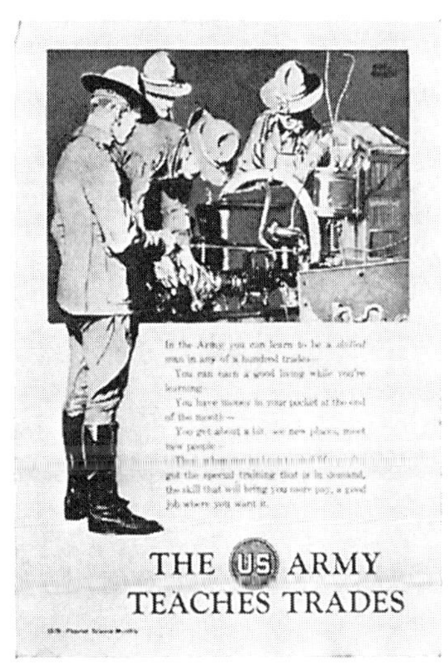

81

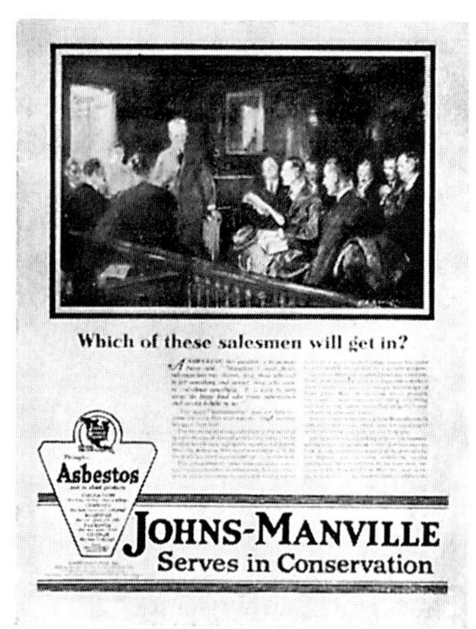

82

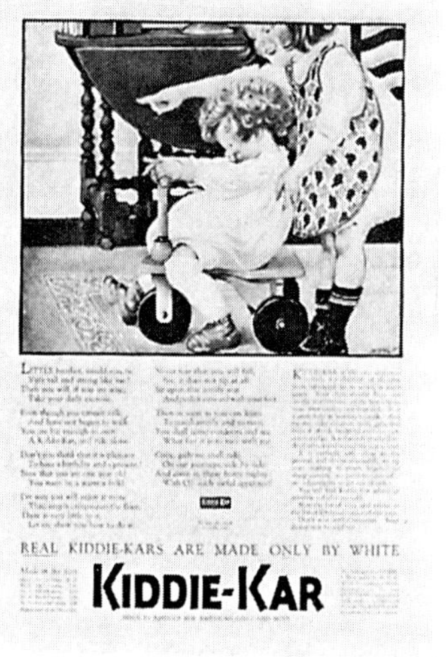

83

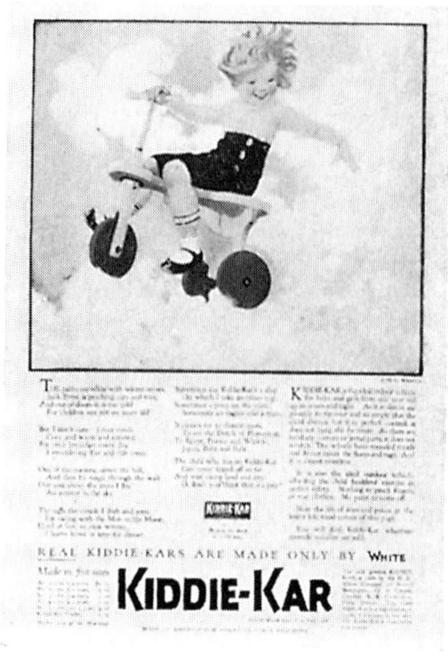

84

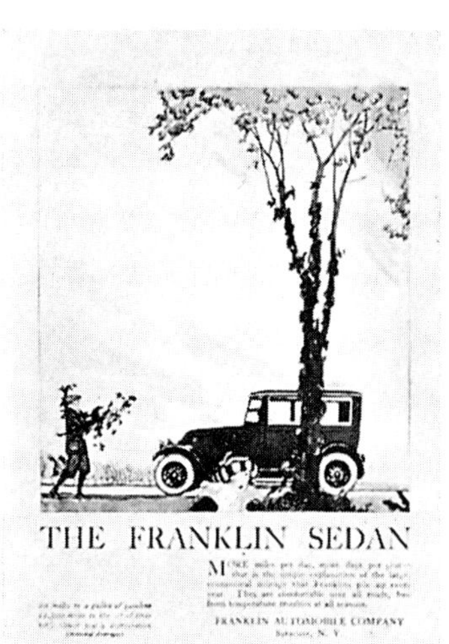

85

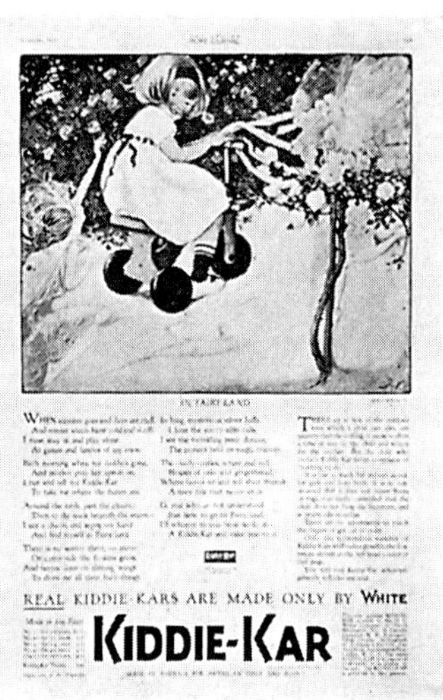

88

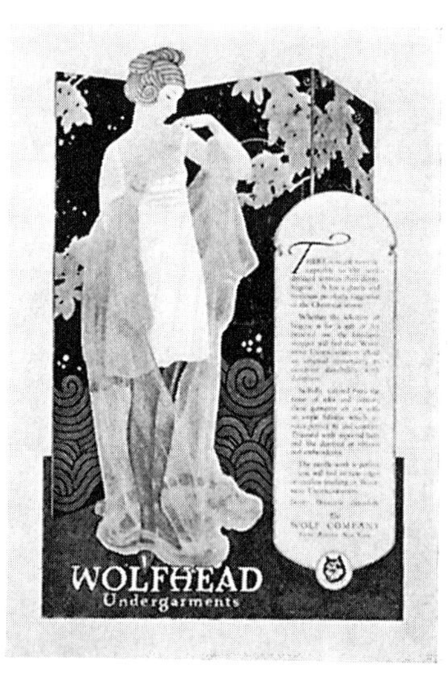

89

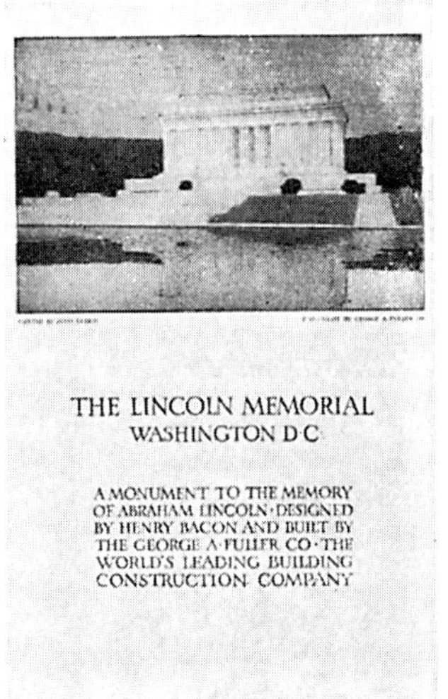

93

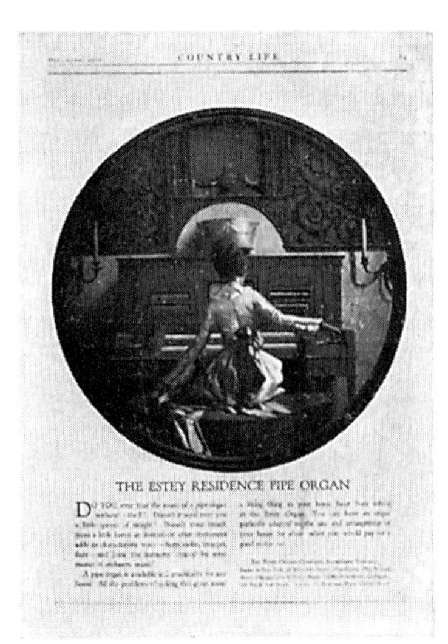

98

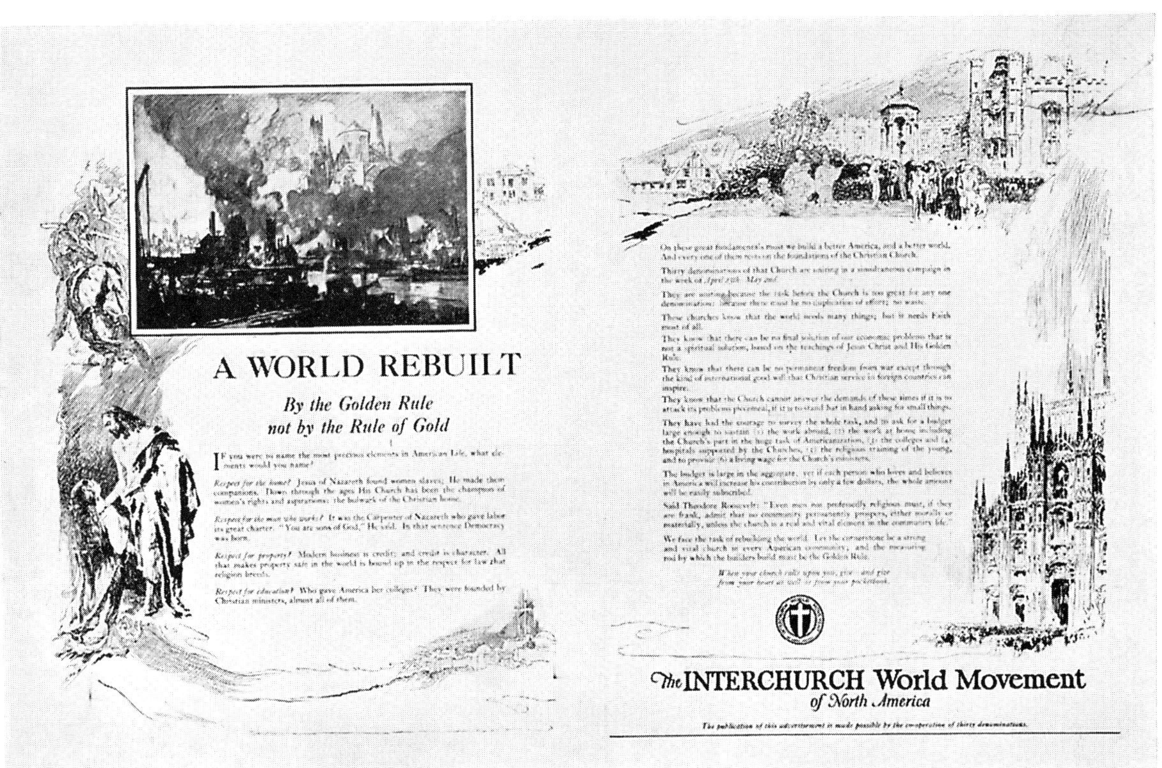

A WORLD REBUILT
By the Golden Rule
not by the Rule of Gold
The INTERCHURCH World Movement
of North America

The Finishing Touch
Vode
KID
The Leather
for Fine Shoes

105

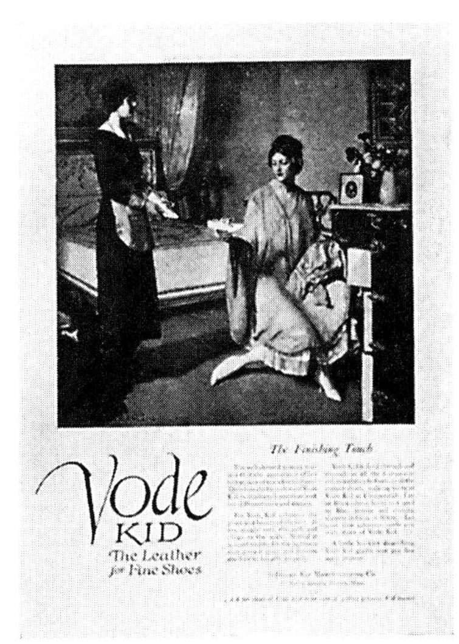

106

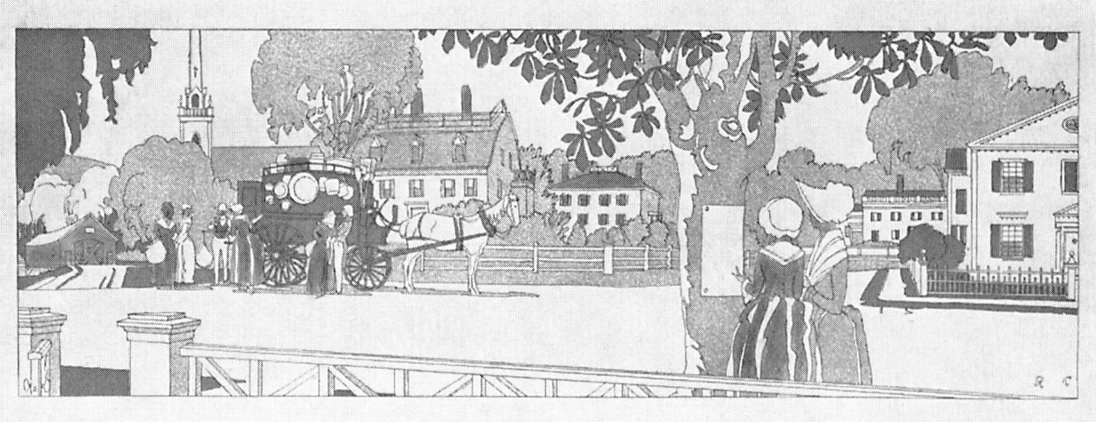

114

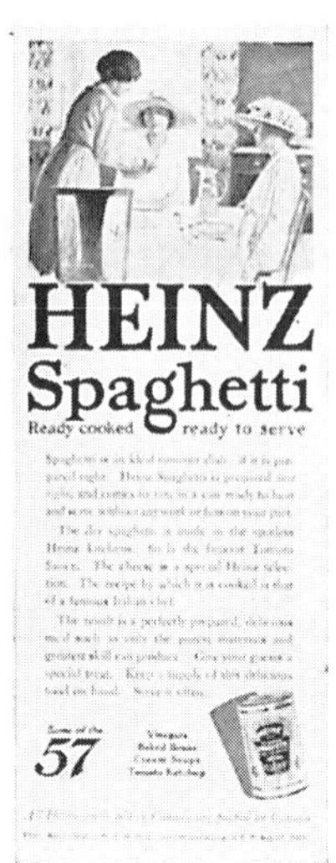

116

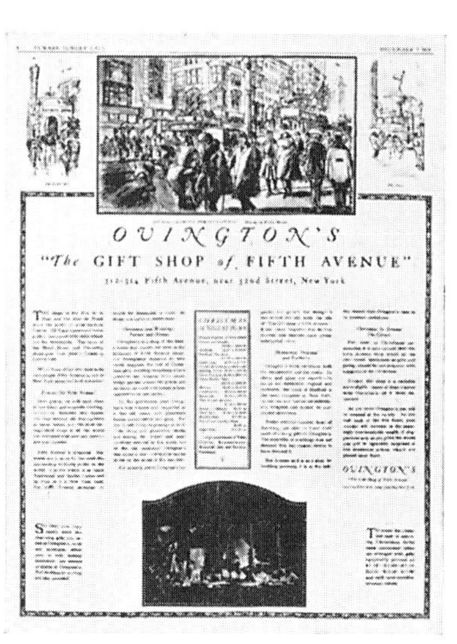

117

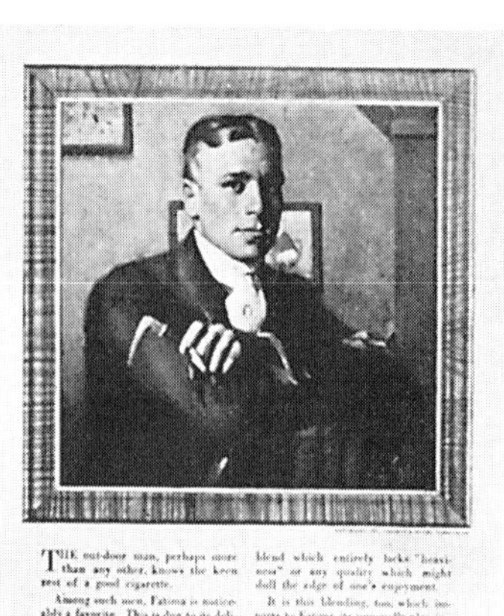

119

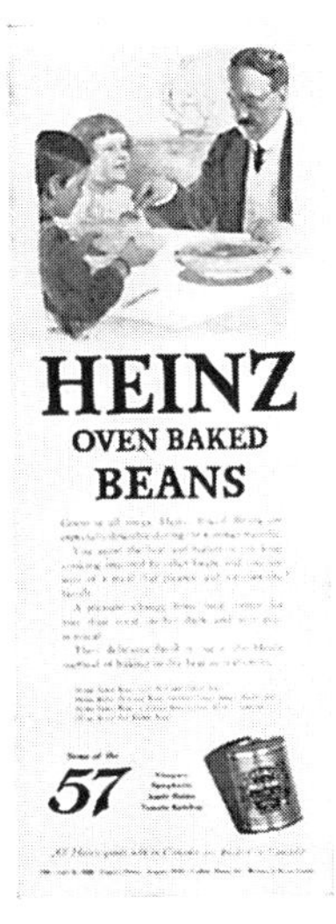

120

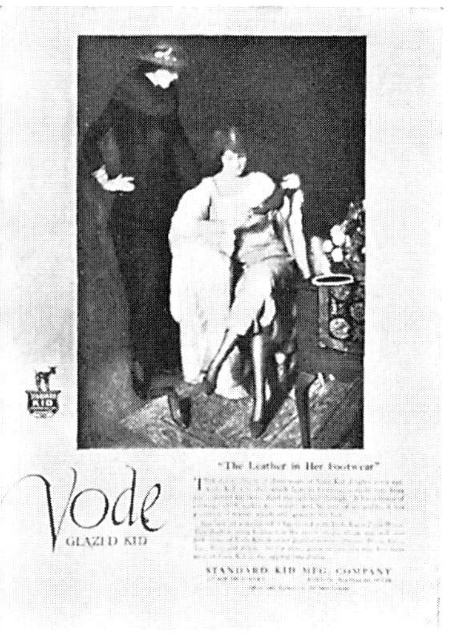

123

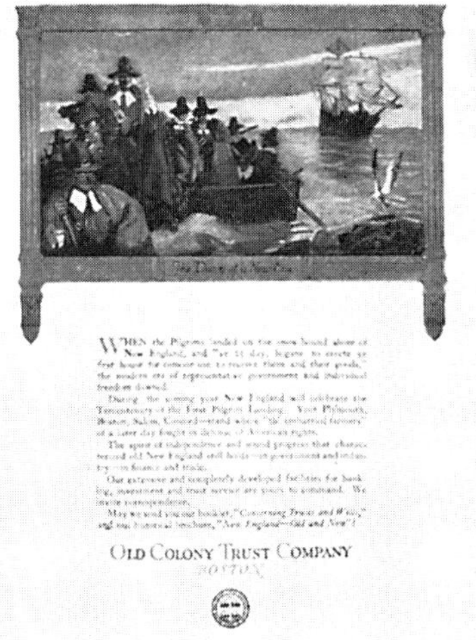

125

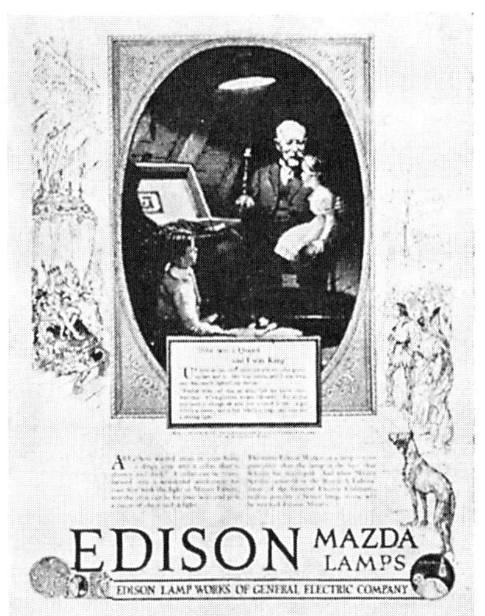

129

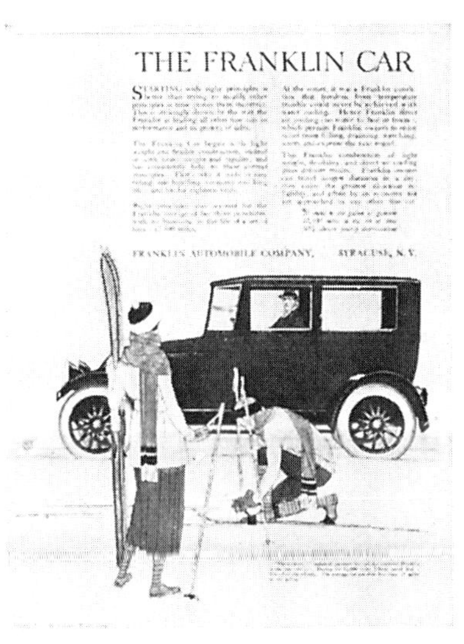

130

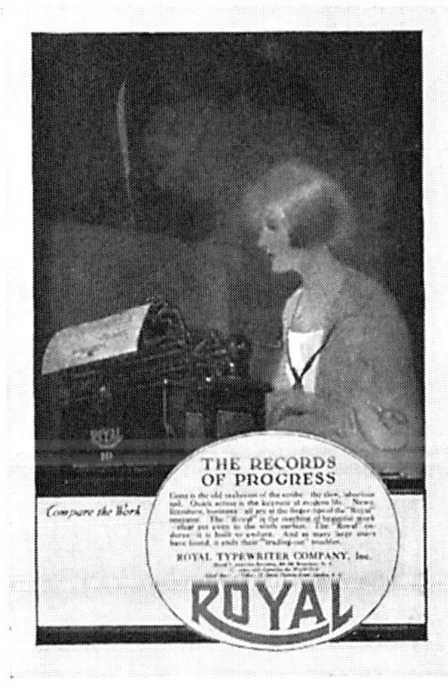

131

151

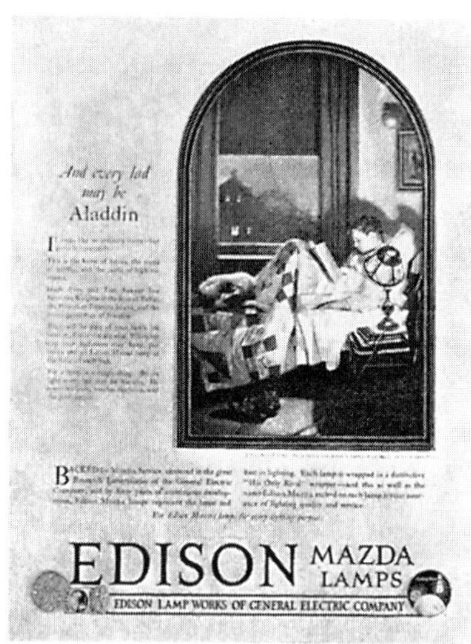

155

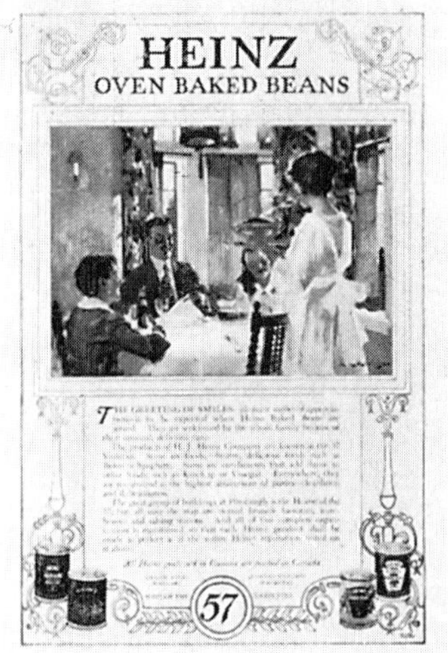

156

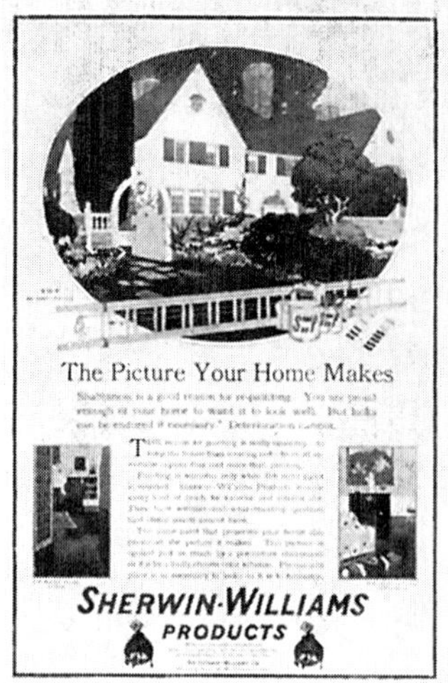

157

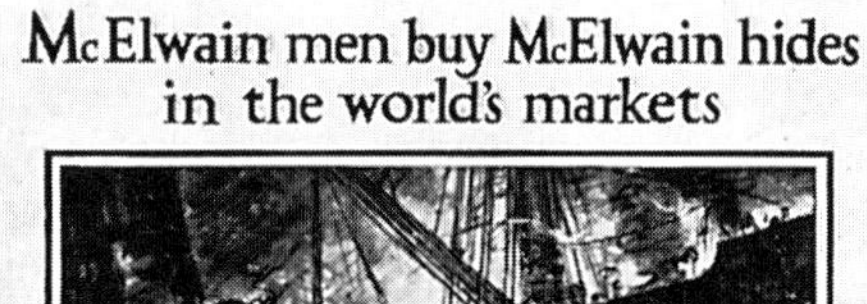
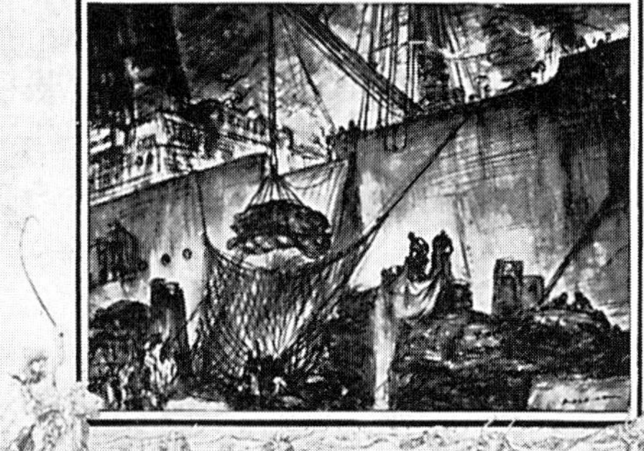

159

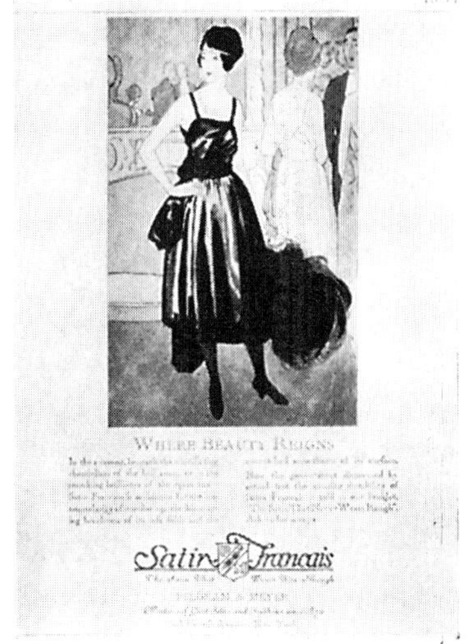

165

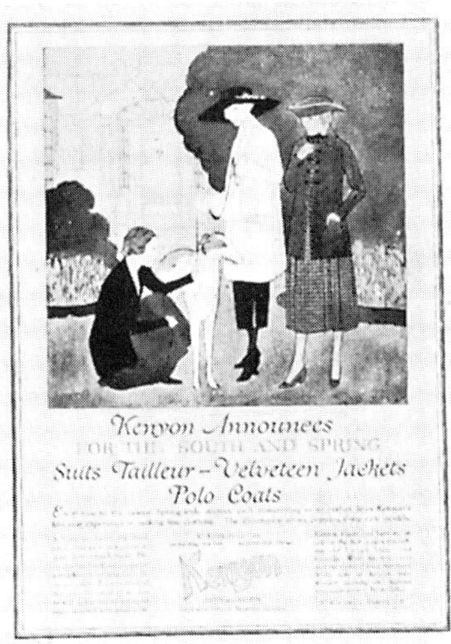

167

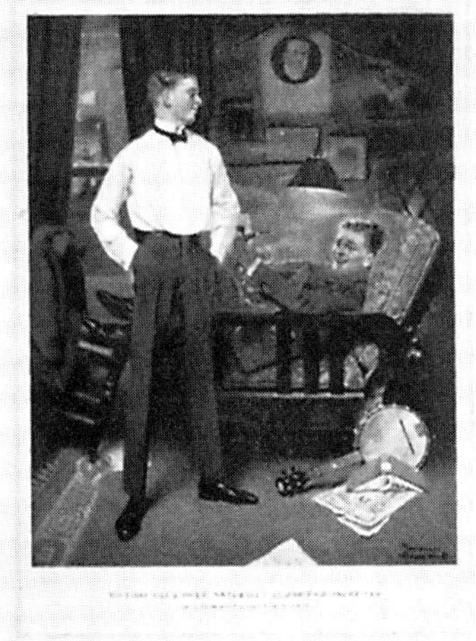

170

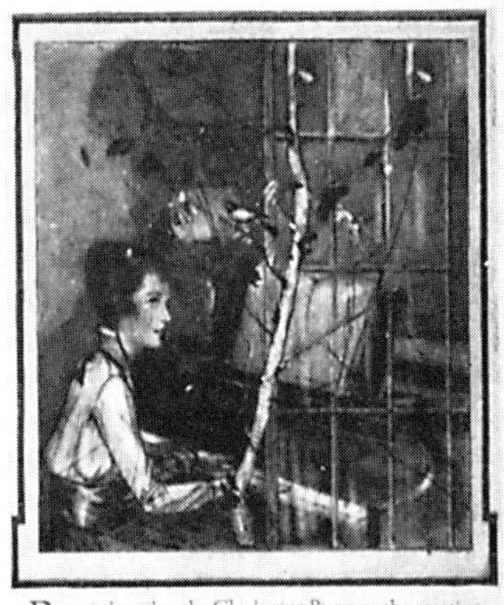

178

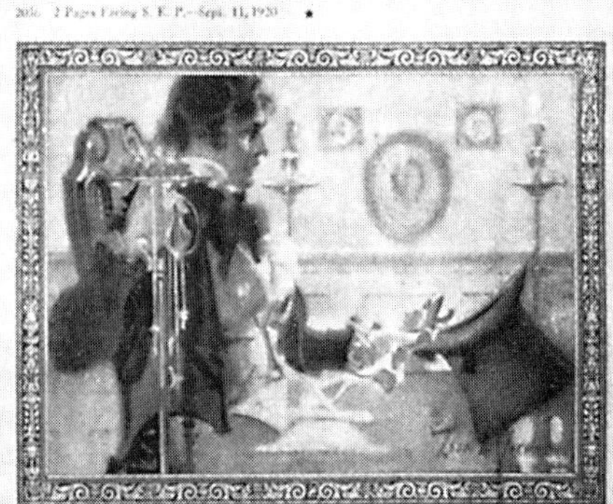

180

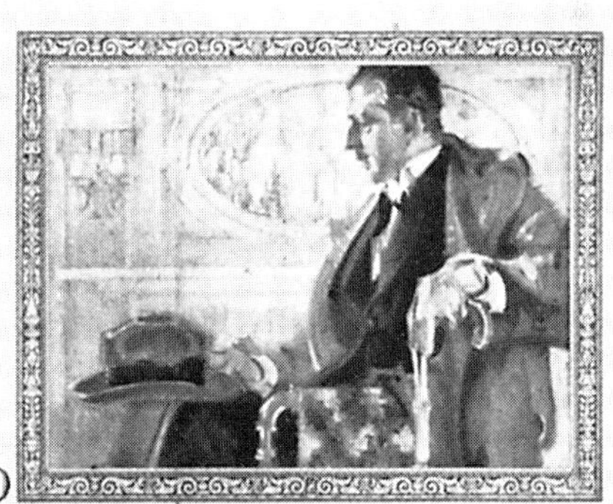

54

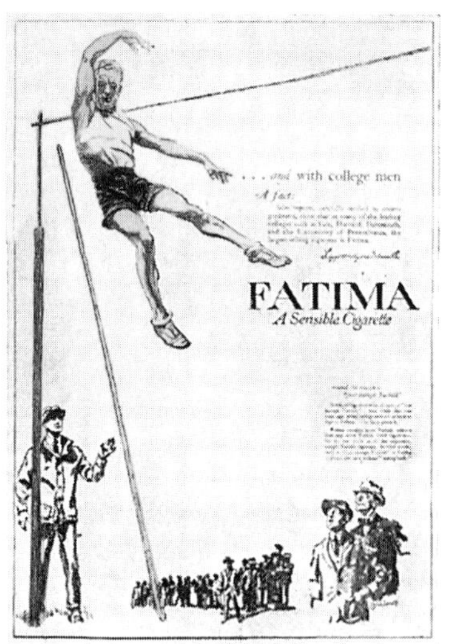

183

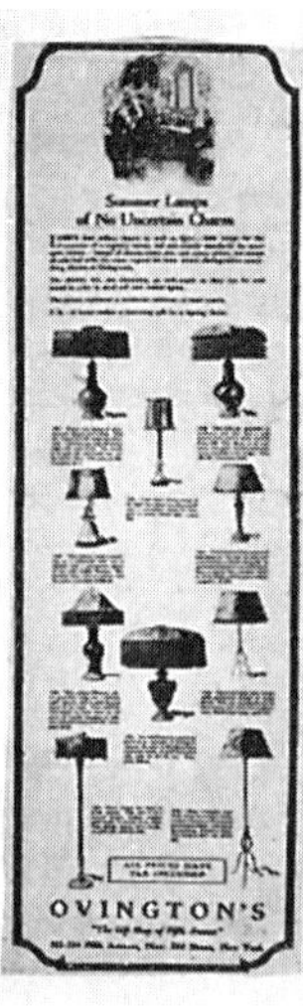

185

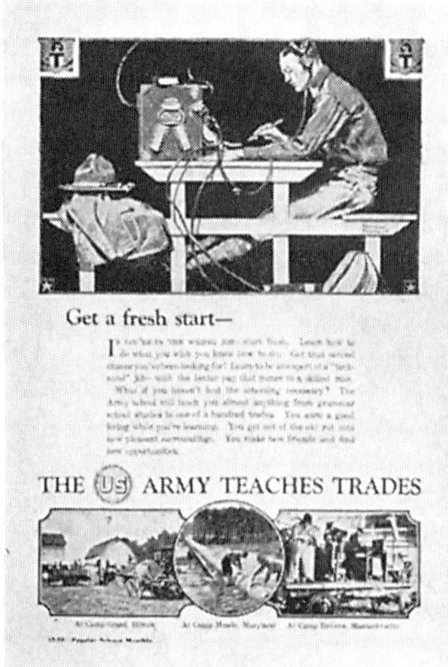

187

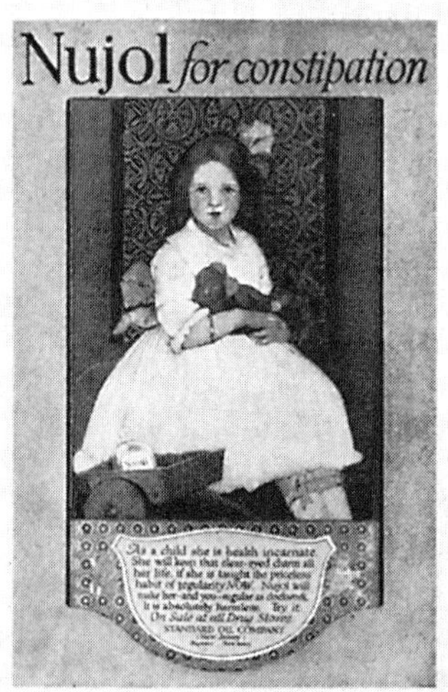

189

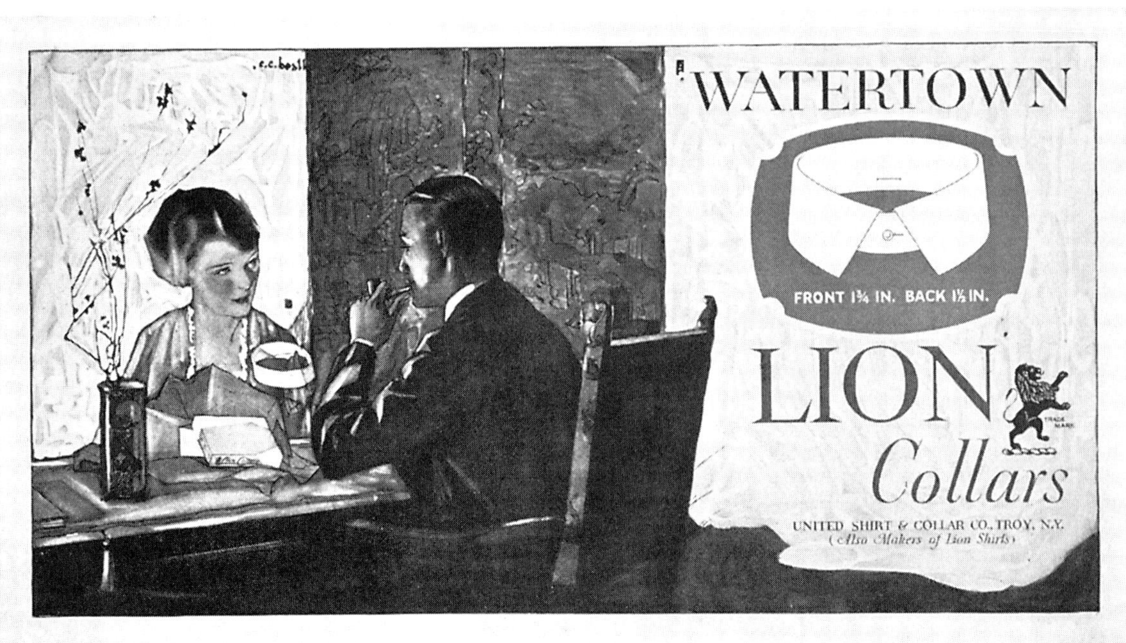

195

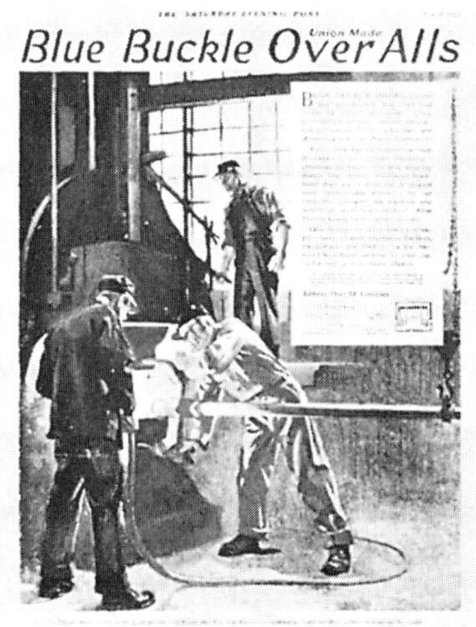

196

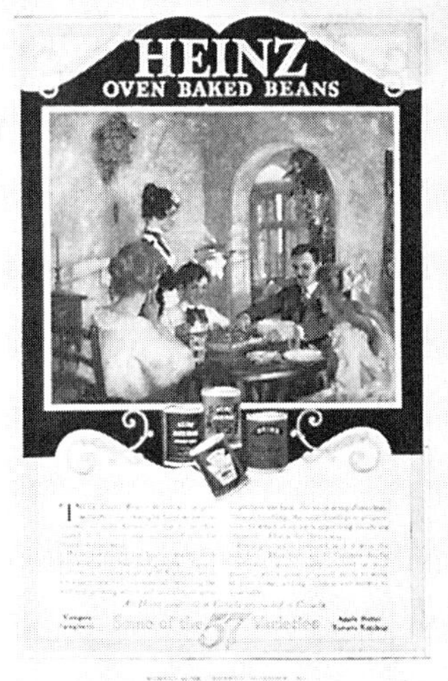

199

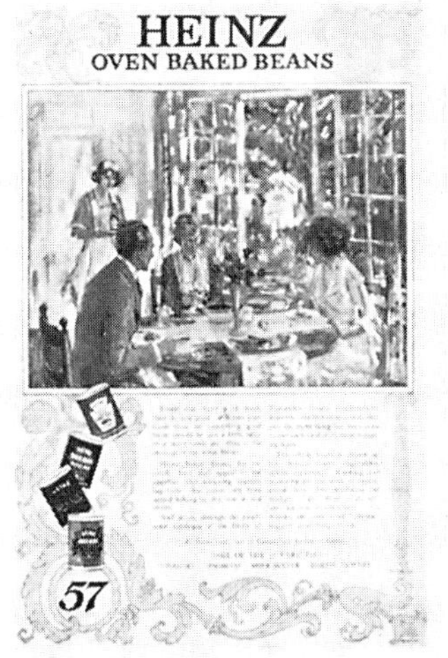

200

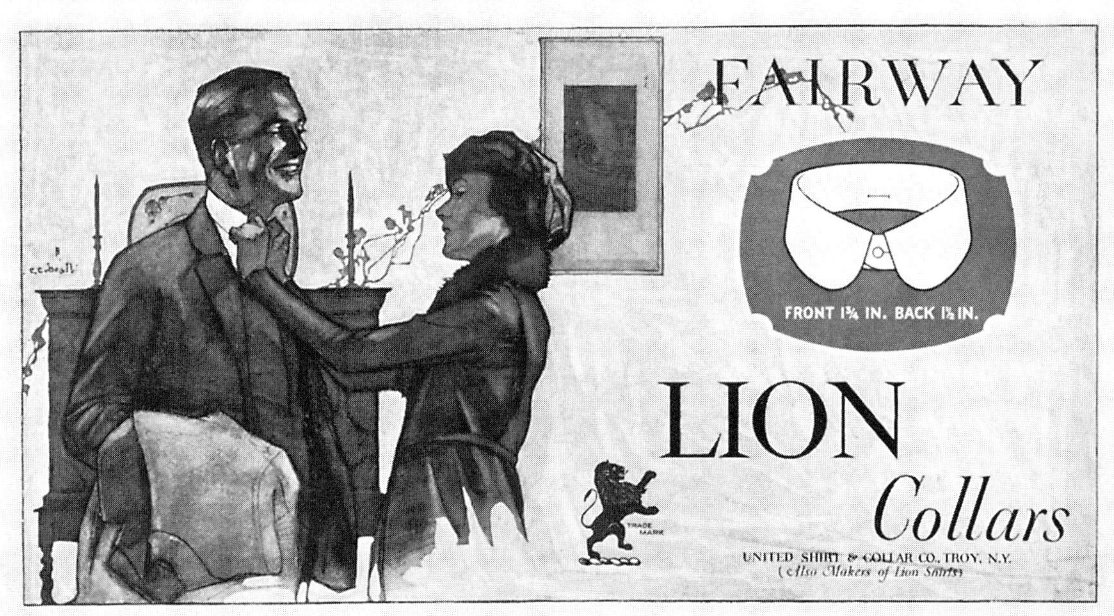

209

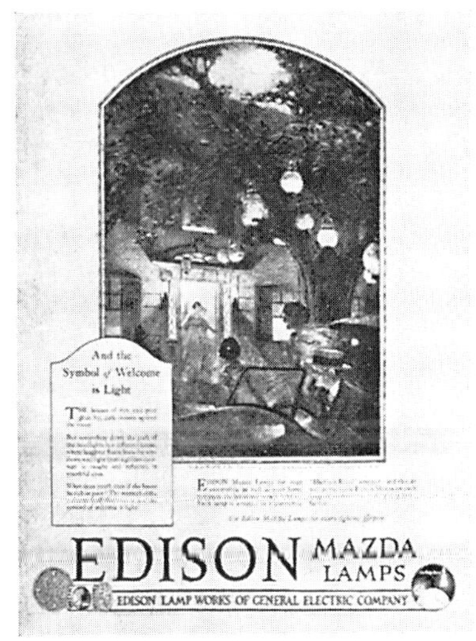

205

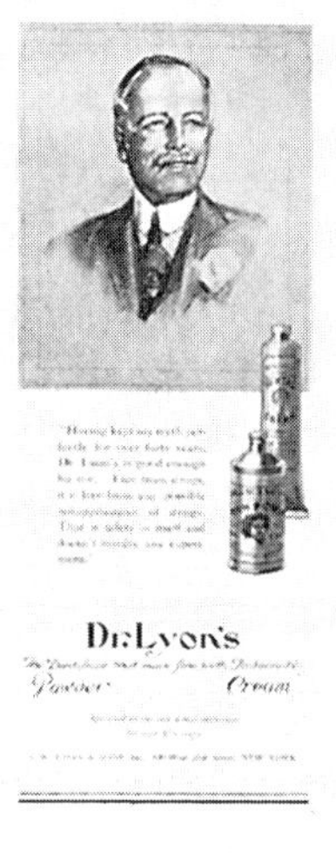

216

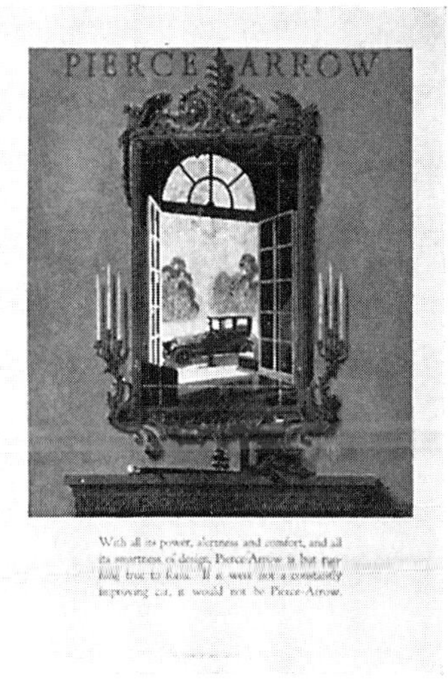

218

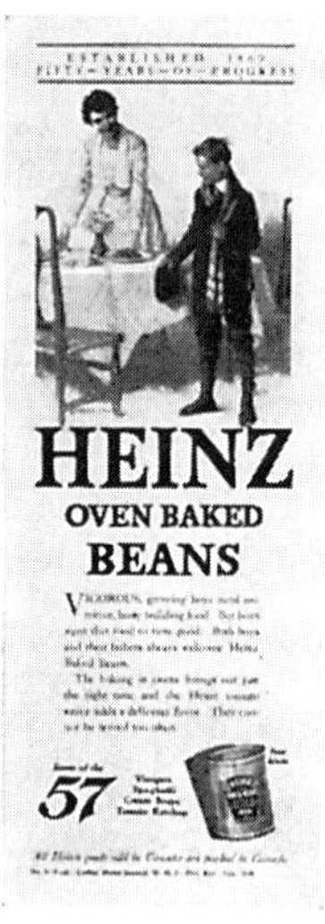

219

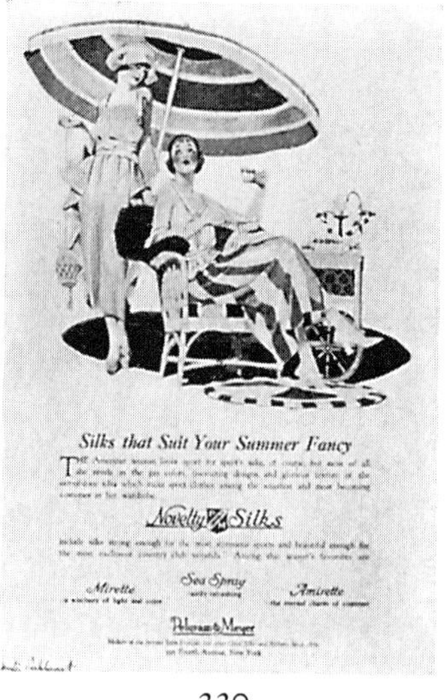

220

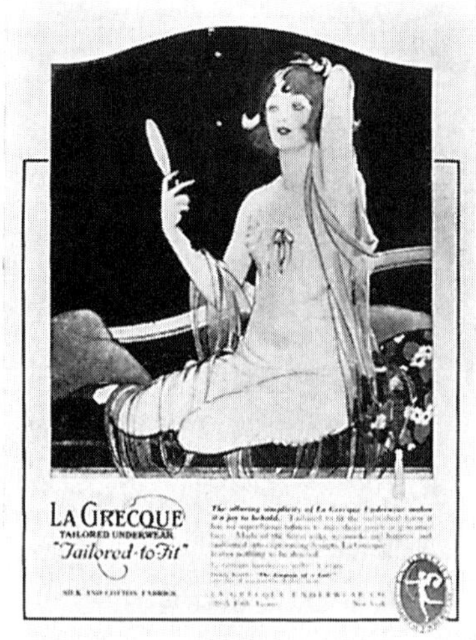

228

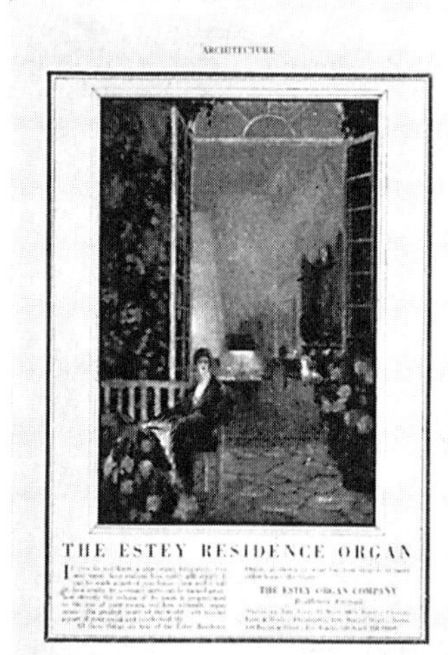

229

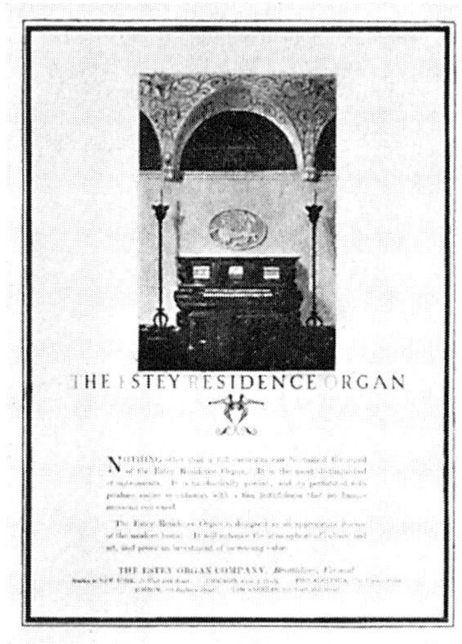

230

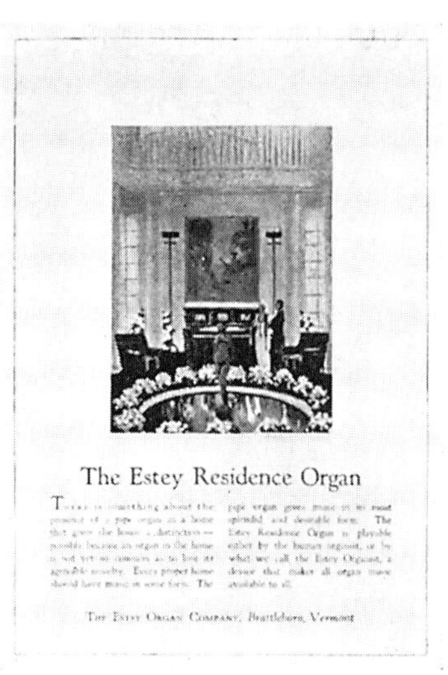

231

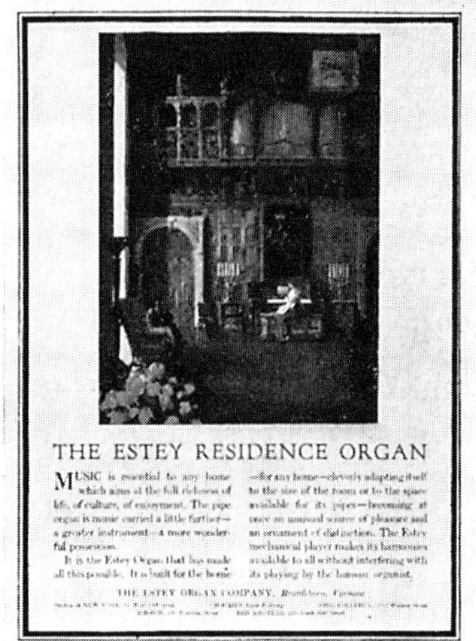

232

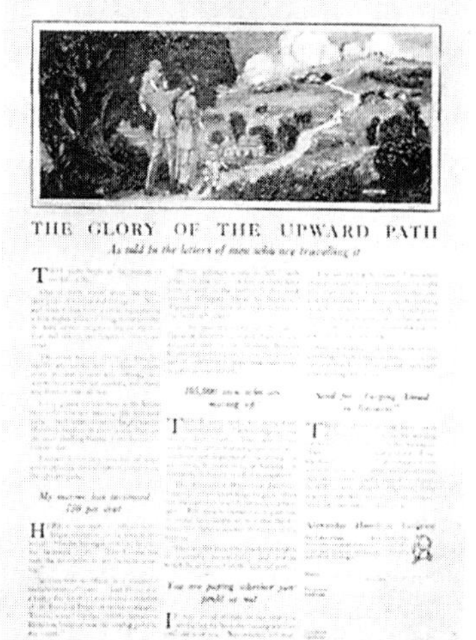

242

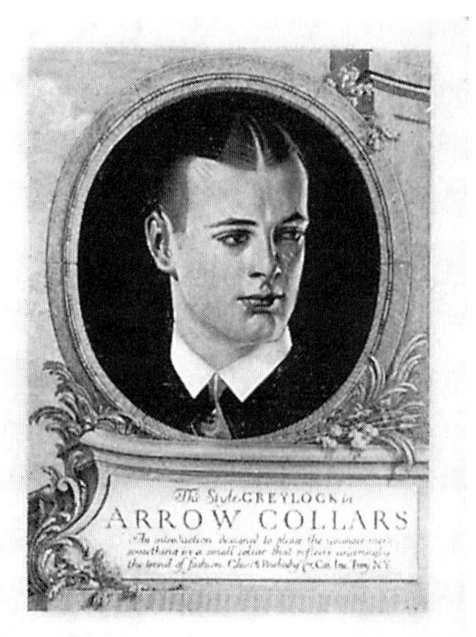

246

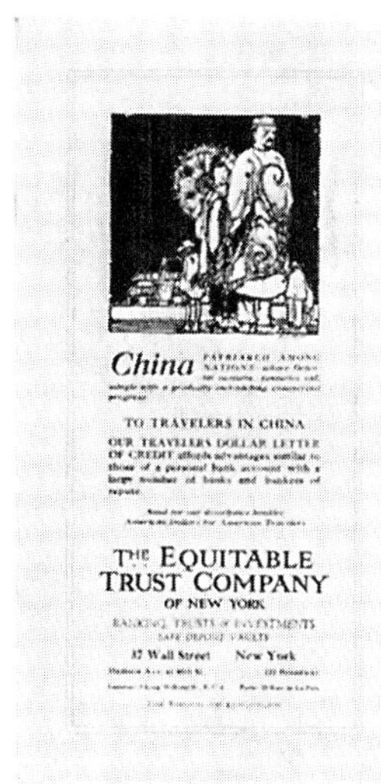

252

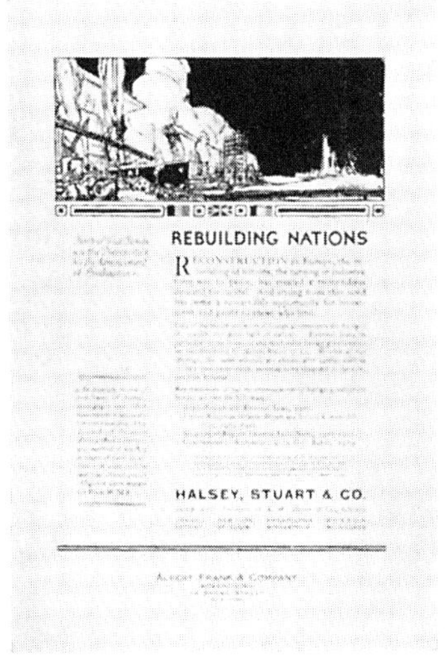

254

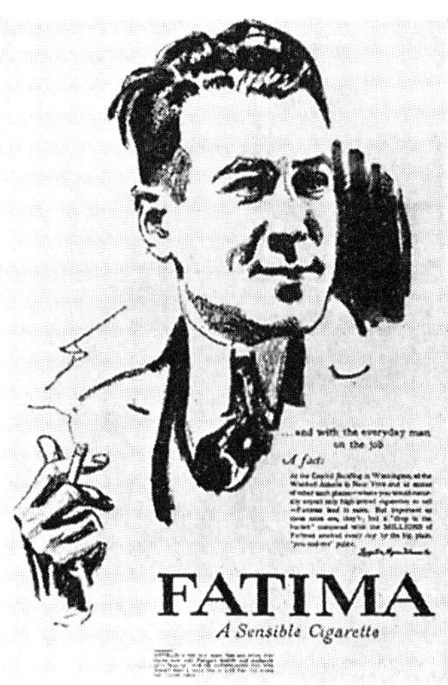

257

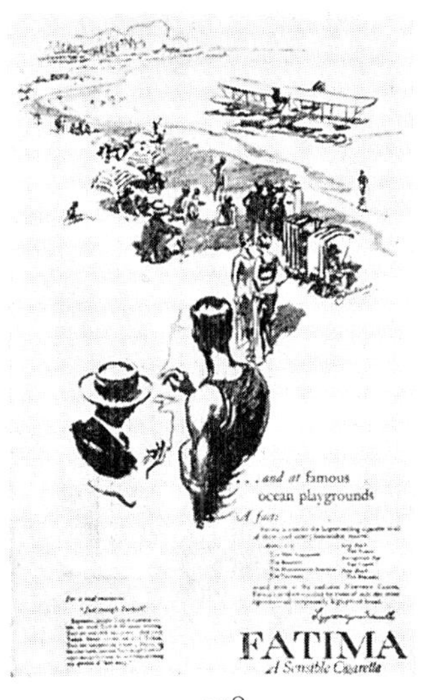

258

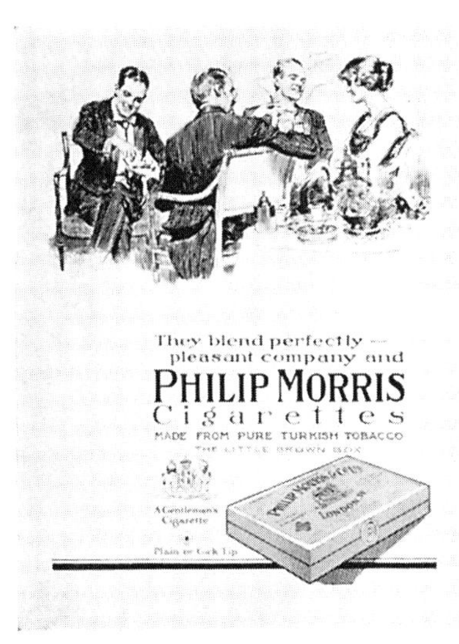

259

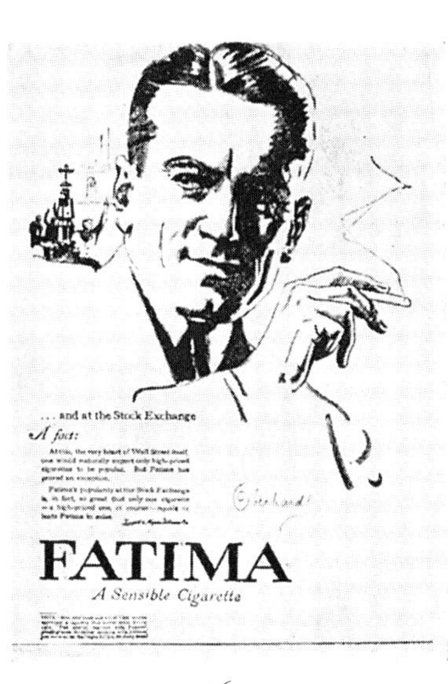

261

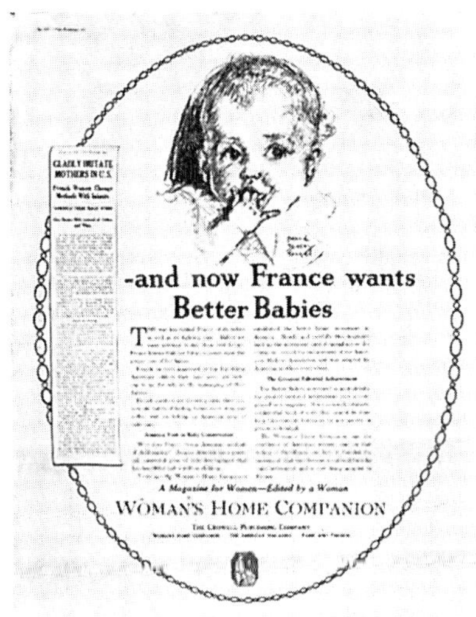

262

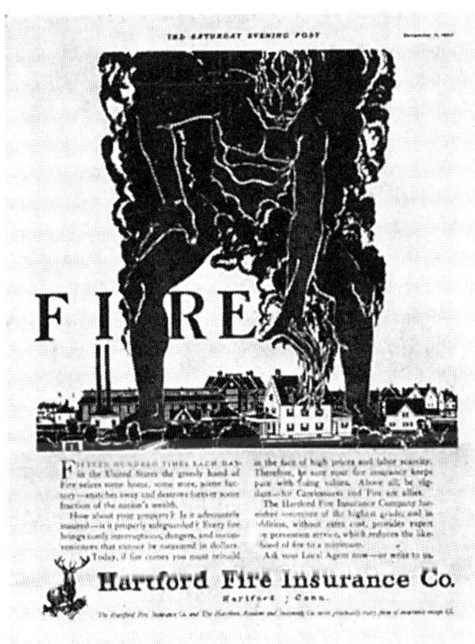

265

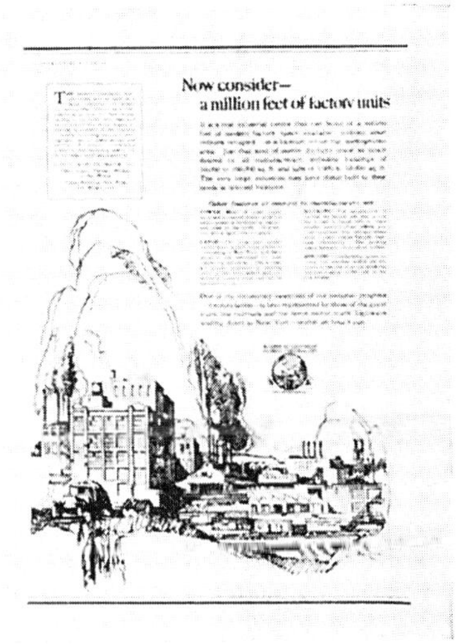

272

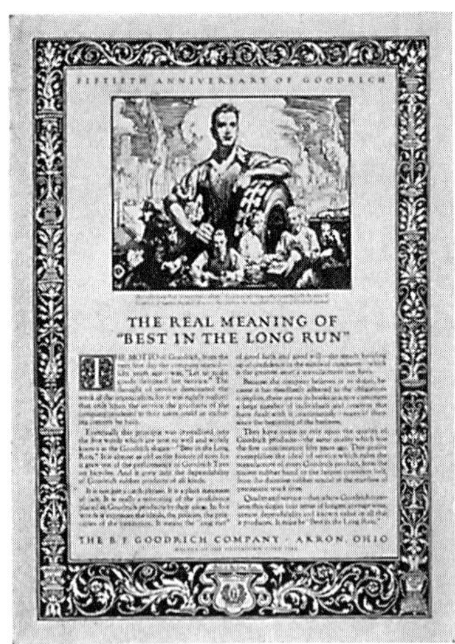

275

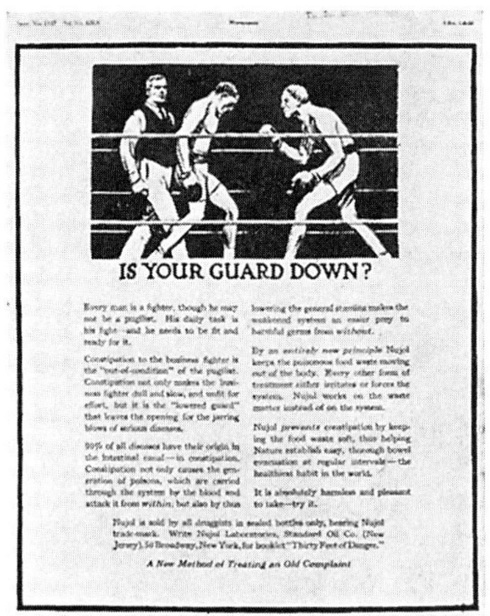

280

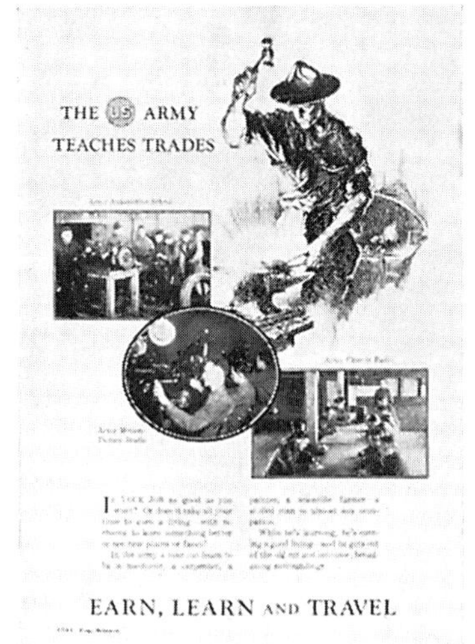

286

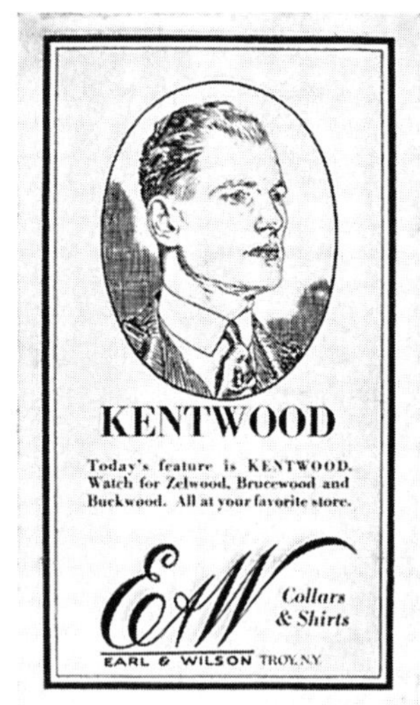

293

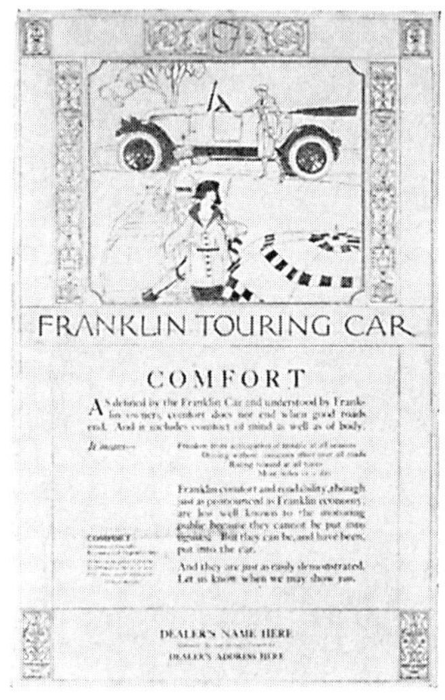

298

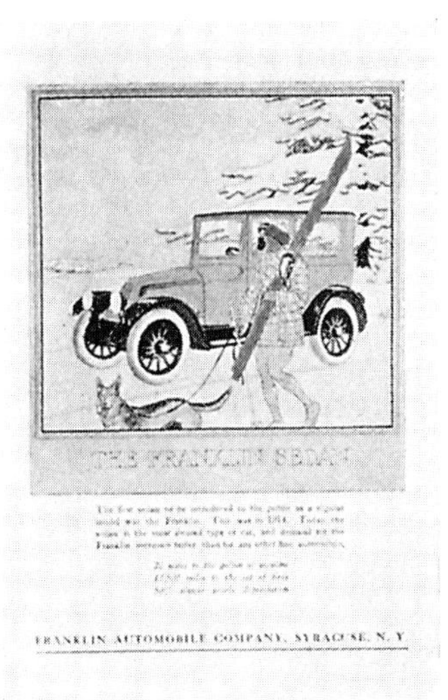

299

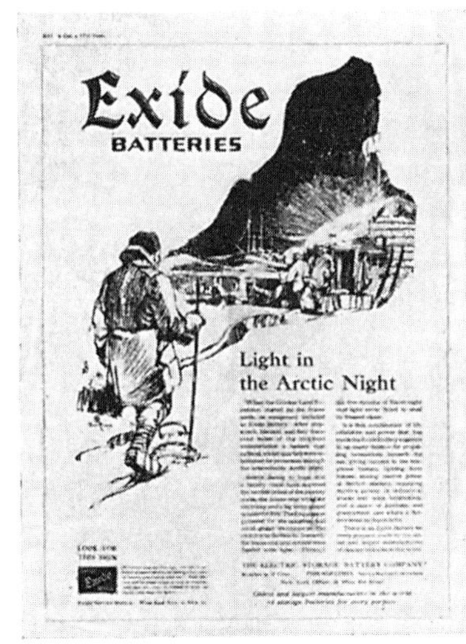

302

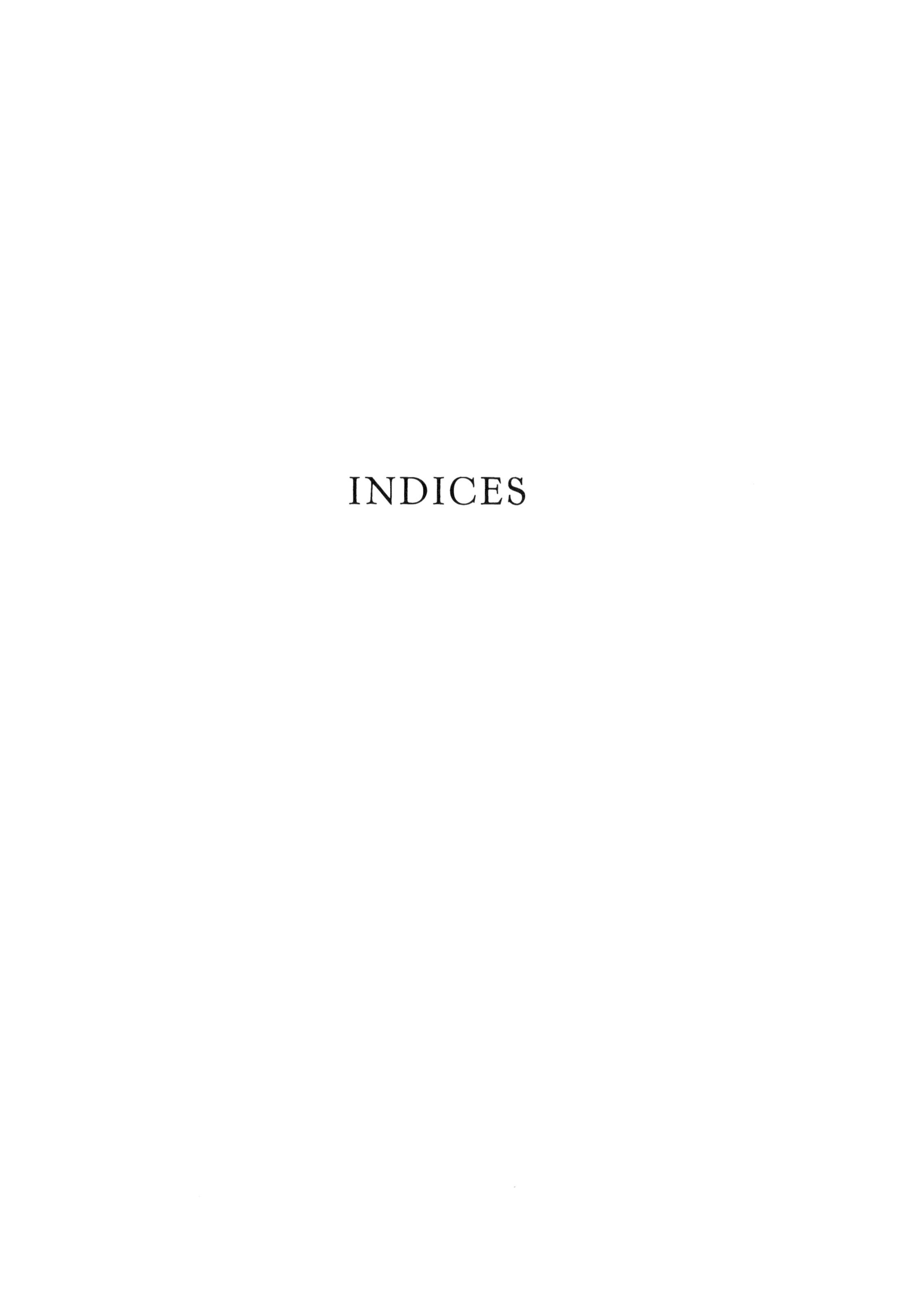

INDICES

INDEX OF PRODUCTS

INDEX OF ARTISTS

The Catalog of the First Exhibition Held by

COLOR
SUPPLEMENT

This section has been added for this edition; the original 1921 catalog did not feature any full-color reproductions, despite the vibrant painting that was exhibited in so many of the entries. To provide better appreciation for these works, a small selection of the advertisements and their art appear here in full color.

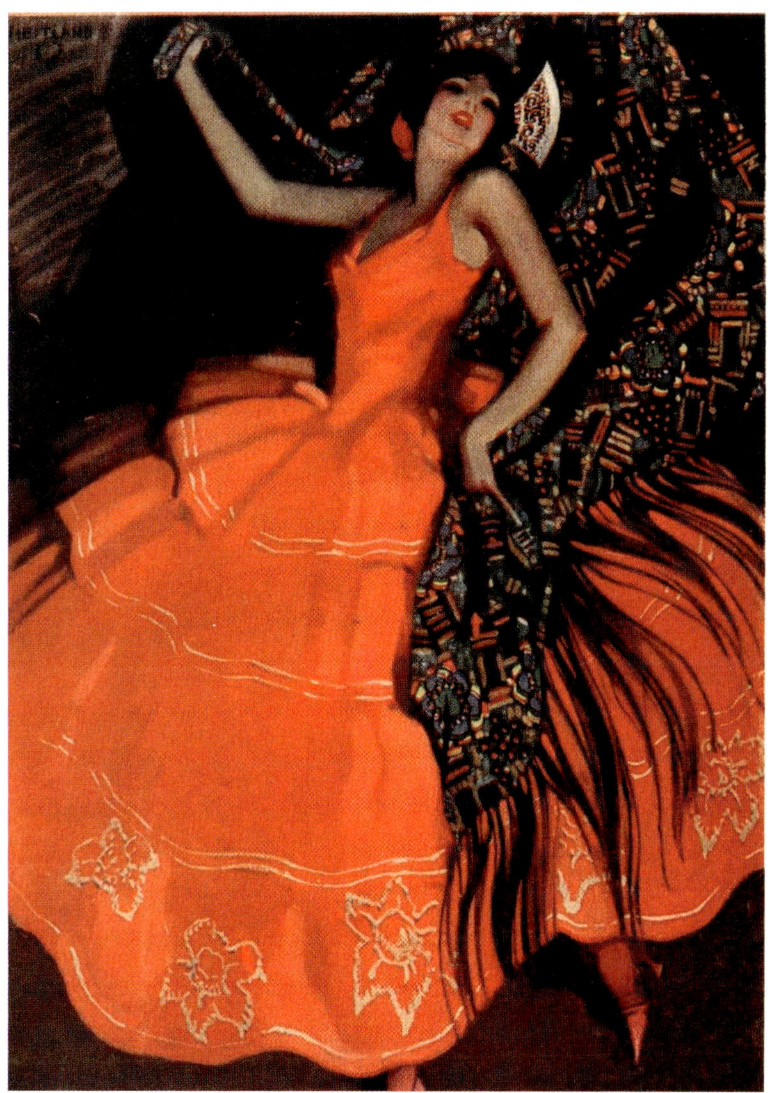

The First Award in Section II for Paintings and Drawings In Color
CARMEN— *W. E. Heitland*
(p. iv)

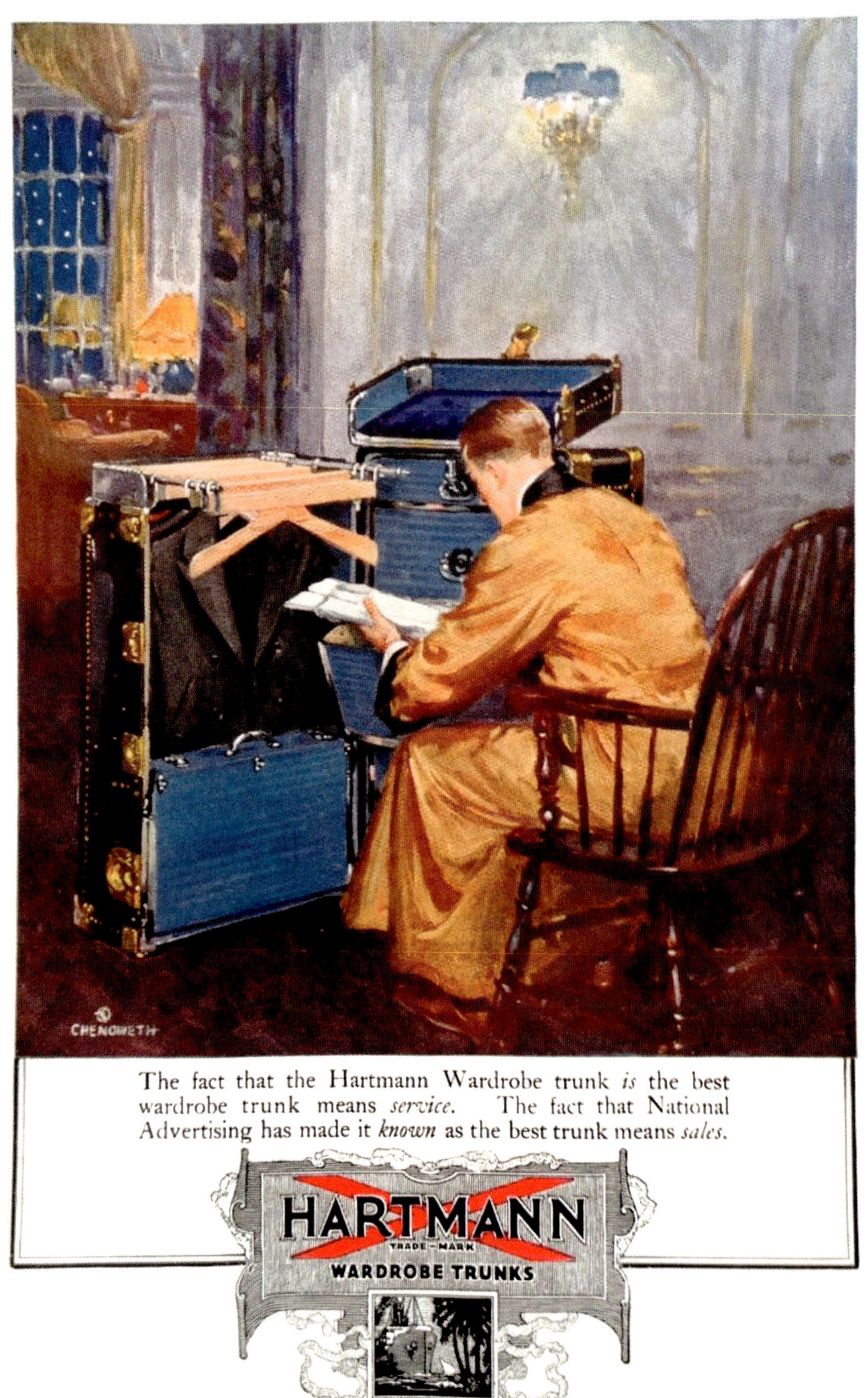

HARTMANN TRUNKS— *J. Chenoweth*

(p. 21)

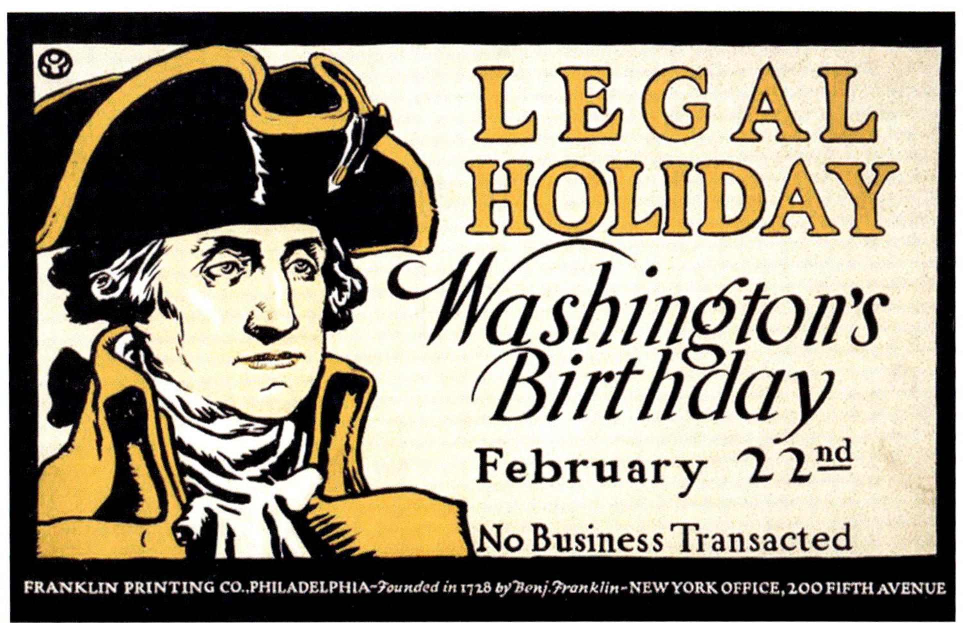

Franklin Printing Company— *Edward Penfield*
(p. 42)

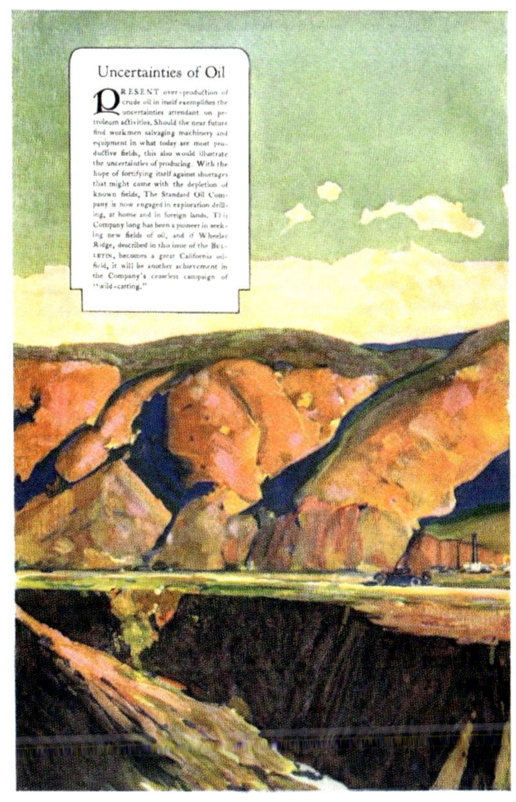

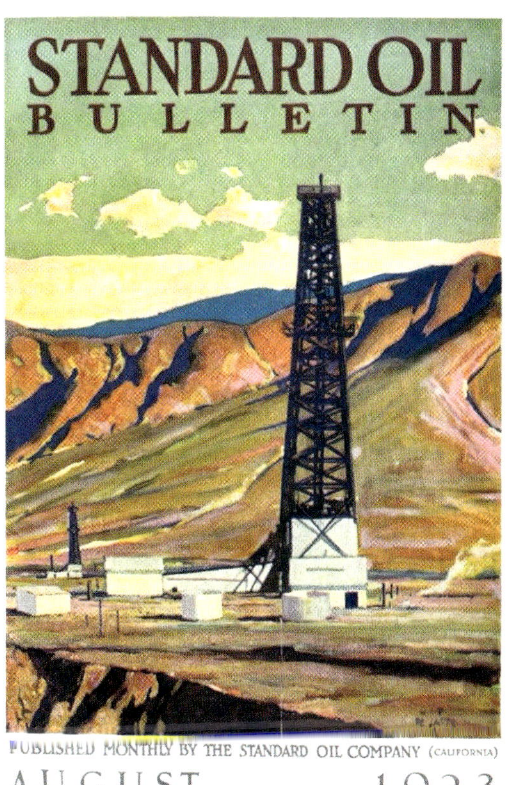

Standard Oil Co., House Organ — *W. R. Delappe*
(p. 73)

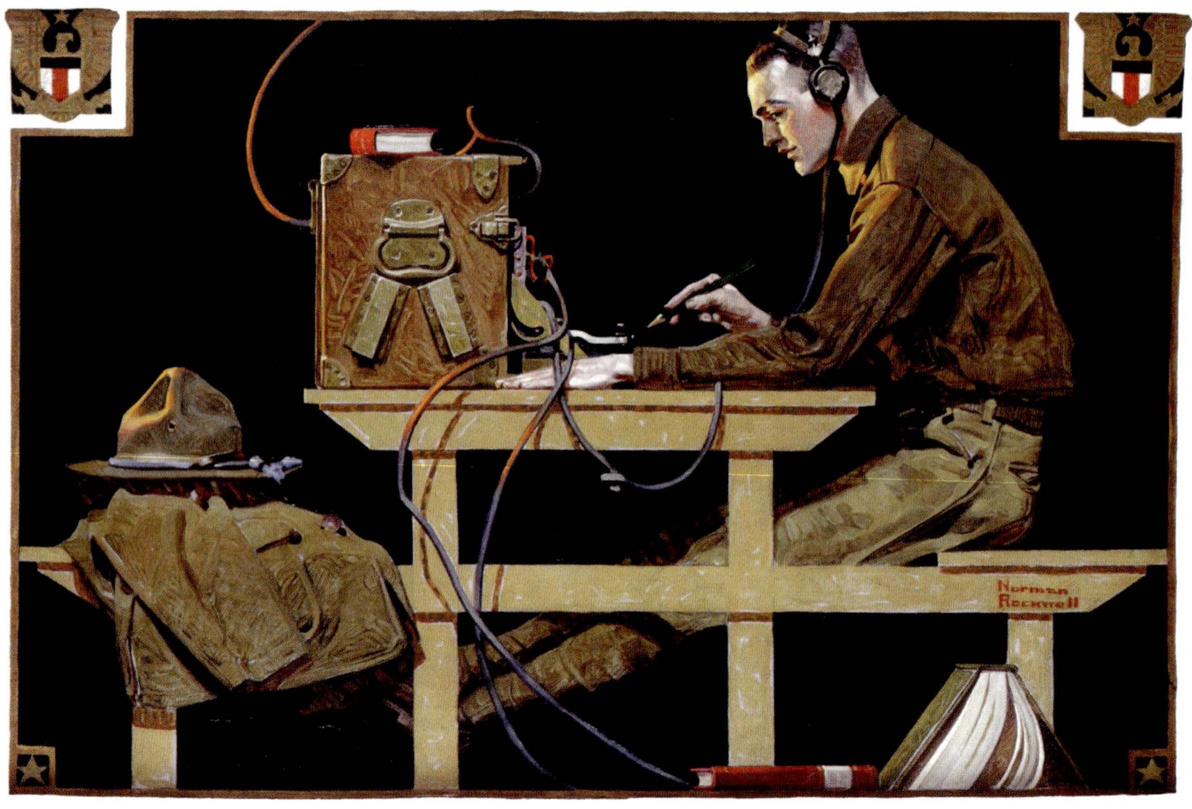

U. S. Army Teaches Trades— *Norman Rockwell*
(p. 63)

Edison Mazda Lamps— *Norman Rockwell*
(p. 43)

Norman Rockwell

Having five illustration pieces in this exhibit of professional work is quite a statement as Rockwell (1894–1978) was all of 27 years old at the time. He was a "mover and shaker" right from the beginning of his career, landing nationally published work, and an Art Director's position at the fledgling *Boys' Life Magazine,* before he was out of his teens.

Rockwell would go on to become one of the most defining illustrators of American culture in the twentieth century.

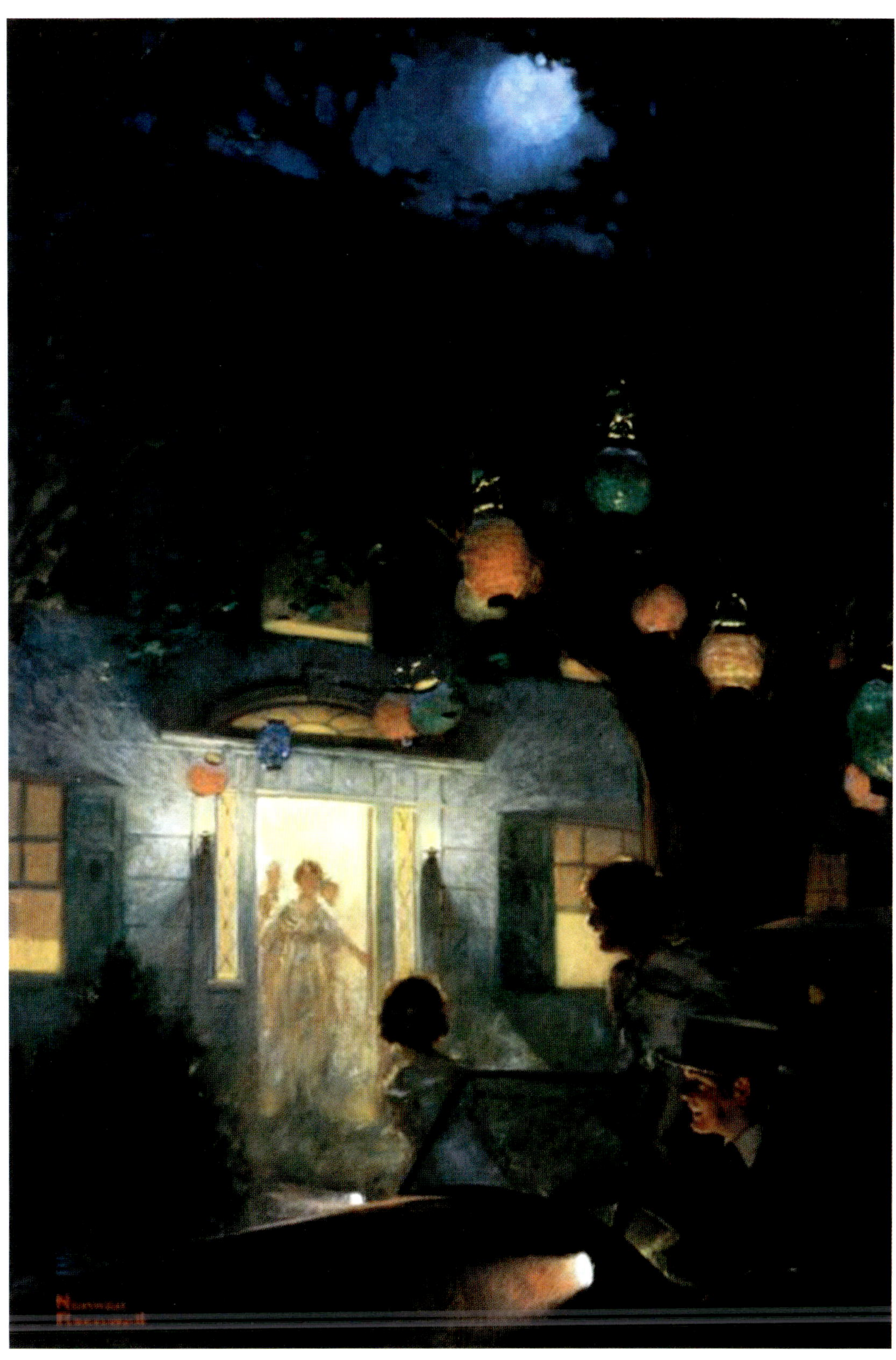

Edison Mazda Lamps— *Norman Rockwell*
(p. 71)

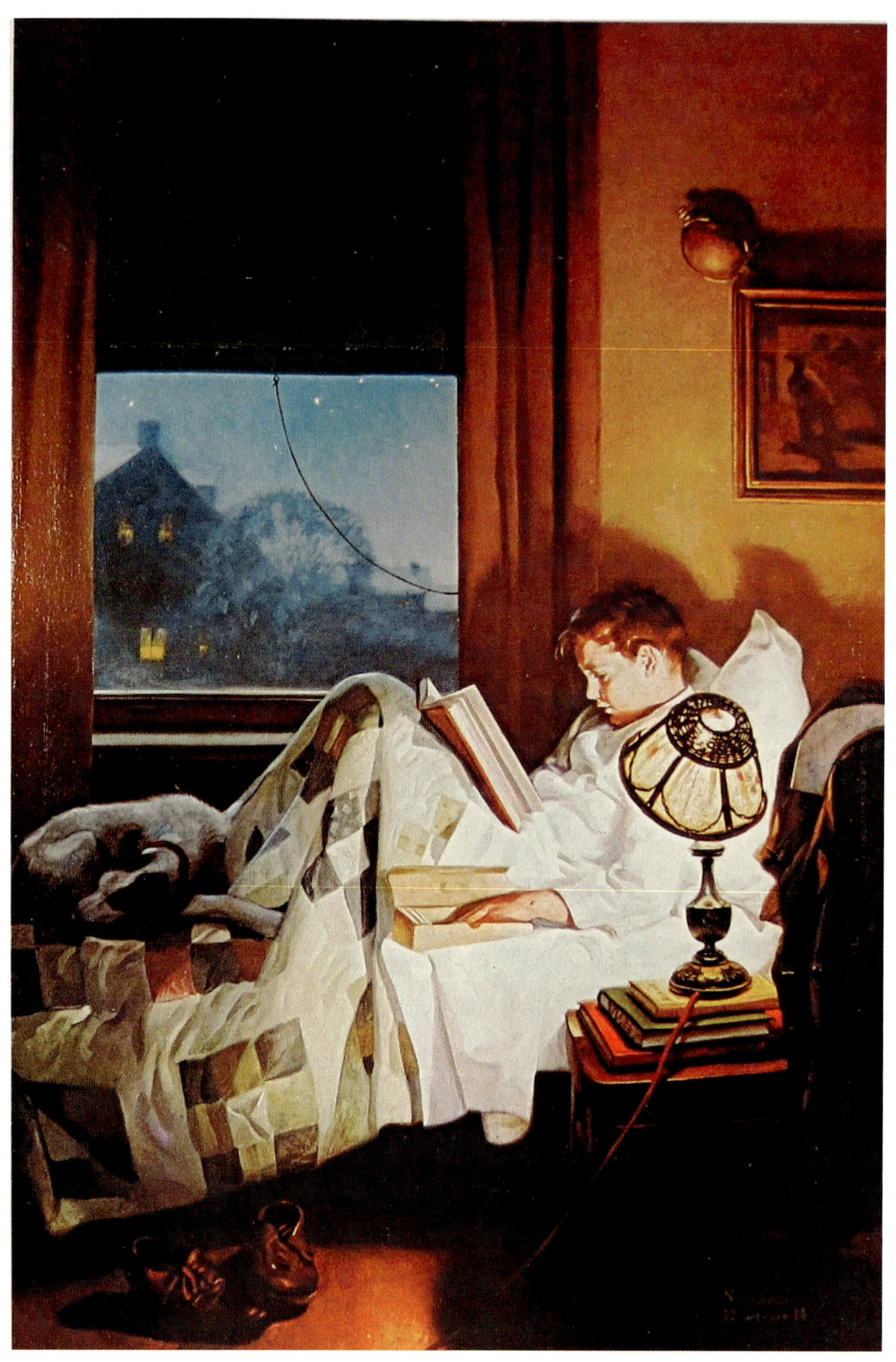

Edison Mazda Lamps— *Norman Rockwell*
(p. 52)

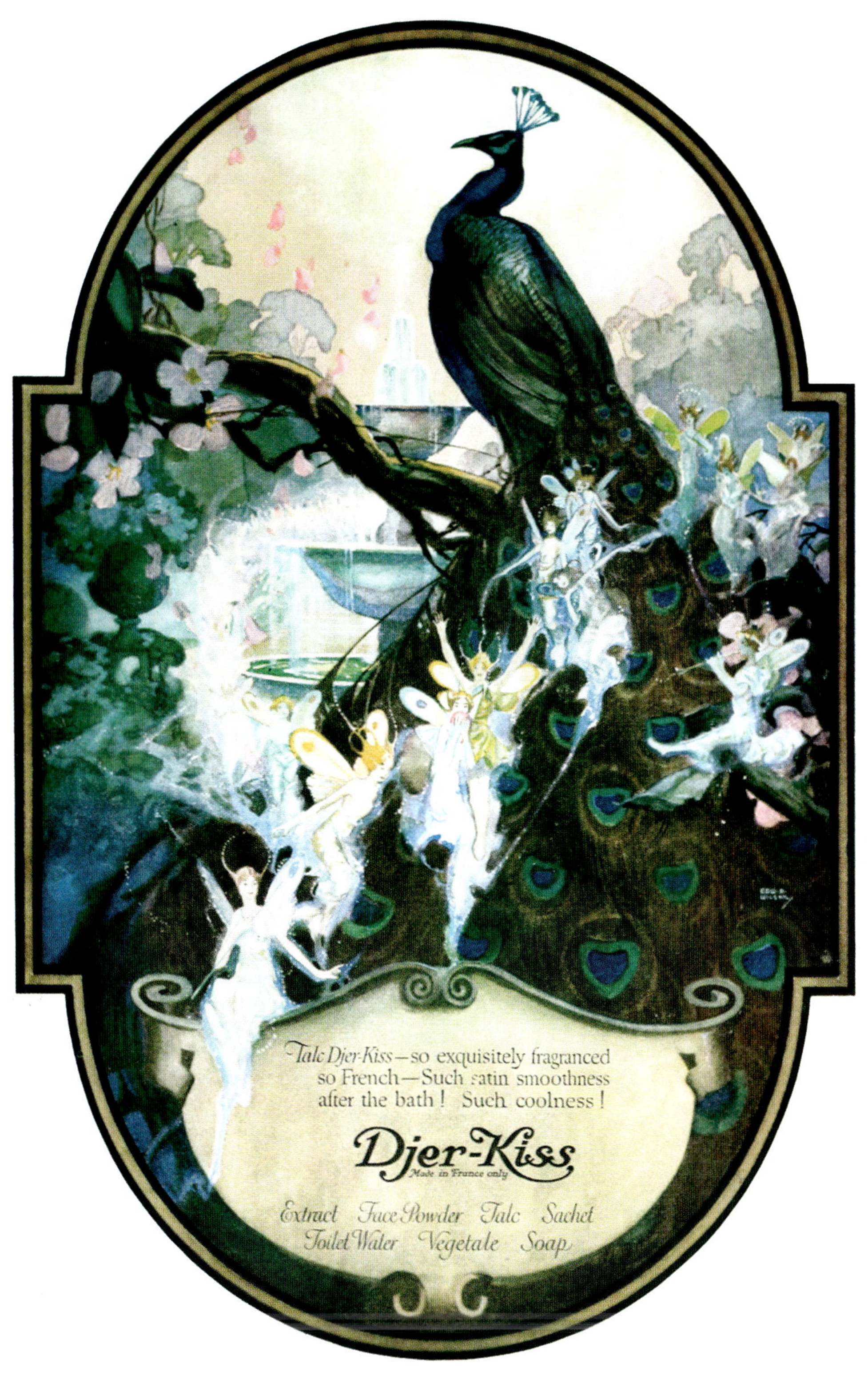

Djer-Kiss— *Edward A. Wilson*

(p. 44)

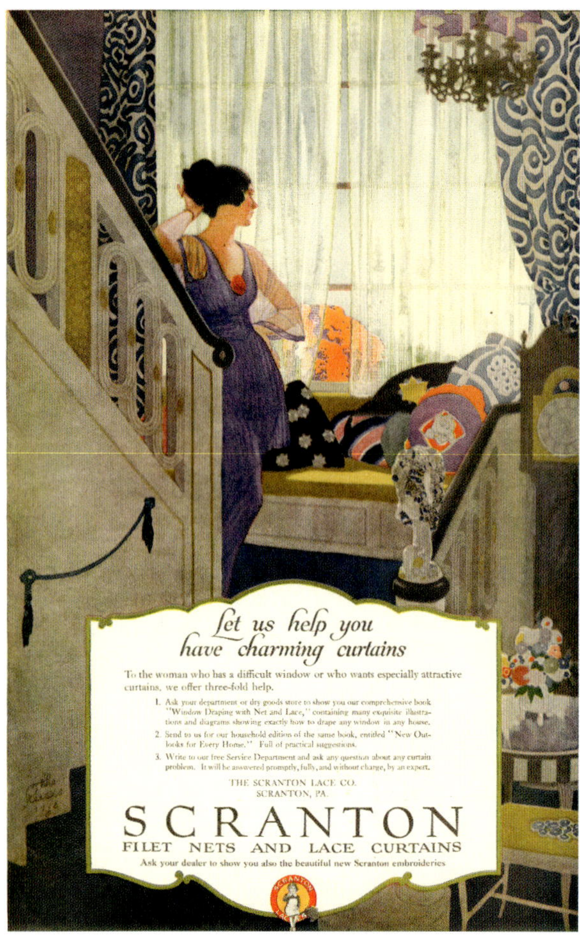

LACE CURTAINS— *The Reeses*
(p. 49)

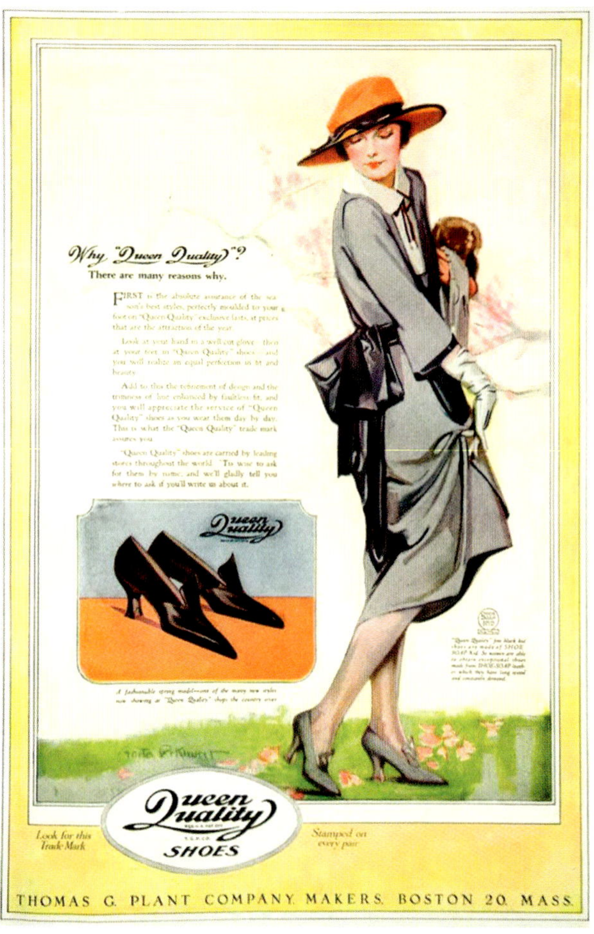

QUEEN QUALITY SHOES— *Anita Parkhurst*
(p. 35)

Fashion Matters

In a time that long proceeded the digital age, and even television, print advertising was how most new products were promoted. There was no better way to introduce an audience to your product than to show them a picture of it. This created an industry for doing just that, providing visual images to announce a new car, a reliable cleanser, or a new style of clothing.

The fashion industry made particularly good use of this medium. From men's hats to ladies' stockings—suits, dresses, and shoes—advertisers like Kuppenheimer, Hart Schaffner & Marx, and Vode Kid Shoes all employed illustrators to present their product and their brand name in the best possible light.

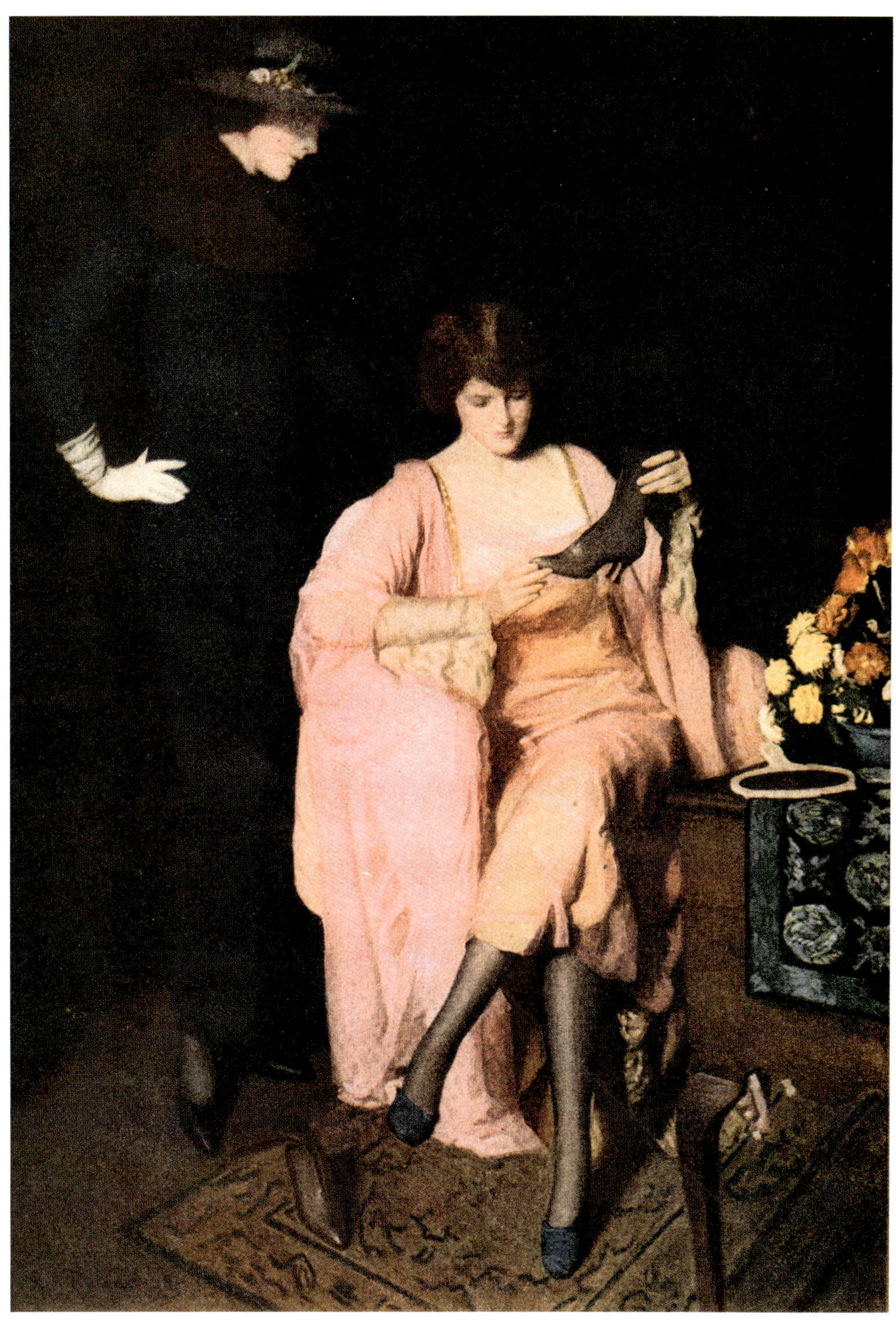

Vode Kid— *R. K. Ryland*

(p. 39)

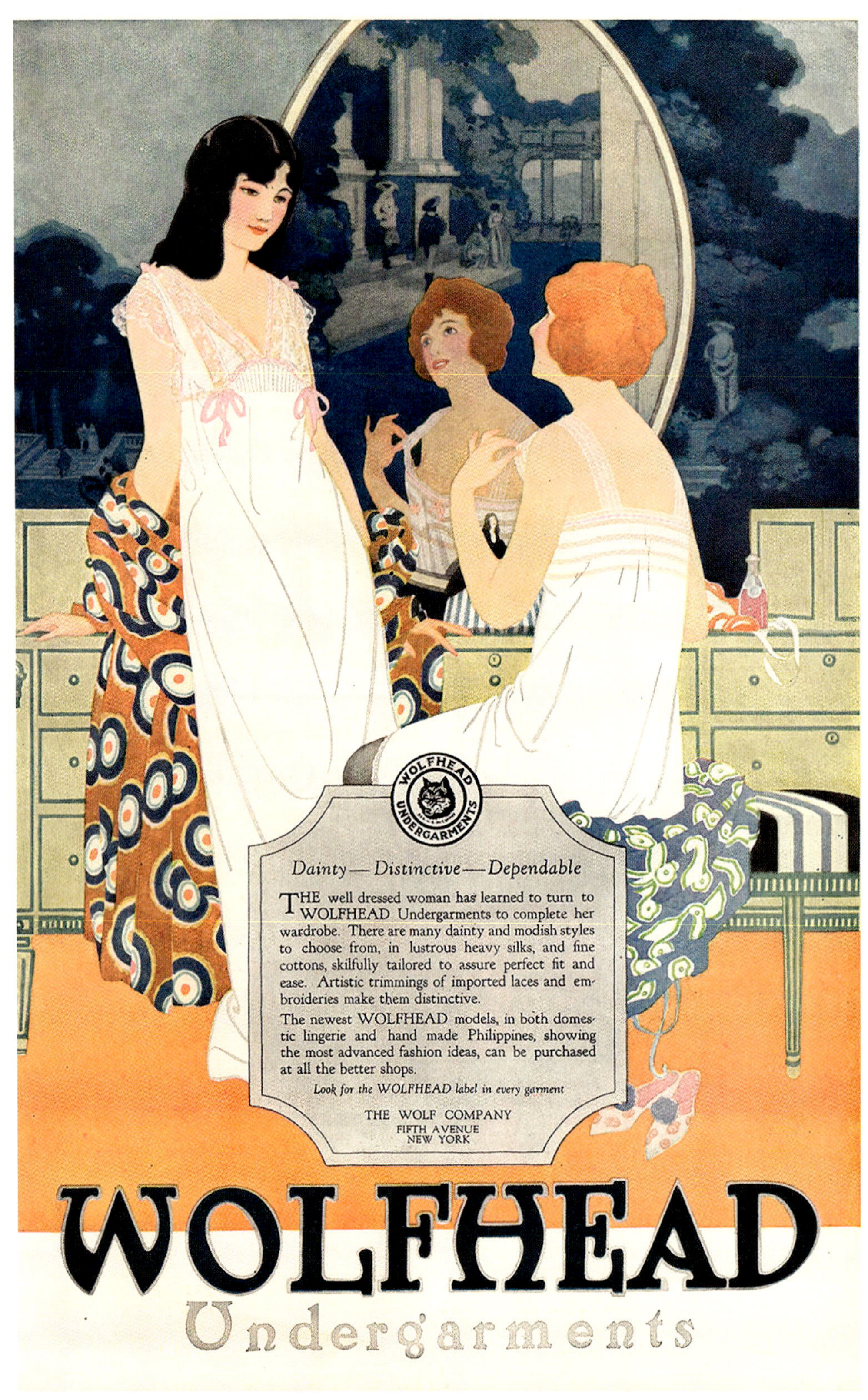
WOLFHEAD
UNDERGARMENTS

Dainty — Distinctive — Dependable

THE well dressed woman has learned to turn to
WOLFHEAD Undergarments to complete her
wardrobe. There are many dainty and modish styles
to choose from, in lustrous heavy silks, and fine
cottons, skilfully tailored to assure perfect fit and
ease. Artistic trimmings of imported laces and em-
broideries make them distinctive.

The newest WOLFHEAD models, in both domes-
tic lingerie and hand made Philippines, showing
the most advanced fashion ideas, can be purchased
at all the better shops.

Look for the WOLFHEAD label in every garment

THE WOLF COMPANY
FIFTH AVENUE
NEW YORK

WOLFHEAD
Undergarments

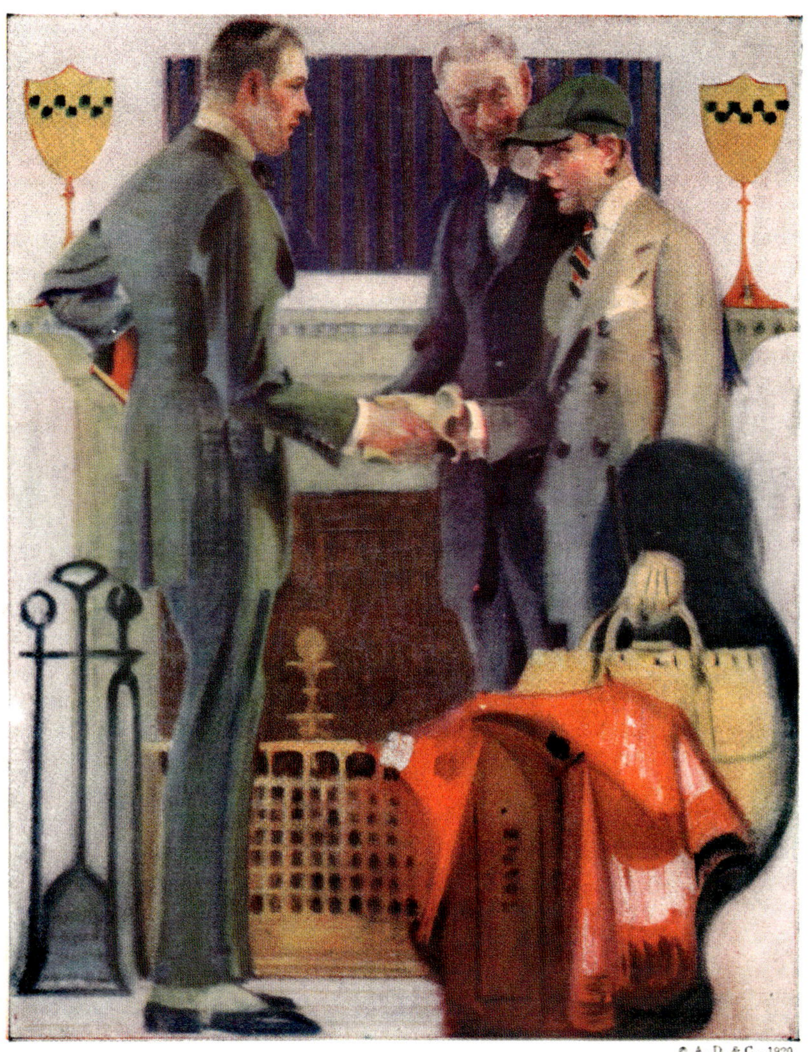

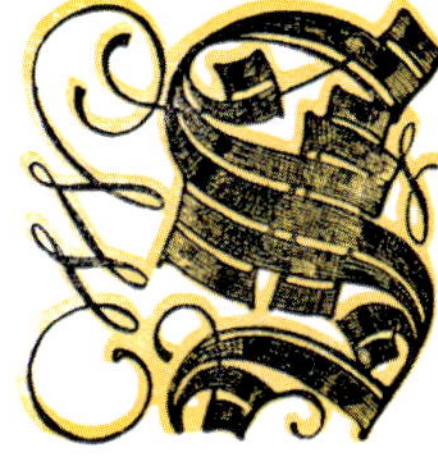

OCIETY BRAND CLOTHES are for young men because their acknowledged style leadership keeps the young man conscious of his good appearance. ¶ They are for men who stay young because staying young consists largely in retaining the confidence and alertness of youth, even after age has swept away the young man's self-consciousness.

With the Varied Grades of Clothing Flooding the Market, Look for the Label as Your Guide

ALFRED DECKER & COHN, Makers, Chicago, New York
In Canada· SOCIETY BRAND CLOTHES, Limited, Montreal

Society Brand Clothes

FOR YOUNG MEN AND MEN WHO STAY YOUNG

Society Brand Clothing — Leon M. Gordon

(p. 57)

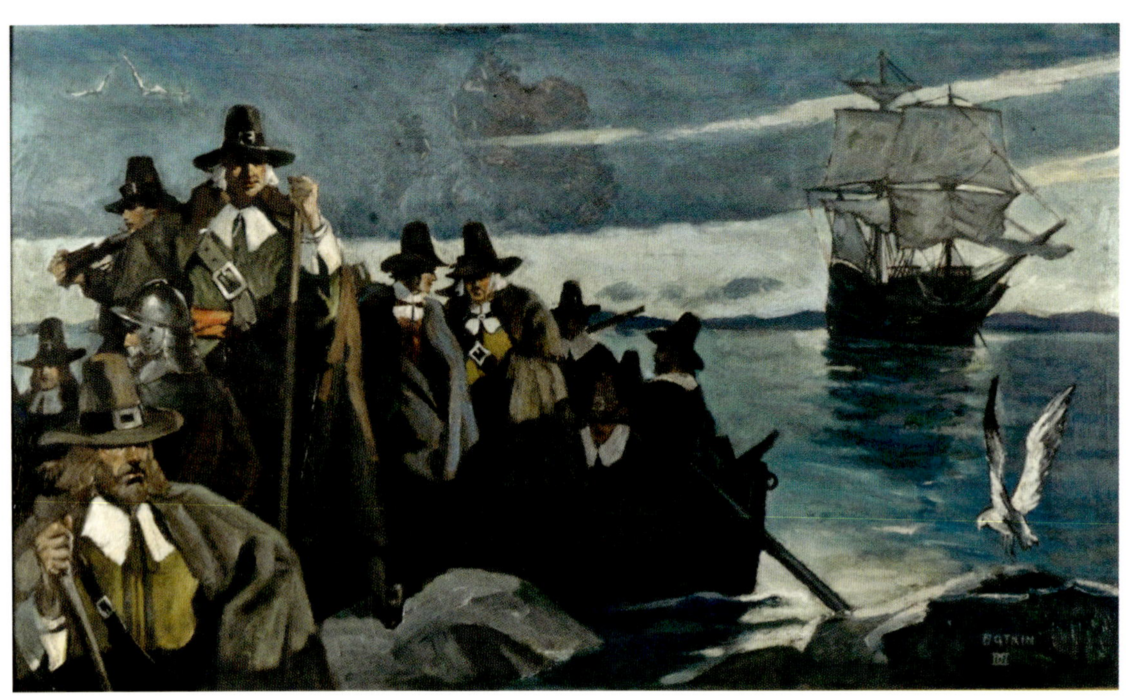

OLD COLONY TRUST CO. — *Henry A. Botkin*
(p. 41)

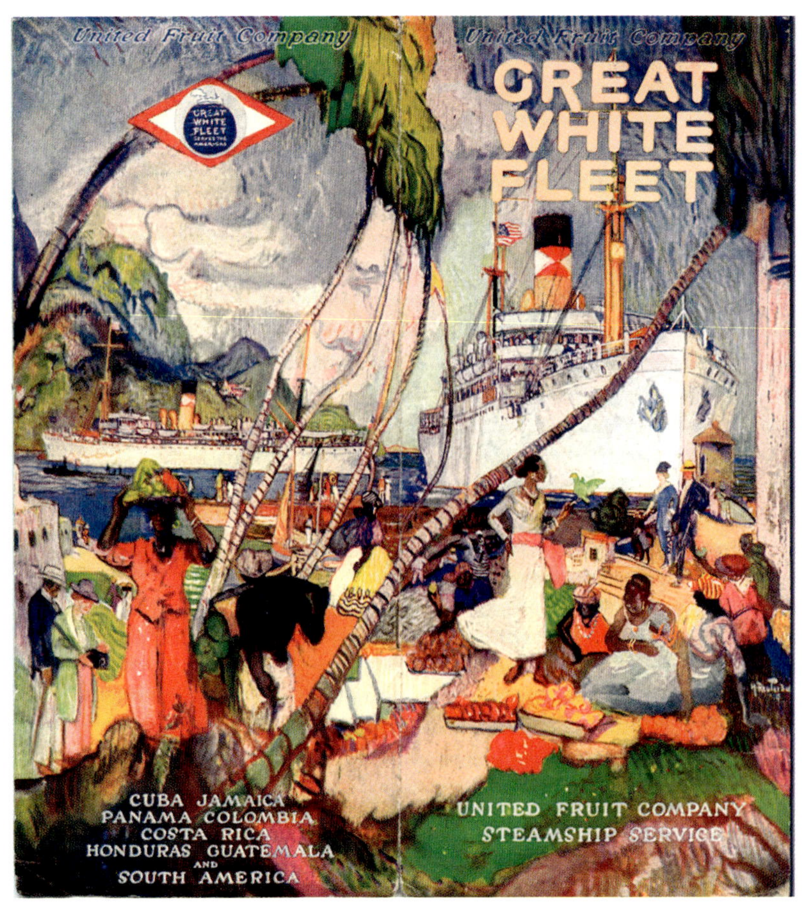

GREAT WHITE FLEET— *Henry Reuterdahl*
(p. 74)

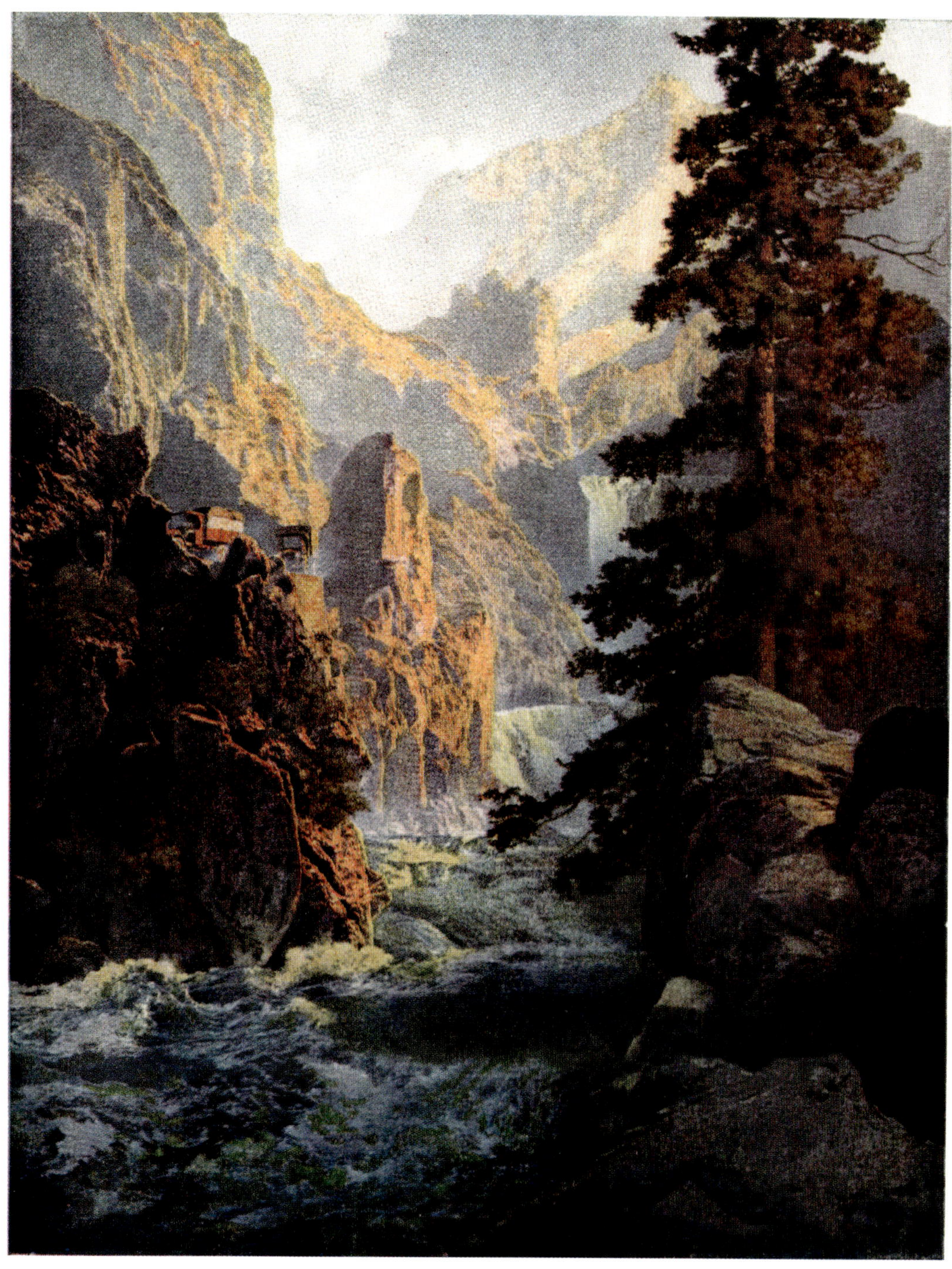

Maxfield Parrish

Already a household name by 1921, Maxfield Parrish (1870-1966) had a unique and attractive style. He depicted his realistic figures in dreamlike idyllic settings, which caught the imagination of his viewers and the attention of advertisers. Edison Mazda Lamps asked Parrish to create a series of calendar images, illustrating the history of mankind's use of light.

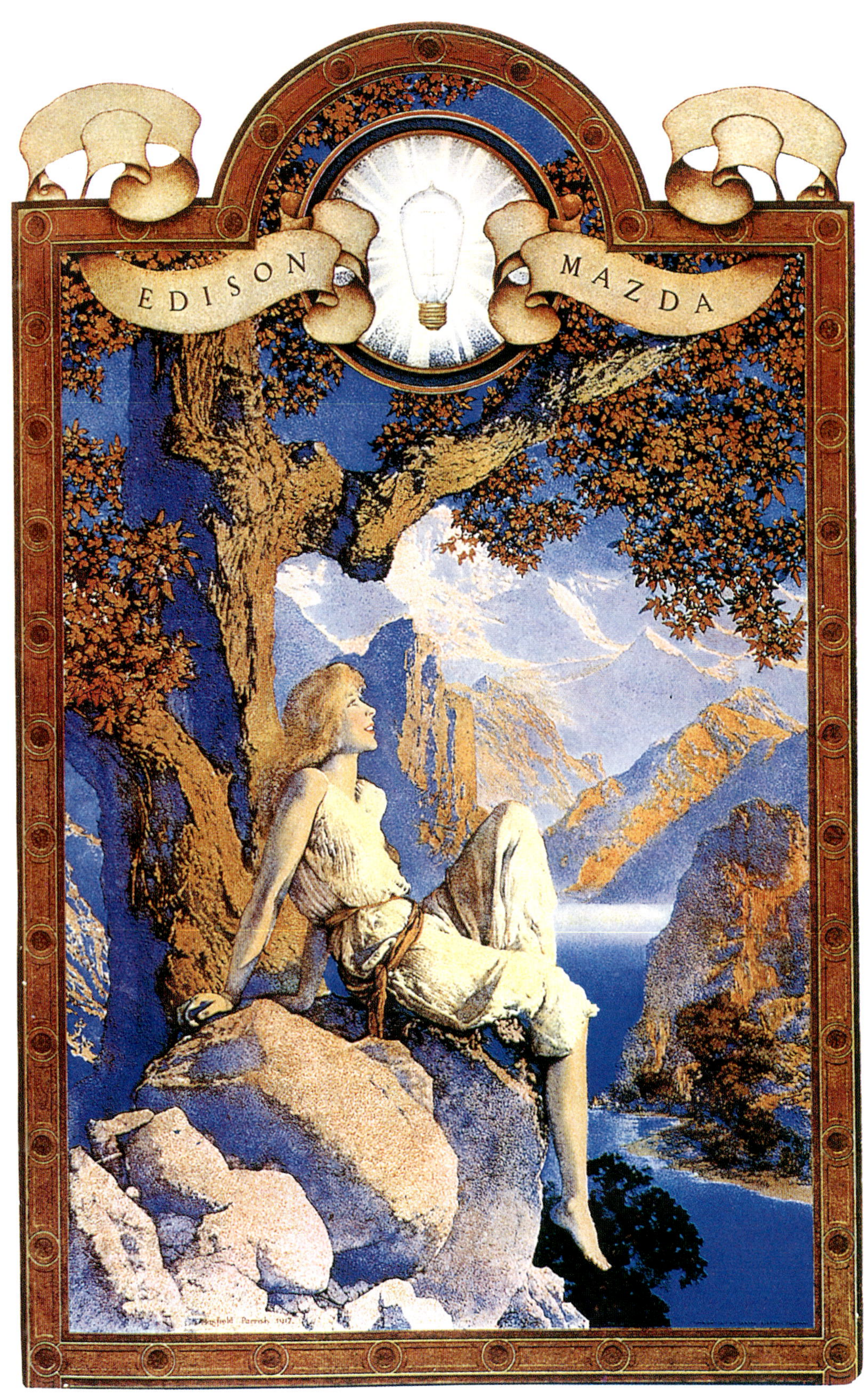

Edison Mazda Lamps— *Maxfield Parrish*

(p. 29)

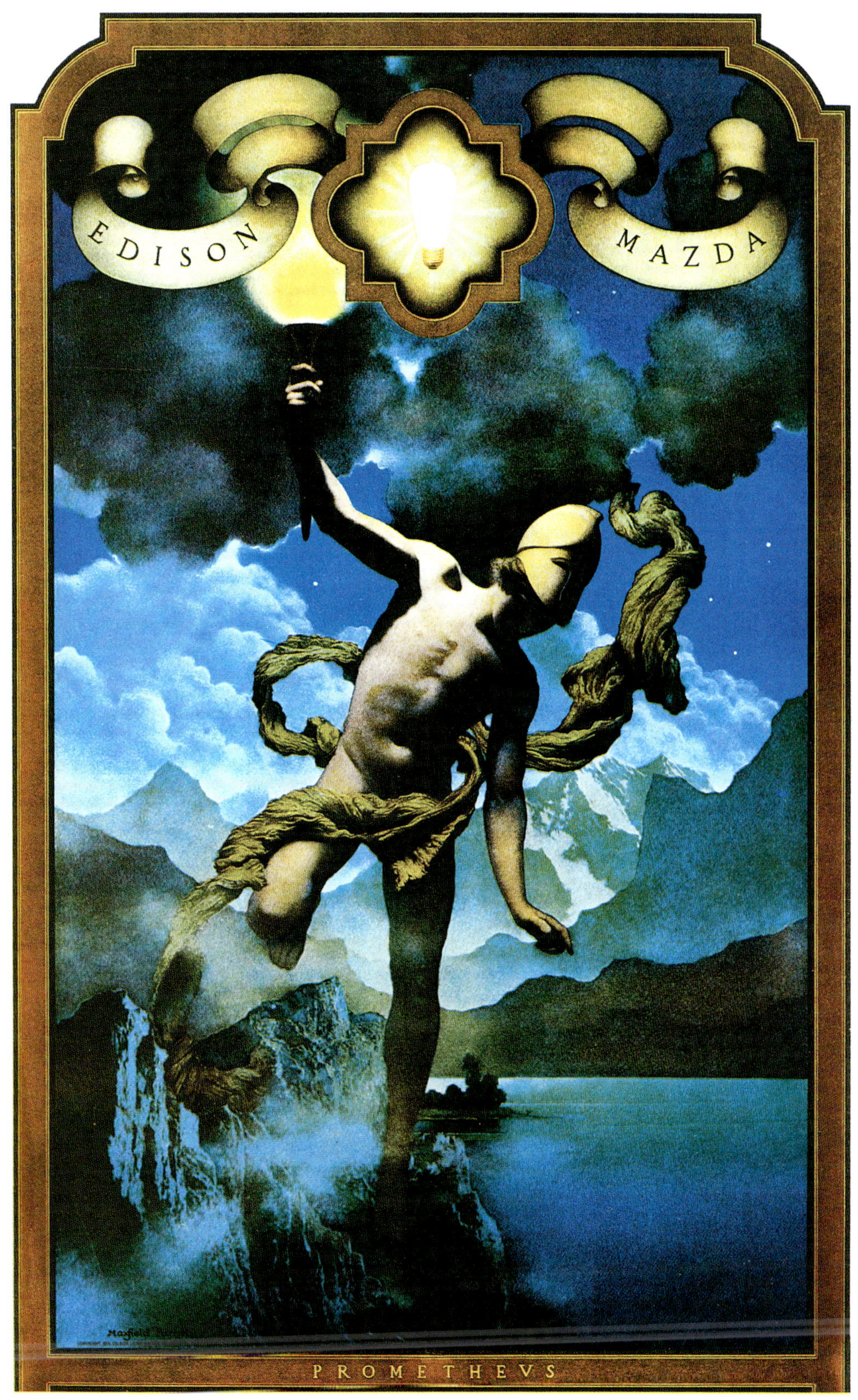

Edison Mazda Lamps— *Maxfield Parrish*
(p. 22)